5 STEPS TO A 5

AP Microeconomics/ Macroeconomics

2010-2011

Other books in McGraw-Hill's **5 STEPS TO A 5** series include:

AP Biology

AP Calculus AB/BC

AP Chemistry

AP Computer Science

AP English Language

AP English Literature

AP Environmental Science

AP Physics B and C

AP Psychology

AP Spanish Language

AP Statistics

AP U.S. Government and Politics

AP U.S. History

AP World History

Writing the AP English Essay

5 STEPS TO A 5

AP Microeconomics/ Macroeconomics

2010–2011

Eric R. Dodge

New York   Chicago   San Francisco   Lisbon   London   Madrid   Mexico City
Milan   New Delhi   San Juan   Seoul   Singapore   Sydney   Toronto

Copyright © 2010 by The McGraw-Hill Companies, Inc. All rights reserved. Printed in the
United States of America. Except as permitted under the United States Copyright Act of
1976, no part of this publication may be reproduced or distributed in any form or by any
means, or stored in a data base or retrieval system, without the prior written permission of
the publisher.

1 2 3 4 5 6 7 8 9 10 11 12 13 14 15 16 17 18 19 20   WDQ/WDQ 0 9

ISBN 978-0-07-162186-1
MHID   0-07-162186-5
ISSN 1949-1689

The series editor was Grace Freedson, and the project editor was Del Franz.
Series design by Jane Tenenbaum.

McGraw-Hill books are available at special quantity discounts to use as premiums and
sales promotions or for use in corporate training programs. To contact a representative,
please e-mail us at bulksales@mcgraw-hill.com.

AP, Advanced Placement Program, and *College Board* are registered trademarks of the
College Entrance Examination Board, which was not involved in the production of, and
does not endorse, this product.

ABOUT THE AUTHOR

Eric R. Dodge was born in Portland, Oregon and attended high school in Tigard, Oregon. He received a bachelor's degree in Business Administration from the University of Puget Sound in Tacoma, Washington before attending the University of Oregon for his master's and doctoral degrees in Economics. While at the University of Oregon he received two graduate student awards for teaching and became a die-hard fan of the Ducks. Since 1995 he has been teaching economics at Hanover College in Hanover, Indiana, the oldest private college in the state. The author teaches principles of microeconomics and macroeconomics, intermediate microeconomic theory, labor economics, environmental economics, industrial organization, statistics, and econometrics. Since 2000 he has served as a faculty consultant for the Educational Testing Service reading AP free-response exams. He lives in Madison, Indiana.

CONTENTS

PREFACE

So, you've decided to bite the bullet and invest in a book designed to help you earn a 5 on your AP Microeconomics and Macroeconomics exams. Congratulations! You have taken the first of many small steps toward this goal. An important question remains: Why this book?

Priority number one, both for your AP course and for this book, is to prepare you to do well enough on the AP Microeconomics and Macroeconomics exams to earn college credit. I firmly believe that this book has a comparative advantage over your other options. First, I have written this text with a certain conversational approach, rather than a flurry of formulas and diagrams that you must remember. Sure, some memorization is required for any standardized test, but a memorizer of formulas is in deep trouble when asked to analyze the relative success of several possible economic policies or to draw fine distinctions between competing economic theories. Using this book to supplement and reinforce your understanding of the theories and relationships in economics will allow you to apply your analytical skills to the exam, and this gives you a significant advantage over the formula-memorizing exam taker. If you spend less time memorizing formulas and take the extra time to understand the basics, you will get along just fine with this book, and you will do extremely well on the AP Economics exams.

Second, as a college professor who has taught economics to thousands of students, I have a strong understanding of where the learning happens and where the mistakes are made.

Third, as a reader of AP exams, I can tell you where points are lost and where a 5 is made on the free-response questions. Most importantly, I am a realist. You want to know what it takes to earn a 5 and not necessarily the finer points of the Federal Reserve System, the Sherman Antitrust Act, or the NAFTA.

Take the time to read the first four chapters of this book, which are designed to help you understand the challenge that lies ahead and to provide you with tips for success on the exam.

Take each diagnostic exam to see where you stand before beginning your review. The bulk of this book is a comprehensive review of economics with practice questions at the end of each chapter. These questions are designed to quickly test your understanding of the material presented in each chapter, not necessarily to mirror the AP exams. For exam questions that are more typical of what you will experience in May, I have provided you with two practice exams in both microeconomics and macroeconomics. These are practice exams complete with essay questions, sample responses, and scoring guidelines.

There have been several important updates since the first edition. The second edition included expanded coverage of game theory, reflecting the growing use of game theory in the AP Microeconomics curriculum. In that edition, I included a free-response question involving game theory because the people who develop the AP exam had been urging high school AP teachers to devote more time to game theory. Such urgings are usually a strong hint of a future free-response question and indeed in 2007 the Microeconomics exam included, for the first time, a free-response game-theory question. Also for the second edition, I increased the degree of difficulty on the Macroeconomics free-response questions, based on the input of respected high school economics teachers.

For the third edition (2010–2011), I have expanded coverage of the balance of payments and provided an explanation for how changes to the current account affect changes to the capital (or financial) account. Because I have seen first-hand the subtle changes in recent AP exams, I have modified a macroeconomics free-response question to address this topic in order to make sure the book stays abreast of the topics most likely to be covered on the exam.

I do not see any reason to continue talking about the book when we could just dive in. I hope that you enjoy this book and that you find it a useful resource. Good luck!

ACKNOWLEDGMENTS

The third edition of this book was greatly improved by input from the following outstanding teachers of economics: Michael Brody at the Menlo School in Atherton, California; David Burgin at Science Hill High School in Johnson City, Tennessee; and David Mayer at Winston Churchill High School in San Antonio, Texas. Gentlemen, our many conversations about teaching and economics have convinced me that Walter Mondale was one of our most underrated public servants. My son, Eli, continues to provide comic relief, inspiration, and joy throughout projects such as these. Thank you for being my "best buddy."

INTRODUCTION: THE FIVE-STEP PROGRAM

The Basics

Not too long ago, you agreed to enroll in AP Microeconomics or Macroeconomics. Maybe you saw a flyer and the allure of economic knowledge was just too much to resist, or maybe a respected teacher encouraged you to challenge yourself and you took the bait. Either way, you find yourself here, flipping through a book that promises to help you culminate this life-changing experience with the highest of honors, a 5 in AP Economics.[1] Can it be done without this book? Sure, there are many excellent teachers of AP Economics out there who teach, coax, and cajole their students into a 5 every year. But for the majority of students in your shoes, the marginal benefits of buying this book far outweigh the marginal costs.

Introducing The Five-Step Preparation Program

This book is organized as a five-step program to prepare you for success on the exams. These steps are designed to provide you with the skills and strategies vital to the exam and the practice that can lead you to that perfect 5. Each of the five steps will provide you with the opportunity to get closer and closer to that prize trophy 5. Here are the five steps.

Step 1: Set Up Your Study Program

In this step you'll read a brief overview of the AP Economics exams both in microeconomics and in macroeconomics, including an outline of topics and the approximate percentage of the exam that will test knowledge of each topic. You will also follow a process to help determine which of the following preparation programs is right for you:

- Full school year: September through May.
- One semester: January through May.
- Six weeks: Basic training for the exam.

Step 2: Determine Your Test Readiness

In this step you'll take diagnostic exams in microeconomics and macroeconomics. These pre-tests should give you an idea of how prepared you are to take both of the real exams before beginning to study for them.

- Go through each diagnostic exam step-by-step and question-by-question to build your confidence level.
- Review the correct answers and explanations so that you see what you do and do not yet fully understand.

---

[1]There are two AP exams in economics: Microeconomics and Macroeconomics. When I refer to both exams, I just call them the AP Economics exams.

Step 3: Develop Strategies for Success

In this step you'll learn strategies that will help you do your best on the exam. These strategies cover both the multiple-choice and free-response sections of the exam. Some of these tips are based upon my understanding of how the questions are designed, and others have been gleaned from my years of experience reading (grading) the AP Economics exams.

- Learn to read multiple-choice questions.
- Learn how to answer multiple-choice questions, including whether or not to guess.
- Learn how to plan and write the free-response questions.

Step 4: Review the Knowledge You Need to Score High

In this step you'll learn or review the material you need to know for the test. This review section takes up the bulk of this book. It contains:

- A comprehensive review of microeconomics.
- A comprehensive review of macroeconomics.

Studying for one exam is daunting enough, but studying for two exams, in one subject area, can be unsettling. There is a lot of material here, enough to summarize a year-long experience in AP Microeconomics and Macroeconomics and highlight the, well, highlights. Some AP courses will have covered more material than yours, some will have covered less, but the bottom line is that if you thoroughly review this material, you will have studied all that is tested on the exam, and you will have significantly increased your chances of scoring well. This 2008–2009 edition gives new emphasis to some areas of the microeconomic and macroeconomic content to bring your review more in line with recent exams. For example, there is more discussion of efficiency and game theory in the microeconomics review and more discussion of the market for loanable funds in the macroeconomics review.

Step 5: Build Your Test-Taking Confidence

In this step you'll complete your preparation by testing yourself on practice exams. This section contains two complete exams in microeconomics and macroeconomics, solutions, and, sometimes more importantly, advice on how to avoid the common mistakes. Once again, the 2008–2009 edition of this book has updated the free-response exams to more accurately reflect the content tested on recent AP exams. Be aware that these practice exams are *not* reproduced questions from actual AP Economics exams, but they mirror both the material tested by AP and the way in which it is tested.

Lastly, at the back of this book you'll find additional resources to aid your preparation. These include:

- A summary of formulas related to the AP Economics exams.
- A glossary of terms related to the AP Economics exams.
- A list of Web sites related to the AP Economics exams.
- A brief bibliography.

Introduction to the Graphics Used in this Book

To emphasize particular skills and strategies, we use several icons throughout this book. An icon in the margin will alert you to pay particular attention to the accompanying text. We use these three icons:

This icon indicates a very important concept or fact that you should not pass over.

This icon calls your attention to a strategy that you might want to try.

This icon alerts you to a tip that you might find useful.

Boldfaced words indicate terms that are included in the glossary at the end of this book. Throughout the book you will also find marginal notes, boxes, and starred areas. Pay close attention to these areas because they can provide tips, hints, strategies, and further explanations to help you reach your full potential.

5 STEPS TO A 5

AP Microeconomics/ Macroeconomics

2010–2011

STEP 1

Set Up Your Study Program

CHAPTER 1

What You Need to Know About the AP Economics Exams

IN THIS CHAPTER

Summary: Learn what topics are tested, how the test is scored, and basic test-taking information.

Key Ideas
- ✪ Most colleges will award credit for a score of 4 or 5.
- ✪ Multiple-choice questions account for two-thirds of your final score.
- ✪ One-quarter of a point is deducted for each wrong answer on multiple-choice questions.
- ✪ Free-response questions account for one-third of your final score.
- ✪ Your composite score on the two test sections is converted to a score on the 1-to-5 scale.

Background Information

The AP Economics exams that you are taking were first offered by the College Board in 1989. Since then, the number of students taking the tests has grown rapidly. In 1989, 3,198 students took the Macroeconomics exam, and by 2008 that number had increased to 68,009.

Some Frequently Asked Questions About the AP Economics Exams

Why Take the AP Economics Exams?

While there might be some altruistic motivators, let's face it: most of you take the AP Economics exams because you are seeking college credit. The majority of colleges and universities will accept a 4 or 5 as acceptable credit for their Principles of Microeconomics or Macroeconomics courses. Many private colleges will give you credit if you take both exams and receive a combined score of a 9 or 10. A small number of schools will even accept a 3 on an exam. This means you are one or two courses closer to graduation before you even begin working on the "freshman 15." Even if you do not score high enough to earn college credit, the fact that you elected to enroll in AP courses tells admission committees that you are a high achiever and serious about your education. In recent years close to two-thirds of students have scored a 3 or higher on their AP Microeconomics or Macroeconomics exams.

What Is the Format of the Exams?

Table 1.1 Summarizes the format of the AP Macroeconomics and Microeconomics exams

AP MACROECONOMICS		
Section	*Number of Questions*	*Time Limit*
I. Multiple-Choice Questions	60	1 hour and 10 minutes
II. Free-Response Questions	3	Planning time: 10 minutes Writing time: 50 minutes

AP MICROECONOMICS		
Section	*Number of Questions*	*Time Limit*
I. Multiple-Choice Questions	60	1 hour and 10 minutes
II. Free-Response Questions	3	Planning time: 10 minutes Writing time: 50 minutes

Who Writes the AP Economics Exams?

Development of each AP exam is a multi-year effort that involves many education and testing professionals and students. At the heart of the effort is the AP Economics Development Committee, a group of college and high school economics teachers who are typically asked to serve for three years. The committee and other college professors create a large pool of multiple-choice questions. With the help of the testing experts at Educational Testing Service (ETS), these questions are then pre-tested with college students enrolled in Principles of Microeconomics and Macroeconomics for accuracy, appropriateness, clarity, and assurance that there is only one possible answer. The results of this pre-testing allow each question to be categorized by degree of difficulty. Several more months of development and refinement later, Section I of the exam is ready to be administered.

The free-response essay questions that make up Section II go through a similar process of creation, modification, pre-testing, and final refinement so that the questions cover the necessary areas of material and are at an appropriate level of difficulty and clarity. The committee also makes a great effort to construct a free-response exam that will allow for clear and equitable grading by the AP readers.

At the conclusion of each AP reading and scoring of exams, the exam itself and the results are thoroughly evaluated by the committee and by ETS. In this way, the College Board can use the results to make suggestions for course development in high schools and to plan future exams.

What Topics Appear on the Exams?

Excellent question. The College Board, after consulting with teachers of economics, develops a curriculum that covers material that college professors expect to cover in their first-year classes. Based upon this outline of topics, the multiple-choice exams are written such that those topics are covered in proportion to their importance to the expected economics understanding of the student. Confused? Suppose that faculty consultants agree that environmental issues are important to the microeconomics curriculum, maybe to the tune of 10 percent. If 10 percent of the curriculum in an AP Microeconomics course is devoted to environmental issues, you can expect roughly 10 percent of the multiple-choice exam to address environmental issues. Below are the general outlines for the Microeconomics and Macroeconomics curriculum and exams. Remember this is just a guide and each year the exam differs slightly in the percentages.

Microeconomics

Content Area	Approximate percentage for exam (multiple-choice)
I. Basic Economic Concepts	8–14%
A. Scarcity, choice, and opportunity cost	
B. Production possibilities curve	
C. Comparative advantage, specialization, and trade	
D. Property rights and role of incentives	
E. Marginal analysis	
II. The Nature and Functions of Product Markets	70%
A. Supply and demand (15–20%)	
1. Market equilibrium	
2. Determinants of supply and demand	
3. Price and quantity controls	
4. Elasticity	
a. Price, income, and cross-price elasticities of demand	
b. Price elasticity of supply	
5. Consumer surplus, producer surplus, and market efficiency	
6. Tax incidence and dead weight loss	
B. Theory of consumer choice (5–10%)	
1. Total utility and marginal utility	
2. Utility maximization: equalizing marginal utility per dollar	

       3. Individual and market demand curves
       4. Income and substitution effects
    C. Production and costs (10–15%)
       1. Production functions: short and long run
       2. Marginal product and diminishing returns
       3. Short-run costs
       4. Long-run costs and economies of scale
       5. Cost minimizing input combination
    D. Firm behavior and market structures (25–35%)
       1. Profit
          a. Accounting versus economic profits
          b. Normal profit
          c. Profit maximization: MR = MC rule
       2. Perfect competition
          a. Profit maximization
          b. Short-run supply and shutdown decision
          c. Firm and market behaviors in short-run and long-run equilibria
          d. Efficiency and perfect competition
       3. Monopoly
          a. Sources of market power
          b. Profit maximization
          c. Inefficiency of monopoly
          d. Price discrimination
       4. Oligopoly
          a. Interdependence, collusion, and cartels
          b. Game theory and strategic behavior
       5. Monopolistic competition
          a. Product differentiation and role of advertising
          b. Profit maximization
          c. Short-run and long-run equilibria
          d. Excess capacity and inefficiency

III. Factor Markets   10–18%
    A. Derived factor demand
    B. Marginal revenue product
    C. Labor market and firms' hiring of labor
    D. Market distribution of income

IV. Market Failure and the Role of Government   12–18%
    A. Externalities
       1. Marginal social benefit and marginal social cost
       2. Positive externalities
       3. Negative externalities
       4. Remedies
    B. Public goods
       1. Public versus private goods
       2. Provision of public goods
    C. Public policy to promote competition
       1. Antitrust policy
       2. Regulation

    D. Income distribution
      1. Equity
      2. Sources of income inequality

Macroeconomics

Content Area	Approximate percentage for exam (multiple-choice)
I. Basic Economic Concepts	8–12%
A. Scarcity, choice, and opportunity cost	
B. Production possibilities curve	
C. Comparative advantage, specialization, and trade	
D. Demand, supply, and market equilibrium	
E. Macroeconomic issues: business cycles, unemployment, inflation, growth	
II. Measurement of Economic Performance	12–16%
A. National income accounts	
1. Circular flow	
2. Gross domestic product	
3. Components of gross domestic product	
4. Real versus nominal gross domestic product	
B. Inflation measurement and adjustment	
1. Price indices	
2. Nominal and real values	
3. Costs of inflation	
C. Unemployment	
1. Definition and measurement	
2. Types of unemployment	
3. Natural rate of unemployment	
III. National Income and Price Determination	10–15%
A. Aggregate demand	
1. Determinants of aggregate demand	
2. Multiplier and crowding-out effects	
B. Aggregate supply	
1. Short-run and long-run analyses	
2. Sticky versus flexible wages and prices	
3. Determinants of aggregate supply	
C. Macroeconomic equilibrium	
1. Real output and price level	
2. Short and long run	
3. Actual versus full-employment output	
4. Economic fluctuations	
IV. Financial Sector	15–20%
A. Money, banking, and financial markets	
1. Definition of financial assets: money, stocks, bonds	

    2. Time value of money
    3. Measures of money supply
    4. Banks and the creation of money
    5. Money demand
    6. Money market
    7. Loanable funds market
  B. Central bank and control of the money supply
    1. Tools of central bank policy
    2. Quantity theory of money
    3. Real versus nominal interest rates

  V. Inflation, Unemployment, and Stabilization Policies   20–30%
  A. Fiscal and monetary policies
    1. Demand-side effects
    2. Supply-side effects
    3. Policy mix
    4. Government deficits and debt
  B. Inflation and unemployment
    1. Types of inflation
      a. Demand-pull inflation
      b. Cost-push inflation
    2. The Phillips curve: short-run versus long-run
    3. Role of expectations

  VI. Economic Growth and Productivity   5–10%
  A. Investment in human capital
  B. Investment in physical capital
  C. Research and development, and technological progress
  D. Growth policy

  VII. Open Economy: International Trade and Finance   10–15%
  A. Balance of payments accounts
    1. Balance of trade
    2. Current account
    3. Capital account
  B. Foreign exchange market
    1. Demand for and supply of foreign exchange
    2. Exchange rate determination
    3. Currency appreciation and depreciation
  C. Net exports and capital flows
  D. Links to financial and goods markets

Who Grades My AP Economics Exam?

From confidential sources, I can tell you that over 100,000 free-response essay booklets are dropped from a three-story building, and those that fall into a small cardboard box are given a 5, those that fall into a slightly larger box are given a 4, and so on until those that fall into a dumpster receive a 1. It's really quite scientific!

Every June a group of economics teachers gather for a week to assign grades to your hard work. Each of these "Faculty Consultants" spends a day or so getting trained on one question and one question only. Because each reader becomes an expert on that question, and because each exam book is anonymous, this process provides a very consistent and unbiased scoring of that question. During a typical day of grading, a random sample of each reader's scores is selected and cross-checked by other experienced "Table Leaders" to insure that the consistency is maintained throughout the day and the week. Each reader's scores on a given question are also statistically analyzed to make sure that they are not giving scores that are significantly higher or lower than the mean scores given by other readers of that question. All measures are taken to maintain consistency and fairness for your benefit.

Will My Exam Remain Anonymous?

Absolutely. Even if your high school teacher happens to randomly read your booklet, there is virtually no way he or she will know it is you. To the reader, each student is a number and to the computer, each student is a bar code.

What About That Permission Box on the Back?

The College Board uses some exams to help train high school teachers so that they can help the next generation of economics students to avoid common mistakes. If you check this box, you simply give permission to use your exam in this way. Even if you give permission, your anonymity is still maintained.

How Is My Multiple-Choice Exam Scored?

The multiple-choice section of each Economics exam is 60 questions and is worth two-thirds of your final score. Your answer sheet is run through the computer, which adds up your correct responses and subtracts a fraction for each incorrect response. For every incorrect answer that you give, one-quarter of a point is deducted and the total is a raw score. This formula looks something like this:

$$\text{Section I Raw Score} = N_{right} - 0.25 N_{wrong}$$

How Is My Free-Response Exam Scored?

Your performance on the free-response section is worth one-third of your final score. The Economics exam in both microeconomics and macroeconomics consists of three questions. Because the first question is longer than the other two, and therefore scored on a higher scale, it is given a different weight in the raw score. For example, question #1 might be graded on a scale of 10 points while question #2 is graded on a scale of 7 points and question #3 on a scale of 5 points. Every year, ETS, the Economics Development Committee, and the Chief Faculty Consultant tinker with the weighting formulas. However, if you use the following sample formula as a rough guide, you'll be able to gauge your approximate score on the practice questions.

$$\text{Section II Raw Score} = (1.50 \times \text{Score \#1}) + (1.0714 \times \text{Score \#2}) + (1.50 \times \text{Score \#3})$$

So How Is My Final Grade Determined and What Does It Mean?

With a total composite score of 90 points, and 60 being determined on Section I, the remaining 30 must be divided among the three essay questions in Section II. The total composite score is then a weighted sum of the multiple-choice and the free-response sections.

In the end, when all of the numbers have been crunched, the Chief Faculty Consultant converts the range of composite scores to the 5-point scale of the AP grades.

Table 1.2 gives you a very rough example of a conversion and as you complete the practice exams, you may use this to give yourself a hypothetical grade, keeping in mind that every year the conversion changes slightly to adjust for the difficulty of the questions from year to year. You should receive your grade in early July.

Table 1.2

MICROECONOMICS		MACROECONOMICS		
Composite Score Range	AP Grade	Composite Score Range	AP Grade	Interpretation
73–90	5	71–90	5	Extremely well qualified for college credit
58–72	4	53–70	4	Well qualified
45–57	3	43–52	3	Qualified
33–44	2	31–42	2	Possibly qualified
0–32	1	0–30	1	No recommendation

Example:

In Section I, you receive 50 correct and 10 incorrect responses on the macroeconomics practice exam. In Section II, your scores are 7/10, 6/7, and 5/5.

$$\text{Weighted Section I} = 50 - 0.25 \times 10 = 47.5$$

$$\text{Weighted Section II} = (1.50 \times 7) + (1.0714 \times 6) + (1.50 \times 5)$$
$$= 10.50 + 6.4284 + 7.5 = 24.4284$$

Composite Score = 47.5 + 24.4284 = 71.9284, rounded to 72, which would be assigned a 5.

How Do I Register and How Much Does It Cost?

If you are enrolled in AP Economics in your high school, your teacher is going to provide all of these details, but a quick summary wouldn't hurt. After all, you do not have to enroll in the AP course to register for and complete the AP exam. When in doubt, the best source of information is the College Board's Web site: www.collegeboard.com.

In 2008 the fee for taking the morning Macroeconomics and afternoon Microeconomics exams was $86 for each exam. Students who demonstrate financial need may receive a $22 refund to help offset the cost of testing. There are also several *optional* fees that *can* be paid if you want your scores rushed to you or if you wish to receive multiple grade reports.

The coordinator of the AP program at your school will inform you where and when you will take the exam. If you live in a small community, your exam might not be administered at your school, so be sure to get this information.

What If My School Only Offered AP Macroeconomics and Not AP Microeconomics, or Vice Versa?

Because of budget and personnel constraints, some high schools cannot offer both Microeconomics and Macroeconomics. The majority of these schools choose the macro side of the AP program, but some choose the micro side. This puts students at a significant disadvantage when they sit down for the Microeconomics exam without having taken the course. Likewise, Macroeconomics test takers have a rough time when they have not taken the Macroeconomics course. If you are in this situation, and you put in the necessary effort, I assure you that buying this book will give you more than a fighting chance on either exam even if your school did not offer that course.

What Should I Bring to the Exam?

On exam day, I suggest bringing the following items:

- Several pencils and an eraser that doesn't leave smudges.
- Black or blue colored pens for the free-response section. Some students like to use two colors to make their graphs stand out for the reader.
- A watch so that you can monitor your time. You never know if the exam room will, or will not, have a clock on the wall. Make sure you turn off the beep that goes off on the hour.
- Your school code.
- Your photo identification and social security number.
- Tissues.
- Your quiet confidence that you are prepared!

What Should I NOT Bring to the Exam?

It's probably a good idea to leave the following items at home:

- A calculator is not allowed on the Microeconomics or Macroeconomics exam.
- A cell phone, beeper, PDA, or walkie-talkie.
- Books, a dictionary, study notes, flash cards, highlighting pens, correction fluid, a ruler, or any other office supplies.
- Portable music of any kind. No CD players, MP3 players, or iPods are allowed.
- Clothing with any economics on it.
- Panic or fear. It's natural to be nervous, but you can comfort yourself that you have used this book well and that there is no room for fear on your exam.

CHAPTER 2

How to Plan Your Time

IN THIS CHAPTER

Summary: The right preparation plan for you depends on your study habits and the amount of time you have before the test.

Key Idea

✪ Choose the study plan that's right for you.

Three Approaches to Preparing for AP Exams

What kind of preparation program for the AP exam should you follow? Should you carefully follow every step, or are there perhaps some steps you can bypass? That depends not only on how much time you have, but also on what kind of student you are. No one knows your study habits, likes, and dislikes better than you do. So you are the only one who can decide which approach you want and/or need to adopt. This chapter presents three possible study plans, labeled A, B, and C. Look at the brief profiles below. These will help you determine which of these three plans is right for you.

You're a full-school-year prep student if:

1. You are the kind of person who likes to plan for everything very far in advance.
2. You buy your best friend a gift two months before his or her birthday because you know exactly what to choose, where you will buy it, and how much you will pay for it.
3. You like detailed planning and everything in its place.
4. You feel that you must be thoroughly prepared.
5. You hate surprises.

If you fit this profile, consider **Plan A**.

You're a one-semester prep student if:

1. You buy your best friend a gift one week before his or her birthday because it sort of snuck up on you, yet you have a clear idea of exactly what you will be purchasing.
2. You are willing to plan ahead to feel comfortable in stressful situations, but are okay with skipping some details.
3. You feel more comfortable when you know what to expect, but a surprise or two is cool.
4. You're always on time for appointments.

If you fit this profile, consider **Plan B**.

You're a 6-week prep student if:

1. You buy your best friend a gift for his or her birthday, but you need to include a belated card because you missed it by a couple of days.
2. You work best under pressure and tight deadlines.
3. You feel very confident with the skills and background you've learned in your AP Economics classes.
4. You decided late in the year to take the exam.
5. You like surprises.
6. You feel okay if you arrive 10 to 15 minutes late for an appointment.

If you fit this profile, consider **Plan C**.

Table 2.1 Three Different Study Schedules

MONTH	PLAN A: FULL SCHOOL YEAR	PLAN B: ONE SEMESTER	PLAN C: 6 WEEKS
September to October	Introduction; Chapters 1 to 4	—	—
November	Chapters 5 to 7	—	—
December	Chapters 8 to 9	—	—
January	Chapters 10 to 11	Chapters 1 to 4	—
February	Chapters 12 to 13; Micro Practice Exam 1	Chapters 5 to 11; Micro Practice Exam 1	—
March	Chapters 14 to 15	Chapters 12 to 14	—
April	Chapters 16 to 17; Macro Practice Exam 1	Chapters 15 to 17; Macro Practice Exam 1	Skim Chapters 1 to 11; all rapid reviews; take both Practice Exams 1
May	Review everything; take both Practice Exams 2	Review everything; take both Practice Exams 2	Skim Chapters 12 to 17; take both Practice Exams 2

Calendar For Each Plan

Plan A: You Have a Full School Year to Prepare

Use this plan to organize your study during the coming school year.

SEPTEMBER–OCTOBER (Check off the activities as you complete them.)

_____ Determine the student mode (A, B, or C) that applies to you.

_____ Carefully read Chapters 1 to 4 of this book.

_____ Take the Diagnostic Exams.

_____ Pay close attention to your walk through of the Diagnostic Exams.

_____ Get on the Web and take a look at the AP Web site(s).

_____ Skim the review chapters in Step 4 of this book. (Reviewing the topics covered in this section will be part of your year-long preparation.)

_____ Buy a few color highlighters.

_____ Flip through the entire book. Break the book in. Write in it. Toss it around a little bit … highlight it.

_____ Get a clear picture of your own school's AP Economics curriculum.

_____ Begin to use this book as a resource to supplement the classroom learning.

NOVEMBER (the first 10 weeks have elapsed)

_____ Read and study Chapter 5, Fundamentals of Economic Analysis.

_____ Read and study Chapter 6, Demand, Supply, Market Equilibrium, and Welfare Analysis.

_____ Read and study Chapter 7, Elasticity, Microeconomic Policy, and Consumer Theory.

DECEMBER

_____ Read and study Chapter 8, The Firm, Profit, and the Costs of Production.

_____ Read and study Chapter 9, Market Structures, Perfect Competition, Monopoly and Things Between.

_____ Review Chapters 5 to 7.

JANUARY (20 weeks have elapsed)

_____ Read and study Chapter 10, Factor Markets.

_____ Read and study Chapter 11, Public Goods, Externalities, and the Role of Government.

_____ Review Chapters 5 to 9.

FEBRUARY

_____ Take Microeconomics Practice Exam 1 in the first week of February.

_____ Evaluate your Micro strengths and weaknesses.

_____ Study appropriate chapters to correct your Micro weaknesses.

_____ Read and study Chapter 12, Macroeconomic Measures of Performance.

_____ Read and study Chapter 13, Consumption, Saving, Investment and the Multiplier.

_____ Review Chapters 5 to 11.

MARCH (30 weeks have now elapsed)

_____ Read and study Chapter 14, Aggregate Demand and Aggregate Supply.

_____ Read and study Chapter 15, Fiscal Policy, Economic Growth and Productivity.

_____ Review Chapters 5 to 13.

APRIL

_____ Read and study Chapter 16, Money, Banking and Monetary Policy.

_____ Read and study Chapter 17, International Trade.

_____ Review Chapters 5 to 15.

_____ Take Macroeconomics Practice Exam 1 in the last week of April.

_____ Evaluate your Macro strengths and weaknesses.

_____ Study appropriate chapters to correct your Macro weaknesses.

MAY (first 2 weeks) (THIS IS IT!)

_____ Review Chapters 5 to 17 – all the material!

_____ Take both Practice Exams 2.

_____ Score yourself.

_____ Get a good night's sleep before the exam. Fall asleep knowing that you are well prepared.

GOOD LUCK ON THE TEST!

Plan B: You Have One Semester to Prepare

If you have already completed one semester of economic studies, the following plan will help you use those skills you've been practicing to prepare for the May exam.

JANUARY–FEBRUARY

_____ Carefully read Chapters 1 to 4 of this book.

_____ Take the Diagnostic Exams.

_____ Pay close attention to your walk through of the Diagnostic Exams.

_____ Read and study Chapter 5, Fundamentals of Economic Analysis.

_____ Read and study Chapter 6, Demand, Supply, Market Equilibrium, and Welfare Analysis.

_____ Read and study Chapter 7, Elasticity, Microeconomic Policy, and Consumer Theory.

_____ Read and study Chapter 8, The Firm, Profit, and the Costs of Production.

_____ Read and study Chapter 9, Market Structures, Perfect Competition, Monopoly and Things Between.

_____ Read and study Chapter 10, Factor Markets.

_____ Read and study Chapter 11, Public Goods, Externalities, and the Role of Government.

_____ Take Microeconomics Practice Exam 1 in the last week of February.

_____ Evaluate your Micro strengths and weaknesses.

_____ Study appropriate chapters to correct your Micro weaknesses.

MARCH (10 weeks to go)

_____ Read and study Chapter 12, Macroeconomic Measures of Performance.

_____ Read and study Chapter 13, Consumption, Saving, Investment and the Multiplier.

_____ Read and study Chapter 14, Aggregate Demand and Aggregate Supply.

_____ Review Chapters 5 to 11.

APRIL

_____ Read and study Chapter 15, Fiscal Policy.

_____ Read and study Chapter 16, Money, Banking and Monetary Policy.

_____ Read and study Chapter 17, International Trade.

_____ Take Macroeconomics Practice Exam 1 in the last week of April.

_____ Evaluate your Macro strengths and weaknesses.

_____ Study appropriate chapters to correct your Macro weaknesses.

_____ Review Chapters 12 to 17.

MAY (first 2 weeks) (THIS IS IT!)

_____ Review Chapters 5 to 17 – all the material!

_____ Take both Practice Exams 2.

_____ Score yourself.

_____ Get a good night's sleep before the exam. Fall asleep knowing that you are well prepared.

GOOD LUCK ON THE TEST!

Plan C: You Have Six Weeks to Prepare

Use this plan if you have been studying economics for 6 months or more and intend to use this book primarily as a specific guide to the AP Economics exams. If you have only 6 weeks to prepare, now is not the time to try to learn everything. Focus instead on the essential points you need to know for the test.

APRIL 1–15

_____ Skim Chapters 1 to 4 of this book.

_____ Skim Chapters 5 to 11.

_____ Carefully go over the Rapid Review sections of Chapters 5 to 11.

_____ Complete the Microeconomics Practice Exam 1.

_____ Score yourself and analyze your errors.

_____ Skim and highlight the Glossary at the end of the book.

APRIL 15–MAY 1

_____ Skim Chapters 12 to 17.

_____ Carefully go over the Rapid Review sections of Chapters 12 to 17.

_____ Complete the Macroeconomics Practice Exam 1.

_____ Score yourself and analyze your errors.

_____ Continue to skim and highlight the Glossary at the end of the book.

MAY (first 2 weeks) (THIS IS IT!)

_____ Carefully go over the Rapid Review sections of Chapters 5 to 17.

_____ Take both Practice Exams 2.

_____ Score yourself and analyze your errors.

_____ Get a good night's sleep before the exam. Fall asleep knowing that you are well prepared.

GOOD LUCK ON THE TEST!

STEP **2**

Determine Your Test Readiness

CHAPTER **3**   Take Diagnostic Exams

CHAPTER 3

Take Diagnostic Exams

IN THIS CHAPTER

Summary: Because you are studying for two exams, this chapter includes a diagnostic exam for both microeconomics and macroeconomics. These are each half the length of the real thing and are restricted to multiple-choice questions. They are intended to give you an idea of where you stand with your economics preparation. The questions have been written to approximate the coverage of material that you will see on the AP exams and are similar to the review questions that you see at the end of each chapter in this book. Once you are done with both exams, check your work against the given answers, which also indicate where you can find the corresponding material in this book. Also provided is a way to convert your score to a rough AP score.

Key Ideas

✪ Practice the kind of multiple-choice questions you will be asked on the real exam.

✪ Answer questions that approximate the coverage of topics on the real exam.

✪ Check your work against the given answers.

✪ Determine your areas of strength and weakness.

✪ Earmark the pages which you must give special attention.

Diagnostic Exams: Answer Sheet

Record your responses to the exams in the spaces below.

MICROECONOMICS—SECTION I

1 Ⓐ Ⓑ Ⓒ Ⓓ Ⓔ	11 Ⓐ Ⓑ Ⓒ Ⓓ Ⓔ	21 Ⓐ Ⓑ Ⓒ Ⓓ Ⓔ
2 Ⓐ Ⓑ Ⓒ Ⓓ Ⓔ	12 Ⓐ Ⓑ Ⓒ Ⓓ Ⓔ	22 Ⓐ Ⓑ Ⓒ Ⓓ Ⓔ
3 Ⓐ Ⓑ Ⓒ Ⓓ Ⓔ	13 Ⓐ Ⓑ Ⓒ Ⓓ Ⓔ	23 Ⓐ Ⓑ Ⓒ Ⓓ Ⓔ
4 Ⓐ Ⓑ Ⓒ Ⓓ Ⓔ	14 Ⓐ Ⓑ Ⓒ Ⓓ Ⓔ	24 Ⓐ Ⓑ Ⓒ Ⓓ Ⓔ
5 Ⓐ Ⓑ Ⓒ Ⓓ Ⓔ	15 Ⓐ Ⓑ Ⓒ Ⓓ Ⓔ	25 Ⓐ Ⓑ Ⓒ Ⓓ Ⓔ
6 Ⓐ Ⓑ Ⓒ Ⓓ Ⓔ	16 Ⓐ Ⓑ Ⓒ Ⓓ Ⓔ	26 Ⓐ Ⓑ Ⓒ Ⓓ Ⓔ
7 Ⓐ Ⓑ Ⓒ Ⓓ Ⓔ	17 Ⓐ Ⓑ Ⓒ Ⓓ Ⓔ	27 Ⓐ Ⓑ Ⓒ Ⓓ Ⓔ
8 Ⓐ Ⓑ Ⓒ Ⓓ Ⓔ	18 Ⓐ Ⓑ Ⓒ Ⓓ Ⓔ	28 Ⓐ Ⓑ Ⓒ Ⓓ Ⓔ
9 Ⓐ Ⓑ Ⓒ Ⓓ Ⓔ	19 Ⓐ Ⓑ Ⓒ Ⓓ Ⓔ	29 Ⓐ Ⓑ Ⓒ Ⓓ Ⓔ
10 Ⓐ Ⓑ Ⓒ Ⓓ Ⓔ	20 Ⓐ Ⓑ Ⓒ Ⓓ Ⓔ	30 Ⓐ Ⓑ Ⓒ Ⓓ Ⓔ

MACROECONOMICS—SECTION I

1 Ⓐ Ⓑ Ⓒ Ⓓ Ⓔ	11 Ⓐ Ⓑ Ⓒ Ⓓ Ⓔ	21 Ⓐ Ⓑ Ⓒ Ⓓ Ⓔ
2 Ⓐ Ⓑ Ⓒ Ⓓ Ⓔ	12 Ⓐ Ⓑ Ⓒ Ⓓ Ⓔ	22 Ⓐ Ⓑ Ⓒ Ⓓ Ⓔ
3 Ⓐ Ⓑ Ⓒ Ⓓ Ⓔ	13 Ⓐ Ⓑ Ⓒ Ⓓ Ⓔ	23 Ⓐ Ⓑ Ⓒ Ⓓ Ⓔ
4 Ⓐ Ⓑ Ⓒ Ⓓ Ⓔ	14 Ⓐ Ⓑ Ⓒ Ⓓ Ⓔ	24 Ⓐ Ⓑ Ⓒ Ⓓ Ⓔ
5 Ⓐ Ⓑ Ⓒ Ⓓ Ⓔ	15 Ⓐ Ⓑ Ⓒ Ⓓ Ⓔ	25 Ⓐ Ⓑ Ⓒ Ⓓ Ⓔ
6 Ⓐ Ⓑ Ⓒ Ⓓ Ⓔ	16 Ⓐ Ⓑ Ⓒ Ⓓ Ⓔ	26 Ⓐ Ⓑ Ⓒ Ⓓ Ⓔ
7 Ⓐ Ⓑ Ⓒ Ⓓ Ⓔ	17 Ⓐ Ⓑ Ⓒ Ⓓ Ⓔ	27 Ⓐ Ⓑ Ⓒ Ⓓ Ⓔ
8 Ⓐ Ⓑ Ⓒ Ⓓ Ⓔ	18 Ⓐ Ⓑ Ⓒ Ⓓ Ⓔ	28 Ⓐ Ⓑ Ⓒ Ⓓ Ⓔ
9 Ⓐ Ⓑ Ⓒ Ⓓ Ⓔ	19 Ⓐ Ⓑ Ⓒ Ⓓ Ⓔ	29 Ⓐ Ⓑ Ⓒ Ⓓ Ⓔ
10 Ⓐ Ⓑ Ⓒ Ⓓ Ⓔ	20 Ⓐ Ⓑ Ⓒ Ⓓ Ⓔ	30 Ⓐ Ⓑ Ⓒ Ⓓ Ⓔ

Diagnostic Exam: AP Microeconomics

SECTION I

Time—35 Minutes
30 Questions

For the following multiple-choice questions, select the best answer choice and record your choice on the answer sheet provided.

1. Scarcity is best defined as

    (A) the difference between limited wants and limited economic resources.
    (B) the difference between the total benefit of an action and the total cost of that action.
    (C) the difference between unlimited wants and limited economic resources.
    (D) the opportunity cost of pursuing a given course of action.
    (E) the difference between the marginal benefit and marginal cost of an action.

2. Which of the following statements describes a capitalist market economy?

    I. Economic resources are allocated based upon relative prices.
    II. Private property is fundamental to innovation, growth, and trade.
    III. A central government plans the production and distribution of goods.

    (A) I only
    (B) II only
    (C) III only
    (D) I and II only
    (E) I and III only

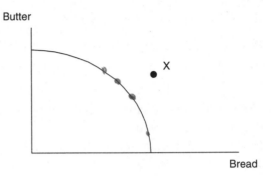

Figure D.1

3. The graph above (Figure D.1) shows a nation's production possibility frontier (PPF) for the production of bread and butter. Which of the following is true?

    (A) The opportunity cost of producing more butter is a decreasing amount of bread.
    (B) Point X represents unemployed economic resources.
    (C) The opportunity cost of producing more butter is a constant amount of bread.
    (D) Point X represents a labor force that has become less productive.
    (E) The opportunity cost of producing more butter is an increasing amount of bread.

4. Which of the following is true of equilibrium in a purely (or perfectly) competitive market for good X?

    (A) A shortage of good X exists.
    (B) The quantity demanded equals the quantity supplied of good X.
    (C) A surplus of good X exists.
    (D) The government regulates the quantity of good X produced at the market price.
    (E) Dead weight loss exists.

5. The competitive market for gasoline is currently in a state of equilibrium. Which of the following would most likely increase the price of gasoline?

   (A) Household income falls.
   (B) Technology used to produce gasoline improves.
   (C) The price of subway tickets and other public transportation falls.
   (D) The price of crude oil, a raw material for gasoline, rises.
   (E) The price of car insurance rises.

6. If the demand for grapes increases simultaneously with an increase in the supply of grapes, we can say that

   (A) equilibrium quantity rises, but the price change is ambiguous.
   (B) equilibrium quantity falls, but the price change is ambiguous.
   (C) equilibrium quantity rises, and the price rises.
   (D) equilibrium quantity falls, and the price falls.
   (E) the quantity change is ambiguous, but the equilibrium price rises.

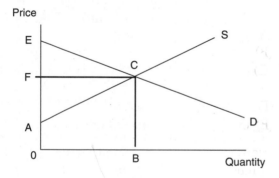

Figure D.2

7. In Figure D.2 above, identify the area of consumer surplus.

   (A) 0ACB
   (B) 0FCB
   (C) AFC
   (D) ACE
   (E) FCE

8. Suppose the price of beef rises by 10 percent and the quantity demanded of beef falls by 20 percent. We can conclude that

   (A) demand for beef is price elastic and consumer spending on beef is falling.
   (B) demand for beef is price elastic and consumer spending on beef is rising.
   (C) demand for beef is price inelastic and consumer spending on beef is falling.
   (D) demand for beef is price inelastic and consumer spending on beef is rising.
   (E) demand for beef is unit elastic and consumer spending on beef is constant.

9. If the price of firm A's long-distance service rises by 5 percent and the quantity demanded for firm B's long-distance service increases by 10 percent, we can say that

   (A) demand for firm B is price elastic.
   (B) supply for firm B is price elastic.
   (C) firms A and B are substitutes because the cross-price elasticity is greater than zero.
   (D) firms A and B are complements because the cross-price elasticity is less than zero.
   (E) firms A and B are complements because the cross-price elasticity is greater than zero.

10. Which of the following describes the theory behind the demand curve?

   (A) Decreasing marginal utility as consumption rises.
   (B) Increasing marginal cost as consumption rises.
   (C) Decreasing marginal cost as consumption rises.
   (D) Increasing total utility at an increasing rate as consumption rises.
   (E) The substitution effect is larger than the income effect.

11. If a consumer is not required to pay a monetary price for each cookie she consumes, the consumer will stop eating cookies when

(A) the total utility from eating cookies is equal to zero.
(B) the substitution effect outweighs the income effect from eating cookies.
(C) the ratio of marginal utility divided by total utility is equal to one.
(D) the marginal utility from eating the last cookie is zero.
(E) the marginal utility from eating the next cookie is increasing at a decreasing rate.

12. In the short run, a firm employs labor and capital to produce gadgets. If the annual price of capital increases, what will happen to the short-run cost curves?

(A) The marginal cost and average variable cost curves will shift upward.
(B) The average fixed cost and average total cost curves will shift upward.
(C) The marginal cost and average fixed cost curves will shift upward.
(D) The marginal cost, average fixed cost, average variable cost, and average total cost curves will all shift upward.
(E) Only the average fixed cost curve will shift upward.

Questions 13 to 15 are based on the table of costs below for a perfectly competitive firm.

OUTPUT	AVERAGE FIXED COST	AVERAGE VARIABLE COST	MARGINAL COST
0			
1	$10	$5	$5
2	$5	$3.50	$2
3	$3.33	$4.33	$6
4	$2.50	$5	$7
5	$2	$5.60	$8

13. The total fixed cost of producing a quantity of 4 is

(A) $5
(B) $7.50
(C) $7
(D) $2.50
(E) $10

14. The range of diminishing marginal productivity begins at what level of output?

(A) 1
(B) 2
(C) 3
(D) 4
(E) 5

15. At a quantity of 4, what is the total cost of production?

(A) $7.50
(B) $2.50
(C) $15
(D) $30
(E) $14.50

16. Monopolistic competition is often characterized by

(A) strong barriers to entry.
(B) long-run price that exceeds average total cost.
(C) price that exceeds average variable cost, causing excess capacity.
(D) a homogenous product.
(E) many resources devoted to advertising.

Questions 17 to 18 are based on Figure D.3 below, which illustrates the short-run cost curves of a perfectly competitive firm.

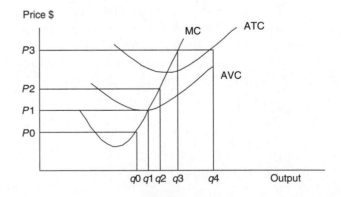

Figure D.3

17. The shutdown point is seen at:

    (A) $P0, q0$
    (B) $P1, q1$
    (C) $P2, q2$
    (D) $P3, q3$
    (E) $P3, q4$

18. If the market price of the output increases from $P1$ to $P3$, the profit-maximizing firm will

    (A) increase output from $q1$ to $q4$ and earn positive economic profits.
    (B) increase output from $q1$ to $q4$ and earn a normal profit.
    (C) increase output from $q1$ to $q3$ and earn positive economic profits.
    (D) increase output from $q1$ to $q3$ and earn a normal profit.
    (E) increase output from $q1$ to $q2$ and earn economic losses.

19. If the perfectly competitive price is currently below minimum average total cost, we can expect which of the following events in the long run?

    (A) The price will rise and each firm's output will fall as firms exit the industry.
    (B) Market equilibrium quantity will increase as firms exit the industry.
    (C) Nothing. The industry is currently in long-run equilibrium.
    (D) Profits will fall as the market price increases.
    (E) The price will rise to the breakeven point as firms exit the industry.

20. Which of the following statements describes a profit-maximizing monopolist?

    I.   Output is set where marginal revenue equals marginal cost, creating an efficient allocation of economic resources.
    II. Dead weight loss is eliminated in the long run.
    III. Price is set above marginal cost, creating allocative inefficiency.

    (A) I only
    (B) II only
    (C) III only
    (D) I and II only
    (E) II and III only

21. Which of the following is necessarily a characteristic of oligopoly?

    (A) Free entry into and exit from the market.
    (B) A few large producers.
    (C) One producer of a good with no close substitutes.
    (D) A homogenous product.
    (E) No opportunities for collusion between firms.

22. The market structures of perfect competition and monopolistic competition share which of the following characteristics?

    (A) Ease of entry and exit in the long run.
    (B) Homogenous products.
    (C) Perfectly elastic demand for the firm's product.
    (D) Long-run positive profits.
    (E) Rigid or "sticky" prices.

23. If the government wishes to regulate a natural monopoly so that it produces an efficient level of output it would be

    (A) where price is equal to average total cost.
    (B) where marginal revenue equals marginal cost.
    (C) where normal profits are made.
    (D) where price is equal to average variable cost.
    (E) where price is equal to marginal cost.

24. Which of the following is most likely to decrease the demand for kindergarten teachers?

    (A) An increase in K–12 funding.
    (B) Increased immigration of foreign citizens and their families.
    (C) A decrease in the average number of children per household.
    (D) Subsidies given to college students who major in elementary education.
    (E) The state decreases the number of classes required to receive a teaching certificate.

25. Which of the following statements is true about the demand for labor?

    (A) It rises if the price of a substitute resource falls and the output effect is greater than the substitution effect.
    (B) It falls if the price of the output produced rises.
    (C) It falls if the price of a complementary resource falls.
    (D) It falls if the demand for the output produced by labor increases.
    (E) It falls if the labor becomes more productive.

Questions 26 to 27 are based on the table of employment data below.

WAGE (W)	QUANTITY OF LABOR SUPPLIED	MARGINAL REVENUE PRODUCT OF LABOR (MRP$_L$)
$4	0	
$5	10	$7
$6	20	$6
$7	30	$5
$8	40	$4

26. If a firm is hiring labor in the perfectly competitive labor market, the wage and employment will be

(A) $4 and zero.
(B) $5 and 10.
(C) $6 and 20.
(D) $7 and 30.
(E) $8 and 40.

27. If the above firm were a monopsonist, the wage would be _____ and employment would be _____ the competitive outcome.

(A) greater than; less than
(B) less than; greater than
(C) greater than; greater than
(D) less than; less than
(E) less than; the same as

28. Which of the following is the best example of a public good?
(A) A visit to the orthodontist.
(B) A session at the tanning salon.
(C) A large pizza.
(D) A cup of coffee.
(E) The Hubble telescope.

29. A negative externality from the production of a good exists when

(A) the market overallocates resources to the production of this good.
(B) spillover benefits are received by society.
(C) the marginal social benefit equals the marginal social cost.
(D) total welfare is maximized.
(E) the marginal private cost exceeds the marginal social cost.

30. Which of the following tax systems is designed to redistribute income from the wealthy to the poor?
(A) A progressive tax system.
(B) A regressive tax system.
(C) A proportional tax system.
(D) An excise tax system.
(E) A tariff system.

Once you have completed the Diagnostic Exam in Microeconomics, take a short break before restarting the clock and completing the Macroeconomics exam. Wait until you are done with both exams before you score them. Again, the questions on this Macroeconomics exam will approximate the coverage of material that you will see on the actual AP exam and are similar to the review questions that you will see at the end of each chapter of review material.

Diagnostic Exam: AP Macroeconomics

SECTION I
Time—35 Minutes
30 Questions

For the following multiple-choice questions, select the best answer choice and record your choice on the answer sheet provided.

1. Which of the following resources are examples of capital?

   I. An electric typewriter
   II. A barrel of crude oil
   III. A registered nurse
   IV. A share of corporate stock

   (A) I only
   (B) II only
   (C) III only
   (D) II and IV only
   (E) I and IV only

Question 2 is based on the production possibilities of two nations that can produce both crepes and paper.

NATION X		NATION Y	
Crepes	Paper	Crepes	Paper
0	3	0	5
9	0	5	0

2. Which of the following statements is true of these production possibilities?

   (A) Nation *X* has comparative advantage in paper production and should trade paper to Nation *Y* in exchange for crepes.
   (B) Nation *X* has comparative advantage in crepe production and should trade crepes to Nation *Y* in exchange for paper.
   (C) Nation *X* has absolute advantage in paper production and Nation *Y* has absolute advantage in crepe production. No trade is possible.
   (D) Nation *Y* has absolute advantage in paper production and Nation *X* has absolute advantage in crepe production. No trade is possible.
   (E) Nation *Y* has comparative advantage in crepe production and should trade paper to Nation *X* in exchange for crepes.

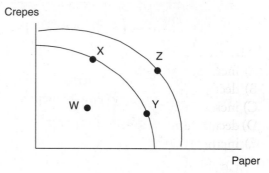

Crepes

Paper

Figure D.4

3. Using the graph above (Figure D.4), which of the following movements would be described as economic growth?
   (A) W to X
   (B) X to Y
   (C) W to Y
   (D) Z to W
   (E) X to Z

4. If DVD players are a normal good, an increase in household income will

   (A) increase the equilibrium quantity and increase the price.
   (B) decrease the equilibrium quantity and increase the price.
   (C) increase the equilibrium price, but the change in quantity is ambiguous.
   (D) decrease the equilibrium quantity and decrease the price.
   (E) increase the equilibrium quantity but the change in price is ambiguous.

5. If an American firm moves a plant from the U.S. to Brazil,

   (A) U.S. GDP falls and Brazil's GDP falls.
   (B) U.S. GDP rises and Brazil's GDP falls.
   (C) U.S. GDP falls and U.S. GNP rises.
   (D) U.S. GDP falls and Brazil's GDP rises.
   (E) U.S. GDP rises and Brazil's GDP rises.

6. For years you work as a grocery checker at a supermarket and one day you are replaced by self-serve checkout stations. What type of unemployment is this?

(A) Cyclical
(B) Structural
(C) Seasonal
(D) Frictional
(E) Discouraged

7. If the CPI increases by 2 percent and your nominal income increases by 8 percent, your real income has

(A) increased by 4 percent.
(B) decreased by 4 percent.
(C) increased by 6 percent.
(D) decreased by 6 percent.
(E) increased by 10 percent.

8. To deflate nominal GDP, you must

(A) divide nominal GDP by the GDP deflator.
(B) multiply real GDP by the GDP deflator.
(C) divide real GDP by the GDP deflator.
(D) multiply nominal GDP by the GDP deflator.
(E) divide nominal GDP by real GDP.

9. A stronger stock market is likely to cause which of the following changes in the consumption function, the MPC, and aggregate demand?

CONSUMPTION FUNCTION	MPC	AGGREGATE DEMAND
(A) Increase	Increase	Increase
(B) No change	No change	No change
(C) Increase	Decrease	No change
(D) Increase	No change	Increase
(E) Decrease	No change	Decrease

10. An increase in investor optimism will have which of the following effects in the market for loanable funds?

(A) An increase in supply, lowering the interest rate.
(B) A decrease in demand, increasing the interest rate.
(C) An increase in both supply and demand, and an ambiguous change in interest rates.
(D) A decrease in supply, decreasing the interest rate.
(E) An increase in demand, increasing the interest rate.

11. If the economy is operating below full employment, which of the following will have the greatest positive impact on real GDP?

(A) The government decreases spending with no change in taxes.
(B) The government increases spending with no change in taxes.
(C) The government decreases spending and matches it with a decrease in taxes.
(D) The government holds spending constant while decreasing taxes.
(E) The government increases spending and matches it with an increase in taxes.

12. Suppose the economy is operating beyond full employment. Which of the following is true at this point?

(A) The short-run AS curve is horizontal.
(B) Further increases in AD will result in a lower price level.
(C) A decrease in AD will result in a lower price level if prices are sticky.
(D) Further increases in AD will not lower the unemployment rate, but will create inflation.
(E) The unemployment rate is higher than the natural rate of unemployment.

13. The spending multiplier is often smaller than predicted because of

(A) lower taxes.
(B) increasing net exports.
(C) falling unemployment.
(D) lower interest rates.
(E) rising price levels.

14. The best example of a negative supply shock to the economy would be

    (A) a decrease in government spending.
    (B) a decrease in the real interest rate.
    (C) an increase in the money supply.
    (D) unexpectedly higher resource prices.
    (E) technological improvements.

15. The Phillips curve represents the relationship between

    (A) inflation and the money supply.
    (B) unemployment and the money supply.
    (C) the money supply and the real interest rate.
    (D) inflation and unemployment.
    (E) investment and the real interest rate.

16. If the economy is experiencing a recession, how will a plan to decrease taxes for consumers and increase spending on government purchases affect real GDP and the price level?

    (A) GDP rises and the price level falls.
    (B) GDP falls and the price level rises.
    (C) GDP rises and the price level rises.
    (D) GDP falls and the price level falls.
    (E) GDP stays the same and the price level rises.

17. Of the following choices, the one most likely to be preferred by supply-side economists would be

    (A) increased government spending.
    (B) higher tariffs on imported goods.
    (C) lower taxes on household income.
    (D) higher welfare payments.
    (E) a tax credit on capital investment.

18. Automatic stabilizers in the economy serve an important role in

    (A) increasing the length of the business cycle.
    (B) balancing the budget.
    (C) increasing a budget surplus in a recession.
    (D) decreasing net tax revenue during economic growth.
    (E) lessening the impact of a recession.

19. The "crowding out" effect is the result of

    (A) decreasing interest rates from contractionary fiscal policy.
    (B) increasing interest rates from expansionary fiscal policy.
    (C) increasing interest rates from expansionary monetary policy.
    (D) increasing unemployment rates from expansionary monetary policy.
    (E) a depreciating dollar versus other currencies.

20. In a recession, expansionary monetary policy is designed to

    (A) decrease AD so that real prices will decrease, which is good for the economy.
    (B) increase AD, which will increase real GDP and increase employment.
    (C) increase unemployment, but low prices negate this effect.
    (D) keep interest rates high, which attracts foreign investment.
    (E) boost the value of the dollar in foreign currency markets.

21. A contractionary monetary policy will cause the nominal interest rate, aggregate demand, output, and the price level to change in which of the following ways?

NOMINAL INTEREST RATE	AGGREGATE DEMAND	OUTPUT	PRICE LEVEL
(A) Decrease	Increase	Increase	Increase
(B) Decrease	Decrease	Decrease	Increase
(C) Increase	Decrease	Decrease	Increase
(D) Increase	Decrease	Decrease	Decrease
(E) Increase	Increase	Increase	Increase

22. Which of the following is a tool used by the Fed to increase the money supply?

    (A) A lower discount rate
    (B) Selling Treasury securities to commercial banks
    (C) A higher reserve ratio
    (D) A lower personal income tax rate
    (E) A lower investment income tax rate

23. Which of the following monetary policies would lessen the effectiveness of expansionary fiscal policy?

    (A) Decreasing the value of the domestic currency.
    (B) Lowering the income tax rate.
    (C) Selling Treasury securities to commercial banks.
    (D) Lowering the discount rate.
    (E) Lowering the reserve ratio.

24. Which of the following is an accurate statement of the money supply in the U.S.?

    (A) The money supply is backed by gold reserves.
    (B) The least liquid measure of money is $M2$.
    (C) $M1$ is larger than $M3$.
    (D) Paper money can be exchanged at commercial banks for an equal amount of gold.
    (E) The most liquid measure of money is $M1$.

25. Excess reserves in the banking system will increase if

    (A) the reserve ratio is increased.
    (B) the checking deposits increase.
    (C) the discount rate is increased.
    (D) the Fed sells Treasury securities to commercial banks.
    (E) income tax rates increase.

26. If a bank has $1000 in checking deposits and the bank is required to reserve $250, what is the reserve ratio? How much does the bank have in excess reserves? What is the size of the money multiplier?

    (A) 25%, $750, $M = ¼$
    (B) 75%, $250, $M = 4$
    (C) 25%, $750, $M = 4$
    (D) 75%, $750, $M = ¼$
    (E) 25%, $250, $M = 4$

27. Suppose the reserve ratio is 10 percent and the Fed buys $1 million in Treasury securities from commercial banks. If money demand is perfectly elastic, which of the following is likely to occur?

    (A) Money supply increases by $10 million, lowering the interest rate and increasing AD.
    (B) Money supply remains constant, the interest rate does not fall, and AD does not increase.
    (C) Money supply increases by $10 million, the interest rate does not fall, and AD does not increase.
    (D) Money supply decreases by $10 million, raising the interest rate and decreasing AD.
    (E) Money supply decreases by $10 million, the interest rate does not rise, and AD does not decrease.

28. If the world price of copper exceeds the domestic (U.S.) price of copper, we would expect

    (A) The U.S. to be a net exporter of copper.
    (B) The U.S. to impose a tariff on imported copper to protect domestic producers.
    (C) The demand for U.S. copper to fall.
    (D) A growing trade deficit in the U.S. in goods and services.
    (E) The dollar to depreciate relative to the currencies of other copper-producing nations.

29. Suppose the Japanese economy is suffering a prolonged recession. Lower Japanese household incomes will affect U.S. exports to Japan, demand for the dollar, and the value of the dollar relative to the yen in which of the following ways?

	EXPORTS TO JAPAN	DEMAND FOR $	VALUE OF $
(A)	Decrease	Decrease	Decrease
(B)	Decrease	Decrease	Increase
(C)	Decrease	Increase	Decrease
(D)	Increase	Decrease	Decrease
(E)	Increase	Decrease	Increase

30. Which of the following is a likely effect of a higher tariff imposed by the U.S. on imported automobiles?
    (A) Net exports will fall and the dollar will appreciate in value.
    (B) Net exports will fall and the dollar will depreciate in value.
    (C) The price of automobiles in the U.S. will fall.
    (D) Net exports will rise and the dollar will depreciate in value.
    (E) Net exports will rise and the dollar will appreciate in value.

Microeconomics Answers and Explanations, Section I

This Diagnostic Exam was designed to test you on topics that you will see on the AP Microeconomics exam in the approximate proportions that you will see them. Chronologically they appear in the approximate order of their review in Step 4 of this book, but this is not the case on the AP exam. Topics on the practice exams are shuffled.

Questions from Chapter 5

1. **C**—This is the definition of scarcity.

2. **D**—In a capitalistic market economy the central government has minimal roles in the production and distribution of goods. Resources are allocated based on relative, not absolute, prices. The role of private property is central to capitalism.

3. **E**—A concave, or bowed out, PPF illustrates the principle of increasing opportunity costs. It is more and more difficult (costly) to produce increasing amounts of a good.

Questions from Chapter 6

4. **B**—In a market free of price controls or other distortions, equilibrium occurs at a price where $Q_d = Q_s$. Graphically this is where the demand curve intersects the supply curve. Here, social welfare is maximized, allocative efficiency is attained, and there exists no dead weight loss.

5. **D**—If the price of a production input (or resource) increases, the supply curve shifts leftward and the price of gasoline rises. Hint: Having a strong grasp of what shifts supply and demand curves will really pay off. Draw these shifting curves in the margin of the exam book!

6. **A**—Increased demand, by itself, increases equilibrium quantity and increases the price of grapes. Increased supply, by itself, increases equilibrium quantity and decreases the price of grapes. So quantity definitely increases, but the price change is unknown because it depends on how far the curves shift in relation to each other. Quickly draw these in the exam book.

7. **E**—Consumer surplus is the area above the price and below the demand curve. It is the difference between the price consumers would have paid and the price they did pay.

Questions from Chapter 7

8. **A**—If the percentage change in Q_d is greater than the percentage change in price, the good is elastic. In this situation of rising prices, total spending on beef will fall because the upward effect of prices is outweighed by the downward effect of quantity.

9. **C**—The cross-price elasticity measures how sensitive the Q_d of good X is to a change in the price of good Y. If this elasticity is greater than zero, the two goods are substitutes and if it is negative, the two goods are complements.

10. **A**—One of the foundations of the Law of Demand is falling marginal utility as more of a good is consumed. You can eliminate any choices that refer to marginal cost and a downward sloping demand curve would not be the result of total utility that increases at an increasing rate.

11. **D**—A consumer stops eating cookies when total utility is maximized, which corresponds to when MU = 0. Because marginal utility falls with consumption, the very next cookie will give the consumer disutility (MU < 0) so she stops.

Questions from Chapter 8

12. **B**—An increase in the price of capital is an increase in total fixed costs. This increases AFC. Since ATC = AFC + AVC, it also increases ATC. Because fixed costs do not change with output, marginal cost and variable cost remain the same.

13. **E**—TFC are constant so if AFC = $10 at $q = 1$, and AFC = TFC/q, TFC must be $10. Know the way in which all total and average costs are related.

14. **B**—This question tests whether you know the relationships between production and cost. Marginal cost and marginal product are inverses of each other. Since the point of diminishing marginal productivity is where MP is at a maximum, look for the point where MC is at a minimum.

15. **D**—At a quantity of 4, TFC = $10 and TVC = AVC * q = $5 * 4 = $20. Since TC = TFC + TVC, TC = $30.

Questions from Chapter 9

16. **E**—Monopolistic competition is characterized by product differentiation. One way that firms differentiate their products and protect market share is through extensive advertising.

17. **B**—The shutdown point is at minimum AVC. If the price falls below this point, the firm finds it rational to produce nothing in the short run and incur losses equal to TFC.

18. **C**—When the price rises, the perfectly competitive firm finds a higher level of output where $P =$ MR = MC. Since this price lies above the ATC curve, positive economic profits are possible.

19. **E**—The question describes a situation where short-run losses are being incurred. In the long run, firms exit, shifting market supply leftward, increasing market price until the firms earn normal, or breakeven, profits.

20. **C**—One of the important results of monopoly is that, while output is set where MR = MC, price is set from the demand curve, so $P >$ MC. This creates inefficient resource allocation and dead weight loss that is not eliminated in the long run.

21. **B**—Oligopolies are industries dominated by a few large firms, but can have either homogenous or differentiated products. All other choices describe other market structures in the chapter.

22. **A**—These two market structures are fairly similar and free entry and exit is one of the characteristics that they share. They also share the characteristic of normal profits in the long run, but do not share homogenous products or efficiency.

23. **E**—In perfect competition, $P =$ MR = MC and resources are allocated efficiently. Since a monopoly will not have the situation where $P =$ MR, regulators might try to force the firm to produce where $P =$ MC. This point may or may not insure a long-run profit for the firm.

Questions from Chapter 10

24. **C**—Demand for a type of labor is derived from the demand for the good or service that the labor produces. With fewer children in the household, there will be less demand for kindergarten classes and teachers.

25. **A**—When the price of a substitute resource (like capital) falls, two effects move the demand for labor in opposite directions. The firm wants to substitute for more capital and less labor, but lower costs prompt more output to be produced, and this can require more labor. If the output effect outweighs the substitution effect, demand for labor may increase even if capital is less expensive. Labor demand will increase if the labor becomes more productive or if the price of the output produced rises.

26. **C**—Competitive labor markets are characterized by hiring where $W =$ MRPL. This is another example of decision-making where marginal costs (wage paid) equal marginal benefits (MR * MPL).

27. **D**—A monopsonist is like a monopolist on the hiring side of the firm. Monopsonists hire where MFC = MRPL and because MFC lies above the labor supply curve, this means that they will hire fewer workers and pay lower wages than the competitive outcome.

Questions from Chapter 11

28. **E**—Public goods cannot be divided between consumers. If one consumes a public good, the next person is not denied consumption of it. All other choices are goods and services that are both rival and excludable.

29. **A**—When individuals and firms exchange a good that imposes costs on third parties, they have created a negative externality. The market produces "too much" because these spillover costs are not reflected in the private (or market) supply curve. Resources are overallocated to the production of this good.

30. **A**—A progressive tax system means that higher levels of income pay higher proportions of their income to the tax collector. This system is designed to redistribute income from higher tax brackets to lower tax brackets.

Macroeconomics Answers and Explanations, Section I

This test was designed to test you on topics that you will see on the AP Macroeconomics exam in the approximate proportions that you will see them. Chronologically they appear in the approximate order of their review in Step 4 of this book, but this is not the case on the AP exam. Topics on your practice exams will be shuffled.

Questions from Chapter 5

1. **A**—Economic capital includes machinery used to produce goods and services. A barrel of oil is a natural resource and a nurse is a unit of labor. A share of corporate stock is a financial instrument used to raise money so that a firm can purchase more economic resources.

2. **B**—A quick calculation of opportunity costs shows that the opportunity cost of one more paper is three crepes in Nation X and one crepe in Nation Y. The opportunity cost of one more crepe is one-third paper in Nation X and one crepe in Nation Y. Nations benefit by specializing in the goods for which they have comparative advantage. Thus Nation Y can specialize in paper production and Nation X can specialize in crepe production. Nation X trades some crepes to Nation Y in exchange for paper.

3. **E**—Economic growth occurs when the production possibility frontier shifts outward. A movement from W to X or to Y is an improved allocation of unemployed resources, but the potential production has not grown for this nation.

Questions from Chapter 6

4. **A**—If DVDs are normal goods, an increase in household income increases demand for DVDs, which increases quantity and price. Even though this is a macroeconomics exam, be prepared for simple supply and demand questions to test your understanding of markets.

Questions from Chapter 12

5. **D**—GDP in a nation includes production done within the borders of that nation, regardless of the nationality of the owners. If a U.S. factory moves to Brazil, U.S. GDP falls and it rises in Brazil. This does not change U.S. GNP since GNP includes all production of U.S. firms, even if they are located abroad.

6. **B**—Structural unemployment is the result of changing demand for skills, not the business cycle. Automation decreases the demand for human grocery checkers and this trend is unlikely to reverse itself.

7. **C**—The change in real income is equal to the change in nominal income minus the change in the price level.

8. **A**—Nominal values do not take into account rising prices. To deflate nominal values to real, divide the nominal value by the price index (in hundredths).

Questions from Chapter 13

9. **D**—A strong stock market increases consumer wealth and optimism, shifting the consumption function upward. The slope of that function (MPC) is unlikely to change. Since AD includes consumption, AD increases.

10. **E**—In the market for loanable funds, investment (I) represents demand and saving represents supply. More $I increases the demand for loanable funds and increases the interest rate.

11. **B**—The spending multiplier is larger than the tax multiplier, which is larger than the balanced budget multiplier (equals 1). If you want the largest increase in real GDP, you should increase government spending and leave taxes unchanged. The largest impact would be seen if we increased spending and decreased taxes, but this is not one of your options.

Questions from Chapter 14

12. **D**—If the economy is beyond real GDP, the AS curve is nearly vertical. At this point, increasing AD cannot increase output, and will only increase prices.

13. **E**—The full multiplier is only felt if AS is horizontal. Any increase in the price level decreases the impact of the spending multiplier.

14. **D**—Higher resource prices shift AS to the left. All other choices either do not impact the AS curve, or they would act as positive shocks to the AS curve.

15. **D**—The Phillips curve shows the short-run inverse relationship between the inflation rate and the unemployment rate. In the long run this curve is vertical at the natural rate of unemployment.

Questions from Chapter 15

16. **C**—Using AD and AS, lower taxes and more government spending increases AD. This rightward shift increases real GDP and begins to increase the price level.

17. **E**—Supply-side economists advocate increased AS through incentives for investment and productivity. These would likely come in the form of lower taxes or tax credits for investment.

18. **E**—As a recession deepens, a progressive tax system and transfer programs like welfare assistance kick in and shorten the downturn in the business cycle. These automatic stabilizers produce recessionary deficits and inflationary surpluses.

19. **B**—Expansionary fiscal policy that requires borrowing increases interest rates, and lessens private I and C. The decrease in C and I weakens the impact of fiscal policy, intended to increase AD.

Questions from Chapter 16

20. **B**—Increasing the money supply lowers interest rates, increases I, AD, real GDP, and employment.

21. **D**—A contractionary money supply increases nominal interest rates, decreases AD and real GDP, and decreases the price level.

22. **A**—A lower discount rate increases excess reserves by making it less costly for commercial banks to borrow from the Fed. This is one of the Fed's tools of monetary policy. Remember that the Fed does not impact taxes, as taxes are fiscal policy made by the executive and legislative branches.

23. **C**—Selling securities would draw down excess reserves in the banks, decrease the money supply, and increase the interest rate. This would work counter to expansionary fiscal policy.

24. **E**—Nearest to cash, $M1$ is the most liquid of monetary measures. The U.S. dollar is not backed by gold. Our fiat money has value because the Fed assures stable prices.

25. **B**—When more deposits are made, the bank increases required reserves by the fraction of the reserve ratio, and increased excess reserves are loaned to create more money.

26. **C**—The reserve ratio is required reserves divided by deposits so rr = .25. With $250 in required reserves, excess reserves are $750. The money multiplier is equal to 1/rr = 4.

27. **C**—The money multiplier is 10 because the reserve ratio is .10. If money demand is horizontal, a $1 million increase in excess reserves shifts the money supply curve rightward by $10 million, but will not lower the nominal interest rate. If the interest rate does not fall, AD does not rise.

Questions from Chapter 17

28. **A**—Nations are net exporters of a good when the world price is greater than the domestic price. A higher world price creates a surplus in the domestic market and the surplus is exported. This situation improves the U.S. balance of trade and would not foster any U.S. protective trade policy. In currency markets, the dollar likely appreciates as foreign consumers need dollars to buy U.S. copper.

29. **A**—When relative incomes are falling in Japan, fewer U.S. goods are demanded so U.S. exports fall. The decrease in the demand for U.S. dollars causes the dollar to depreciate.

30. **E**—A tariff causes imports to fall, so net exports rise for the U.S. With fewer consumers demanding foreign-built cars, the demand for foreign currency falls, decreasing the value of foreign currency, appreciating the value of the U.S. dollar.

Scoring and Interpretation

Now that you have completed each Diagnostic Exam and checked your answers, it is time to assess your knowledge and preparation. If you saw some questions that caused you to roll your eyes and mutter "What the . . . ?" then you can focus your study on those areas. If you breezed through some questions, great!

For each of these two exams, calculate your raw score with the formula below. If you left any questions blank, there is no penalty. Take this raw score on each Diagnostic Exam and compare it to the table below to estimate where you might score at this point.

$$\text{Section I Raw Score} = N_{right} - .25 * N_{wrong}$$

MICROECONOMICS		MACROECONOMICS	
Raw Diagnostic Score	*AP Grade*	*Raw Diagnostic Score*	*AP Grade*
23.5–30	5	23.25–30	5
18–23.25	4	18–23	4
14–17.75	3	15–17.75	3
9.5–13.75	2	9.75–14.75	2
0–9.25	1	0–9.5	1

Remember on the real exam, Section I will account for two-thirds of your composite score, with one-third coming from the free-response Section II. Given this important difference between your Diagnostic Exam and the real thing, the table above is a *very* preliminary way to convert your Diagnostic raw score to an AP grade. No matter how you scored on the Diagnostic Exams, it is time to begin to review for your AP Microeconomics and Macroeconomics Exams.

Microeconomics
Chapters 5 to 11

Macroeconomics
Chapters 5 to 6/12 to 17

STEP **3**

Develop Strategies
for Success

CHAPTER **4**   How to Approach Each Question Type

CHAPTER 4

How to Approach Each Question Type

IN THIS CHAPTER

Summary: Use these question-answering strategies to raise your AP score.

Key Ideas

Multiple-Choice Questions
✪ Read the question carefully.
✪ Try to answer the question yourself before reading the answer choices.
✪ Guess if you can eliminate one or more answer choices.
✪ Drawing a picture can help.
✪ Don't spend too much time on any one question.

Free-Response Questions
✪ Write clearly and legibly.
✪ Be consistent from one part of your answer to another.
✪ Draw a graph if one is required.
✪ If the question can be answered with one word or number, don't write more.
✪ If a question asks "how," tell "why" as well.

Section I: Multiple-Choice Questions

Because you are a seasoned student accustomed to the educational testing machine, you have surely participated in more standardized tests than you care to count. You probably know some students who always seem to ace the multiple-choice questions and some students who would rather set themselves on fire than sit for another round of "bubble trouble." I hope that, with a little background and a few tips, you might improve your scores in this important component of the AP Economics exams.

First, the background. Every multiple-choice question has three important parts:

1. The **stem** is the basis for the actual question. Sometimes this comes in the form of a fill-in-the-blank statement, rather than a question.

Example

Average fixed cost is computed by dividing total fixed cost by:

Example

If the economy is operating below full employment, which of the following fiscal policies is most likely to decrease the unemployment rate?

2. The **correct answer option**. Obviously, this is the one selection that best completes the statement, or responds to the question in the stem. Because you have purchased this book, you will select this option many, many times.

3. **Distractor options**. Just as it sounds, these are the incorrect answers intended to distract the person who decided not to purchase this book. You can locate this person in the exam room by searching for the individual who is repeatedly smacking his or her forehead on the desktop.

Students who do well on multiple-choice exams are so well prepared that they can easily find the correct answer, but other students do well because they are savvy enough to identify and avoid the distractors. Much research has been done on how to best study for, and complete, multiple-choice questions. You can find some of this research by using your favorite Internet search engine, but here are a few tips that many economics students find useful.

1. *Let's be careful out there*. You must carefully read the question. This sounds pretty obvious, but you would be surprised how tricky those test developers can be. For example, rushing past, and failing to see, the use of a negative can throw a student.

Example

Which of the following is *not* true of firms in perfect competition?

   a. Firms produce a homogenous good.
   b. Firms engage in price discrimination.
   c. Firms earn a normal profit in the long run.
   d. Firms have no ability to influence the market price.
   e. Firms produce the output where price is equal to marginal cost.

A student who is going too fast, and ignores the negative *not*, might select option (a) because it is true of perfectly competitive firms and it was the first option that the student saw.

2. *See the answer, be the answer*. Many people find success when they carefully read the question and, before looking at the alternatives, visualize the correct answer. This allows the person to narrow the search for the correct option, and identify the distractors. Of course this visualization tip is most useful for students who have used this book to thoroughly review the economic content.

Example

The profit-maximizing monopolist sets output where

> Before you even look at the options, you should know that the answer is where MR = MC. Find that option, and then quickly confirm to yourself that the others are indeed wrong.

3. *Never say never.* Words like "never" and "always" are called absolute qualifiers. If these words are used in one of the choices, it is rarely the correct choice.

Example

Which of the following is true about production in the short run?

a.   MP is always greater than AP.
b.   MP is never increasing.

> If you can think of any situation where the statements in (a) and (b) are untrue, then you have discovered distractors and can eliminate these as valid choices.

4. *Easy is as easy does.* It's exam day and you're all geared up to set this very difficult test on its ear. Question number one looks like a no-brainer. Of course! The answer is 7, choice c. But rather than smiling at the satisfaction that you knew the answer, you doubt yourself. Could it be that easy? Sometimes they are just that easy.

5. *Sometimes a blind squirrel finds an acorn.* Should you guess? If you have *absolutely* no clue which choice is correct, guessing is a poor strategy. With five choices, your chance of getting the question wrong is 80%, and every wrong answer costs you one-quarter of a point. In this case, leave it blank with no penalty. Guessing becomes a much better gamble if you can eliminate even one obviously incorrect response. If you can narrow the choices down to three possibilities by eliminating obvious wrong answers, you might just find that acorn.

6. *Draw it, nail it.* Many questions can be easily answered if you do a quick sketch in the margins of your test book. Hey, you paid for that test book, you might as well use it.

Example

In an economy with a vertical aggregate supply curve, a decrease in consumer confidence will cause output and the price level to change in which of the following ways?

	OUTPUT	PRICE LEVEL
(A)	No change	Increase
(B)	Decrease	Decrease
(C)	Increase	No change
(D)	No change	No change
(E)	No change	Decrease

> These types of questions are particularly difficult because the answer requires two ingredients. It also requires a very thorough understanding of the AD/AS model and here is where your graph comes in. The first thing you should do is quickly draw the situation given to you in the question: a vertical AS curve.

Show a downward-sloping AD curve shifting to the left and you can see that option (e) is correct. The graph speaks for itself.

7. *Come back Lassie, come back!* There are 60 questions and none of these is worth more than the other. If you are struggling with a particular question, circle it in your exam book and move on. Another question deeper into the exam might jog a memory of a theory you studied or something you learned from a practice exam in this book. You can then go back and quickly slay the beast. But if you spend a ridiculous amount of time on one question, you will feel your confidence and your time slipping away. Which leads me to my last tip.

8. *Timing is everything, kid.* You have about 70 seconds of time for each of the 60 questions. Keep an eye on your watch as you pass the halfway point. If you are running out of time and you have a few questions left, skim them for the easy (and quick) ones so that the rest of your scarce time can be devoted to those that need a little extra reading or thought.

Other things to keep in mind:

- Take the extra half of a second required to clearly fill in the bubbles.
- Don't smudge anything with sloppy erasures. If your eraser is smudgy, ask the proctor for another.
- Absolutely, positively, check that you are bubbling the same line on the answer sheet as the question you are answering. I suggest that every time you turn the page you double-check that you are still lined up correctly.

Section II: Free-Response Questions

Your score on the FRQs amount to one-third of your grade and, as a long-time reader of essays, I assure you that there is no other way to score highly than to know your stuff. While you can guess on a multiple-choice question and have a one-in-five chance of getting the correct answer, there is no room for guessing in this section. There are however, some tips that you can use to enhance your FRQ scores.

1. *Easy to Read = Easy to Grade.* Organize your responses around the separate parts of the question and clearly label each part of your response. In other words, do not hide your answer; make it easy to find and easy to read. It helps you and it helps the reader to see where you're going. *Trust me, helping the reader can never hurt.* Which leads me to a related tip . . . Write in English, not Sanskrit. Even the most levelheaded and unbiased reader has trouble keeping his or her patience while struggling to read your handwriting. I have seen three readers waste almost 10 minutes using the Rosetta stone to decipher a paragraph of text that was obviously written by a time-traveling student from the Byzantine Empire.

2. *Consistently wrong can be good.* The free-response questions are written in several parts, each building upon the first. If you are looking at an eight-part question, it can be scary. However, these questions are graded so that you can salvage several points even if you do not correctly answer the first part. The key thing for you to know is that you must be consistent, even if it is consistently wrong. For example, you might be asked to draw a graph showing a monopolist who has chosen the profit-maximizing level of output. Following sections might ask you to label the price, economic profit, consumer surplus,

and deadweight loss—each being determined by the choice of output. So let's say you draw your diagram, but you label an incorrect level of output. Obviously you are not going to receive that point. But, if you proceed by labeling price, economic profit, consumer surplus, and deadweight loss correctly at your *incorrect* quantity, you would be surprised how forgiving the grading rubric can be.

3. *Have the last laugh with a well-drawn graph.* There are some points that require an explanation (i.e. "Describe how . . ."). Not all free-response questions require a graph, but a garbled paragraph of explanation can be saved with a perfect graph that tells the reader you know the answer to the question. This does not work in reverse.

4. *If I say draw, you better draw, Tex.* There are what readers call "graphing points" and these cannot be earned with a well-written paragraph. For example, if you are asked to draw the monopoly scenario that I described above, certain points will be awarded for the graph, and only the graph. A delightfully written, and entirely accurate paragraph of text will not earn the graphing points. You also need to clearly label graphs. You might think that downward sloping line is obviously a demand curve, but some of those graphing points will not be awarded if lines and points are not clearly, and accurately, identified.

5. *Give the answer, not a dissertation.* There are some parts of a question where you are asked to simply "identify" something. Identify the price if this firm were a monopolist. Identify the area that corresponds to dead weight loss. This type of question requires a quick piece of analysis that can literally be answered in one word or number. That point will be given if you provide that one word or number whether it is the only word you write, or the fortieth that you write. For example, you might be given a table that shows how a firm's output changes as it hires more workers. One part of the question asks you to identify the optimal number of workers that the firm should hire. Suppose the correct answer is 4. The point is given if you say "4," "four," and maybe even "iv." If you write a 500-word Magna Carta concluding with the word "four," you will get the point, but will have wasted precious time. This brings me to . . .

6. *Welcome to the magic kingdom.* If you surround the right answer to a question with a paragraph of economic wrongness, you will usually get the point, so long as you say the magic word. The only exception is a direct contradiction of the right answer. For example, suppose that when asked to *identify* the optimal number of workers, you spend a paragraph describing how the workers are unionized and therefore are subject to a price ceiling and that the exchange rate between those workers and the production possibility frontier means the answer is four. You get the point! You said they should hire four and "four" was the magic word. However, if you say that the answer is four, but that it is also five and on Mondays it is seven, you have contradicted yourself and the point will not be given.

7. *Marginally speaking.* This point is made throughout the microeconomics review contained in this book, but it bears repeating here as a valuable test-taking strategy. In economics, anything that is optimal, or efficient, or rational, or cost minimizing, or profit maximizing can be answered by telling the reader that the marginal benefits must equal the marginal costs. Depending upon the situation, you might have to clarify that "marginal benefit" to the firm is "marginal revenue," or to the employer "marginal revenue product." If the question asks you *why* the answer is four, there is always a very short phrase that readers look for so that they may award the point. This answer often includes the appropriate marginal comparison.

8. *Identify, Illustrate, Define, and Explain.* Each part of a free-response question includes a prompt that tells you what the reader will be looking for so that the points can be awarded. If the question asks you to "identify" something, you may need only one word or a short phrase to receive all of the points. Writing a paragraph here will only waste your time. As I mentioned above, any reference to "illustrate" will require you to draw, or redraw, a graph to receive points. If the question asks you to "define" a concept, you will need to devote more time to providing your best definition of that concept. The most time-intensive prompt is usually one that involves "explain." Suppose you are told that the Canadian dollar is appreciating relative to the U.S. dollar. Then you are asked to explain how this will impact domestic output and the price level in the U.S. To give yourself the best chance at receiving all of the points, your response must provide two parts. First, give a clear statement of what exactly will happen; second, explain why it is going to happen.

Other things to keep in mind:

- The free-response section begins with a 10-minute reading period. Use this time well to jot down some quick notes to yourself so that when you actually begin to respond, you will have a nice start.
- The first parts of the free-response questions are the easiest parts. Spend just enough time to get these points before moving on to the more difficult sections.
- The questions are written in logical order. If you find yourself explaining Part C before responding to Part B, back up and work through the logical progression of topics.
- Abbreviations are your friends. You can save time by using commonly accepted abbreviations for economic variables and graphical curves and you will get more adept at their use as your mastery improves. For example, in macroeconomics you can save some time by using "OMO" rather than "Open Market Operation" and in microeconomics you can use "MRP" rather than "Marginal Revenue Product."

Review the Knowledge You Need to Score High

CHAPTER 5

Fundamentals of Economic Analysis

IN THIS CHAPTER

Summary: If there are two concepts that you should have down pat, they are: (1) scarce resources require decision makers to make decisions that involve costs and benefits, and (2) these decisions are best made when the additional benefits of the action are exactly offset by the additional costs of the action. This chapter presents material that, at least on the surface, appears to be "Econ-lite." Some readers might make the mistake of simply glossing over it on the way to meatier topics. I urge you to take the time to reinforce these early concepts for they should, like a bad commercial jingle, stick in your subconscious throughout your preparation for the AP exam.

Key Ideas

✪ Scarcity
✪ Opportunity Cost
✪ Marginal Analysis
✪ Production Possibilities
✪ Functions of Economic Systems

5.1 Scarce Resources

Main Topics: *Resources, Scarcity, Trade-Offs, Opportunity Cost, Marginal Analysis*

Economic Resources

Economics is the study of how people, firms, and societies use their scarce productive resources to best satisfy their unlimited material wants.

Resources, or Factors of Production, are commonly separated into four groups:

- *Labor:* human effort and talent, physical and mental. This can be augmented by education and training (human capital).
- *Land* or *Natural Resources:* any resource created by nature. This may be arable land, mineral deposits, oil and gas reserves, or water.
- *Physical capital:* manmade equipment like machinery, but also buildings, roads, vehicles, and computers.
- *Entrepreneurial ability:* the effort and know-how to put the other resources together in a productive venture.

Scarcity

All of the above resources are scarce, or in limited supply. Since productive resources are scarce, it makes sense that the production of goods and services must be scarce.

Example:

Sometimes it is easier to see this if you look at the production of something familiar, like the production of a term paper.

- *Labor:* your hours of research, writing, and rewriting. As we all know, these hours are scarce, or limited to the number of waking hours in the day.
- *Land/Natural Resources:* paper (trees), electricity (rivers, coal, natural gas, wind, solar). Not only are these in scarce supply, but your ability to acquire these resources is limited by your income, which is a result of using some of your scarce labor hours to work for a wage.
- *Capital:* your computer, printer, desk, pens and pencils, the library and sources within.
- *Entrepreneurial ability:* the skill that it takes to compile the research into a coherent, thoughtful, and articulate piece of academic work.

Trade-Offs

The fact that we are faced with scarce resources implies that individuals, firms, and governments are constantly faced with trade-offs.

Individuals

Consumers choose between housing arrangements, transportation options, grocery store items, and many other daily purchases. Do I rent an apartment or buy a home? Workers must choose from a wide range of employment opportunities. Do I pursue my MBA or Ph.D.? Do I pick up an extra shift?

Firms

For the firm, decisions are often centered upon which good or service can be provided, how much should be produced, and how to go about producing those goods and services.

A local restaurant considers whether or not to stay open later on Saturday night. Do we open a steel plant in Indiana or Indonesia?

Governments

Every society, in one form or another, places many tough decisions in the hands of government, both local and national. Not surprisingly, local government is faced with issues that are likely to have an immediate impact on the lives of local citizens. Should we use tax revenues to pave potholes in the streets or buy a new city bus? At the national level, not all citizens might/would feel the impact immediately, but the stakes are likely much higher. Should we open protected wilderness areas to oil and gas exploration? Should we impose a tariff on imported rice?

Regardless of the decision maker—individual, firm, or government—the reality of scarce resources creates a trade-off between the opportunity that is taken, and the opportunity that was not taken and thus forgone. The value of what was given up is called the opportunity cost.

Opportunity Cost

At the most basic level, the opportunity cost of doing something is what you sacrifice to do it. In other words, if you use a scarce resource to pursue activity X, the opportunity cost of activity X is activity Y, the next best use of that resource.

> **Example:**
> You have one scarce hour to spend between studying for an exam or working at a coffee shop for $6 per hour. If you study, the opportunity cost of studying is $6.

> **Example:**
> You have one scarce hour to spend between studying for an exam or working at a coffee shop for $6 per hour or mowing your uncle's lawn for $10 per hour. If you choose to study, what is the opportunity cost of studying?
>
> *Be careful!* A common mistake is to add up the value of *all* of your other options ($16), but this misses an important point. In this scenario, and in many others, you have one hour to allocate to one activity, thus giving up the others. By choosing to study, you really only gave up one thing: mowing the lawn *or* serving cappuccinos, not both.
>
> The opportunity cost of using your resource to do activity X is the value the resource would have in its *next best alternative use*. Therefore, the opportunity cost of studying is $10, the better of your two alternatives.

"Does everything have a dollar figure attached to it? Can't we just enjoy something without slapping a price tag on it?"

An excellent question and often a difficult point to make. If you have one scarce hour and you could either work at the coffee shop for $6 or take a restful nap, the opportunity cost of working is the nap, which certainly has value. How can we place a dollar value on the nap? Maybe you are giving serious thought to taking the nap, but your employer at the coffee shop really needs you to work. Maybe your employer offers you $10 to forgo the nap and come to work. After some consideration, you still choose the nap. Surely there is a price (the wage) that would be high enough to entice you to come to work at the coffee shop. If your employer offered you just enough to compensate you for the nap you gave up, you have found the value that you placed on the nap.

Marginal Analysis

Most decisions are made based upon a change in the status quo. You have one cup of coffee (the status quo) and are deciding whether to have another. You have studied five hours for an economics exam (the status quo) and need to decide if it is in your best interest to study another hour.

These decisions are said to be made at the margin. The next cup of coffee brings with it *additional* benefits to the consumer, but comes at *additional* costs. The rational consumer weighs the additional benefits against the additional costs.

Marginal: "the next one," or "additional," or "incremental."

While this is a concept that is seen throughout economics, and throughout this book, let us briefly look at **marginal analysis** from a consumer's point of view.

Marginal Cost (MC): The additional cost incurred from the consumption of the next unit of a good or service.

Marginal Benefit (MB): The additional benefit received from the consumption of the next unit of a good or service.

Example:

The soda machine down the hall charges me $1.00 for every can of pop. The decision to buy another soda is another example of marginal analysis. If I expect to receive at least $1 in additional benefit, buying another soda is a rational decision. This decision can be seen in Figure 5.1.

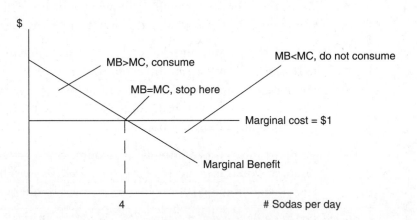

Figure 5.1

So how many sodas will I consume in a typical day? For each of the first three sodas, my MB > $1, the marginal cost of the next soda. The fourth soda provides me with exactly $1 in marginal benefit, so I find it exactly worth my while to buy it. The fifth soda is not bought because the MC > MB. Notice that my MB declines as I consume more sodas. This is a fairly predictable relationship since I am likely to enjoy my first soda of the day more than my fifth.

Rule:

Do something if the marginal benefits ≥ marginal costs of doing it.

Stop doing something when the marginal benefits = marginal costs of doing it.

Never do something when the marginal benefits < marginal costs of doing it.

You will find this to be true in consumption, production, hiring, and many other economic decisions.

5.2 Production Possibilities

Main Topics: *Production Possibilities Curves, Resource Substitutability, Law of Increasing Costs, Absolute Advantage, Comparative Advantage, Efficiency, Growth*

Production Possibilities Curve

To examine production and opportunity cost, economists find it useful to create a simplified model of an individual, or a nation, that can choose to allocate its scarce resources between the production of two goods or services. For now we assume that those resources are being fully employed and used efficiently.

Example:

The owner of a small bakery can allocate a fixed amount of labor (the chef and her helpers), capital (mixers, pans, and ovens), natural resources (raw materials), and her entrepreneurial talent toward the production of pastries and pizza crusts.

The **production possibilities table** (Table 5.1) lists the different combinations of pastries and crusts that can be produced with a fixed quantity of scarce resources.

Table 5.1

PASTRIES	PIZZA CRUST
0	10
1	8
2	6
3	4
4	2
5	0

If the chef wishes to produce one more pastry, she must give up two pizza crusts. If she wishes one more crust, she must give up one-half of a pastry.

In other words:

The opportunity cost of a pastry is two crusts.
The opportunity cost of a pizza crust is one-half of a pastry.

We can graphically depict Table 5.1 in a **production possibility curve.** Each point on the curve represents some maximum output combination of the two products. Some refer to this curve as a **production possibility frontier** because it reflects the outer limit of production. Any point outside the frontier (e.g., 4, 8) is currently unattainable and any point inside the frontier (e.g., 1, 2) fails to use all of the bakery's available resources in an efficient way. We talk more about efficiency at the end of this section.

"Why is there a limit to the production of these goods? In other words, why doesn't the frontier just expand to allow an unlimited amount of either?"

Over the course of time, the frontier is believed to expand. But at any given point in time, we must confront the scarcity problem again. The resources used to produce these goods are scarce, and thus the production frontier is going to act as a binding constraint. The concept of economic growth is introduced in this chapter and also discussed in the coverage of macroeconomics, but for the time being, the frontier looks like Figure 5.2

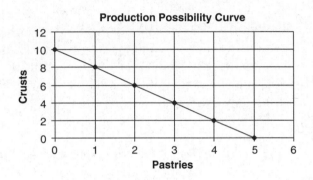

Figure 5.2

The opportunity cost of each good is also apparent in the production possibility curve itself.

- The slope of the curve, 2 in our case, measures the opportunity cost of the good on the *x* axis.
- The inverse of the slope, ½ in our case, measures the opportunity cost of the good on the *y* axis.

Notice that with a straight line, the opportunity cost of producing more of each good is always a constant. Is this realistic?

Resource Substitutability

Suppose our bakery chef is currently producing 10 pizza crusts and zero pastries. But today she decides that she should produce one pastry and eight crusts. In Figure 5.2 above, this decision appears fairly straightforward.

What we often forget is that resources must be reallocated from pizza crust production to pastry production. Labor, capital, and natural resources must be removed from crust production and moved into pastry production.

Perhaps some of the capital (i.e., pans) in the bakery are better suited to pizza crust production than pastry production. Certainly raw materials like chocolate and frosting are not very useful for pizza crust production, but extremely valuable to the pastry production.

The same could be said for individual laborers. Maybe the entrepreneur herself was trained as a French pastry chef and can make pizza crusts, but not as well as she can make éclairs. The fact that these resources are better suited to the production of one good, and less easily adaptable to the production of the other good, gives us the concept of . . .

Law of Increasing Costs

Law of Increasing Costs tells us that the more of a good that is produced, the greater its opportunity cost. This reality gives us a production possibility curve that is concave, or *bowed outward*, as seen in Figure 5.3 below.

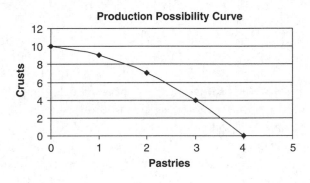

Figure 5.3

Now as the bakery produces more pastries, the opportunity cost (slope) begins to rise. Of course the same is happening if the chef chooses to produce more crusts.

- Because resources are not perfectly adaptable to alternative uses, our production possibility curve is unlikely to be linear.

Comparative Advantage and Specialization

I went to the dentist's office the other day. For 30 minutes the dental hygienist took an X-ray, and then cleaned and flossed my teeth. When she was done, the dentist popped in, peeked at her handiwork, studied my X-ray and sent me on my way with a new toothbrush. Why does the dentist let the hygienist do all the cleaning and flossing, when he is perfectly capable of doing the task? Because the dentist's scarce time resource is better used performing tasks like oral surgery. The opportunity cost of the dentist flossing my teeth is the revenue earned from a procedure that only he is qualified to perform. Forgoing the revenue from the oral surgery is avoided by assigning the cleaning tasks to the hygienist, whose specialty is oral hygiene, but not oral surgery.

The Law of Increasing Costs tells us that it becomes more costly to produce a good as you produce more of it. This reality prompts us to find other, less expensive, ways to get our hands on additional units. The concepts of **specialization** and **comparative advantage** describe the way that individuals, nations, and societies can acquire more goods at lower cost.

Example:
Suppose our bakery, which can produce both pizza crust and pastries, shares the local market with a pizza parlor. The pizza parlor can also produce pastries, but they might rather produce pizza crusts. Each firm would like to produce more goods at lower cost. Table 5.2 shows the production possibilities of these two firms and the opportunity costs of producing more of each good.

Table 5.2

BAKERY		PIZZA PARLOR	
Pastries	*Crusts*	*Pastries*	*Crusts*
10	0	5	0
0	5	0	10
OPPORTUNITY COSTS		**OPPORTUNITY COSTS**	
1 pastry costs	1 crust costs	1 pastry costs	1 crust costs
½ crust	2 pastries	2 crusts	½ pastry

Because the bakery can produce more pastries than the pizza parlor, the bakery has **absolute advantage** in pastry production. The pizza parlor has absolute advantage in crust production. Simply being able to produce more of a good does not mean that the firm produces that good at a lower opportunity cost.

Both producers could produce pastries, but the bakery can produce pastries at lower opportunity cost (0.5 crusts vs. 2 crusts). The bakery is said to have **comparative advantage** in the production of pastries. Likewise, the table illustrates that the pizza parlor has the comparative advantage in pizza crusts (0.5 pastries vs. 2 pastries). These producers can, and indeed should, **specialize** by producing only pastries at the bakery and only crusts at the pizza parlor. Because these firms are specializing and producing at lower cost, not only do they benefit by earning more profit, but consumers across town benefit from purchasing goods at lower prices.

In microeconomics, the principle of comparative advantage explains why the pediatrician delivers the babies while the electrician wires the house, and not the other way around. In macroeconomics, this principle is the basis for showing how nations can gain from free trade. We explore trade between nations in the last chapter. To see the microeconomics gains from specialization, we do a game called "before and after."

Before: Each firm devotes half of its resources to pastry production and half to crust production.

> Total Citywide Pastry Production = 5 + 2.5 = 7.5
> Total Citywide Crust Production = 2.5 + 5 = 7.5

After: Each firm specializes in the production of the good for which they have comparative advantage.

> Total Citywide Pastry Production = 10 + 0 = 10
> Total Citywide Crust Production = 0 + 10 = 10

Figure 5.4 shows both production possibility frontiers and how a combination of 10 crusts and 10 pastries (specialization) was previously unattainable and is superior to when each firm produced at the midpoint (50/50) of their individual frontiers.

"Know the different ways of showing comparative advantage. This is a potential free-response question."
—*AP Teacher*

- If firms and individuals produce goods based upon their comparative advantage, society gains more production at lower cost.

 KEY IDEA

Efficiency

If not all available resources are being used to their fullest, the economy is operating at some point inside the production possibility frontier. This is clearly inefficient. But even if the

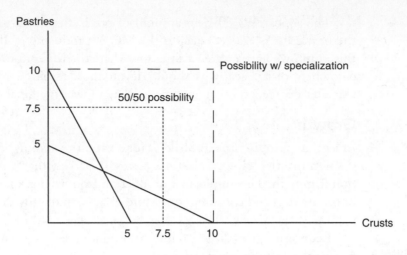

Figure 5.4

economy is operating at some point on the frontier, who is to say that it is the point that is most desired by the citizens? If it does not happen to be the point that society most wants, we are also facing an inefficient situation. There are two types of efficiency.

Productive efficiency: The economy is producing the maximum output for a given level of technology and resources. All points on the production frontier are productively efficient.

Allocative efficiency: The economy is producing the optimal mix of goods and services. By optimal, we mean that it is the combination of goods and services that provides the most net benefit to society. If society is allocatively efficient, it is operating at the best point on the frontier.

How do we determine which point is the optimal point? Remember how I determined the optimal number of sodas to consume every day? Suppose we could measure, society-wide, the marginal benefit received from the consumption of pizza crusts. Like my MB for sodas, the societal MB for crusts is falling as more crusts are consumed. We already know that the marginal cost of producing pizza crusts increases. The marginal cost of producing and marginal benefit of consuming more pizza crusts are illustrated in Figure 5.5.

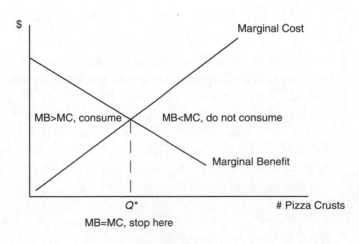

Figure 5.5

The allocatively efficient amount of pizza crusts is Q^*, the quantity where the MB of the next crust is exactly equal to the MC of producing it. If we produce anything beyond this point, we have created a situation where the MC of producing it exceeds our marginal enjoyment of it. Clearly we should devote those resources to other goods that we desire to a greater degree, and that are produced at a lower marginal cost.

Growth

At a given point in time, the bakery (or a nation's economy) cannot operate beyond the production frontier. However as time passes, it is likely that firms and nations experience economic growth. This results in a production frontier that moves outward, expanding the set of production and consumption. More discussion of growth follows in the macroeconomic section of the review.

Economic growth, the ability to produce a larger total output over time, can occur if one or all of the following occur:

- An increase in the quantity of resources. For example, the bakery acquires another oven.
- An increase in the quality of existing resources. For example, the chef acquires the best assistants in the city.
- Technological advancements in production. For example, electric mixers versus hand mixers.

Figure 5.6 below illustrates economic growth for the bakery.

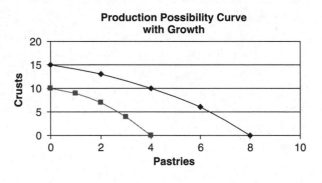

Figure 5.6

Notice that the above frontier has not increased proportionally. The maximum number of crusts that could possibly be produced has increased by 50 percent while the maximum number of pastries has increased by 100 percent.

Economic growth almost always occurs in this way. For example, technological advancements in wireless technology have certainly increased the nation's capacity to produce cell phones and PDAs, but has not likely measurably increased our capacity to produce tomatoes.

5.3 Functions of Economic Systems

Main Topic: *The Market System*

Market Systems

In the twenty-first century, most industrially advanced nations have gravitated towards a **market economy—capitalism.**

Keys to a Market System

- *Private Property:* individuals, not government, own most economic resources. This private ownership encourages innovation, investment, growth, and trade.

  Example:

  If the state owned the bakery ovens, mixers and even the building itself, how much of an incentive would our entrepreneur have to maintain the equipment, the inventory, or even the quality of the product? Knowing that the state could take these resources with very little notice, our chef might just do the bare minimum and, if this situation happened all over town, the local economy would languish.

- *Freedom:* individuals are free to acquire resources to produce goods and services, and free to choose which of their resources to sell to others so that they may buy their own goods and services.

  Example:

  The bakery can freely use its resources to produce rolls, pastries, croissants, and anything else it believes leads to profitability. Of course this freedom is limited by legal constraints. The bakery cannot sell illegal drugs from the back door and the chef is not free to offer open-heart surgery with her bagels.

- *Self-Interest and Incentives:* individuals are motivated by self-interest in their use of resources. Entrepreneurs seek to maximize profit while consumers seek to maximize happiness; with these incentives, goods are sold and bought.

  Example:

  Our bakery owner, motivated by profit, seeks to offer products that appeal to her customers. Customers, seeking to maximize their happiness, consume these bakery products only if they satisfy their personal tastes and wants.

- *Competition:* buyers and sellers, acting independently, and motivated by self-interest, freely move in and out of individual markets. Again, the issue of incentives is powerful. A new firm, eager to compete in a market, only enters that market if profits are available.

  Example:

  Competition implies that prices are determined in the marketplace and not controlled by individual sellers, buyers, or the government. Our bakery owner employs labor at the going market wage, which is determined in the competitive local labor market. She offers baked products at the going price, which is determined in the competitive local market for those goods.

- *Prices:* Prices send signals to buyers and sellers, and resource allocation decisions are made based upon this information. Prices also serve to ration goods to those consumers who are most willing and able to pay those prices. Prices coordinate the decentralized economic activity of millions of individuals and firms in a way that no one central economic figure can hope to achieve. Prices, not just for goods and services, but also for labor and other resources, are the delivery mechanism for the above incentives—profit for the firm and happiness for the consumer.

Example:

As the price of labor, relative to capital, changes, the bakery chef might be motivated to readjust her employment of assistants. Changes in the relative price of her products might prompt consumers to readjust their purchasing decisions.

› Review Questions

1. Economics is best described as

(A) the study of how scarce material wants are allocated between unlimited resources.

(B) the study of how scarce labor can be replaced by unlimited capital.

(C) the study of how decision makers choose the best way to satisfy their unlimited material wants with a scarce supply of resources.

(D) the study of how unlimited material wants can best be satisfied by allocating limitless amounts of productive resources.

(E) the study of how capitalism is superior to any other economic system.

2. A student decides that, having already spent three hours studying for an exam, she should spend one more hour studying for the same exam. Which of the following is most likely true?

(A) The marginal benefit of the fourth hour is certainly less than the marginal cost of the fourth hour.

(B) The marginal benefit of the fourth hour is at least as great as the marginal cost of the fourth hour.

(C) Without knowing the student's opportunity cost of studying, we have no way of knowing whether or not her marginal benefits outweigh her marginal costs.

(D) The marginal cost of the third hour was likely greater than the marginal cost of the fourth hour.

(E) The marginal benefit of the third hour was less than the marginal cost of the third hour.

The island nation of Beckham uses economic resources to produce tea and crumpets. Use the following production possibilities frontier for questions 3–4.

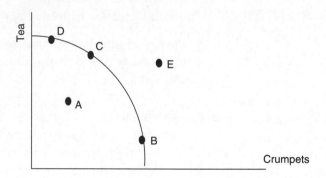

3. Economic growth is best represented by a movement from

(A) A to B

(B) B to C

(C) C to D

(D) D to E

(E) E to A

4. The shape of this PPF tells us that

(A) economic resources are perfectly substitutable from production of tea to production of crumpets.

(B) citizens prefer that an equal amount of tea and crumpets be produced.

(C) the opportunity cost of producing crumpets rises as more crumpets are produced.

(D) the opportunity cost of producing crumpets is constant along the curve.

(E) the opportunity cost of producing tea falls as you produce more tea.

5. Ray and Dorothy can both cook and can both pull weeds in the garden on a Saturday afternoon. For every hour of cooking, Ray can pull 50 weeds and Dorothy can pull 100 weeds. Based on this information,

(A) Ray pulls weeds since he has absolute advantage in cooking.
(B) Dorothy pulls weeds since she has absolute advantage in cooking.
(C) Dorothy cooks since she has comparative advantage in cooking.
(D) Ray cooks since he has comparative advantage in cooking.
(E) Dorothy pulls weeds since she has comparative advantage in cooking.

› Answers and Explanations

1. **C**—It is important to remember that society has a limitless desire for material wants, but satisfaction of these wants is limited by scarce economic resources. Economics studies how to solve this problem in the best possible way.

2. **B**—If we observe her studying for the fourth hour, then it must be the case that the MB ≥ MC of studying for that next hour. If we observe her putting her books away and doing something else, the opposite must be true.

3. **D**—Economic growth is an outward expansion of the entire PPF. A movement from the interior to the frontier (A to B) is not growth, it just tells us that some unemployed resources (A) are now being used to their full potential (B).

4. **C**—When the PPF is concave (or bowed outward) it is an indicator of the Law of Increasing Costs. This is a result of economic resources not being perfectly substitutable between tea and crumpets. A baking sheet used to bake crumpets might be quite useless in producing tea leaves.

5. **D**—For Ray, the opportunity cost of cooking is 50 weeds, while Dorothy's opportunity cost of cooking is 100 unpulled weeds. Ray does not pull weeds because he has comparative advantage in cooking. Dorothy does not cook because she has comparative advantage in weed pulling.

› Rapid Review

Economics: the study of how people, firms, and societies use their scarce productive resources to best satisfy their unlimited material wants.

Resources: called factors of production, these are commonly grouped into the four categories of labor, physical capital, land or natural resources, and entrepreneurial ability.

Scarcity: the imbalance between limited productive resources and unlimited human wants. Because economic resources are scarce, the goods and services a society can produce are also scarce.

Trade-offs: scarce resources imply that individuals, firms, and governments are constantly faced with difficult choices that involve benefits and costs.

Opportunity cost: the value of the sacrifice made to pursue a course of action.

Marginal: the next unit or increment of an action.

Marginal Benefit (MB): the additional benefit received from the consumption of the next unit of a good or service.

Marginal Cost (MC): the additional cost incurred from the consumption of the next unit of a good or service.

Marginal Analysis: making decisions based upon weighing the marginal benefits and costs of that action. The rational decision maker chooses an action if the MB ≥ MC.

Production Possibilities: different quantities of goods that an economy can produce with a given amount of scarce resources. Graphically, the trade-off between the production of two goods is portrayed as a Production Possibility Curve or Frontier (PPF).

Law of Increasing Costs: the more of a good that is produced, the greater the opportunity cost of producing the next unit of that good.

Absolute Advantage: exists if a producer can produce more of a good than all other producers.

Comparative Advantage: A producer has comparative advantage if he can produce a good at lower opportunity cost than all other producers.

Specialization: When firms focus their resources on production of goods for which they have comparative advantage, they are said to be specializing.

Productive Efficiency: production of maximum output for a given level of technology and resources. All points on the PPF are productively efficient.

Allocative Efficiency: production of the combination of goods and services that provides the most net benefit to society. The optimal quantity of a good is achieved when the MB = MC of the next unit. This only occurs at one point on the PPF.

Economic Growth: occurs when an economy's production possibilities increase. This can be a result of more resources, better resources, or improvements in technology.

Market Economy (Capitalism): an economic system based upon the fundamentals of private property, freedom, self-interest, and prices.

CHAPTER 6

Demand, Supply, Market Equilibrium, and Welfare Analysis

IN THIS CHAPTER

Summary: A thorough understanding of the way in which the market system determines price and quantity pays dividends both in microeconomics and macroeconomics. In the absence of government intervention and/or externalities, the competitive market also provides the most efficient outcome for society.

Key Ideas
✪ Demand
✪ Supply
✪ Equilibrium
✪ Consumer and Producer Surplus

6.1 Demand

Main Topics: *Law of Demand, Income and Substitution Effects, Demand Curves, Determinants of Demand*

For many years now, you have understood the concept of demand. On the surface, the concept is rather simple: people tend to purchase fewer items when the price is high than they do when the price is low. This is such an intuitively appealing concept that your typical consumer cares little about the rationale and still manages to live a happy life. As someone knee-deep in reviewing to take the AP exams, you need to go "behind the scenes" of demand. Intuition will take you only so far: you need to know the underlying theory of what is perhaps the most widely understood, and sometimes misunderstood, economic concept.

Law of Demand

Let's get this part out of the way. The **Law of Demand** is commonly described as: *"Holding all else equal, when the price of a good rises, consumers decrease their quantity demanded for that good."* In other words, there is an inverse, or negative, relationship between the price and the quantity demanded of a good.

"Holding all else equal"? Economic models—demand is just one of many such models—are simplified versions of real behavior. In addition to the price, there are many factors that influence how many units of a good consumers purchase. In order to predict how consumers respond to changes in one variable (price), we must assume that all other relevant factors are held constant. Say we observed that last month, the price of orange juice fell, consumer incomes rose, the price of apple juice increased, and consumers bought more orange juice. Was this increased orange juice consumption because the price fell, because incomes rose, or was it because apple juice became more expensive? Maybe it increased for all of these reasons. Maybe for none of these reasons. It is impossible to isolate and measure the effect of one variable (i.e., orange juice prices) on the consumption of orange juice if we do not control (hold constant) these other external factors. At the heart of the Law of Demand is a consumer's willingness and ability to pay the going price. If the consumer becomes more willing, or more able, to consume a good, then either the price has fallen, or one of these external factors has changed. We spend more time on these demand "determinants" a little later in this chapter.

Income and Substitution Effects

One of the important things behind the scenes of the Law of Demand is the economic mantra *"only relative prices matter."* I'm sure you have heard the stories from your parents or grandparents about how the price of a cup of coffee "back in the good old days" was just a nickel. Today you might get the same coffee for $1.75. These prices are simply **money** (or **absolute**, or **nominal**) **prices**, and when it comes to a demand decision, a money price alone is near useless. However, if you think about the money price in terms of: (1) what other goods $1.75 could buy, or (2) how much of your income is absorbed by $1.75, then you're talking **relative** (or **real**) **prices**. These are what matter. The number of units of any other good Y that must be sacrificed to acquire the first good X, measures the relative price of good X.

Example:

Let's keep things simple and say that you divide your $10 daily income between apple fritters at today's prices of $1 each and chocolate chip bagels at $2 each. These are the money prices of your labor and of these two yummy snacks.

Table 6.1

	MONEY PRICE		RELATIVE PRICE		SHARE OF INCOME	
	Today	*Tomorrow*	*Today*	*Tomorrow*	*Today*	*Tomorrow*
Fritter	$1	$2	1/2 bagel	1 bagel	1/10	1/5
Bagel	$2	$2	2 fritters	1 fritter	1/5	1/5

Today at the price of $1, the relative cost of a fritter is one-half of a bagel (see Table 6.1). Relative to your income, it amounts to one-tenth of your budget.

Tomorrow, when the price doubles to $2 per fritter, two things happen to help explain, and lay the foundation for, the Law of Demand.

1. The relative price of a fritter has risen to one bagel and the relative price of a bagel has fallen from two fritters to one fritter. Since fritters are now *relatively more expensive,* we would expect you to consume more bagels and fewer fritters. This is known as the ***substitution effect.***

2. Relative to your income, the price of a fritter has increased from one tenth to one fifth of your budget. In other words, if you were to buy only fritters, today you can purchase 10 but tomorrow the same income would only buy you 5. This lost purchasing power is known as the ***income effect.***

- ***Substitution effect:*** the change in quantity demanded resulting from a change in the price of one good relative to the price of other goods.
- ***Income effect:*** the change in quantity demanded resulting from a change in the consumer's purchasing power (or real income).

When the price of fritters increased, both of these effects caused our consumer (you) to decrease the quantity demanded, thus predicting a response consistent with the Law of Demand.

"*How would a consumer react if the prices of fritters and bagels, and daily income had all doubled?*"

Since the price of fritters, relative to the price of bagels, and relative to daily income, has not changed, the consumer is unlikely to alter behavior. This is why we say that only relative prices matter.

The Demand Curve

The residents of small midwestern town love to quench their summer thirsts with lemonade. Table 6.2 summarizes the townsfolk's daily consumption of cups of lemonade at several prices, holding constant all other factors that might influence the overall demand for lemonade. This table is sometimes referred to as a **demand schedule**.

Table 6.2

PRICE PER CUP ($)	QUANTITY DEMANDED (CUPS PER DAY)
.25	120
.50	100
.75	80
1.00	60
1.25	40

The values in Table 6.2 reflect the Law of Demand: "*Holding all else equal, when the price of a cup of lemonade rises, consumers decrease their quantity demanded for lemonade.*" It is often quite useful to convert a demand schedule like the one above into a graphical representation, the **demand curve** (Figure 6.1).

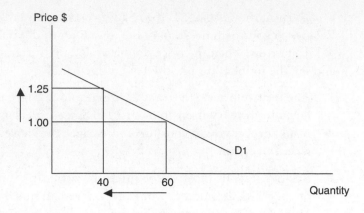

Figure 6.1

Quantity Demanded versus Demand

The Law of Demand predicts a downward (or negative) sloping demand curve (Figure 6.1) If the price moves from $1 to $1.25, and all other factors are held constant, we observe a decrease in the *quantity demanded* from 60 to 40 cups. It is important to place special emphasis on "quantity demanded." If the price of the good changes and all other factors remain constant, the demand curve is held constant and we simply observe the consumer moving along the fixed demand curve. If one of the external factors change, the entire demand curve shifts to the left or right.

Determinants of Demand

So what are all of these factors that we insist on holding constant? These **determinants of demand** influence both the willingness and ability of the consumer to purchase units of the good or service. In addition to the price of the product itself, there are a number of variables that account for the total demand of a good like lemonade. These are:

- Consumer income.
- The price of a substitute good such as iced tea.
- The price of a complementary good such as a popsicle.
- Consumer tastes and preferences for lemonade.
- Consumer expectations about future prices of lemonade.
- Number of buyers in the market for lemonade.

- *Consumer Income*

Demand represents the consumer's willingness and ability to pay for a good. Income is a major factor in that "ability" to pay component. For most goods, when income increases, demand for the good increases. Thus, for these **normal goods**, increased income results in a graphical rightward shift in the entire demand curve. There are other **inferior goods**, fewer in number, where higher levels of income produce a decrease in the demand curve.

Example:
When looking to furnish a first college apartment, many students increase their demand for used furniture at yard sales. Upon graduation and employment in their first real job, new graduates increase their demand for new furniture and decrease their demand for used furniture. For them, new furniture is a normal good while used furniture is an inferior good.

- An *increase in demand* is viewed as a *rightward shift* in the demand curve. There are two ways to think about this shift.

  a. At all prices, the consumer is willing and able to buy more units of the good. In Figure 6.2 below you can see that at the constant price of $1, the quantity demanded has risen from two to three.

  b. At all quantities, the consumer is willing and able to pay higher prices for the good.

- Of course the opposite is, true of a *decrease in demand*, or *leftward shift* of the demand curve. In Figure 6.2 you can see that at the constant price of $1, the quantity demanded has fallen from two to one.

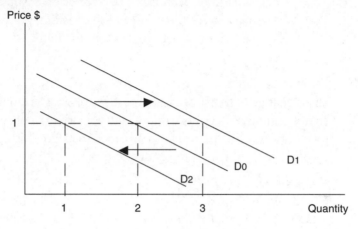

Figure 6.2

- *Price of Substitute Goods*

Two goods are substitutes if the consumer can use either to satisfy the same essential function, therefore experiencing the same degree of happiness (utility). If the two goods are substitutes, and the price of one good X falls, the consumer demand for the substitute good Y decreases.

Example:

Mammoth State University (MSU) and Ivy Vine College (IVC) are considered substitute institutions of higher learning in the same geographical region. Ivy Vine College, shamelessly (wink, wink) seeking to increase its reputation as an "elite" institution, increases tuition while Mammoth State's tuition remains the same. We expect to see, holding all else constant, a decrease in quantity demanded for IVC degrees, and an increase in the overall demand for MSU degrees. (See Figures 6.3 and 6.4.)

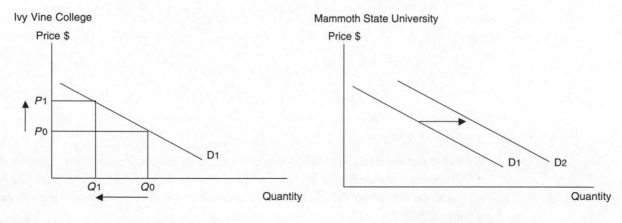

Figure 6.3   **Figure 6.4**

- *Price of Complementary Goods*

Two goods are complements if the consumer receives more utility from consuming them together than she would receive consuming each separately. I enjoy consuming tortilla chips by themselves, but my utility increases if I combine those chips with a complementary good like salsa or nacho cheese dip. If any two goods are complements, and the price of one good *X* falls, the consumer demand for the complement good *Y* increases.

> *"Finally, something in a textbook that I can fathom!"*
> *—Adam, AP Student*

Example:

College students love to order late night pizza delivered to their dorm rooms. The local pizza joint decreased the price of breadsticks, a complement to the pizzas. We expect to see, holding all else constant, an increase in quantity demanded for breadsticks, and an increase in the demand for pizzas.

- *Tastes and Preferences*

We have different internal tastes and preferences. Collectively, consumer tastes and preferences change with the seasons (more gloves in December, fewer lawn chairs); with fashion trends (increased popularity of tattoos, return of bell-bottoms); or with advertising (low-carb foods). A stronger preference for a good is an increase in the willingness to pay for the good, which increases demand.

- *Future Expectations*

The future expectation of a price change or an income change can cause demand to shift today. Demand can also respond to an expectation of the future availability of a good.

Example:

On a Wednesday, you have reason to believe that the price of gasoline is going to rise $.05 per gallon by the weekend. What do you do? Many consumers, armed with this expectation, increase their demand for gasoline today. We might predict the opposite behavior, a decrease in demand today, if consumers expect the price of gasoline to fall a few days from now.

Demand can also be influenced by future expectations of an income change.

Example:

One month prior to your college graduation day you land your first full-time job. You have signed an employment contract that guarantees a specific salary, but you will not receive your first paycheck until the end of your first month on the job. This future expectation of a sizeable increase in income often prompts consumers to increase their demand for normal goods now. Maybe you would start shopping for a car, a larger apartment, or several business suits.

Example:

For years, auto producers have been promising more alternative fuel cars, but so far these cars are relatively difficult to find on dealership lots. Suppose the "Big 3" promise widespread availability of affordable electric and hydrogen fuel cell cars in the next 12 months. This expectation of increased availability in the future will likely decrease the demand of these cars today.

- *Number of Buyers*

An increase in the number of buyers, holding other factors constant, increases the demand for a good. This is often the result of demographic changes or increased availability in more markets.

Example:

When the Soviet Union fractured and the Russian government began allowing more foreign investment, corporations such as Coca-Cola, IBM, and McDonald's found millions of new buyers for their products. Globally, the demand for colas, PCs, and burgers increased.

6.2 Supply

Main Topics: *Law of Supply, Increasing Marginal Costs, Supply Curves, Determinants of Supply*

Fred and Wilma, Woodward and Bernstein, Ross and Rachel, Bill and Monica, Mercedes and Benz, Ben and Jerry, Sex Symbol and Economist. What do they have in common? They are all famous, or infamous, partners. If there are three words that you need to have in your arsenal for the AP exams, they are "Demand and Supply," or "Supply and Demand" if you are the rebellious type. The previous section has covered the demand half of this duo and so it stands to reason that we should spend a little time studying the other side. Unlike demand, few of us have ever had up close and personal experience as suppliers. Lacking such personal experience with supply, it is helpful to try to put yourself in the shoes of someone who wishes to profit from the production and sale of a product. If something happens that would increase your chances of earning more profit, you increase your supply of the product. If something happens that will hurt your profit opportunities, you decrease your supply of the product.

Law of Supply

Drumroll, please. **The Law of Supply** is commonly described as: "*Holding all else equal, when the price of a good rises, suppliers increase their quantity supplied for that good.*" In other words, there is a direct, or positive, relationship between the price and the quantity supplied of a good.

Again, we insist on qualifying our law with the phrase, "*Holding all else equal.*" Similar to the *demand model,* the *supply model* is a simplified version of real behavior. In addition to the price, there are several factors that influence how many units of a good producers supply. In order to predict how producers respond to fluctuations in one variable (price), we must assume that all other relevant factors are held constant. Before we talk about these external supply determinants, let's examine what is happening behind the scenes of the Law of Supply.

Increasing Marginal Costs

The more you do something (e.g., a physical activity), the more difficult it becomes to do the next unit of that activity. Anyone who has run laps around a track, lifted weights, or raked leaves in the yard understands this. If you were asked to rake leaves, as more hours of raking are supplied, it becomes physically more and more difficult to rake the next hour. We also include the opportunity cost of the time involved in the raking, and you surely know that time is precious to a student. If you have a paper to write or an exam to cram for, raking leaves for an hour comes at a dear cost. In terms of forgone opportunities, the marginal cost of raking leaves rises as you postpone that paper or study session.

When we discussed production possibilities in Chapter 5, we addressed a key economic concept: as more of a good is produced, the greater is its marginal cost.

- As suppliers increase the quantity supplied of a good, they face rising marginal costs.
- As a result, they only increase the quantity supplied of that good if the price received is high enough to at least cover the higher marginal cost.

The Supply Curve

A small town has a thriving summer sidewalk lemonade stand industry. Table 6.3 summarizes the daily quantity of lemonade cups offered for sale at several prices, holding constant all other factors that might influence the overall supply of lemonade. This table is sometimes referred to as a **supply schedule**.

Table 6.3

PRICE PER CUP ($)	QUANTITY SUPPLIED (CUPS PER DAY)
.25	40
.50	60
.75	80
1.00	100
1.25	120

"Make sure on the AP test to include all labels, especially arrows." —Adam, AP Student

The values in this table reflect the Law of Supply: *"Holding all else equal, when the price of a cup of lemonade rises, suppliers increase their quantity supplied for lemonade."* Remember those profit opportunities? If kids can sell more cups of lemonade at a higher price, they will do so. It is often quite useful to convert a supply schedule like the one in Table 6.3 into a graphical representation, the **supply curve** (Figure 6.5).

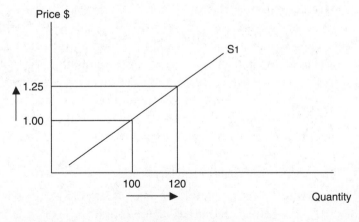

Figure 6.5

Quantity Supplied versus Supply

"This is an important distinction to make." —AP Teacher

The Law of Supply predicts an upward (or positive) sloping supply curve (Figure 6.5). When the price moves from $1 to $1.25, and all other factors are held constant, we observe an increase in the *quantity supplied* from 100 cups to 120 cups. Just as with demand, it is important to place special emphasis on "quantity supplied." When the price of the good changes, and all other factors are held constant, the supply curve is held constant; we simply observe the producer moving along the fixed supply curve. If one of the external factors changes, the entire supply curve shifts to the left or right.

Determinants of Supply

Lemonade producers are willing and able to supply more lemonade if something happens that promises to increase their profit opportunities. In addition to the price of the product itself, there are a number of variables, or **determinants of supply**, that account for the total supply of a good like lemonade. These factors are:

- The cost of an input (e.g., sugar) to the production of lemonade.
- Technology and productivity used to produce lemonade.
- Taxes or subsidies on lemonade.
- Producer expectations about future prices.
- The price of other goods that could be produced.
- The number of lemonade stands in the industry.

- *Cost of Inputs*
If the cost of sugar, a key ingredient in lemonade, unexpectedly falls, it has now become less costly to produce lemonade and so we should expect producers all over town, seeing the profit opportunity, to increase the supply of lemonade at all prices. This results in a graphical rightward shift in the entire supply curve.

- An *increase in supply* is viewed as a *rightward shift* in the supply curve. There are two ways to think about this shift.

  a. At all prices, the producer is willing and able to supply more units of the good. In Figure 6.6 you can see that at the constant price of $1, the quantity supplied has risen from two to three.

  b. At all quantities, the marginal cost of production is lower, so producers are willing and able to accept lower prices for the good.

- Of course the opposite is true of a *decrease in supply*, or *leftward shift* of the supply curve. In Figure 6.6 you can see that at the constant price of $1, the quantity supplied has fallen from two to one.

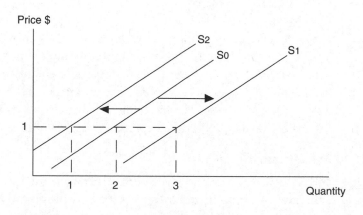

Figure 6.6

- *Technology or Productivity*
A technological improvement usually decreases the marginal cost of producing a good, thus allowing the producer to supply more units, and is reflected by a rightward shift in the

supply curve. If kids all over town began using electric lemon squeezers rather than their sticky bare hands, the supply of lemonade would increase.

> "Remember, the tax goes to the government and is NOT included in the profit."
> —Hillary, AP Student

- *Taxes and Subsidies*

A per unit tax is treated by the firm as an additional cost of production and would therefore decrease the supply curve, or shift it leftward. Mayor McScrooge might impose a 25 cent tax on every cup of lemonade, decreasing the entire supply curve. A subsidy is essentially the anti-tax, or a per unit gift from the government because it lowers the per unit cost of production.

- *Price Expectations*

A producer's willingness to supply today might be affected by an expectation of tomorrow's price. If it were the 2nd of July, and lemonade producers expected a heat wave and a 4th of July parade in two days, they might hold back some of their supply today and hope to sell it at an inflated price on the holiday. Thus today's quantity supplied at all prices would decrease.

- *Price of Other Outputs*

Firms can use the same resources to produce different goods. If the price of a milkshake were rising and profit opportunities were improving for milkshake producers, the supply of lemonade in a small town would decrease and the supply of milkshakes would increase.

- *Number of Suppliers*

When more suppliers enter a market, we expect the supply curve to shift to the right. If several of our lemonade entrepreneurs are forced by their parents to attend summer camp, we would expect the entire supply curve to move leftward. Fewer cups of lemonade would be supplied at each and every price.

6.3 Market Equilibrium

Main Topics: *Equilibrium, Shortages, Surpluses, Changes in Demand, Changes in Supply, Simultaneous Changes*

Demanders and suppliers are both motivated by prices, but from opposite camps. The consumer is a big fan of low prices; the supplier applauds high prices. If a good were available, consumers would be willing to buy more of it, but only if the price is right. Suppliers would love to accommodate more consumption by increasing production, but only if justly compensated. Is there a price and a compatible quantity where both groups are content? Amazingly enough, the answer is a resounding "maybe." Discouraged? Don't be. For now we assume that the good is exchanged in a free and competitive market, and if this is the case, the answer is "yes." We explore the "maybes" in a later chapter.

Equilibrium

The market is in a state of **equilibrium** when the quantity supplied equals the quantity demanded at a given price. Another way of thinking about equilibrium is that it occurs at the quantity where the price expected by consumers is equal to the price required by suppliers. So if suppliers and demanders are, for a given quantity, content with the price, the market is in a state of equilibrium. If there is pressure on the price to change, the market has not yet reached equilibrium. Let's combine our lemonade tables from the earlier sections in Table 6.4.

Table 6.4

PRICE PER CUP ($)	QUANTITY DEMANDED (CUPS PER DAY)	QUANTITY SUPPLIED (CUPS PER DAY)	Q_d-Q_s	SITUATION	PRICE SHOULD
.25	120	40	80	Shortage	Rise
.50	100	60	40	Shortage	Rise
.75	80	80	0	Equilibrium	Stable
1.00	60	100	−40	Surplus	Fall
1.25	40	120	−80	Surplus	Fall

At a price of 75 cents, the daily quantity demanded and quantity supplied are both equal to 80 cups of lemonade. The equilibrium (or market clearing) price is therefore 75 cents per cup. In Figure 6.7 the equilibrium price and quantity are located where the demand curve intersects the supply curve. Holding all other demand and supply variables constant, there exists no other price where $Q_d = Q_s$.

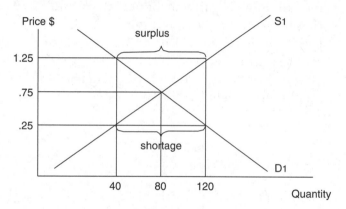

Figure 6.7

Shortage

A **shortage** exists at a market price when the quantity demanded exceeds the quantity supplied. This is why a shortage is also known as **excess demand**. At prices of 25 cents and 50 cents per cup, you can see the shortage in Figure 6.7. Remember that consumers love low prices so the quantity demanded is going to be high. However, suppliers are not thrilled to see low prices and therefore decrease their quantity supplied. At prices below 75 cents per cup, lemonade buyers and sellers are in a state of **disequilibrium**. The disparity between what the buyers want at 50 cents per cup and what the suppliers want at that price should remedy itself. Thirsty demanders offer lemonade stand owners prices slightly higher than 50 cents and, receiving higher prices, suppliers accommodate them by squeezing lemons. With competition, the shortage is eliminated at a price of 75 cents per cup.

Surplus

A **surplus** exists at a market price when the quantity supplied exceeds the quantity demanded. This is why a surplus is also known as **excess supply**. At prices of $1 and

$1.25 per cup, you can see the surplus in Figure. 6.7. Consumers are reluctant to purchase as much lemonade as suppliers are willing to supply and, once again, the market is in disequilibrium. To entice more consumers to buy lemonade, lemonade stand owners offer slightly discounted cups of lemonade and buyers respond by increasing their quantity demanded. Again, with competition, the surplus would be eliminated at a price of 75 cents per cup.

TIP

- Shortages and surpluses are relatively short-lived in a free market as prices rise or fall until the quantity demanded again equals the quantity supplied.

Changes in Demand

"Explain your logic every time you shift a curve, no matter what!"
—Jake, AP Student

While our discussion of market equilibrium implies a certain kind of stability in both the price and quantity of a good, changing market forces disrupt equilibrium, either by shifting demand, shifting supply, or shifting both demand and supply.

Increase in Demand

About once a winter a freak blizzard hits southern states like Georgia and the Carolinas. You can bet that the national media shows video of panicked southerners scrambling for bags of rock salt and bottled water. Inevitably a bemused reporter tells us that the price of rock salt has "skyrocketed" to $17 per bag. What is happening here? In Figure 6.8, the market for rock salt is initially in equilibrium at a price of $2.79 per bag. With a forecast of a blizzard, consumers expect a lack of future availability for this good. This expectation results in a feverish increase in the demand for rock salt and, at the original price of $2.79, there is a shortage and the market's cure for a shortage is a higher equilibrium price. (Note: The equilibrium quantity of rock salt might not increase much since blizzards are short-lived and the supply curve might be nearly vertical.)

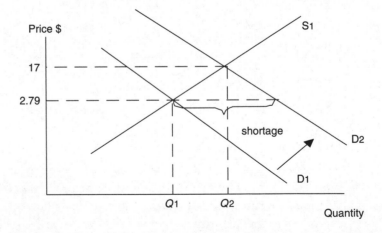

Figure 6.8

Decrease in Demand

The most recent recession was damaging to the automobile industry. When average household incomes fell in the United States, the demand for cars, a normal good, decreased. Manufacturers began offering deeply discounted sticker prices, zero-interest financing, and other incentives to reluctant consumers so that they might purchase a new car. In Figure 6.9 you can see that the original price of a new car was $18,000. Once the demand for new cars fell, there was a surplus of cars on dealer lots at the original price. The market cure for a surplus is a lower equilibrium price, therefore fewer new cars were bought and sold.

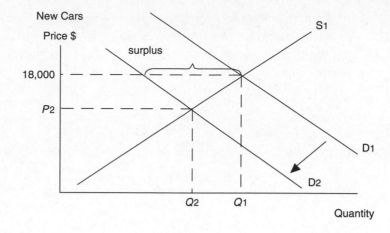

Figure 6.9

- When demand increases, equilibrium price and quantity both increase.
- When demand decreases, equilibrium price and quantity both decrease.

Changes in Supply

Increase in Supply

Advancements in computer technology and production methods have been felt in many markets. Figure 6.10 illustrates how, because of better technology, the supply of laptop computers has increased. At the original equilibrium price of $4000, there is now a surplus of laptops. To eliminate the surplus the market price must fall to P_2 and the equilibrium quantity must rise to Q_2.

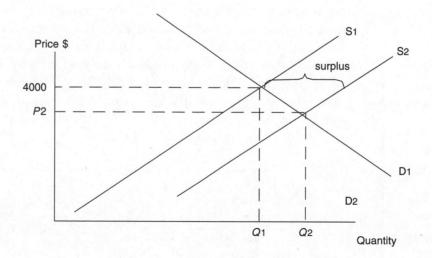

Figure 6.10

Decrease in Supply

Geopolitical conflict in the Middle East usually slows the production of crude oil. This decrease in the global supply of oil can be seen in Figure 6.11. At the original equilibrium price of $20 per barrel, there is now a shortage of crude oil on the global market. The market eliminates this shortage through higher prices and, at least temporarily, the equilibrium quantity of crude oil falls.

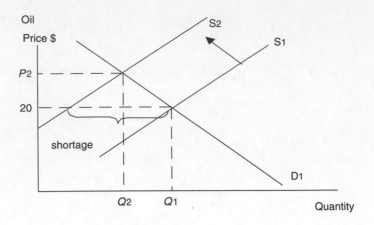

Figure 6.11

- When supply increases, equilibrium price decreases and quantity increases.
- When supply decreases, equilibrium price increases and quantity decreases.

Simultaneous Changes in Demand and Supply

When both demand and supply change at the same time, predicting changes in price and quantity becomes a little more complicated. An example should illustrate how you need to be careful.

An extremely cold winter results in a higher demand for energy such as natural gas. At the same time, environmental safeguards and restrictions on drilling in protected wilderness areas have limited the supply of natural gas. An increase in demand, by itself, creates an increase in both price and quantity. However, a decrease in supply, by itself, creates an increase in price and a decrease in quantity. When these forces are combined, we see a double-whammy on higher prices. But when trying to predict the change in equilibrium quantity, the outcome is uncertain and depends upon which of the two effects is larger.

One possible outcome is shown in Figure 6.12 where the initial equilibrium outcome is labeled E_1. A relatively large increase in demand with a fairly small decrease in supply results in more natural gas being consumed. The new equilibrium outcome is labeled E_2.

The other possibility is that the increase in demand is relatively smaller than the decrease in supply. This is seen in Figure 6.13 and, while the price is going to increase again, the equilibrium quantity is lower than before.

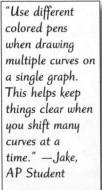

"Use different colored pens when drawing multiple curves on a single graph. This helps keep things clear when you shift many curves at a time." —Jake, AP Student

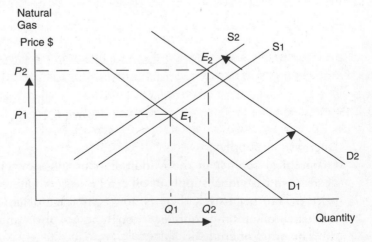

Figure 6.12

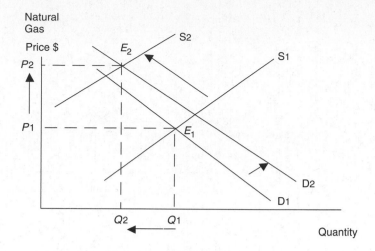

Figure 6.13

- When both demand and supply are changing, one of the equilibrium outcomes (price or quantity) is predictable and one is ambiguous.
- Before combining the two shifting curves, predict changes in price and quantity for each shift, by itself.
- The variable that is rising in one case and falling in the other case is your ambiguous prediction.

6.4 Welfare Analysis

Main Topics: *Total Welfare, Consumer Surplus, Producer Surplus*

Total Welfare

The competitive market, free of government and externalities, produces an equilibrium outcome that provides the maximum amount of total welfare for society. Society consists of all consumers and all producers and, in the marketplace, each party seeks the other so that they can make an acceptable transaction at the going market price. Each party expects to gain in these transactions. **Total welfare** is the sum of two measures of these gains: consumer surplus and producer surplus.

Consumer Surplus: You know that great feeling you get when you pay a price that is lower than you expected, or is lower than you were willing to pay? That's **consumer surplus**, the difference between your willingness to pay and the price you actually pay. The market demand curve, at each quantity, measures, society's willingness to pay (the price). You can see consumer surplus in Figure 6.14. At a price of $5, three units of the good are purchased. The first two units receive some amount of consumer surplus because the willingness to pay exceeds $5. The consumer of the third unit pays a price exactly equal to his willingness to pay so he earns no consumer surplus. Total consumer surplus is the total amount earned by these three consumer transactions.

Producer Surplus: Producers are ecstatic when they receive a price for their product that is above the marginal cost of producing it. This is **producer surplus**, the difference between the price received and the marginal cost of producing the good. The market supply curve, at each quantity, measures society's marginal cost. You can see producer surplus in Figure 6.15. At a price of $5, three units of the good are produced. The first two units earn producer surplus because $5 is above the marginal cost. The third unit earns no additional producer surplus since the marginal cost is exactly equal to the price received. Total producer surplus is the total amount earned by these three producer transactions.

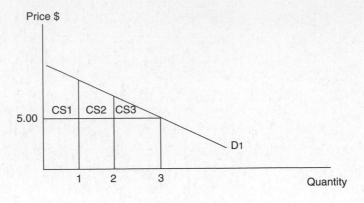

Figure 6.14

- The area under the demand curve and above the market price is equal to total consumer surplus.

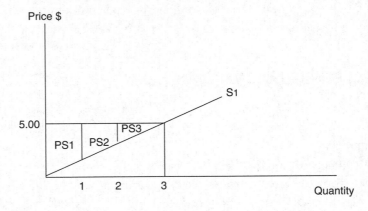

Figure 6.15

- The area above the supply curve and below the market price is equal to total producer surplus.

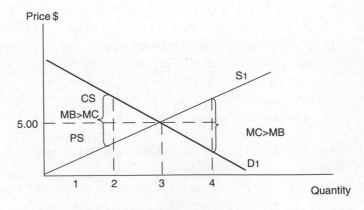

Figure 6.16

So, is market equilibrium conducive to increasing total welfare for society? Combining Figures 6.14 and 6.15 completes the market pictured in Figure 6.16. We see that the combined consumer and producer surplus, or total welfare, is greatest at the equilibrium price of $5 and quantity of three units.

At a lesser quantity (e.g., two units), the combined area is smaller than at a quantity of three. At greater quantities (i.e., $q = 4$) the price of $5 exceeds MB so consumer surplus is being lost. If this weren't bad enough, the MC exceeds the price at $q = 4$ so producer surplus is being lost. Thus, if total welfare is falling at quantities less than three and at quantities greater than three, total welfare must be maximized at the market equilibrium quantity of three and price of $5.

› Review Questions

1. When the price of pears increases, we expect the following:

   (A) quantity demanded of pears rises.
   (B) quantity supplied of pears falls.
   (C) quantity demanded of pears falls.
   (D) demand for pears falls.
   (E) supply of pears rises.

2. If average household income rises and we observe that the demand for pork chops increases, pork chops must be

   (A) an inferior good.
   (B) a normal good.
   (C) a surplus good.
   (D) a necessity.
   (E) a shortage good.

3. Suppose that aluminum is a key production input in the production of bicycles. If the price of aluminum falls, and all other variables are held constant, we expect

   (A) the demand for aluminum to rise.
   (B) the supply of bicycles to rise.
   (C) the supply of bicycles to fall.
   (D) the demand for bicycles to rise.
   (E) the demand for bicycles to fall.

4. The market for denim jeans is in equilibrium, and the price of polyester pants, a substitute good, rises. In the jean market

   (A) supply falls, increasing the price and decreasing the quantity.
   (B) supply falls, increasing the price and increasing the quantity.
   (C) demand falls, increasing the price and decreasing the quantity.
   (D) demand rises, increasing the price and increasing the quantity.
   (E) supply and demand both fall, causing an ambiguous change in price but a definite decrease in quantity.

5. The apple market is in equilibrium. Suppose we observe that apple growers are using more pesticides to increase apple production. At the same time, we hear that the price of pears, a substitute for apples, is rising. Which of the following is a reasonable prediction for the new price and quantity of apples?

   (A) Price rises, but quantity is ambiguous.
   (B) Price falls, but quantity is ambiguous.
   (C) Price is ambiguous, but quantity rises.
   (D) Price is ambiguous, but quantity falls.
   (E) Both price and quantity are ambiguous.

6. The competitive market provides the best outcome for society because

   (A) consumer surplus is minimized while producer surplus is maximized.
   (B) the total welfare is maximized.
   (C) producer surplus is minimized while consumer surplus is maximized.
   (D) the difference between consumer and producer surplus is maximized.
   (E) the total cost to society is maximized.

› Answers and Explanations

1. **C**—If the price of pears rises, either quantity demanded falls or quantity supplied rises. Entire demand or supply curves for pears can shift, but only if an external factor, not the price of pears, changes.

2. **B**—When income increases and demand increases, the good is a normal good. Had the demand for pork chops decreased, they would be an inferior good.

3. **B**—This is a determinant of supply. If the raw material becomes less costly to acquire, the marginal cost of producing bicycles falls. Producers increase the supply of bicycles. Recognizing this as a supply determinant allows you to quickly eliminate any reference to a demand shift.

4. **D**—When a substitute good becomes more expensive the demand for jeans rises, increasing price and quantity.

5. **C**—Increased use of pesticides increases the supply of apples. If the price of a substitute increases, the demand for apples increases. Combining these two factors predicts an increase in the quantity of apples, but an ambiguous change in price. *To help you see this, draw these situations in the margin of the exam.*

6. **B**—When competitive markets reach equilibrium, no other quantity can increase total welfare (consumer + producer surplus). Total welfare, under the supply and demand curves, is maximized at that point.

› Rapid Review

Law of Demand: holding all else equal, when the price of a good rises, consumers decrease their quantity demanded for that good.

All else equal: to predict how a change in one variable affects a second, we hold all other variables constant. This is also referred to as the "ceteris paribus" assumption.

Absolute (or money) prices: the price of a good measured in units of currency.

Relative prices: the number of units of any other good Y that must be sacrificed to acquire the first good X. Only relative prices matter.

Substitution effect: the change in quantity demanded resulting from a change in the price of one good relative to the price of other goods.

Income effect: the change in quantity demanded that results from a change in the consumer's purchasing power (or real income).

Demand schedule: a table showing quantity demanded for a good at various prices.

Demand curve: a graphical depiction of the demand schedule. The demand curve is downward sloping, reflecting the Law of Demand.

Determinants of demand: the external factors that shift demand to the left or right.

Normal goods: a good for which higher income increases demand.

Inferior goods: a good for which higher income decreases demand.

Substitute goods: two goods are consumer substitutes if they provide essentially the same utility to the consumer. A Honda Accord and a Toyota Camry might be substitutes for many consumers.

Complementary goods: two goods are consumer complements if they provide more utility when consumed together than when consumed separately. A 35 mm camera and a roll of film are complementary goods.

Law of Supply: holding all else equal, when the price of a good rises, suppliers increase their quantity supplied for that good.

Supply schedule: a table showing quantity supplied for a good at various prices.

Supply curve: a graphical depiction of the supply schedule. The supply curve is upward sloping, reflecting the Law of Supply.

Determinants of supply: one of the external factors that influences supply. When these variables change, the entire supply curve shifts to the left or right.

Market equilibrium: exists at the only price where the quantity supplied equals the quantity demanded. Or, it is the only quantity where the price consumers are willing to pay is exactly the price producers are willing to accept.

Shortage: also known as *excess demand,* a shortage exists at a market price when the quantity demanded exceeds the quantity supplied. The price rises to eliminate a shortage.

Disequilibrium: any price where quantity demanded is not equal to quantity supplied.

Surplus: also known as *excess supply,* a surplus exists at a market price when the quantity supplied exceeds the quantity demanded. The price falls to eliminate a surplus.

Total welfare: the sum of consumer surplus and producer surplus. The free market equilibrium provides maximum combined gain to society.

Consumer surplus: the difference between your willingness to pay and the price you actually pay. It is the area below the demand curve and above the price.

Producer surplus: the difference between the price received and the marginal cost of producing the good. It is the area above the supply curve and under the price.

CHAPTER ▶ 7

Elasticity, Microeconomic Policy, and Consumer Theory

IN THIS CHAPTER

Summary: It is critical to remember that behind the faceless supply and demand curves are individuals making decisions. These decisions are made with the rational decision maker's best interests at the top of the agenda, but are influenced by many variables. This chapter begins by focusing on how sensitive consumer decisions are to external forces, how policies might affect the market and influence those choices, and concludes by analyzing the theory behind how consumers make choices to maximize their happiness.

Key Ideas
✪ Price Elasticity of Demand
✪ Income Elasticity
✪ Cross-Price Elasticity
✪ Price Elasticity of Supply
✪ The Impact of Taxes and Subsidies
✪ The Impact of Price Controls
✪ Utility Maximization

7.1 Elasticity

Main Topics: *Price Elasticity of Demand, Determinants of Elasticity, Total Revenue, Income Elasticity, Cross-Price Elasticity of Demand, Elasticity of Supply*

Studying the economic concept of elasticity is much like a corporate executive workshop, the topic of which is "Sensitivity Training." When we observe a consumer's purchase decision, say for good X, change in response to a change in some external variable (the price of good X or her income), **elasticity** helps us measure the sensitivity of her consumption to that external change. We also examine the sensitivity of suppliers of good X to a change in the price of good X. We use basic mathematical relationships to measure elasticity, but it is useful to remember that all elasticity formulas measure sensitivity to a change.

Price Elasticity of Demand

The Law of Demand tells us that: "*all else equal, when the price of a particular good falls, the quantity demanded for that good rises.*" But what it fails to answer for us is: "by how much"? Will it be a relatively large increase in quantity demanded or will it be almost negligible? In other words, we would like to measure how sensitive consumers are to a change in the price of this good.

Price Elasticity of Demand Formula

$$E_d = (\%\Delta \text{ in quantity demanded of good } X)/(\%\Delta \text{ in the price of good } X)$$

Note: The Law of Demand insures that E_d is negative, but, for ease of interpretation, economists usually ignore the fact that price elasticity of demand is negative and simply use the absolute value. The greater this ratio, the more sensitive, or responsive, consumers are to a change in the price of good X.

Range of Price Elasticity

Economists like to classify things. It's a sickness, but it is usually done for a reason. (You do need to know these for the exam.) For example, we classify elasticities based upon how sizeable the reaction of consumers is to a change in the price. Rather than describing consumers as "really responsive" or "really, really responsive" or "super duper responsive," we classify consumer responses as elastic or inelastic. The examples below should clarify things.

> **Example:**
> The price of a laptop computer increases by 10 percent and we observe a 20 percent decrease in quantity demanded. Using the above formula:
> $$E_d = (-20\%)/(+10\%) = -2 \text{ or simply } E_d = 2$$

- If $E_d > 1$, demand is said to be "**price elastic**" for good X. The responsiveness of the consumer exceeded, in percentage terms, the initial change in the price.

> **Example:**
> The price of a package of chewing gum increases by 10 percent and we observe a 5 percent decrease in quantity demanded. Using the above formula:
> $$E_d = (5\%)/(10\%) = 1/2$$

- If $E_d < 1$, demand is said to be "**price inelastic**" for good X. The initial change in the price exceeded, in percentage terms, the responsiveness of the consumer.

> **Example:**
> The price of oranges increases by 5 percent and the quantity demanded decreases by 5 percent. Using our elasticity formula:
> $$E_d = (5\%)/(5\%) = 1$$

- If $E_d = 1$, demand is said to be **"unit elastic"** for good X. The initial change in the price is exactly equal to, in percentage terms, the responsiveness of the consumer.

When describing or calculating elasticity measures you *must* use percentage changes.

Elasticity on the Demand Curve

Take a very simple demand curve for cheeseburgers: $P = 6 - Q_d$, and plot this demand curve below (Figure 7.1).

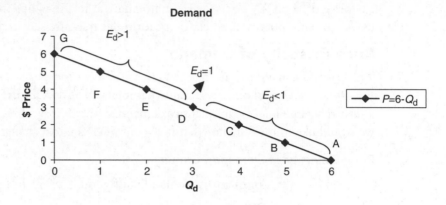

Figure 7.1

Table 7.1 summarizes changes in price, quantity demanded and price elasticity at each point on the demand curve.[1]

As you can see, in Figure 7.1, the price elasticity of demand is not constant at points A through G on the demand curve. Specifically, as the price rises, E_d rises, telling us that consumers are more price sensitive at higher prices than they are at lower prices. This makes good intuitive sense. When the price is relatively low (e.g., point B) a 50 percent increase in price might be almost negligible to consumers. But if the original price is quite high (point F) then a 50 percent increase in the price is pretty drastic. In fact, if we divide the demand curve in half, you can see that above the midpoint (point D), demand is price elastic and below the midpoint, demand is price inelastic. At the midpoint, demand is unit elastic.

Table 7.1

POINT	PRICE PER CHEESEBURGER	QUANTITY DEMANDED OF CHEESEBURGERS	PRICE ELASTICITY (E_d)
A	0	6	= 0
B	1	5	= .2
C	2	4	= .5
D	3	3	= 1
E	4	2	= 2
F	5	1	= 5
G	6	0	= ∞

[1]Note: To calculate the elasticity at each point on the demand curve in Figure 7.1, I used an equivalent way of calculating percentage change. Your AP test does not include these calculations, but you do need to know how elasticity changes along a demand curve.

Special Cases

If it is true that any increase in the price results in no decrease in the quantity demanded, then we are describing the special case where demand for the good is **perfectly inelastic:** Figure 7.2 shows the demand for a life-saving pharmaceutical, for which there is no substitute, and without which the patient dies. A vertical demand curve (D_0) tells us that no matter what percentage increase, or decrease, in price, the quantity demanded remains the same. Mathematically speaking, $E_d = 0$.

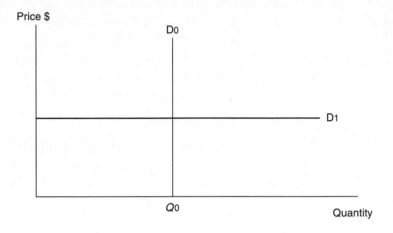

Figure 7.2

In the case where a decrease in the price causes the quantity demanded to increase without limits, then we have the special case where demand is **perfectly elastic** for that good. Figure 7.2 shows demand for a good (D_1), maybe one farmer's grain, which has many substitutes. A horizontal demand curve tells us that even the smallest percentage change in price causes an infinite change in quantity demanded. Mathematically speaking, $E_d = \infty$.

Comparing the vertical (perfectly inelastic) demand curve to the horizontal (perfectly elastic) demand curve allows us to draw an important generalization. As a demand curve becomes more vertical, the price elasticity falls and consumers become more price inelastic. The opposite generalization can be made as the demand curve becomes more horizontal. Figure 7.3 illustrates some general points about slope and elasticity.

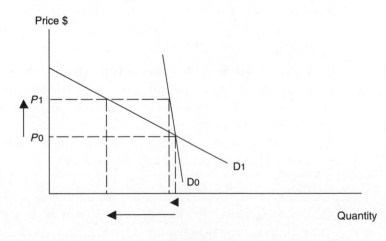

Figure 7.3

- In general, the more vertical a good's demand curve (D_0), the more inelastic the demand for that good.
- The more horizontal a good's demand curve (D_1), the more elastic the demand for that good.
- Despite this generalization, be careful, elasticity and slope are *not* equivalent measures.

Determinants of Elasticity

Perfectly elastic and perfectly inelastic demand curves are usually reserved for the hypothetical example, but they illustrate that E_d differs across consumer goods. Your intuition is that consumers respond to a price change in different ways. A 10 percent increase in the price of a car might have a drastically different consumer response from what we observe from a 10 percent increase in the price of a college education, a package of mechanical pencils or a hotel stay in Fort Lauderdale. Let's look at some general explanations for why elasticity differs.

1. Number of Good Substitutes

   If the price of good X increases, and many substitutes exist, the decrease in quantity demanded can be quite elastic. For this reason we expect E_d of orange juice to be high since there are many substitutes available to drinkers of fruit juice.

   Corollary: Often times you hear of a good that is a "necessity" or a "frivolity." These adjectives are reiterating a relative lack of or a relative wealth of good substitutes.

   Example:
   The more narrowly the product is defined, the more elastic it becomes. If we narrow our focus from orange juice down to one brand of orange juice (i.e., Minutemaid), the number of substitutes grows and we predict that so too does the price elasticity of demand for Minutemaid brand orange juice. Likewise, the demand for blue Chevrolet SUVs is more elastic than the demand for Chevrolet SUVs which, in turn, is more elastic than the demand for all SUVs.

2. Proportion of Income

   If the price of a good increases, the consumer loses purchasing power. If that good takes up a large proportion of the consumer's income, he greatly feels the pinch of the income effect, and his responsiveness might be significant. If the price of toothpicks increased by 10 percent, the typical household probably would not feel the lost purchasing power and E_d would be low. The opposite would be true if the price of food items increased by 10 percent.

   Example:
   A young full-time college student is purchasing her education by the credit-hour and supporting herself with a part-time job on the weekends and evenings. Since the student is living on a relatively small monthly income, if the price of a credit-hour increases, the response might be very elastic. The student might drop down to part-time status or drop out of college altogether so that she can save enough money to return next quarter.

3. Time

   Consumers faced by a rising price are usually fairly resourceful in their ability to find a way of decreasing the quantity demanded of a good. The difficulty faced by consumers is that they might not have time, at least not initially, to find a substitute for the more expensive good. We expect price elasticity to increase as more time passes after the initial increase in the price.

Example:

If the price of gasoline rises, consumers driving large SUVs do not immediately switch to small cars and E_d is low. But given enough time, if the gas price remains high, the E_d for gasoline increases.

Total Revenue and Elasticity

Discussing price elasticity and making simple calculations is not just a delightful academic exercise for students. Knowing how sensitive consumers are to changes in price is important to those who benefit from selling goods to those consumers—the sellers. Sellers compute total revenues collected from selling goods.

$$\text{Total Revenue} = \text{Price} * \text{Quantity demanded}$$

A seller might think, "If I continue to raise the price, my total revenues must continue to rise." A student of microeconomics knows that this is flawed logic, because quantity demanded falls when the price rises, making the impact on total revenue uncertain.

$$\text{Here's what's happening: (Price}\uparrow) * (\text{Quantity demanded}\downarrow)$$
$$= \text{Total Revenue } \updownarrow$$

With price going up and quantity demanded going down, it's like a tug-of-war between two teams, with total revenue being pulled in the direction of the strongest team.

Whether or not the total revenue increases with a price increase depends upon whether or not the gain from the higher price offsets the loss from lower quantity demanded. Price elasticity is an excellent way to predict how total revenue changes with a price change. This is sometimes called the total revenue test. Table 7.2 extends our earlier table by adding a column for total revenue at points A through G.

Table 7.2

POINT	PRICE PER CHEESEBURGER	QUANTITY DEMANDED OF CHEESEBURGERS	TOTAL = REVENUE $P * Q_d$	PRICE ELASTICITY (E_d)
A	$0	6	$0	0
B	1	5	5	0.2
C	2	4	8	0.5
D	3	3	9	1
E	4	2	8	2
F	5	1	5	5
G	6	0	0	∞

As you can see, if the price rises in the inelastic range of the demand curve, total revenues rise. However, if the price continues to rise into the elastic range, total revenues begin to fall. Why? Maybe a reminder of what it means for demand to be elastic helps to predict which team wins the tug-of-war.

- Inelastic demand $E_d < 1$: % ΔQ_d < % ΔP so Total Revenue increases with a price increase.
- Elastic demand $E_d > 1$: % ΔQ_d > % ΔP so Total Revenue decreases with a price increase.
- Unit elastic demand $E_d = 1$: % ΔQ_d = % ΔP so Total Revenue remains the same.

In Figures 7.4 and 7.5, we can graphically illustrate the connection between the demand curve, elasticity, and total revenue.

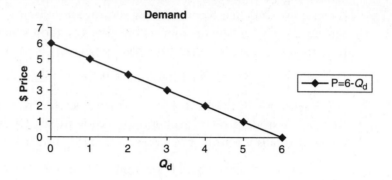

Figure 7.4

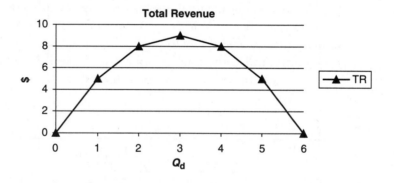

Figure 7.5

Income Elasticity of Demand

In the case of the **income elasticity**, it is a measure of how sensitive consumption of good X is to a change in a consumer's income.

$$E_I = (\% \Delta Q_d \text{ good } X)/(\% \Delta \text{ Income})$$

Example:

Jason's income rises 5 percent and we see his consumption of fast food meals rise 10 percent.

$$E_I = 10\%/5\% = 2$$

So what do we make of this? First, because E_I is greater than zero, we can determine that fast food meals are a normal good for Jason. Second, at least in this example, the consumption of fast food meals is quite income elastic. A relatively small percentage increase in income causes a large, in fact twofold, percentage increase in fast food meals. Some refer to these goods as **luxuries**.

Example:
Jen's income rises 5 percent and we observe her consumption of bread rise 1 percent.

$$E_I = 1\%/5\% = .2$$

Once again, this measure would indicate that bread is a normal good as more income prompts more bread consumption. However, the relatively small increase in consumption compared to the increase in income tells us that bread is relatively income inelastic. This makes sense, after all, how much more bread does one really wish to consume as their income rises? If Jen's income doubled, would she double, or more than double, her consumption of bread? These goods are often referred to as **necessities**.

Example:
Consumer income increases by 5 percent and we observe consumption of packaged bologna decrease by 2 percent.

$$E_I = -2\%/5\% = -.4$$

Again, there are two important observations that can be made here. First, because consumption of bologna decreased with an increase in income, we can conclude that bologna, in this example, is an inferior good. Second, there is a relatively inelastic response in bologna consumption to a change in income.

- If $E_I > 1$, the good is normal and income elastic (a luxury).
- If $1 > E_I > 0$, the good is normal but income inelastic (a necessity).
- If $E_I < 0$, the good is inferior.

Cross-Price Elasticity of Demand

Consumers also change their consumption of good X when the price of a related good, good Y changes. The sensitivity of consumption of good X to a change in the price of good Y is called the **cross-price elasticity of demand.**

$$E_{x,y} = (\% \Delta Q_d \text{ good } X)/(\% \Delta \text{ Price good } Y)$$

Example:
The price of eggs increases by 1 percent and the consumption of bacon falls 2 percent. The fact that bacon consumption fell when eggs became more expensive tells us that these goods are complementary goods.

$$E_{x,y} = (\% \Delta Q_d \text{ bacon})/(\% \Delta \text{ Price eggs}) = -2\%/1\% = -2$$

Example:
The price of Honda cars increases 2 percent and consumption of Ford cars increases 4 percent. Because Ford cars saw increased consumption when Honda cars got more expensive, the two goods are substitutes.

$$E_{x,y} = (\% \Delta Q_d \text{ Ford})/(\% \Delta \text{ Price Honda}) = 2\%/1\% = +2$$

> - A cross-price elasticity of demand less than zero identifies complementary goods.
> - A cross-price elasticity of demand greater than zero identifies substitute goods.

Price Elasticity of Supply

Now that we have addressed the sensitivity of consumer consumption of good X, let us discuss elasticity from the supplier's perspective. When the price of good X changes, we expect quantity supplied to change. The Law of Supply predicts that as the price of good X increases, so too does quantity supplied. But what we do not know is, "by how much?" The price elasticity of supply helps to measure this response.

Price Elasticity of Supply Formula

$$E_s = (\% \ \Delta \text{ in quantity supplied of good } X)/(\% \ \Delta \text{ in the price of good } X)$$

Note: The Law of Supply insures that E_s is positive. The greater this ratio, the more sensitive, or responsive, suppliers are to a change in the price of good X.

The Element of Time

Perhaps the most important determinant of how price elastic suppliers are in a particular industry is the time that it takes suppliers to change the quantity supplied once the price of the good itself has changed. This flexibility of course is different for different types of producers.

Example:

A local attorney produces hours of legal service in a small midwestern town from her small office. At the current market price for an hour of legal advice, she works a 40-hour workweek with the help of one clerical employee. If the price of an hour of legal assistance rises by 10 percent in the local market, initially our attorney responds by working a few additional hours each weekday evening and on Saturday, but the constraints of the calendar allow for only an increase of 5 percent in the hours that she supplies.

$$\text{Short term } E_s = 5\%/10\% = .5$$

If this higher price is maintained for a month or two, the attorney might ask her employee to work additional hours, thus allowing the small office to increase the quantity of hours supplied by 10 percent. And, if the price continues to stay at the higher rate, she might expand the office and employ a junior associate and thus increase the hours supplied by 20 percent.

$$\text{Long term } E_s = 20\%/10\% = 2$$

Because suppliers, once the price of the good has changed, usually cannot quickly change the quantity supplied, economists predict that the price elasticity of supply increases as time passes. Figure 7.6 illustrates the short-term (S_{SR}) and long-term (S_{LR}) supply curves for our attorney. In general, the less steep the supply curve, the more elastic suppliers are in response to a change in the price.

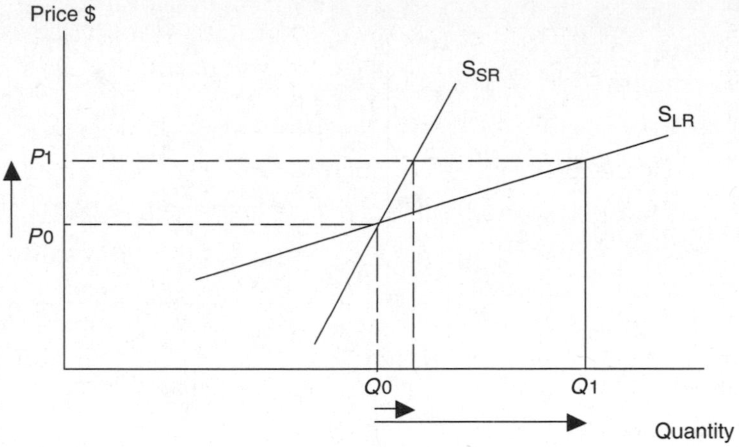

Price $

S_{SR}

S_{LR}

$P1$

$P0$

$Q0$ $Q1$

Quantity

Figure 7.6

7.2 Microeconomic Policy and Applications of Elasticity

Main Topics: *Excise Taxes, Government Subsidies, Price Floors, Price Ceilings*

Excise Taxes

Government occasionally imposes an **excise tax** on the production of a good or service. Because it is a per unit tax on production, the firm responds as if the marginal cost of producing each unit has risen by the amount of the tax. Graphically this results in a vertical shift in the supply curve by the amount of the tax. The reasons for this tax are usually twofold: (1) to increase revenue collected by the government and/or (2) to decrease consumption of a good that might be harmful to some members of society. For these reasons, tobacco is a good example of an excise tax. Can an excise tax on tobacco raise money for government? Can it deter people from smoking? Let's use our two extreme demand curves to see where these goals might, or might not, be achieved, and how the price elasticity of demand plays a critical role on where the burden, or **incidence**, of the tax rests. Economists commonly express the incidence of the tax as the percentage of the tax paid by consumers, in the form of a higher price.

Demand is Perfectly Inelastic

If the demand for cigarettes is perfectly inelastic ($E_d = 0$) then the demand curve (D_0) is vertical. With an untaxed supply (S_0) of cigarettes, the initial price of a pack of cigarettes is P_0 and Q_0 packs of cigarettes are consumed every day. If a per unit tax of T is imposed on the producers of cigarettes, the supply curve shifts upward by T. *Be careful! This is not an "increase in supply"!* Because the demand is perfectly inelastic, the equilibrium quantity remains at Q_0, but the new price rises to P_0 +T. Total dollars spent on cigarettes increases from $P_0 * Q_0$ to $(P_0+T) * Q_0$. The revenue collected by the government is equal to the area of the rectangle T $* Q_0$.

Did our excise tax accomplish our goals? Since quantity remained constant, the tax did nothing to decrease the harmful effects of smoking in society and only increased tax revenues for the government. In fact, because the quantity demanded did not fall, this scenario creates the largest revenue rectangle collected by the government. Who paid the burden of the tax? In Figure 7.7, you can see that the entire tax was paid by consumers in the form of a new price exactly equal to the old price plus the tax.

Demand is Perfectly Elastic

Figure 7.8 shows that if the demand for cigarettes is perfectly elastic ($E_d = \infty$), then the demand curve (D_0) is horizontal. With an untaxed supply (S_0) of cigarettes, the initial price of a pack of cigarettes is P_0 and Q_0 packs of cigarettes are consumed daily. The per unit tax of T shifts the supply curve upward by T, but with a perfectly elastic demand curve, the

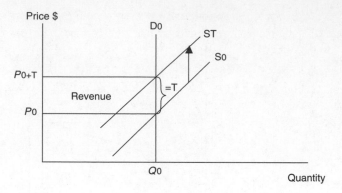

Figure 7.7

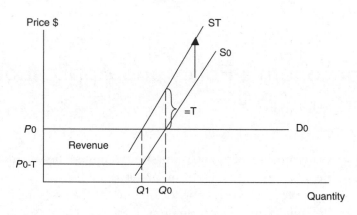

Figure 7.8

equilibrium price of cigarettes does not change, while equilibrium quantity demanded falls to Q_1. Total spending by consumers falls to the area $P_0 * Q_1$. Tax revenue for the government is a much smaller rectangle $T * Q_1$.

Who paid for the tax in this case? Because the price of a pack of cigarettes did not increase after the tax, it was not the consumers. Each producer receives a price of P_0 but must then pay T to the government so the net price received from each pack of cigarettes is $(P_0 - T)$. So the producer pays the entire share of the tax when demand is perfectly elastic. Compared to the perfectly inelastic scenario, the government collected much fewer tax revenue dollars, but the maximum decrease in harmful cigarette consumption is a definite plus.

With these two extreme cases as benchmarks, we can conclude that as demand is more inelastic, consumers pay a higher share of an excise tax. Government revenues from the excise tax increase with inelastic demand, but the goal of decreasing consumption sees only minimal success. Table 7.3 summarizes the effects of a higher excise tax and how these depend upon the price elasticity of demand.

Table 7.3

PRICE ELASTICITY OF DEMAND	GOVERNMENT REVENUE	DECREASE IN CONSUMPTION	INCIDENCE OF TAX PAID BY CONSUMERS	INCIDENCE OF TAX PAID BY SUPPLIERS
$E_d = \infty$	The least	The most	0%	100%
$E_d > 1$	Falling	Sizeable	Less than 50%	More than 50%
$E_d < 1$	Rising	Minimal	More than 50%	Less than 50%
$E_d = 0$	The most	Zero	100%	0%

Since cigarette demand is usually inelastic, significant improvements in the health of consumers is probably not the primary outcome of higher excise taxes, although they would seem to be effective revenue generating devices. Ironically, although the tax is actually imposed on suppliers of cigarettes, most of the burden of the tax falls upon consumers. Figure 7.9 illustrates an inelastic demand for cigarettes, before and after an excise tax.

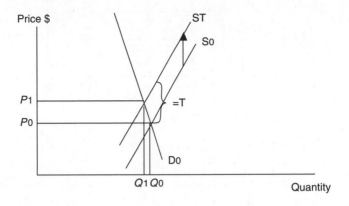

Figure 7.9

The Role the Supply Curve Plays in the Impact of an Excise Tax

We have seen that the greater the price elasticity of demand, the smaller the portion of the tax paid by consumers. It is also true that the price elasticity of supply plays a role in determining how much a tax will cause the price to increase and therefore helps to determine which group, consumers or producers, pay a higher burden of a tax.

It again helps to see if we look at two extremes: a perfectly elastic supply curve and a perfectly inelastic supply curve.

A perfectly elastic, or horizontal, supply curve tells us that even a very small change in the price will cause an infinitely large change in the quantity supplied. A per unit tax T imposed on suppliers causes this horizontal supply curve to shift upward by the amount of the tax. In Figure 7.10, you can see that the new equilibrium price is exactly T higher than the old price P_0 so consumers pay the entire burden of the tax. The equilibrium quantity decreases from Q_0 to Q_1 and the government collects tax revenue equal to $T*Q_1$.

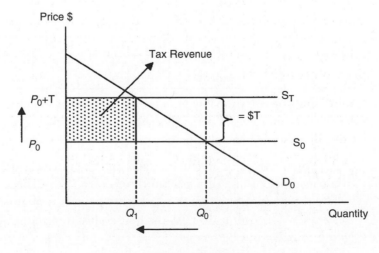

Figure 7.10

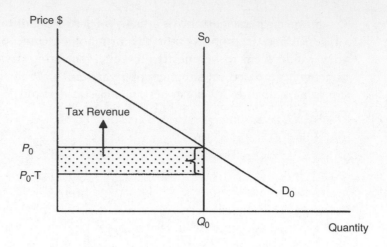

Figure 7.11

A perfectly inelastic, or vertical, supply curve illustrates the special case where any change in the price creates absolutely no change in quantity supplied. Figure 7.11 shows that in this case, the supply curve cannot vertically shift. At the equilibrium quantity Q_0, suppliers would like to charge a higher price than P_0, but any price above P_0 creates a surplus, and this surplus will clear only at the equilibrium price P_0. Therefore the firms must pay T to the government for each of the Q_0 units that are sold and consumers continue to pay the original price of P_0. In this special case, producers pay the entire burden of the tax because, after paying the tax, they receive only $(P_0 - T)$ on each unit. The government collects total revenue equal to T^*Q_0.

Table 7.4 summarizes the effects of a higher excise tax and how these depend upon the price elasticity of supply.

Table 7.4

PRICE ELASTICITY OF SUPPLY	GOVERNMENT REVENUE	DECREASE IN CONSUMPTION	INCIDENCE OF TAX PAID BY CONSUMERS	INCIDENCE OF TAX PAID BY PRODUCERS
$E_s = \infty$	The least	The most	100%	0%
$E_s > 1$	Falling	Sizeable	More than 50%	Less than 50%
$E_s < 1$	Rising	Minimal	Less than 50%	More than 50%
$E_s = 0$	The most	Zero	0%	100%

By now you are probably wondering: "How can I keep all of this straight?" If we consider the extreme cases of perfectly elastic and perfectly inelastic demand and supply curves, we can draw some general conclusions.

- As the price elasticity of demand falls, and the price elasticity of supply rises, the greater the consumer's share of a per unit excise tax. Why? Because this describes a situation where the consumer response to a higher price is negligible and the producer's response is sizeable. The group that has the best ability to respond to the higher post-tax price is going to make out better.

- Conversely, as the price elasticity of demand rises, and the price elasticity of supply falls, the greater the producer's share of a per unit excise tax.

Loss to Society

There is also a cost to society when an excise tax is imposed on a competitive market. In the hypothetical soda market depicted in Figure 7.12, the equilibrium quantity is 100 and the equilibrium price is $1. At this point, the marginal benefit to society exactly equals the marginal cost and net benefit; total welfare (combined consumer and producer surplus) is the greatest. When a $1 excise tax is imposed, the price of sodas increases to $1.80 and the amount of sodas consumed decreases to 80. The government collects $80 = $1 * 80 in tax revenue. With the tax, consumers and producers demand and supply 20 fewer units than without the tax. For these 20 units that go unproduced, the marginal benefit to consumers exceeds the marginal costs to producers. The fact that these 20 units go unproduced and unconsumed results in an inefficient outcome. The triangle labeled DWL used to be earned by society in the form of consumer and producer surplus. With the excise tax, society loses this area; it goes to no one. Economists call this area **dead weight loss** (DWL) or the net benefit sacrificed by society when such a per unit tax is imposed. Since the key to dead weight loss is a large decrease in quantity below the untaxed outcome, the area of dead weight loss to society increases as the demand or supply curves get more elastic.

Note: Taxes such as these are not the only sources of distortions away from market efficiency. For example, production often generates pollution (a negative externality), which creates a situation where harmful spillover costs are incurred by third parties. Left unregulated, these costs are not captured by the market price and the market will not produce the "correct" amount of a good. These sources of inefficiency, or market failures, are addressed in Chapter 11.

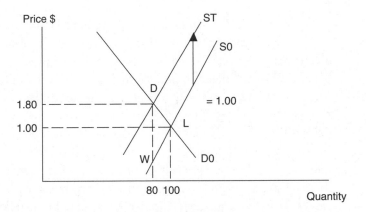

Figure 7.12

- Taxes create lost efficiency by moving away from the equilibrium market quantity where MB = MC to society.
- The area of dead weight loss (triangle DWL) increases as the quantity moves further from the competitive market equilibrium quantity.

Subsidies

A per unit **subsidy** on good X has the opposite effect of an excise tax, because firms respond as if the subsidy has lowered the marginal cost of production, therefore resulting in a downward vertical shift in the supply curve for good *X. Be careful here! This is not a "decrease in supply"!* Since subsidies come from the government, they are certainly not designed as revenue-generating devices. Ideally, their primary goal is to support producers of a good or service that has significant benefit to society so that it can be produced in greater quantities and at lower prices to consumers. This form of positive externality is also explored in Chapter 11. Public university education is a common example of this type of subsidy.

Figure 7.13 illustrates the market for public university education where the demand (D_0) and unsubsidized supply (S_0) curves produce an equilibrium price P_0 (tuition) and quantity Q_0 (degrees earned). If government decides that provision of bachelor's degrees is a beneficial service to society, a per student subsidy U is given to the public university system. The subsidy decreases tuition and increases the number of undergraduate degrees received.

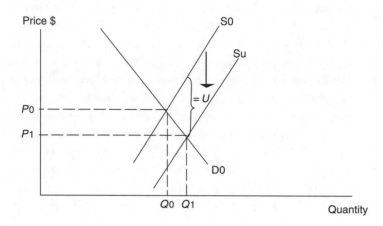

Figure 7.13

How does the price elasticity of demand factor into this outcome? If the demand for public university education is elastic, then a relatively small percentage decrease in the price of tuition creates a sizeable percentage increase in the number of degrees earned by members of society. If demand is price inelastic, it takes a much larger percentage decrease in the price to achieve the same percentage increase in degrees earned.

Price Floors

In some cases, the market-determined equilibrium price P_0 is deemed "too low" by some members of society. Typically, suppliers who feel that the market price is not high enough to cover production costs and earn a decent living make this argument. If the government agrees with this argument, a **price floor** may be installed at some level above the equilibrium price. A price floor is a legal minimum price below which the product cannot be sold. Another example is a minimum wage in a market for labor. A price floor in the market for milk is seen in Figure 7.14.

The resulting surplus of milk is not eliminated through the market and the government usually agrees, as part of the price floor arrangement, to purchase the surplus milk. For consumers, the result of the policy is a higher price of milk (and other dairy products) at grocery stores, a decrease in milk consumption and an increase in taxpayer-supported government spending. The amount of government spending to purchase the surplus is equal to (P_F) * surplus. If the price elasticities of demand or supply are large, the surplus, and resulting government spending, rises.

By providing an incentive for producers to produce beyond where the MB = MC, efficiency is lost with the price floor. For gallons of milk above Q_0, MC > MB; there is an

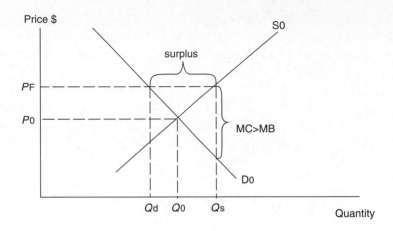

Figure 7.14

overallocation of resources to milk production. Quite simply, the policy produces a situation where "too much" milk is produced.

- A price floor is installed when producers feel the market equilibrium price is "too low."
- A price floor creates a permanent surplus at a price above equilibrium.
- If the government purchases the surplus, taxpayers eventually pay the bill.
- The more price elastic the demand and supply curves, the greater the surplus and the greater the government spending to purchase the surplus.
- The price floor reduces net benefit by overallocating resources to the production of the good.

Price Ceilings

For some goods and services, the market equilibrium price is judged to be "too high." Consumers who feel that the price is so high that it prevents a significant fraction of citizens from being able to consume a good, usually express this sentiment. If the government agrees with this argument, a **price ceiling** may be installed at a level below the equilibrium price. A price ceiling is a legal maximum price above which the product cannot be bought and sold. A price ceiling in the market for rental apartments (rent control) is seen in Figure 7.15.

The resulting shortage of rent-controlled apartments is not eliminated through the market and this creates a sticky situation for low-income households, the group for which the policy was intended. Many suppliers completely remove their rental units from the market, converting them into office space or condominiums. Others attempt to increase profits by lowering levels of health and safety maintenance, or by charging exorbitant fees for a key to the apartment. For families lucky enough to find rent-controlled space, the result of this policy is certainly lower rents, but the shortage also tends to create an underground or "black" market for apartments where a vacant apartment might go to the highest bidder, regardless of financial need. If the price elasticities of demand or supply are large, the shortage, and the negative consequences of it, increase.

Again, this form of price control results in lost efficiency for society. When suppliers reduce their quantity supplied below the competitive equilibrium quantity, there is a situation

"Always remember on the graphs that floors are HIGH and ceilings are LOW."
—Kristy, AP Student

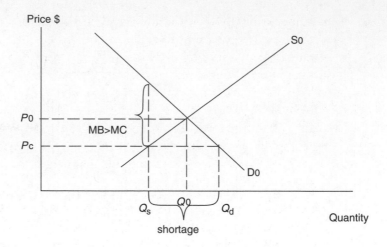

Figure 7.15

where the MB > MC, and we see an underallocation of resources in the rental apartment market. This policy, intended to help low-income families, creates a situation where "too little" of the good is produced.

- A price ceiling is installed when consumers feel the market equilibrium price is "too high."
- A price ceiling creates a permanent shortage at a price below equilibrium.
- The more price elastic the demand and supply curves, the greater the shortage.
- The price ceiling reduces net benefit by underallocating resources to the production of the good.

7.3 Consumer Choice

Main Topics: *Total and Marginal Utility, Unconstrained Choice, Law of Diminishing Marginal Utility, Constrained Choice, Utility Maximizing Rule*

Utility

If you pull back the curtain on the Law of Demand to study how consumers behave, much insight can be gained. It's important to remember that people demand things because *those things make those people happy.* We choose to consume mundane items like electricity or crackers, or luxury items like trans-Atlantic flights and tickets to an NFL game, because they provide us with happiness. In economics, we call this happiness (or benefit, or satisfaction, or enjoyment) **utility**.

While in the course of a week, consumption of more and more pints of Cherry Garcia ice cream is likely to increase our **total utility**, it is probably safe to say that the first pint in a week provides more **marginal utility** than the second, third, or fourth pint. If you recall from Chapter 5, analysis of marginal changes is extremely important in modeling how individuals make decisions.

- Total utility (TU) is the total amount of happiness received from the consumption of a certain amount of a good.

- Marginal utility (MU) is the additional utility received (or sometimes lost) from the consumption of the *next* unit of a good.
- Mathematically speaking: $MU = \Delta TU/\Delta Q$ (this ΔQ is likely to equal 1 if you are consuming one additional unit at a time).

Example:

Table 7.5 summarizes the utility gained from consumption of successive cups of coffee in a typical morning at work. Some choose to measure utility in hypothetical "**utils**," but I like to think about these as "happy points."

As our coffee drinker (Joe) goes from zero to one cup of coffee, his total happiness from coffee drinking increases from zero to 20 happy points. The incremental, or marginal, change is also 20 points. The marginal utility is simply calculated as the difference between the totals as Joe consumes consecutive cups of coffee.

Table 7.5

# CUPS(Q)	TOTAL UTILITY (TU) ("HAPPY POINTS")	MARGINAL UTILITY (MU)
0	0	—
1	20	20
2	35	15
3	45	10
4	50	5
5	45	−5
6	35	−10

Unconstrained Consumer Choice

So how much coffee should our desk jockey consume in a typical morning? Assuming that he does not have to pay for each cup and can freely use the coffee machine, one might assume that Joe consumes unlimited amounts of coffee. Using Table 7.5 or Figure 7.16, you can easily see that total utility initially rises, peaks, and then begins to fall as more coffee is consumed. If Joe is a consumer who seeks to maximize happiness, and this seems a reasonable aim, he would not consume more than four cups of coffee, even if he were not asked to pay for each cup.

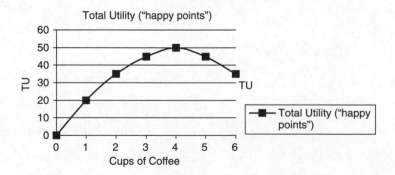

Figure 7.16

- Even if the monetary price of good X is zero, the rational consumer stops consuming good X at the point where total utility is maximized.

Diminishing Marginal Utility

From the above diagram (Figure 7.16), you can see a relationship between total utility and coffee consumption. There is the obvious rise, peak and fall of total utility as the number of cups increases. But closer inspection reveals that, as more coffee is consumed, total utility rises at a slower and slower rate. Since marginal utility is the rate at which total utility changes, marginal utility must be falling.

The **Law of Diminishing Marginal Utility** says that in a given time period, the marginal utility from consumption of one more of that item falls. A graphical depiction of marginal utility, also the slope of total utility, is seen in Figure 7.17.

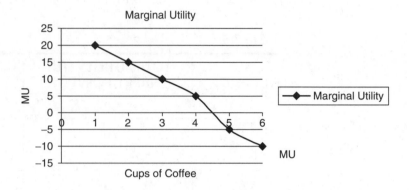

Figure 7.17

Constrained Utility Maximization

Now we require Joe to pay a price P_c for additional cups of coffee. With a fixed daily income and a price that must be paid, this individual is now a **constrained utility maximizer**. Joe must ask himself: "Does the next cup of coffee provide at least $\$P_c$ worth of additional happiness?" If Joe answers "Yes" to this question for the first three cups of coffee, he maximizes his utility by stopping at three cups. If his answer is "No" to the fourth cup, he does not consume it.

Does this sound familiar? It should, as it is another example of how a consumer never does something if the marginal benefit (in this case, utility) gained is exceeded by the marginal cost incurred.

- When required to pay a price, the utility maximizing consumer stops consuming when: $MB = P$.

Demand Curve Revisited

Using the logic outlined above as an example, what would happen if the price of coffee fell? If Joe was facing a new lower price, you should expect that Joe would rationally increase his daily consumption of cups of coffee. Have you heard this behavior described before? Sure! It's the Law of Demand and it has a tight connection to the Law of Diminishing Marginal Utility.

Imagine you are a consumer who has already paid for, and consumed the first pint of ice cream this week. Would you pay the same price for the second pint of ice cream? Doubtful, because the second pint does not provide the same marginal utility as the first.

In order to entice you to purchase and consume additional pints of Cherry Garcia ice cream, the price must fall to compensate you for your falling marginal utility.

This Law of Diminishing Marginal Utility is the backbone of the Law of Demand. To convert the relationship between marginal utility and quantity consumed at any price, we might ask you how much you are willing to pay to consume successive pints of ice cream. Because of diminishing marginal utility, you offer to pay less for additional units. Thus, we can then construct your monthly demand curve for ice cream. Figure 7.18 illustrates how diminishing marginal utility from consumption of a good can be converted to a demand curve for that good.

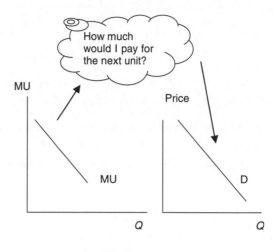

Figure 7.18

Constrained Utility Maximization, Two Goods

Economists see a consumer, constrained by income and prices, as living within a budget constraint. In a simple case where one good is consumed, the consumer maximizes utility by buying units of good X up to the point where the marginal utility of the last unit of good X is equal to the price. Most consumers allocate limited income between many goods and services, each with a price that must be paid. To see how a consumer maximizes utility in this situation, we consider a two-good case where, in addition to daily cups of coffee, Joe also purchases scones. We start with a "rule" and then proceed to solve a couple of problems.

Utility Maximizing Rule

Given limited income, consumers maximize utility when they buy amounts of goods X and Y so that the marginal utility per dollar spent is equal for both goods. Another way to think about it is that they seek the most "bang for their bucks." Mathematically, this **utility maximizing rule** is expressed:

$$\text{MU}_x/P_x = \text{MU}_y/P_y \text{ or } \text{MU}_x/\text{MU}_y = P_x/P_y$$

If the consumer has used all income and the above ratios are equal, they are said to be in equilibrium. Under this condition, no other combination of X and Y provides more total utility.

Example:

Joe has daily income of $20, each cup of coffee costs $P_c = \$2$ and each scone costs $P_s = \$4$. Table 7.6 provides us with Joe's marginal utility received in the consumption of each good.

Table 7.6

CUPS OF COFFEE	MU OF COFFEE	# OF SCONES	MU OF SCONES
1	10	1	30
2	8	2	24
3	6	3	20
4	4	4	16
5	2	5	14
6	1	6	8

- It is very important to remember that consuming more of one good causes the *marginal utility* to fall, but the *total utility* to rise.

In order to maximize Joe's utility, he seeks a combination of coffee and scones so that $MU_c/\$2 = MU_s/\$4$ and spends exactly his income of $20. Another way to solve this problem is to rearrange these ratios so that:

$$MU_c/MU_s = \$2/\$4 = .5$$

There are several combinations of coffee and scones in Table 7.6 where the ratio of marginal utilities is one-half. For example, Joe could consume one cup of coffee (MU = 10) and three scones (MU = 20) for a total utility of 84 (10+30+24+20). But this combination would only spend a total of $14, and surely Joe would be happier if he used all of his income.

- To find the total utility of consuming two cups of coffee, sum up the marginal utility of the first and the second. Do the same for scones to calculate total utility.

Another possibility is to consume two cups of coffee (MU = 8) with four scones (MU = 16). This does indeed spend exactly $20. The total utility of 108 confirms that Joe is happier with this combination of coffee and scones. There exists one other combination of goods that satisfies our rule: four cups of coffee (MU = 4) with six scones (MU = 8) expends too much money ($32) for Joe's income.

So according to our rule, Joe's utility maximizing decision would be to use his income of $20 to consume two cups of coffee and four scones. What if he decided to experiment and reallocate his consumption, while still spending only $20 on coffee and scones? For example, four cups of coffee (MU = 4) and three scones (MU = 20) fails our rule, but still would spend $20. On closer inspection, this is a poor decision because total utility falls to 102.

Example:
Now the price of a cup of coffee falls to $1. Joe needs to reexamine his utility maximizing combination of coffee and scones.

$$MU_c/MU_s = \$1/\$4 = .25$$

Again, there are three possibilities, but only one uses exactly $20 of income. If Joe buys four cups of coffee (MU = 4) and four scones (MU = 16), he spends exactly his income and receives total utility of 118. The combination of three cups of coffee and two scones does not use all of the income and the combination of five cups of coffee and six scones exceeds the income constraint.

Connection Back to Demand Curves

Joe, as a utility maximizing consumer, chooses two cups of coffee at a price of $2 and four cups of coffee at a price of $1. This sounds familiar! What Joe has done, simply by responding in a utility maximizing way, is illustrate the Law of Demand. The two combinations of price and quantity demanded are two points on Joe's coffee demand curve. By connecting these points, we trace out his demand curve (Figure 7.19).

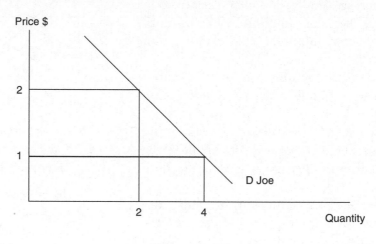

Figure 7.19

Individual and Market Demand Curves

We can take the individual decisions made by consumers like Joe and expand the analysis to build a market demand curve for coffee and other goods. This process is called **horizontal summation.** At every price, we would simply add the quantity demanded for all individual consumers.

- Utility maximizing behavior of individuals creates individual demand curves.
- Summing the quantity demanded by individuals at each price creates market demand curves.

❯ Review Questions

1. If the price of corn rises 5 percent and the quantity demanded for corn falls 1 percent, then

   (A) $E_d = 5$ and demand is price elastic.
   (B) $E_d = 1/5$ and demand is price elastic.
   (C) $E_d = 5$ and demand is price inelastic.
   (D) $E_d = 1/5$ and demand is price inelastic.
   (E) $E_d = 5$ and corn is a luxury good.

2. A small business estimates price elasticity for the product to be 3. To raise total revenue, owners should

   (A) decrease price as demand is elastic.
   (B) decrease price as demand is inelastic.
   (C) increase price as demand is elastic.
   (D) increase price as demand is inelastic.
   (E) do nothing; they are already maximizing total revenue.

3. Mrs. Johnson spends her entire daily budget on potato chips, at a price of $1 each, and onion dip at a price of $2 each. At her current consumption bundle, the marginal utility of chips is 12 and the marginal utility of dip is 30. Mrs. Johnson should

(A) do nothing; she is consuming her utility maximizing combination of chips and dip.

(B) increase her consumption of chips until the marginal utility of chip consumption equals 30.

(C) decrease her consumption of chips until the marginal utility of chip consumption equals 30.

(D) decrease her consumption of chips and increase her consumption of dip until the marginal utility per dollar is equal for both goods.

(E) increase her consumption of chips and increase her consumption of dip until the marginal utility per dollar is equal for both goods.

4. A consequence of a price floor is

(A) a persistent shortage of the good.

(B) an increase in total welfare.

(C) a persistent surplus of the good.

(D) elimination of dead weight loss.

(E) an increase in quantity demanded and a decrease in quantity supplied.

Use the figure below to respond to the next two questions.

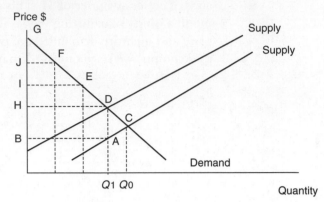

5. The competitive market equilibrium is at point C. If a per unit excise tax is imposed on the production of this good, the dead weight loss is

(A) the area BDE.

(B) the area BADH.

(C) the area GDH.

(D) the area DAC.

(E) the area GDAB.

6. The competitive market equilibrium is at point C. If a per unit excise tax is imposed on the production of this good, the revenue collected by the government is

(A) the area BDE.

(B) the area BADH.

(C) the area GDH.

(D) the area DAC.

(E) the area GDAB.

› Answers and Explanations

1. **D**—You must know the formula for elasticity: $E_d = (\%\Delta Q_d)/(\%\Delta P) = 1/5$. Since $E_d < 1$, this is inelastic demand, and you can quickly eliminate any reference to elastic demand. Although calculators are not allowed on the AP exam, simple calculations can be made in the margins of your exam.

2. **A**—If you know your elasticity measures, you see that with $E_d = 3$ you can eliminate any reference to inelastic demand. Choice E is incorrect as total revenue is maximized at the midpoint of the demand curve where $E_d = 1$. If $E_d > 1$, the firm increases total revenue by decreasing the price because the quantity demanded rises by a greater percentage than the fall in price.

3. **D**—Mrs. Johnson needs to find the combination of chips and dip where the ratio of marginal utility per dollar is equated. Currently $MU_c/P_c = 12$ and $MU_d/P_d = 15$ so choice A is ruled out. Since she is receiving more "bang for her buck" from dip consumption, she increases dip consumption and therefore decreases chip consumption. MU_d falls and MU_c rises. She adjusts her spending until $MU_c/P_c = MU_d/P_d$.

4. **C**—Price floors are installed when the market equilibrium price is believed to be "too low." This price lies above the equilibrium price, decreasing Q_d and increasing Q_s, thus creating a surplus. Price controls worsen total welfare and create dead weight loss.

5. **D**—Dead weight loss is total welfare that used to be gained by society prior to the tax. When looking for dead weight loss, narrow your focus by comparing the quantity produced with and without the tax. The horizontal distance between Q_0 and Q_1 is the unattained output from the tax. The vertical distance between points D and A illustrates that the MB>MC and is therefore an inefficient outcome.

6. **B**—Revenue collected by the government is equal to the per unit tax multiplied by the new quantity. The vertical distance between supply curves is the tax.

› Rapid Review

Elasticity: measures the sensitivity, or responsiveness, of a choice to a change in an external factor.

Price elasticity of demand (E_d): measures the sensitivity of consumer quantity demanded for good X when the price of good X changes.

Price elasticity formula: $E_d = (\%\Delta Q_d)/(\%\Delta P)$. Ignore the negative sign.

Price elastic demand: $E_d > 1$ or the $(\%\Delta Q_d) > (\%\Delta P)$. Consumers are price sensitive.

Price inelastic demand: $E_d < 1$ or the $(\%\Delta Q_d) < (\%\Delta P)$. Consumers are not price sensitive.

Unit elastic demand: $E_d = 1$ meaning the $(\%\Delta Q_d) = (\%\Delta P)$.

Perfectly inelastic: $E_d = 0$. In this special case, the demand curve is vertical and there is absolutely no response to a price change.

Perfectly elastic: $E_d = \infty$. In this special case, the demand curve is horizontal meaning consumers have an instantaneous and infinite response to a price change.

Slope and elasticity: in general, the more vertical a good's demand curve, the more inelastic the demand for that good. The more horizontal a good's demand curve, the more elastic the demand for that good. Despite this generalization, be careful as elasticities and slopes are *not* equivalent measures.

Determinants of elasticity: if a good has more readily available substitutes (luxuries vs. necessities), it is likely that consumers are more price elastic for that good. If a high proportion of a consumer's income is devoted to a particular good, consumers are generally more price elastic for that good. When consumers have more time to adjust to a price change, their response is usually more elastic.

Total Revenue: $TR = P * Q_d$.

Total Revenue Test: total revenue rises with a price increase if demand is price inelastic and falls with a price increase if demand is price elastic.

Elasticity and demand curves: at the midpoint of a linear demand curve, $E_d = 1$. Above the midpoint demand is elastic and below the midpoint demand is inelastic.

Income elasticity: a measure of how sensitive consumption of good X is to a change in the consumer's income.

Income elasticity formula: $E_I = (\%\Delta Q_d \text{ good } X)/(\%\Delta \text{ Income})$.

Luxury: a good for which the income elasticity is greater than one.

Necessity: a good for which the income elasticity is above zero, but less than one.

Values of Income Elasticity: if $E_I > 1$, the good is normal and a luxury. If $1 > E_I > 0$, the good is normal and income inelastic (necessity). If $E_I < 0$, the good is inferior.

Cross-Price Elasticity of Demand: a measure of how sensitive consumption of good X is to a change in the price of good Y.

Cross-Price elasticity formula: $E_{x,y} = (\%\Delta\ Q_d\ \text{good}\ X)/(\%\ \Delta\ \text{Price}\ Y)$.

Values of Cross-Price Elasticity of Demand: If $E_{x,y} > 0$, goods X and Y are substitutes. If $E_{x,y} < 0$, goods X and Y are complementary.

Price Elasticity of Supply: measures the sensitivity of quantity supplied for good X when the price of good X changes.

Price elasticity of supply formula: $E_s = (\%\Delta Q_s)/(\%\Delta P)$.

Excise tax: a per unit tax on production results in a vertical shift in the supply curve by the amount of the tax.

Incidence of Tax: the proportion of the tax paid by consumers in the form of a higher price for the taxed good is greater if demand for the good is inelastic and supply is elastic.

Dead Weight Loss: the lost net benefit to society caused by a movement away from the competitive market equilibrium. Policies like excise taxes create lost welfare to society.

Subsidy: has the opposite effect of an excise tax, as it lowers the marginal cost of production, resulting in a downward vertical shift in the supply curve for good X.

Price Floor: a legal minimum price below which the product cannot be sold. If a floor is installed at some level above the equilibrium price, it creates a permanent surplus.

Price Ceiling: a legal maximum price above which the product cannot be sold. If a ceiling is installed at a level below the equilibrium price, it creates a permanent shortage.

Utility: happiness, benefit, satisfaction, or enjoyment gained from consumption.

Total utility: total happiness received from consumption of a number of units of a good.

Marginal utility: the incremental happiness received, or lost, when the consumer increases consumption of a good by one unit.

Utils: a unit of measurement often used to quantify utility. A.k.a. "happy points."

Law of Diminishing Marginal Utility: in a given time period, the marginal (additional) utility from consumption of more and more of that item falls.

Constrained utility maximization: for a one-good case. Constrained by prices and income, a consumer stops consuming a good when the price paid for the next unit is equal to the marginal benefit received.

Utility Maximizing Rule: the consumer maximizes utility when they choose amounts of goods X and Y, with their limited income, so that the marginal utility per dollar spent is equal for both goods. Mathematically: $MU_x/P_x = MU_yP_y$, or $MU_x/MU_y = P_x/P_y$.

Horizontal summation: the process of adding, at each price, the individual quantities demanded to find the market demand curve for a good.

CHAPTER 8

The Firm, Profit, and the Costs of Production

IN THIS CHAPTER

Summary: The previous chapter focused on the choices made by consumers and how external forces and microeconomic policies affected those choices. We concluded the chapter by constructing the concept of constrained utility maximization and the utility maximizing rule. Also known as the consumer's equilibrium, it goes a long way towards explaining demand for goods and services. This chapter examines much of the same but for firms, who are assumed to maximize profit by hiring the perfect combination of production inputs at the lowest cost. We begin by introducing the firm, the importance of opportunity costs and the economic view of profits. We proceed by introducing the short-run production function and several principles that flow from production. We then turn to the short-run costs of employing inputs and important principles associated with costs. In particular, these concepts provide the foundation for the supply curve. Lastly, we extend the analysis into the long run.

Key Ideas
- ✪ Economic Profit
- ✪ Short Run vs. Long Run
- ✪ Production in the Short Run
- ✪ Law of Diminishing Marginal Returns
- ✪ Costs in the Short Run
- ✪ Costs in the Long Run

8.1 Firms, Opportunity Costs, and Profits

Main Topics: *The Firm, Accounting and Economic Profit, Explicit and Implicit Costs, Short Run and Long Run*

The Firm

When we talk about consumers, it's very easy to imagine yourself in the leading role. However, when the conversation switches to the firm, it is often much more difficult to visualize what it is, or who we are talking about. The firm can bring to mind many things to many different people. The firm can be an independent bookstore in your town, or it can be Barnes & Noble. It can be a street vendor selling hot dogs or it can be Oscar Mayer. Regardless of the size of the business, a **firm** is defined as: "An organization that employs factors of production to produce a good or service that it hopes to profitably sell."

Profit and Cost: When CPAs and Economists Collide

Before we launch into a technical discussion of production and costs, we need to take care of, well, a technicality. The bottom line is that the accountant sees profit differently than does the economist.

Example:

Upon completion of her undergraduate double major in accounting and economics, Molly creates a firm that sells lemonade on a busy street corner in her small town. Selling cups of lemonade at $1 each, Molly sells 1000 cups per month. The accountant and the economist in her agree (imagine a little devil and little angel on each shoulder—you can decide which is the CPA) that monthly total revenues (TR) = $1 * 1000 cups = $1000.

Molly's accounting textbooks clearly state that profit (π) is calculated by subtracting total production costs (TC) from total revenue. She rents a table from her parents at $75 per month, spends $300 per month on lemons, sugar, and cups, and purchases a monthly vendor's license at $25. These direct, purchased, out-of-pocket costs are referred to as accounting, or **explicit costs**.

$$\text{Accounting } \pi = \text{TR} - \text{explicit cost} = \$1000 - 75 - 300 - 25$$
$$= \$600, \text{ a tidy profit!}$$

The economist on Molly's other shoulder disagrees. Are these the only costs of running the lemonade stand? What about the opportunity costs of resources not accounted for above? For example, Molly has chosen to give up a monthly salary of $1000 at a bank. The economist knows that this opportunity cost must be subtracted from total revenue to better measure profitability. These indirect, non-purchased, opportunity costs, are called economic, or **implicit costs**.

$$\text{Economic } \pi = \text{TR} - \text{explicit cost} - \text{implicit costs} = \$1000 - 75 - 300 - 25 - 1000$$
$$= -\$400, \text{ a painful loss!}$$

Other implicit costs borne by many entrepreneurs include the interest given up when savings are liquidated, or rent forgone if the individual works out of a home or garage. Here's one way to try to keep explicit and implicit costs straight.

- Were the dollars paid to outside resource suppliers (employees, a landlord, a wholesale food store)? Did money actually change hands? **Explicit**.
- Were the resources supplied by the entrepreneur herself (salary or interest given up)? **Implicit**.

So Which Should I Use?

Excellent question. The "quickie" answer is to turn to the title page of this book, and use that method. Of course, as a student of economics, you must include implicit economic costs in calculating economic profit. But why? Well, it's more accurate. An adept student of economics knows that the cost of something goes beyond the price tag. A friend of mine in graduate school once said that "nothing is free, it is just non-priced." If you visit your AP teacher's office, you might not have to pay to pass through the door, but you could be doing something else with your time. This is a non-priced economic cost. Molly's labor and effort at the lemonade stand appear to be free; this is why an accountant does not include that effort in calculating profit. An economist knows that it is not free—it is just non-priced. An economist tries to quantify that price by using the value of Molly's efforts in her next best alternative as the banker. Throughout this book, costs refer to economic costs, and profits refer to economic profits.

Short-Run and Long-Run Decisions

The short run is a time when at least one production input is fixed, and cannot be changed, to respond to a change in product demand. During the holiday season a local gift shop extends hours and increases the workers hired. Much more difficult to change is the total capacity of the shop. The capacity of the shop is fixed in the short run, but can be altered with enough time. The amount of time required to change the plant size is known as the **long run**. In other words, all inputs are variable in the long run. See Table 8.1.

Table 8.1

	PLANT SIZE (CAPITAL)	FIXED COSTS	VARIABLE COSTS	ENTRY/EXIT OF FIRMS
Short Run	Fixed	Some	Some	No
Long Run	Variable	None	All	Yes

Example:

When Molly pays $25 for a monthly vendor's license on January 1st, she is committed for a month. She cannot receive a refund if she fails to operate the lemonade stand and she does not have to pay more if she works 24 hours a day all month. For Molly, the long run is one month. On the other hand, at any point in the month, Molly can choose to purchase more lemons, cups or sugar, or employ assistants, if she is selling more cups of lemonade. This is a short-run decision.

8.2 Production and Cost

Main Topics: *Short-Run Production Functions, Law of Diminishing Returns, Short-Run Costs, Connecting Production and Cost, Long-Run Costs, Economies of Scale*

Short-Run Production Functions

How do economic resources like labor, capital, natural resources, and entrepreneurial talent become a cup of lemonade, or a ton of copper, or a 30-second television commercial? A **production function** is the mechanism for combining production resources, with existing technology, into finished goods and services. In other words, a production function takes inputs and creates output. In a production function that uses only labor (L) and capital (K):

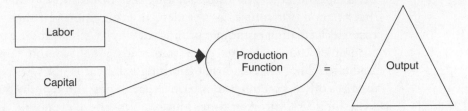

Fixed and Variable Inputs

The short run is a period of time too brief to change the plant capacity. This implies that some production inputs cannot be changed in the short run. These are **fixed inputs**. During the short run, firms can adjust production to meet changes in demand for their output. This implies that some inputs are **variable inputs**. Using only labor and capital, we assume that labor can be changed in the short run, but capital (i.e., the plant capacity) is fixed.

Short-Run Production Measures

By its very nature, production lends itself to be quantified and as a result you need to study these three production measures. To keep it simple, capital is assumed to be fixed while labor can be changed to produce more or less output.

1. **Total Product (TP_L) of Labor** is the total quantity, or total output, of a good produced at each quantity of labor employed.

2. **Marginal Product (MP_L) of Labor** is the change in total product resulting from a change in the labor input. $MP_L = \Delta TP_L / \Delta L$. If labor is changing one unit at time, $MP_L = \Delta TP_L$.

3. **Average Product (AP_L) of Labor** is also a measure of average labor productivity and is total product divided by the amount of labor employed. $AP_L = TP_L / L$.

As you can see, MP_L and AP_L are both derived from TP_L. It is useful to see how these three measures are related with a numerical example.

> **Example:**
> In the production period of a month, Molly's lemonade stand combines variable inputs of her labor (and the raw materials) to the fixed inputs of her table and her license to operate. Molly adds employees to her plant and forecasts the change in production (cups per day) in Table 8.2

Table 8.2

UNITS OF LABOR	TOTAL PRODUCT (TP_L)	MARGINAL PRODUCT (MP_L)	AVERAGE PRODUCT (AP_L)
0	0 cups		
1	5	5–0 = 5	5/1 = 5
2	15	10	7.5
3	30	15	10
4	40	10	10
5	45	5	9
6	40	–5	6.67
7	30	–10	4.29

As Molly employs more workers to the fixed plant capacity (the table on the corner), total product increases, eventually peaks, and then begins to fall. This production function can be seen in Figure 8.1

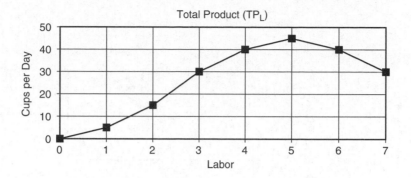

Figure 8.1

Law of Diminishing Marginal Returns

Imagine what happens to the lemonade stand as Molly adds more and more workers. At first, tasks are divided. (For example, Josh squeezes the lemons; Molly adds the sugar; Kelli stirs.) Specialization occurs. The marginal productivity of successive workers is rising in the early stage of production, but at some point, adding more workers increases the total product by a lesser amount. Maybe the fourth worker is pouring the lemonade and stocking while the fifth is taking money and making change. Beyond the fifth worker, the table is too crowded with employees, cups are spilled, product is wasted, and total production actually falls. The marginal contribution of these workers is negative. This illustrates one of the most important production concepts in the short run, the **Law of Diminishing Marginal Returns**, which states that *as successive units of a variable resource are added to a fixed resource, beyond some point the marginal product falls.*

> *"An important principle to know and understand."* —AP Teacher

- Increasing marginal returns: MP_L increase as L increases.
- Diminishing marginal returns: MP_L decreases as L increases.
- Negative marginal returns: MP_L becomes negative as L increases.

Graphically Speaking

Marginal product is the incremental change in total product as one more unit of labor is added. Marginal product is the geometric slope of total product. In Figure 8.1, the total product curve is initially getting steeper as more labor is added. This is seen in Figure 8.2 as increasing marginal product. From the third to the fifth worker, the slope of total product is still positive, but is becoming less steep. In Figure 8.2 marginal product from workers 3 to 5 is still positive but is falling. Beyond the fifth worker, total product is falling and thus has a negative slope. This turn of events is seen below when marginal product becomes negative.

Average product, also plotted below, initially rises, reaches a peak, and then begins to fall. So long as the marginal (next) worker adds production that is above the current average, they are pulling the average up. This is why we see AP_L rising so long as MP_L is above AP_L. If the marginal worker adds production that is below the current average, the worker pulls the average down. Thus when MP_L is below AP_L, you see that AP_L is falling. Logically then, MP_L intersects AP_L at the peak of AP_L. Average product cannot be negative.

- If $MP_L > AP_L$: AP_L is rising.
- If $MP_L < AP_L$: AP_L is falling.
- If $MP_L = AP_L$: AP_L is at the peak.

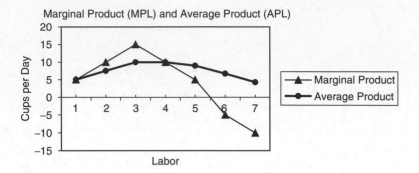

Figure 8.2

Short-Run Costs

It is important to note that we have discussed production theory without including the nagging necessity of paying for our hired inputs. For every employed input, fixed or variable, a cost is incurred.

Total Costs

In the short run, there is at least one input that is fixed and so these costs are also fixed. All inputs that are variable incur variable costs.

1. **Total Fixed Costs (TFC)** are those costs that do not vary with changes in short-run output. They must be paid even when output is zero. These include rent on building or equipment, insurance or licenses.

2. **Total Variable Costs (TVC)** are those costs that change with the level of output. If output is zero, so are total variable costs. They include payment for materials, fuel, power, transportation services, most labor, and similar costs.

3. **Total Cost (TC)** is the sum of total fixed and total variable costs at each level of output.

$$TC = TVC + TFC$$

Table 8.3

TOTAL PRODUCT CUPS PER MINUTE	TOTAL FIXED COST (TFC)	TOTAL VARIABLE COST (TVC)	TOTAL COST (TC = TFC + TVC)
0	$6	$0	$6
1	$6	$5	$11
2	$6	$8	$14
3	$6	$13	$19
4	$6	$19	$25
5	$6	$26	$32
6	$6	$34	$40
7	$6	$43	$49

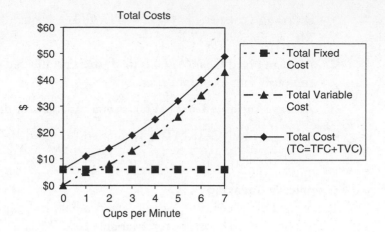

Figure 8.3

Table 8.3 summarizes Molly's costs of producing cups of lemonade per minute. Her total fixed costs are assumed to be $6 per minute and total variable costs increase as production increases.

Figure 8.3 illustrates the three total cost functions. Total fixed cost is a constant at all levels of output. Total variable cost quickly rises at first, briefly slows, and then proceeds to increase at an increasing rate. Total cost is simply the sum of TFC and TVC at every level of output and so it lies parallel to TVC. Thus the vertical distance between TC and TVC is equal to TFC.

Table 8.4

TOTAL PRODUCT CUPS PER MINUTE	MARGINAL COST (MC)	AVERAGE FIXED COST (AFC)	AVERAGE VARIABLE COST (AVC)	AVERAGE TOTAL COST (ATC)
0				
1	$5	$6.00	$5	$11.00
2	$3	$3.00	$4	$7.00
3	$5	$2.00	$4.33	$6.33
4	$6	$1.50	$4.75	$6.25
5	$7	$1.20	$5.20	$6.40
6	$8	$1.00	$5.67	$6.67
7	$9	$0.86	$6.14	$7.00

Marginal and Average Costs

Similar to our discussion of production, we can derive marginal and per unit measures of cost from the total cost functions. These are in Table 8.4.

1. **Marginal Cost** is the additional cost of producing one more unit of output $MC = \Delta TC/\Delta Q$. Since TVC are the only costs that change with the level of output, marginal

cost is also calculated as MC = ΔTVC/ΔQ. If quantity is changing one unit at a time, MC = ΔTC = ΔTVC.

2. **Average Fixed Cost (AFC)** is total fixed cost divided by output. AFC = TFC/Q. It continuously falls as output rises.

3. **Average Variable Cost (AVC)** is total variable cost divided by output. AVC = TVC/Q.

4. **Average Total Cost (ATC)** is total cost divided by output ATC = TC/Q. Note that ATC = AFC + AVC.

Graphically Speaking

> "It's all about the graphs . . . if you can see it, you got it." —Cleo, AP Student

If marginal product is the slope of total product, it should be no surprise that marginal cost is the slope of total cost, or total variable cost. We can see that marginal cost initially falls due to specialization, but soon begins to rise as more output is produced. This is the Law of Increasing Costs and is a direct result of the Law of Diminishing Marginal Returns to production. Both being U-shaped curves, average variable and average total costs initially fall, hit a minimum point, and begin to rise. Average Total Cost is vertically above AVC by the amount of AFC. Figure 8.4 illustrates this.

Marginal cost and average variable and average total cost are related in much the same way as marginal product is related to average product of labor. When the marginal cost of

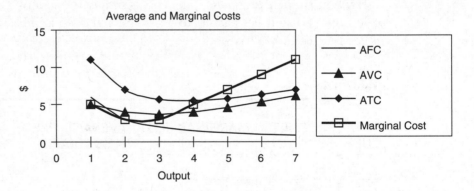

Figure 8.4

producing another cup of lemonade exceeds the current average cost the average is rising. When the marginal cost of producing another cup of lemonade falls below the current average cost the average is falling. Therefore, marginal cost equals average total cost at the minimum of ATC and equals average variable cost at the minimum of AVC.

Bridge over (Troubling) Economic Waters

Many students think that production and cost concepts are two sets of theoretical topics. This separation creates the impression that "there's twice as much to remember." These students are surprised to find out that production and cost are closely connected.

Think about it from Molly's point of view. If the next worker employed has a high marginal product, then the marginal cost of producing that increased product must be quite low. When things are going well with production, they must be going well with cost. Try to see the concepts of production and cost not as two isolated bodies of theory, but as two related sets of concepts that just need to be bridged. Let us try to build this bridge with a little algebra.

Marginal Product and Marginal Cost

$MC = \Delta TVC/\Delta Q$ and since the only variable input is labor being paid a fixed wage w,
$MC = w\Delta L/\Delta Q$ which can be modified as,
$MC = w/(\Delta Q/\Delta L) = w/MP_L$. MC and MP_L are inverses of each other!

- As MP_L is falling (diminishing marginal returns), MC is rising.
- As MP_L is rising (increasing marginal returns), MC is falling.
- When MP_L is highest, MC is lowest.

Average Product and Average Variable Cost

$AVC = TVC/Q$ and with the only variable input being labor paid a fixed wage w,
$AVC = wL/Q$ which can be modified as,
$AVC = w/(Q/L) = w/AP_L$. AVC and AP_L are inverses of each other!

- As AP_L is falling, AVC is rising.
- As AP_L is rising, AVC is falling.
- When AP_L is highest, AVC is lowest.

If we put smoother versions of our production and cost figures together, we can see these relationships in Figures 8.5 and 8.6. The output q_1 where MP_L is at a maximum is the same as the output where MC is at a minimum. Likewise, the output q_2 where AP_L is at a maximum is the same as the output where AVC is at a minimum.

> "Make sure you know the definition for the Law of Diminishing Marginal Returns. It could appear in lots of different questions." —Cassie, AP Student

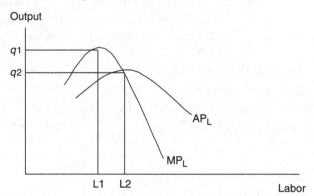

Figure 8.5

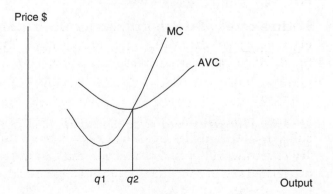

Figure 8.6

Long-Run Costs

Since all inputs are variable in the long run, discussion of production levels isn't so much about output per hour or day; it's more a question of plant size or capacity. In the short run, the firm asks, "With our current plant size, how much must we produce today?" The long run is long enough to adjust the plant capacity so the issue is really one of scale. The firm might ask itself, "At what scale do we want to operate?"

Long-Run Average Cost

I like to think of the firm's short-run average costs as a snapshot of the firm's ability to produce efficiently *at the fixed plant size*. Over time, the firm may grow and expand the plant size and begin to produce efficiently, but at the larger fixed plant size, giving us another snapshot. This process repeats itself as the firm expands or contracts and each time we receive another short-run snapshot of average cost. If we could put these short-run snapshots together into a kind of motion picture, we would see a more continuous long-run home movie of the firm's average costs. The example and Figure 8.7 illustrate the connection between short- and long-run average costs.

> *"Make sure you can differentiate between long-run and short-run curves." —Kristy, AP Student*

Example:

- In year one, Molly's firm operates at a "small" scale, producing on $SRAC_1$.
- In year two, Molly could expand and operate at a "medium" scale, producing on $SRAC_2$, but only if she can sell more than 100 gallons of lemonade. At quantities below 100, $SRAC_1 < SRAC_2$, so expansion would not be wise.
- In year three, Molly might expand to operate at a "large" scale and move to $SRAC_3$, but only if she can sell more than 250 gallons.
- Beyond the "large" scale exists a "grande" scale, but very quickly $SRAC_4 > SRAC_3$ and so this plant capacity actually begins to pay rising per unit costs.

Each of these four short-run snapshots of average costs can be smoothed out into the home movie long-run average cost curve, which is composed of sections of each short-run average cost curve at each of the four plant sizes that Molly might choose for her firm. In Figure 8.7, the long-run average cost curve would lie along the segments a→b→c→d→e.

Economies of Scale

Construction of a smoother version of Figure 8.7 allows us to see more easily some important stages of the long-run average cost curves (Figure 8.8).

1. **Economies of scale** are advantages of increased plant size and are seen on the downward part of the LRAC curve. LRAC falls as plant size rises.
   a. Labor and managerial specialization is one reason for this.
   b. Ability to purchase and use more efficient capital goods also can explain economies of scale.

2. **Constant returns to scale** can occur when LRAC is constant over a variety of plant sizes.

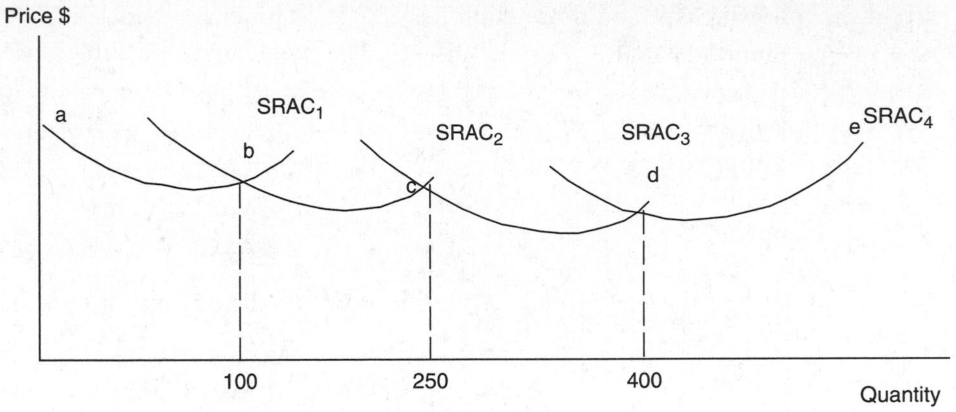

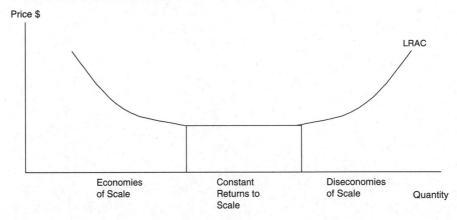

Figure 8.7

3. **Diseconomies of scale** are illustrated by the rising part of the LRAC curve and can occur if a firm becomes too large.
   a. Some reasons for this include distant management, worker alienation, and problems with communication and coordination.

Figure 8.8

› Review Questions

1. Which of the following is most likely an example of production inputs that can be adjusted in the long run, but not in the short run?

   (A) Amount of wood used to make a desk.
   (B) Number of pickles put on a sandwich.
   (C) The size of a McDonald's kitchen.
   (D) Number of teacher's assistants in local high schools.
   (E) The amount of electricity consumed by a manufacturing plant.

2. The Law of Diminishing Marginal Returns is responsible for

   (A) AVC that first rises, but eventually falls, as output increases.
   (B) AFC that first rises, but eventually falls, as output increases.
   (C) MP that first falls, but eventually rises, as output increases.
   (D) MC that first falls, but eventually rises, as output increases.
   (E) ATC that first rises, but eventually falls, as output increases.

3. Which of the following cost and production relationships is inaccurately stated?

   (A) AFC = AVC − ATC
   (B) MC = ΔTVC/ΔQ
   (C) TVC = TC − TFC
   (D) $AP_L = TP_L/L$
   (E) MC = w/MP_L

4. If the per unit price of labor, a variable resource, increases, it causes which of the following?

   (A) An upward shift in AFC.
   (B) An upward shift in MP_L.
   (C) A downward shift in ATC.
   (D) An upward shift in MC.
   (E) A downward shift in AFC.

Use the following figure to respond to questions 5 to 6.

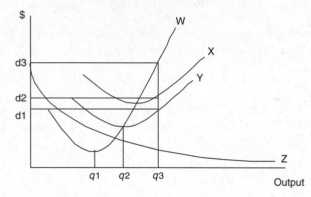

5. The curves labeled W, X, Y, Z refer to which respective cost functions?

   (A) MC, AVC, ATC, and AFC.
   (B) MC, TC, TVC, and AFC.
   (C) MC, ATC, AVC, and AFC.
   (D) MC, ATC, AVC, and TFC.
   (E) ATC, AVC, AFC, and MC.

6. At the $q3$ level of output,

   (A) AFC = $d2 − $d1.
   (B) MC = $d2.
   (C) TVC = $d2.
   (D) ATC = $d3.
   (E) AFC = $d3 − $d2.

❯ Answers and Explanations

1. **C**—The short run is a period of time too short to increase the plant size. All other choices involve decisions that could increase production almost immediately, with no change in the size of the facility. Increasing the size of a McDonald's kitchen takes quite some time and represents an increase in the total capacity of the kitchen to produce.

2. **D**—The Law of Diminishing Marginal Returns says that MP_L eventually falls as you add more labor to a fixed plant. This question tests you on the important connection between production and cost. Remember that we derived this "bridge" and found that MC = w/MP_L. So when MP_L is initially rising, MC is falling. Eventually when MP_L is falling, MC is rising. Choices A, B and E are just flat wrong. All three average costs begin by falling. AFC continues to fall, but AVC and ATC eventually rise.

3. **A**—AFC plus AVC equals ATC. If you do the subtraction, AFC = ATC − AVC, making choice A the only incorrect statement. If you have studied your production and cost relationships, you recognize that choices B, C, D and E are all stated correctly.

4. **D**—When labor is more expensive, the MC of producing the good increases, so the MC curve shifts upward. The price of a variable input has increased, so easily rule out any reference to fixed costs. If anything, a higher wage shifts MP_L downward.

5. **C**—You must be familiar with the graphical representation of marginal and average cost functions.

6. **A**—The vertical distance between ATC and AVC is AFC at any level of output.

› Rapid Review

The firm: an organization that employs factors of production to produce a good or service that it hopes to profitably sell.

Accounting profit: the difference between total revenue and total explicit costs.

Economic profit: the difference between total revenue and total explicit and implicit costs.

Explicit costs: direct, purchased, out-of-pocket costs paid to resource suppliers outside the firm. Also referred to as *accounting costs*.

Implicit costs: Indirect, non-purchased, or opportunity costs of resources provided by the entrepreneur. Also called *economic costs*.

Short Run: a period of time too short to change the size of the plant, but many other, more variable resources can be adjusted to meet demand.

Long Run: a period of time long enough to alter the plant size. New firms can enter the industry and existing firms can liquidate and exit.

Production function: the mechanism for combining production resources, with existing technology, into finished goods and services. Inputs are turned into outputs.

Fixed inputs: production inputs that cannot be changed in the short run. Usually this is the plant size or capital.

Variable inputs: production inputs that the firm can adjust in the short run to meet changes in demand for their output. Often this is labor and/or raw materials.

Total Product of Labor (TP_L): the total quantity, or total output of a good produced at each quantity of labor employed.

Marginal Product of Labor (MP_L): the change in total product resulting from a change in the labor input. $MP_L = \Delta TP_L/\Delta L$, or the slope of total product.

Average Product of Labor (AP_L): total product divided by labor employed. $AP_L = TP_L/L$.

Law of Diminishing Marginal Returns: as successive units of a variable resource are added to a fixed resource, beyond some point the marginal product declines.

Total Fixed Costs (TFC): costs that do not vary with changes in short-run output. They must be paid even when output is zero.

Total Variable Costs (TVC): costs that change with the level of output. If output is zero, so are total variable costs.

Total Cost (TC): the sum of total fixed and total variable costs at each level of output. TC = TVC + TFC.

Marginal Cost (MC): the additional cost of producing one more unit of output. $MC = \Delta TC/\Delta Q = \Delta TVC/\Delta Q$ or the slope of total cost and total variable cost.

Average Fixed Cost (AFC): total fixed cost divided by output. $AFC = TFC/Q$.

Average Variable Cost (AVC): total variable cost divided by output. $AVC = TVC/Q$.

Average Total Cost (ATC): total cost divided by output. $ATC = TC/Q = AFC + AVC$.

Relationship between MP$_L$ and MC: if labor is the variable input being paid a fixed wage (w), MC and MP$_L$ are inverses of each other. MC = $w/(\Delta Q/\Delta L)$ = $w/$MP$_L$.

Relationship between AP$_L$ and AVC: in the simplified case where labor is the variable input being paid a fixed wage (w), AVC and AP$_L$ are inverses of each other. AVC = $w/(Q/L)$ = w/AP$_L$

Economies of scale: the downward part of the LRAC curve where LRAC falls as plant size increases. This is the result of specialization, lower cost of inputs, or other efficiencies from larger scale.

Constant returns to scale: occurs when LRAC is constant over a variety of plant sizes.

Diseconomies of scale: the upward part of the LRAC curve where LRAC rises as plant size increases. This is usually the result of the increased difficulty of managing larger firms, which results in lost efficiency and rising per unit costs.

CHAPTER 9

Market Structures, Perfect Competition, Monopoly, and Things Between

IN THIS CHAPTER

Summary: Chapter 7 presented the relationship between product demand, elasticity and total revenue. Chapter 8 introduced the concept of economic profit and presented the theory behind production and costs. This chapter puts revenue and cost together to examine how a firm chooses the profit maximizing level of output and price of the product. But this profit maximizing decision depends very much upon the structure in which the firm operates. At one extreme there are many perfectly competitive firms, each too small to have a measurable impact on market price, much less each other. At the other extreme there is one firm, a monopolist, that absolutely controls the industry price and output. In between are various shades of each extreme, some closer to monopoly, and some closer to perfect competition. It is important to realize that there is no "representative" industry, or market structure, so we focus on four general models and study how firms in these structures determine price and output. In addition to the extremes of perfect competition and monopoly, we cover the models of monopolistic competition and oligopoly. This chapter also introduces you to some basic game theoretic models.

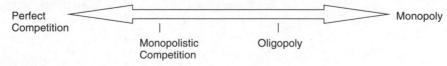

Perfect Competition ⟷ Monopoly

Monopolistic Competition   Oligopoly

Key Ideas

✪ Perfect Competition
✪ Monopoly
✪ Monopolistic Competition
✪ Oligopoly

9.1 Perfect Competition

Main Topics: *Structural Characteristics, Demand, Profit Maximization, Short-Run Profits, Decision to Shut Down, Long-Run Adjustment*

KEY IDEA

Structural Characteristics of Perfect Competition

Each market structure is defined by structural characteristics. These characteristics determine, among other things, how the profit maximizing price and quantity are set in the short run, as well as how profits might be maintained in the long run. Perfect competition is typically described by four characteristics:

- *Many small independent producers and consumers.* Not small like Mini-Me small, but small like each firm is too small to have an impact on market price. No one firm can drive up the price by restricting supply, or drive down the price by flooding the market with output. No one consumer can, by changing the amount of the good that he consumes, impact the price.
- *Firms produce a standardized product.* There exist no real differences between one firm's output and the next.
- *No barriers to entry or exit.* There exist no significant obstacles to the entry of new firms into, or the exit of existing firms out of this industry. Profitability or lack thereof determines whether the industry is expanding or contracting.
- *Firms are "price takers."* This characteristic is actually a result of the first three. Because all firms are too small to affect the price, they must accept the market price and produce as much as they wish at that price. Even if they *could* change the price, they would not do so. To see this, suppose that the market determined competitive price of barley is $5. If farmer Katie increased the price to $5.01, she would now be the high price supplier of barley with thousands of competitors producing an identical product at a lower price; Katie is likely to lose all of her customers. If she lowers her price to $4.99, she would seemingly clean up her competition. But remember, the price-taking characteristic tells us that Katie can sell all she wants at the market price of $5. If you can sell all you want at $5, why would Katie sell even one unit at $4.99?

All four of the characteristics of perfect competition are rarely found in today's industries, but agricultural commodities are usually regarded as approximately perfectly competitive.

> "In order to keep the different types of firms straight, make a table including the firm's definition, what kind of product they produce, barriers, and how they control price. It is the best way to study."
> —Kristy, AP Student

Demand for the Firm

Each perfectly competitive firm produces a standardized, or homogenous, product. Because each firm's output is such a small share of the total market supply, the demand for each firm's output is perfectly elastic. Perfectly competitive firms have no effect on the market price; they simply produce as much as they can at the going price. This implies a horizontal demand curve for their product. This does NOT imply that the market demand curve

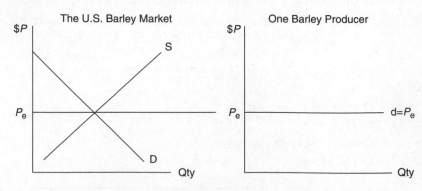

Figure 9.1

is horizontal. If the market price of barley falls, quantity demanded rises. Figure 9.1 illustrates the difference between market demand (D) and the demand for one firm's product (d).

Profit Maximization

Let's get one thing straight. When we say firms *maximize* economic profit, this means they are not going to settle for anything less than the highest possible difference between total revenue and total economic cost. If an additional dollar of profit is to be earned, they take that opportunity. If the maximum profit possible is actually zero, or even negative dollars, they accept this short-run outcome. There are two equivalent ways to maximize economic profit.

The Method of "Totals"

The perfectly competitive firm cannot change the price; it can only adjust output. To maximize profit the firm selects the output to maximize:

$$\text{Economic Profit } (\pi) = \text{Total Revenue} - \text{Total Economic Cost}$$

An example should help to illustrate how a firm goes about maximizing profit.

Example:

A carrot farmer operates in a perfectly competitive market. The going price for a bushel of carrots is $11. Table 9.1 summarizes how total revenue, total cost, and profit differ at various levels of output. Because it is the short run, there exist $16 of fixed costs. All costs reflect the explicit and implicit costs of hiring a resource.

Table 9.1

DAILY BUSHELS OF CARROTS (Q)	PRICE (P)	TOTAL REVENUE (TR)	TOTAL COST (TC)	PROFIT (Π)
0	$11	$0	$16	−$16
1	$11	$11	$22	−$11
2	$11	$22	$27.50	−$5.50
3	$11	$33	$34	−$1
4	$11	$44	$42	$2
5	$11	$55	$53	$2
6	$11	$66	$65	$1

Because the firm is a price taker, the level of output does not affect the going price. Total costs rise as production increases, a concept seen in the previous chapter. As a profit maximizer, our carrot farmer would choose to produce five bushels per day and earn $2 in daily economic profit. This method of profit maximization is much like "trial and error" and is a bit cumbersome. Let's explore an equivalent, and easier way.

The Method of "Marginals"

Throughout this book we have seen illustrations of marginal analysis and this situation is no different. You'll recall that rational decision making implies:

- If MB > MC, do more of it.
- If MB < MC, do less of it.
- If MB = MC, stop here.

Since the only decision to be made by the perfectly competitive firm is to choose the optimal level of output, the firm's rule is:

- **Choose the level of output where MR = MC.**

Table 9.2 can be modified to show the marginal revenue and marginal cost of selling additional bushels of carrots.

"If you only remember one thing, remember this! MR = MC." —Kristy, AP Student

Table 9.2

DAILY BUSHELS OF CARROTS (Q)	PRICE (P)	TOTAL REVENUE (TR)	TOTAL COST (TC)	PROFIT (Π)	MARGINAL REVENUE (MR)	MARGINAL COST (MC)
0	$11	$0	$16	−$16		
1	$11	$11	$22	−$11	$11	$6
2	$11	$22	$27.50	−$5.50	$11	$5.50
3	$11	$33	$34	−$1	$11	$6.50
4	$11	$44	$42	$2	$11	$8
5	$11	$55	$53	$2	$11	$11
6	$11	$66	$65	$1	$11	$12

Notice that in perfect competition, the price is equal to marginal revenue. This is fairly simple if you recall the assumptions of the model. Farmers can sell as much as they want at the market price. If a farmer sells one more bushel, total revenue increases by the price of the bushel; $11 in this case. Sell another bushel; earn another marginal revenue of $11. Price is also equivalent to **average revenue** (AR), or total revenue per unit. These relationships can be seen in Figure 9.2

- $MR = \Delta TR/\Delta Q = P * \Delta Q/\Delta Q = P$
- $AR = TR/Q = P * Q/Q = P$
- $\Pi = MR = AR = $ demand for the firm's product

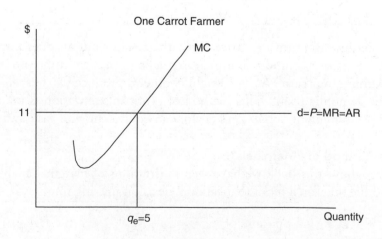

Figure 9.2

Short-Run Profit and Loss

To maximize profit, the firm must choose the level of output (q_e) where MR = MC. But how can we use Figure 9.2 to identify these profits? A little algebra goes a long way.

$\Pi = TR - TC = P * qe - TC$. If you divide both terms by quantity and remember that TC/q = Average Total Cost, you have:

$$\Pi = q_e * (P - ATC)$$

The term ($P - ATC$) is the per unit difference between what the firm receives from the sale of each unit and the average cost of producing it, or profit per unit. When you multiply this per unit profit by the number of units (q_e) produced, you have total profit. Table 9.3 and Figure 9.3 incorporate the ATC into our carrot farmer's table profit maximizing decision.

Table 9.3

DAILY BUSHELS OF CARROTS (Q)	PRICE (P)	TOTAL COST (TC)	AVERAGE TOTAL COST (ATC)	(P–ATC)	PROFIT (Π) = q * (P–ATC)
0	$11	$16			−$16
1	$11	$22	$22	−$11	−$11
2	$11	$27.50	$13.75	−$2.75	−$5.50
3	$11	$34	$11.33	−$.33	−$1
4	$11	$42	$10.50	$.50	$2
5	$11	$53	$10.60	$.40	$2
6	$11	$65	$10.83	$.17	$1

Profit Rectangles and Flying Monkeys

Everyone remembers *The Wizard of Oz* and the critical instructions that the people of Munchkinland gave Dorothy and Toto as they set off to find the Wizard: "Follow the yellow brick road." And when Dorothy, Toto, and friends stayed on the yellow brick road, they

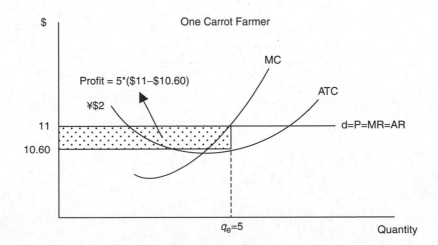

Figure 9.3

were fine. Whenever they ignored these cautionary words and left the yellow brick road, bad things happened—the scariest being the arrival of the flying monkeys. The flying monkeys tore the Scarecrow limb from limb and set the Scarecrow's straw innards on fire. Talk about a Rolaids moment! Very bad things happen when you leave the yellow brick road.

When you find the profit maximizing level of production, q_e, you are locating the yellow brick road for this firm. *Never* leave this level of output, or bad things happen. Finding q_e is the first step in calculating profit with a "profit rectangle." The area of the shaded rectangle is 5 bushels wide, multiplied by 40 cents high. In our case, the price $11 is in Figure 9.3 above the average total cost $10.60 so we have positive economic profits of $2. This does not always occur in the short run. Another look at our per unit equation tells us:

- If $P > $ ATC, $\Pi > 0$.
- If $P < $ ATC, $\Pi < 0$.
- If $P = $ ATC, $\Pi = 0$.

Short-Run Losses

While firms would love to maintain the above scenario where $P > $ ATC and positive economic profits are made, it might not always turn out that way. Due to a failure of the Bugs Bunny diet fad, the market for carrots suffers a dramatic decrease in demand. Plummeting demand decreases the market price to $6.50 per bushel and firms must readjust their profit maximizing output decision.

At the much lower price of $6.50, the firm now finds that MR = MC at an output of three bushels per day. Not surprisingly, the opportunity for positive economic profit has been eliminated. The profit maximizing, or loss minimizing, output of three bushels provides the best possible scenario for the firm; but that scenario involves economic losses of $14.50. The rectangle can still be seen in Figure 9.4, where average total cost is $11.33 per bushel.

Table 9.4

DAILY BUSHELS OF CARROTS (Q)	PRICE (P)	TOTAL REVENUE (TR)	TOTAL COST (TC)	PROFIT (Π)	MARGINAL REVENUE (MR)	MARGINAL COST (MC)
0	$6.50	$0	$16	−$16		
1	$6.50	$6.50	$22	−$15.50	$6.50	$6
2	$6.50	$13	$27.50	−$14.50	$6.50	$5.50
3	*$6.50*	*$19.50*	*$34*	*−$14.50*	*$6.50*	*$6.50*
4	$6.50	$26	$42	−$16	$6.50	$8
5	$6.50	$32.50	$53	−$20.50	$6.50	$11
6	$6.50	$39	$65	−$26	$6.50	$12

- Many AP students lose points because they incorrectly locate and label profit. When finding the profit/loss rectangle, it is important to remember the following.

- Find q_e where $P = $ MR = MC. Once you have found q_e, never leave it.
- Find ATC vertically at q_e. If you move downward, $\Pi > 0$. If you move upward, $\Pi < 0$.
- Move horizontally from ATC to the y axis to complete the rectangle and clearly label it as positive or negative.

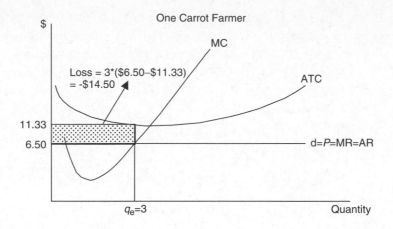

One Carrot Farmer

Loss = 3*($6.50–$11.33) = -$14.50

Figure 9.4

Decision to Shut Down

Firms obviously do not enjoy producing at a loss and desperately hope that the market price improves so that profits are possible. However, if firms are incurring losses, they must decide whether it is economically rational to operate at all. The decision to shut down, or produce zero, in the short run is sometimes the optimal strategy. To see why, consider what happens when a firm begins to produce. When a perfectly competitive firm decides to produce any level of output greater than zero, two things happen.

a. It collects total revenue (TR) = $P * q_e$, and

b. It incurs variable costs (TVC). Of course the firm also incurs total fixed costs, but it incurs those costs anyway, regardless of the level of output.

If the firm, by producing in the short run, can collect total revenues that at least exceed the total variable costs, then it continues to produce, even at a loss. However, if producing output incurs more variable cost than revenue collected, why bother? Shut down, hope for better times, and suffer losses equal to TFC. This comparison provides us a decision rule for shutting down in the short run.

> "This has great potential to be asked on both sections of the exam."
> —AP Teacher

- If TR ≥ TVC, the firm produces q_e where MR = MC.
- If TR < TVC, the firm shuts down and $q = 0$.

The Shutdown Point

We can see the shutdown point in Figure 9.5 by converting the above decision rule into a per unit comparison. Dividing total revenue and total variable cost by q tells us to shut down if $P <$ AVC. This is the identical decision rule; it is just a per unit comparison of revenue and variable cost.

- If $P ≥$ AVC, the firm produces q_e where MR = MC.
- If $P <$ AVC, the firm shuts down and $q = 0$.

In Figure 9.5, there are four prices shown.

- PH is the highest price. At q_h, the firm earns enough total revenue to cover all costs. $\Pi > 0$.
- PM is the middle price. At q_m, the firm's TR exceeds TVC but only covers part of the TFC. $\Pi < 0$.
- PD is the shutdown price. At q_d, the firm's TR just covers TVC and the firm is at the shutdown point. If price falls any lower, the firm does not produce.
- PL is the lowest price. At q_1, the firm's TR cannot even cover TVC and so the firm shuts down, producing $q = 0$. $\Pi = -$TFC.

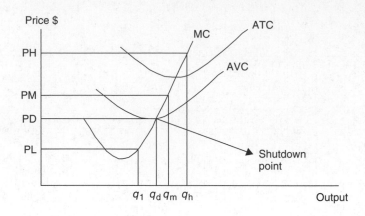

Figure 9.5

Short-Run Supply

As you can see in Figure 9.5, when the price fluctuates between PH and PD, the firm finds a new profit maximizing quantity where P = MR = MC. If price increases, quantity supplied increases. If price decreases, quantity supplied decreases. This is a restatement of the Law of Supply. This movement upward and downward along the marginal cost curve implies that MC serves as the supply curve for the perfectly competitive firm. The only exception is when the price falls below the shutdown point (minimum of AVC) and the firm quickly decides to produce nothing. The market supply curve is simply the summation of all firms' MC curves.

- The MC curve above the shutdown point serves as the supply curve for each perfectly competitive firm.
- The market supply curve is therefore the sum of all of the MC curves. $S = \Sigma\, MC$.

Long-Run Adjustment

The short run is a period of time too brief for firms to change the size of their plants. This means that it is also too short for existing firms to exit the industry in bad times and too short for new entrepreneurs to enter the industry in good times. The "free entry and exit" characteristic of perfect competition assures us that in the long run, we can expect to see firms either exiting or entering, depending upon whether profits or losses are being made in the short run. We'll first examine the case where short-run positive profits are made in the carrot industry and then the situation where short-run losses are incurred.

- In virtually all of the past AP Microeconomics exams, free-response questions have appeared that test the students' knowledge of perfect competition and the difference between the short- and long-run equilibria.

Short-Run Positive Profits

Figure 9.6 illustrates the perfectly competitive carrot industry where the market price is above average total cost. Firms are earning positive short-run profits, as illustrated by the shaded rectangle.

So what next? Well many entrepreneurs on the outside of this market are attracted by the positive short-run profits being made by carrot producers. Given sufficient time (i.e., the long run), these new firms enter the market. With more carrot producers, the market supply curve shifts outward, driving down the price. As the price falls, the profit rectangle

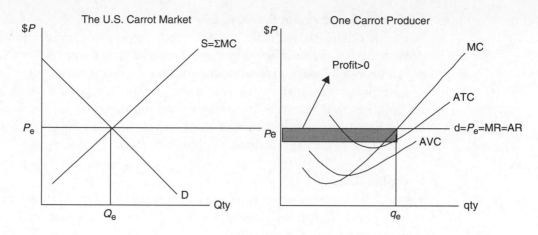

Figure 9.6

gets smaller and smaller until it actually disappears. At the point where $P = MR = MC = ATC$ each carrot farmer is now breaking even with $\Pi = 0$. Would the next potential carrot farmer enter the market? Unlikely, as the entry of one more firm pushes the price down just enough to where losses are actually incurred. Thus this break-even point is described as the long-run equilibrium. The market quantity has increased and each firm produces less at the lower price. Figure 9.7 illustrates the movement toward the long-run equilibrium.

The long-run adjustment to short-run positive profits can be summarized as:

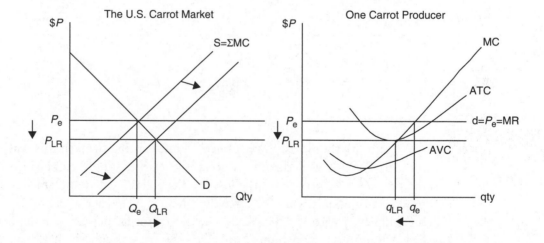

Figure 9.7

- Entry of new firms attracted by economic $\Pi > 0$.
- Increase in market supply.
- A decrease in the market price to P_{LR}.
- Profits fall to the break-even point, $P_{LR} = MR = MC = ATC$ and economic $\Pi = 0$.
- Market quantity increases.
- Individual producer output falls.

What's So Great About Breaking Even?

Remember there is a distinction between accounting profit and economic profit. Economic profit subtracts the next best opportunity costs of your resources from total revenue. If you are still breaking even after subtracting what you might have earned in all of those other opportunities, you can't feel cheated. In other words, you are making a fair rate of return on your invested resources and you have no incentive to take them elsewhere. Sure, you would like to earn more than zero economic profit (a.k.a. "**normal profit**") but the characteristics of perfect competition rule this out.

Short-Run Losses

Figure 9.8 illustrates short-run losses with a price below ATC but above the shutdown point. The long-run adjustment story might sound familiar, only with market forces moving in the opposite direction.

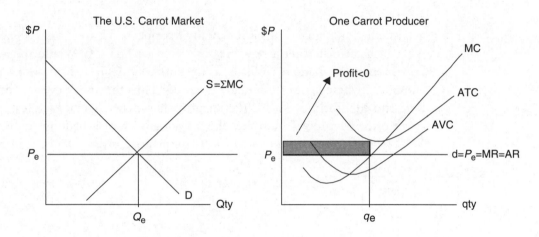

Figure 9.8

Again, we should ask "What next?" Some existing firms in this market begin to exit the industry. With fewer carrot producers, the market supply curve shifts inward, driving up the price. As the price rises, the loss rectangle gets smaller and smaller until again it disappears. At the point where $P_{LR} = MR = MC = ATC$ each remaining carrot farmer is now breaking even with $\Pi = 0$. Would another carrot farmer exit the market? Possibly, but the exit of one more firm bumps up the price just enough so that a small positive profit is earned, prompting one firm to enter and get us back to the break-even point. Arrival at the break-even point is once again the long-run equilibrium. The market quantity has decreased, but each surviving firm produces more at the higher price. Figure 9.9 illustrates the movement toward the long-run equilibrium.

The long-run adjustment to short-run losses can be summarized as:

- Exit of existing firms prompted by economic $\Pi < 0$.
- Decrease in market supply.
- An increase in the market price to P_{LR}.
- Profits increase to the break-even point, $P_{LR} = MR = MC = ATC$ and economic $\Pi = 0$.
- Market quantity decreases.
- Individual producer output rises.

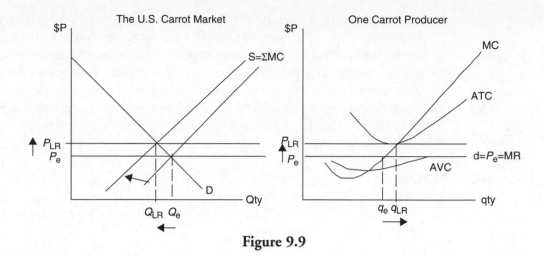

Figure 9.9

Summarizing in Table 9.5, there are four possible short-run scenarios and resulting long-run adjustments to the perfectly competitive equilibrium, which always ends in the same place.

Table 9.5

WHEN THE SHORT RUN …	THE FIRM PRODUCES WHERE …	SHORT-RUN ECONOMIC PROFITS ARE …	IN THE LONG RUN …	THE LONG-RUN OUTCOME IS …
$P > \text{ATC}$	MR = MC	Positive	Firms enter	P_{LR} = MR = MC = ATC and $\Pi = 0$
$P = \text{ATC}$	MR = MC	Zero, break even	No entry or exit	P_{LR} = MR = MC = ATC and $\Pi = 0$
AVC < P < ATC	MR = MC	Negative $0 > \Pi > -\text{TFC}$	Firms exit	P_{LR} = MR = MC = ATC and $\Pi = 0$
$P < \text{AVC}$	Zero, shut down	Negative, (= −TFC)	Firms exit	P_{LR} = MR = MC = ATC and $\Pi = 0$

Are There Variations on This Story and Do I Need to Know Them?

Yes and maybe. Throughout this section we have made an assumption that entry and exit of firms has no impact on the cost curves of firms in the market. In other words, we have been assuming a **constant cost industry**. Recent AP Microeconomics exams have made references to constant cost industries and (maybe) caused unnecessary confusion for test takers. It is always possible that future exams will refer to constant, increasing or decreasing cost industries so you should probably become familiar with these terms. A quick explanation and you will not be one of the confused.

Suppose that entry of new firms into a profitable carrot market increases the demand for key resources like land, labor, and capital. Increased demand for these resources might increase the cost of employing those resources. When this happens, the cost curves for firms in the carrot industry start to shift upward. This situation is described as an **increasing cost industry**. Graphing this situation gets sticky, but if you follow the logic you will be fine. The entry of new firms drives down the price of the output *and* increases the cost curves so the profit is eliminated more quickly than with our constant cost industry. Fewer firms eventually enter this version of the carrot market and the new long-run price is higher than it is in a constant cost industry.

A **decreasing cost industry** is one in which the entry of new firms actually decreases the price of key inputs and causes the cost curves to shift downward. This might occur because producers of the key inputs expand production and experience economies of scale and lower per-unit costs. Since the entry of new firms lowers the price of the output *and* decreases the cost curves, it takes longer for the profit to be eliminated than in our constant cost industry. More firms can eventually enter this market and the new long-run price is lower than it would be in a constant cost industry.

9.2 Monopoly

Main Topics: *Structural Characteristics, Monopoly Demand, Profit Maximization, Efficiency Analysis, Price Discrimination*

Structural Characteristics of Monopoly

Since monopoly is the very opposite of perfect competition in the range of market structures, we can expect that the structural characteristics are also quite different.

- *A single producer.* This is pretty self-explanatory, but a strict definition of monopoly requires that there are no other firms in the industry.
- *No close substitutes.* Consumers cannot find a similar product in other markets.
- *Barriers to entry.* Perhaps the most important characteristic of monopoly is that there exists something that prevents rival firms from entering the market to provide competition to the monopolist and choice to consumers.
- *Market power.* This is the result of the first three characteristics. With no competition and barriers to entry, the unregulated monopolist has **market power**, or monopoly price-setting ability.

Again, it is rare to find a firm that satisfies all of the characteristics of monopoly, but the DeBeers firm holds a near monopoly on global diamond production. The only gas station or bank in a small town might also act as a local monopolist.

Barriers to Entry

If there were no barrier to entry, a monopolist earning positive economic profits would be history and this chapter would be done. So before moving on to the behavior of monopoly, let's talk a little more about this necessary condition for the existence of monopoly.

- *Legal barriers.* In your local television market only one firm is given the right to broadcast on a specific frequency. There might be only one firm given the right to sell liquor in a small community. There are patents, trademarks, and copyright laws to protect inventions and intellectual property. In a move popular with 14-year-old boys everywhere, Carmen Electra was recently given the sole right to the Internet address bearing her name. These legal protections do not provide for absolute monopoly for there are often viable substitutes available to consumers.
- *Economies of scale.* In Chapter 8 this concept was introduced. As a firm grows larger in the long run, average total costs fall, providing the larger firm a cost advantage over smaller firms. If extensive economies of scale exist, an industry could evolve into one with only one enormous producer. A **natural monopoly** is a case where economies of scale are so extensive that it is less costly for one firm to supply the entire range of demand. Power plants are a good example of natural monopoly within a local area.
- *Control of key resources.* If a firm controlled most of the available resources in the production of a good, it would be very difficult for a competitor to enter the market. For example,

if a producer of granulated sugar wanted to monopolize the market, the firm might wish to control all of the sugarcane plantations.

Monopoly Demand

The perfectly competitive firm is a price taker and faces perfectly elastic demand for the product. The firm sells all it wants at the going market price; this decision does not affect the market price. The monopolist is the only provider of that good, making the demand for the product the market demand for that product. The monopolist must pay attention to the Law of Demand, which means that if it wishes to sell more, the monopolist must decrease the price.

Demand, Price, and Marginal Revenue

Price exceeds marginal revenue because the monopolist must lower price to boost sales. The added revenue from selling one more unit is the price of the last unit less the sum of the price cuts that must be taken on all prior units of output. For example, the demand curve for the monopolist's product is: $P = 7 - Q_d$.

The monopolist begins at a price of $6 and sells one unit of the good (see Table 9.6). A price cut to $5 results in one more unit sold, so total revenue increases by $5 on this second unit. However, the first unit previously sold at $6, must also now be sold at $5, which costs the firm $1 in total revenue. With $5 gained ($P$) from the second and $1 lost in total revenue from the first unit, the net or marginal increase (MR) in total revenue is $4 for the second unit. Graphically we can see the revenue effect of selling the second unit in Figure 9.10

Chapter 7 examined the effect that price elasticity of demand (E_d) has on total revenue. Demand is elastic above the midpoint of a linear demand curve like the one in Figure 9.10, so cuts in price increase total revenue. Demand is inelastic below the midpoint; further cuts in price decrease total revenue. At the midpoint, total revenue is maximized and demand is unit elastic. Recognizing this connection, the price-making monopolist is going to avoid the inelastic portion of the demand curve and operate at some point to the left of the midpoint. Figure 9.11 combines demand, marginal revenue, and the total revenue function. You can see that when total revenue is at the maximum, marginal revenue is zero and further price cuts decrease total revenue, making marginal revenue negative.

Table 9.6

P	Q	TR	MR
7	0	0	
6	1	6	6
5	2	10	4
4	3	12	2
3	4	12	0
2	5	10	−2
1	6	6	−4
0	7	0	−6

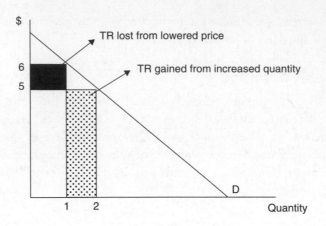

Figure 9.10

> • Demand is horizontal and $P = $ MR in perfect competition.
> • Demand is downward sloping and $P > $ MR in monopoly.
> • The monopolist operates in the elastic (or upper) range of demand.

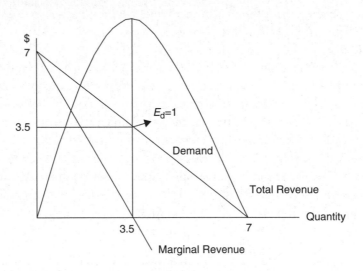

Figure 9.11

Profit Maximization

While demand looks different for the monopolist, the mechanism for maximizing profit is the same for both the monopolist and the perfectly competitive firm. **The firm must set output at the level where MR = MC. At this level of output (Q_m), the monopolist sets the price (P_m) from the demand curve.** Profit is found in the same way by creating the profit rectangle with average total cost. This is seen in Figure 9.12.

The positive monopoly profits illustrated in Figure 9.12 are likely, due to the entry barrier, to last into the long run. Though $\Pi > 0$ is usually the case for a monopoly firm, you might imagine a case where demand plummets, or perhaps production costs increase, to the point where $P <$ ATC and losses are incurred. In the event of persistent losses, we expect the monopolist to exit the industry.

"Understand the profit max rule well. It will help you throughout economics."
—Nick,
AP Student

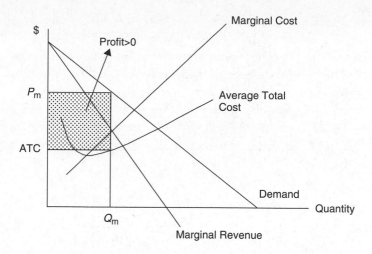

Figure 9.12

- Find Q_m where MR = MC. Once you have found Q_m, never leave it.
- Find P_m vertically from the demand curve above MR = MC.
- Find ATC vertically at Q_m. If you move downward, $\Pi > 0$. If you move upward, $\Pi < 0$.
- Move horizontally from ATC to the y axis to complete the rectangle and clearly label it as positive or negative.

Efficiency Analysis

We refer to efficiency in a couple of different sections of this book and now that we have compared perfect competition to monopoly, it is time for another discussion. Allocative efficiency is achieved when the market produces a level of output where the marginal cost (MC) to society exactly equals the marginal benefit (P) received by society. Total welfare to society is maximized at this outcome, so any movement away from this level of output results in dead weight loss. Productive efficiency is achieved if society has produced a level of output with the lowest possible cost. In perfect competition, the long-run market outcome achieves both of these criteria for efficiency. Figure 9.13 illustrates the competitive and monopoly outcomes.

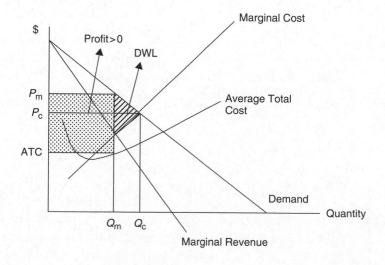

Figure 9.13

Allocative efficiency exists because $P_c = \text{MR} = \text{MC}$ at Q_c and productive efficiency exists because firms produce at minimum ATC.

On the other hand, the monopolist produces at a quantity Q_m where $P_m > \text{MR} = \text{MC}$. This result tells us that consumers would like to consume more of the product; but the monopolist does not produce as much as consumers want. Failing to achieve allocative efficiency creates the dead weight loss (DWL) shown in Figure 9.13. The monopoly output is not at the point where ATC is minimized; thus the monopolist is not productively efficient. A profit earned by the monopolist is a transfer of consumer surplus from consumers to the firm.

- $Q_m < Q_c$
- $P_m > P_c$
- **$P_m > \text{MC}$ so monopoly is not allocatively efficient.**
- Dead weight loss exists with monopoly.
- **$P_m >$ minimum ATC so monopoly is not productively efficient.**
- $\Pi_m > 0$ is a transfer of lost consumer surplus from consumers to the firm.

Price Discrimination

Though it carries a nasty stereotype, **price discrimination** is the selling of the same good at different prices to different consumers. Successful price discrimination is possible if three conditions exist:

1. The firm must have monopoly pricing power.

2. The firm must be able to identify and separate groups of consumers.

3. The firm must be able to prevent resale between consumers.

Common examples of price discrimination include:

- Child and senior discounts at the movie theatre or restaurants
- Airline tickets that are bought three weeks in advance compared to tickets bought one hour in advance
- Long distance calling plans that offer a lower per minute rate at night than during the working day
- Coupons that separate price-sensitive consumers (those who use the coupon) from those who are less price sensitive
- A lower per unit price paid by consumers who buy items in large quantities (like a case of soda) than those paid by consumers who buy in lesser quantities (like a six-pack of soda, or one can from a vending machine).

The airline industry is clearly not perfectly competitive so there must be a degree of monopoly pricing power. The firm creates groupings based upon when consumers purchase tickets. The photo identification requirement for all passengers is an important security measure, but it also prevents the resale of a low-priced ticket to a consumer who is willing to pay a higher price. If resale were possible, the pricing system might break down. It should not surprise you that price discrimination allows firms to earn more profit than if they charged a single price.

9.3 Monopolistic Competition

Main Topics: *Structural Characteristics, Short-Run Profit Maximization, Long-Run Outcome*

Structural Characteristics

Sharing some of the characteristics of both perfect competition and monopoly, the market structure of monopolistic competition provides a description of many modern industries.

- *Relatively large number of firms.* Rather than the thousands of perfectly competitive firms, in monopolistic competition there are perhaps dozens, each with a fairly small share of the total market.
- *Differentiated products.* This characteristic makes monopolistic competition stand out as different from the perfectly competitive market structure and gives firms their ability to set the price above the competitive level.
- *Easy entry and exit.* There are very few barriers to entry in monopolistic competition, perhaps the largest being the need to provide sufficient marketing to differentiate a new firm's product from that of the existing rivals.

The market for shoes closely fits the description of monopolistic competition. While all shoes serve the same basic purpose, to cover and protect the feet, a running shoe, a hiking boot, and a flip-flop are very different and are made by many firms in the global market. The book publishing market is also described as monopolistically competitive.

Short-Run Profit Maximization

Like the monopoly, the firm in monopolistic competition faces a downward sloping demand curve for its differentiated product. Because there are many similar substitutes available to consumers, the demand is fairly elastic. In a recurring theme for profit maximizing behavior, the firm sets Q_{mc} where MR = MC and sets the price from the demand curve. Figure 9.14 illustrates a monopolistically competitive firm that is earning positive short-run economic profits.

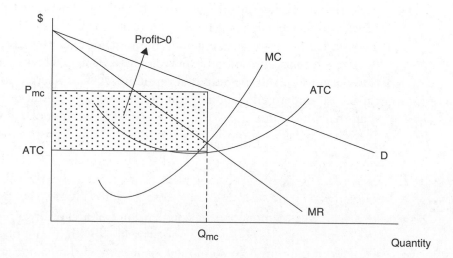

Figure 9.14

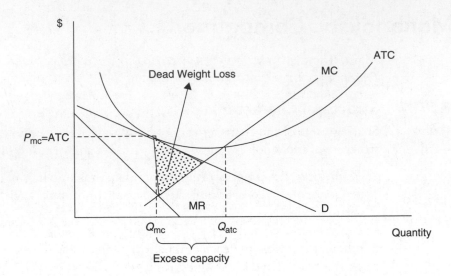

Figure 9.15

Long-Run Adjustment

With easy entry and exit into the monopolistically competitive industry, short-run positive profits like those in Figure 9.14 are not going to last for long. As new firms enter this industry, the market share of all existing firms begins to fall. Graphically we see this as a leftward shift in the demand curve. As the price begins to fall, the profit rectangle begins to shrink. Entry stops when profits are zero and $P = ATC$, or when the demand curve is just tangent to ATC. This adjustment is seen in Figure 9.15

"What About Advertising to Maintain Profits?"

Because easy entry of competitors drives profits down to break-even levels, monopolistically competitive firms typically engage in extensive amounts of advertising to slow down, and even reverse, declining market share. This advertising is realistically only a short-run "fix" as there is no reason to believe that barriers to entry suddenly emerge to prevent the eventual return to break-even profit levels.

Efficiency and Excess Capacity

In long-run monopolistic competition, the firm earns $\Pi = 0$, a characteristic shared by the perfectly competitive firm. But because of the differentiated products, $P > MR = MC$; allocative efficiency is not achieved. The dead weight loss is the shaded area in Figure 9.15. Though the firms are breaking even, they are not operating at the minimum of ATC; productive efficiency is also not achieved. The difference between the monopolistic competition output Q_{mc} and the output at minimum ATC is referred to as **excess capacity**. Excess capacity is underused plant and equipment that is the result of producing at an output less than that which minimizes ATC. The market is over-populated with firms, each producing enough to break even in the long run, but so many firms means that each produces below full capacity.

- $Q_{mc} < Q_c$
- $P_{mc} > P_c$
- $P_{mc} > MC$ so monopolistic competition is not allocatively efficient.
- Dead weight loss exists, but not as much as with monopoly.
- $P_m >$ minimum ATC so monopolistic competition is not productively efficient.
- $\Pi_{mc} = 0$ in the long run.
- Excess capacity is $Q_{atc} - Q_{mc}$.

9.4 Oligopoly

Main Topics: *Structural Characteristics, Industry Concentration, Prisoners' Dilemma, Collusion*
Oligopoly markets are typically farther from perfect competition than the monopolistic market structure, although there is no one model of oligopoly. A couple of oligopoly models are presented; but keep in mind that if one little assumption is relaxed, the predictions of the model can be radically different. For the AP exam you will likely face only these basics.

Structural Characteristics

You can see from these characteristics that oligopoly shares more common ground with monopoly, but these are flexible enough to describe many different and diverse industries.

- *A few large producers.* Can it get more vague than this? Think of the American auto industry, with the "Big 3" producers, or the tobacco industry, also dominated by three huge firms. If the distribution of market share in an industry is top heavy with a few large firms, the industry is described as oligopolistic.
- *Differentiated or standardized product.* Oligopoly industries can come in both flavors. Crude oil is a fairly standard product, but it is very much an oligopoly of large producers. Automobiles, beer, and soft drinks are also oligopoly markets, but with more differentiated products.
- *Entry barriers.* If these industries were fairly easy to enter, we would not see them dominated by a few huge producers.
- *Mutual interdependence.* Because a few large producers control these industries, the action of one firm (price setting or advertising) is likely to affect the others and prompt a response. A good example of this is your local gasoline market. This is very much an oligopoly; when one gas station lowers prices by one cent per gallon, the others usually quickly follow.

Industry Concentration

How does an industry become classified as an oligopoly? Economists have tried to get more specific than a "few large producers" by developing ways to measure how much market share is held by, or concentrated in, the largest of the firms. One way to gauge how powerful the largest of firms might be is to sum up the market share of the top four, or eight or 12 firms and create a **concentration ratio**. If the top four firms in the breakfast cereal industry have a combined market share of 85 percent we say that the four-firm concentration ratio is 85. Some economists use a four-firm concentration ratio of 40 percent as a rough guideline for identifying an oligopolistic industry. We predict that as this concentration ratio increases, the degree of monopoly price-setting power increases.

Game Theory and the Prisoners' Dilemma

Imagine a case where a two-firm oligopoly (a duopoly) engages in a daily pricing decision. Each firm knows that if it sets a price higher than the rival's, it loses sales. Likewise, if it sets a price below the rival's, it steals sales. This non-collusive model of pricing, called the **prisoners' dilemma,** emerges from the following scenario that any fan of *Law and Order* quickly recognizes.

Example:

A college professor suspects two students (Jack and Diane) of cheating on a take-home final exam, but cannot prove guilt with enough certainty to fail both students in the course, or expel them from the school. Without a confession, she will give each student a D in the course. With a confession from one student but not the other, she can reward the confessor with a B. The professor brings both students, one at a time, into her office and gives each the following deal:

- If you remain silent and do not confess, and your classmate implicates you, I will expel you from school and give your friend a B.
- If you confess to cheating and implicate your silent classmate, I will pass you with a B and expel your friend from school.

These options can be depicted in the following matrix.

		JACK'S CHOICES	
		Confess	Stay Silent
DIANE'S CHOICES	Confess	D: Fail the course J: Fail the course	D: Gets a B J: Expelled from school
	Stay Silent	D: Expelled from school J: Gets a B	D: Gets a D J: Gets a D

Diane doesn't know what Jack is going to do when he is in the professor's office. But whatever Jack's decision, Diane should confess. She might be thinking that Jack is going to confess. If so, she confesses because staying silent will get her expelled from school. Maybe she thinks that Jack is going to stay silent. If true, the choice is between a B and a D in the course. Diane would be wise to confess. For Diane, confessing is a **dominant strategy** because no matter what Jack does, confession is always better than staying silent. Likewise for Jack, the dominant strategy is to confess.

This is certainly a dilemma, because if Jack and Diane could only agree to give the professor the silent treatment, they would both walk away with a D, which is much better than failing the course or expulsion from school. Without such a binding agreement, cheating on the pact would be quite tempting, maybe even fairly predictable.

Example:
The owners of two gas stations operate on opposite corners of a busy intersection. Each morning each owner goes out to the sign and sets the price of gasoline, either high or low. Consumers are concerned only about the lowest price of gas. The matrix below summarizes the daily revenues for each station.

		STATION X	
		Price High	Price Low
STATION Y	Price High	X: $2000 Y: $2000	X: $3000 Y: $500
	Price Low	X: $500 Y: $3000	X: $1000 Y: $1000

Can you see the dilemma? Both stations would love to set a high price of gas so that they could earn $2000 in daily revenue. But if the rival were to set the low price, the high price station would be stuck with $500 while the other station cleans up with $3000.

Since both firms recognize that pricing low is the dominant strategy, both earn only $1000 every day. A collusive agreement might emerge.

Use of the previous game matrices assumes that both players in the game make simultaneous choices. Many games involve a series of stages where one player moves first. The second player observes the choice made by the first, and then reacts to it. These sequential games are typically seen as a game tree rather than a game matrix. Let's convert the previous game to a sequential game where gas station *X* gets to move first as shown in Figure 9.16. Station *Y* sees the choice of station *X*, and then sets the price high or low. Payoffs are given at the end of the tree.

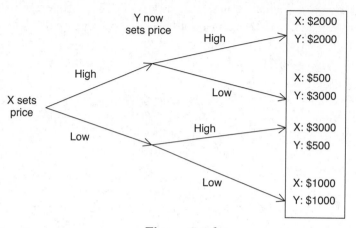

Figure 9.16

Can you see how this game will play out? Gas station *X* knows that its rival, station *Y*, still has a dominant strategy of setting a low price. No matter what the initial decision of station *X*, station *Y* would always see that a low price beats a high price. Because station *X* knows this about its rival, it will select a low price at the beginning of the game. In 2007, the AP Microeconomics exam included simple game theory on the free-response section for the very first time. You should expect this area of microeconomics to be tested again in the future and, in my experience, I predict that the degree of difficulty will gradually increase.

Collusive Pricing

Explicit **collusive** behavior between direct competitors is an illegal business practice, but it does happen (surprise!) from time to time. More common is a kind of tacit, or understood, collusion. Two competitors over time figure out that repeated attempts to undercut the price of their rivals is counterproductive. Eventually they understand that if both set the price high, both firms win. When one cheats on this "understanding," the other inflicts punishment with a retaliatory price cut.

Cartels are more organized forms of collusive oligopoly behavior. Cartels are groups of firms that create a formal agreement not to compete with each other on the basis of price, production, or other competitive dimensions. The general idea of the cartel is that rather than act independently to maximize individual profits, they collectively operate as a monopolist to maximize their joint profits. Each cartel member agrees to a limited level of output and this results in a higher cartel price. Joint profits are maximized and distributed to each member.

In addition to the pesky illegality of forming cartels, these entities face three challenges that are completely unrelated to the Attorney General.

a. Difficulty in arriving at a mutually acceptable agreement to restrict output. Have you ever tried to order pizza or rent a movie with more than two other friends? If so, you get the idea.

b. Punishment mechanism. If the cartel can restrict output and increase the price above the current competitive level, cartel members have an incentive to cheat by producing more than their allotment. There must be some kind of deterrent to cheating.

c. Entry of new firms. If the cartel members are successful in creating monopoly profits, they are faced with new firms eager to enter. If entry occurs, the cartel loses monopoly power and profit.

› Review Questions

1. For a competitive firm, what is the most important thing to consider in deciding whether to shut down in the short run?

(A) Compare AVC to MR.
(B) Compare TR to TC.
(C) Do not produce if the TFC is not covered by revenue.
(D) Produce the highest quantity demanded regardless of price.
(E) Compare P to ATC.

2. Which characteristic is likely a part of a monopoly market but not of monopolistic competition?

(A) Differentiated products
(B) Patents and copyrights
(C) Possibility of profit in the short run
(D) Dead weight loss exists
(E) None of the above

3. If the perfectly competitive price is currently above minimum ATC, we can expect which of the following events in the long run?

(A) Price rises as firms enter the industry.
(B) Market equilibrium quantity rises as firms exit the industry.
(C) Nothing, the industry is currently in long-run equilibrium.
(D) Profits fall as the market price rises.
(E) Price falls as firms enter the industry.

4. Which of these situations is not an example of price discrimination?

(A) Brent works nights so he chooses to buy bread at 7 a.m. rather than at 7 p.m.
(B) Bob and Nancy each receive a "$1 off" coupon in the mail, but Bob redeems it while Nancy does not.
(C) Katie buys 12 Cokes for $3 and Josh buys one Coke at a time for $1.
(D) Velma likes to go to the movies at the lower afternoon matinee price and Rosemary would rather pay more for the evening show.
(E) Jason and Jen go to a popular nightclub. Because it is "Ladies Night" Jen pays no cover charge, but Jason must pay to enter the club.

Two competing firms are deciding whether to launch a huge costly advertising campaign or maintain the status quo. Use the following matrix showing the profits of this duopoly to respond to question 5.

		FIRM X	
		Advertise	Status Quo
FIRM Y	Advertise	X: $4.5 million Y: $4.5 million	X:$1 million Y:$6 million
	Status Quo	X:$6 million Y: $1 million	X:$5 million Y:$5 million

5. If these firms do not collude, the outcome will be:

(A) Both firms maintain the status quo.
(B) Both firms advertise.
(C) Firm X advertises and Firm Y maintains the status quo.
(D) Firm Y advertises and Firm X maintains the status quo.

6. Dead weight loss occurs in

(A) monopolistic competition as $P > MC$.
(B) monopoly markets because $P > MC$.
(C) oligopoly markets because $P > MC$.
(D) all of the above.
(E) none of the above.

› Answers and Explanations

1. **A**—The firm only operates if the total revenue is at least as great as total variable cost. On a per unit basis, the firm must receive a $P = MR$ that is at least as great as AVC. Since firms pay TFC regardless of production, they are not a factor in whether you should shut down. Choices B, C, and E are wrong because TC and ATC include the fixed costs. Choice D is incorrect because it might not be the profitable strategy, but is irrelevant to the shutdown decision.

2. **B**—Monopoly has barriers to entry (i.e., patents) and the monopolistic competitive firm does not. Choices A, C, and D are true of monopolistic competition and monopoly.

3. **E**—With $P > ATC$, you should recognize that positive economic profits exist. Firms enter and price falls toward the break-even point so any mention of exit or rising prices can be eliminated. Entry also increases the market quantity of the good produced.

4. **A**—If Brent chooses to buy his bread early in the morning rather than in the evening, this is not price discrimination. The other choices describe buying in bulk, redeeming a coupon, or paying a lower price because of the time in which one consumes the good. The nightclub example is price discrimination based upon gender.

5. **B**—For each firm, choosing the costly advertising campaign is the dominant strategy. This is an example of the prisoners' dilemma.

6. **D**—Allocative inefficiency and dead weight loss in *any* market structure is when $P > MC$.

› Rapid Review

Perfect competition: the most competitive market structure is characterized by many small price-taking firms producing a standardized product in an industry in which there are no barriers to entry or exit.

Profit Maximizing Rule: all firms maximize profit by producing where $MR = MC$.

Break-even point: the output where ATC is minimized and economic profit is zero.

Shutdown point: the output where AVC is minimized. If the price falls below this point, the firm chooses to shut down or produce zero units in the short run.

Perfectly competitive long-run equilibrium: occurs when there is no more incentive for firms to enter or exit. $P = MR = MC = ATC$ and $\Pi = 0$.

Normal profit: another way of saying that firms are earning zero economic profits or a fair rate of return on invested resources.

Constant cost industry: Entry (or exit) of firms does not shift the cost curves of firms in the industry.

Increasing cost industry: Entry of new firms shifts the cost curves for all firms upward.

Decreasing cost industry: Entry of new firms shifts the cost curves for all firms downward.

Monopoly: the least competitive market structure; it is characterized by a single producer, with no close substitutes, barriers to entry, and price making power.

Market power: the ability to set the price above the perfectly competitive level.

Natural monopoly: the case where economies of scale are so extensive that it is less costly for one firm to supply the entire range of demand.

Monopoly long-run equilibrium: $P_m > MR = MC$, which is not allocatively efficient and dead weight loss exists. $P_m > ATC$, which is not productively efficient. $\Pi_m > 0$ so consumer surplus is transferred to the monopolist as profit.

Price discrimination: the practice of selling essentially the same good to different groups of consumers at different prices.

Monopolistic competition: a market structure characterized by a few small firms producing a differentiated product with easy entry into the market.

Monopolistic competition long-run equilibrium: $P_{mc} > MR = MC$ and $P_{mc} >$ minimum ATC so the outcome is not efficient, but $\Pi_{mc} = 0$.

Excess capacity: the difference between the monopolistic competition output Q_{mc} and the output at minimum ATC. Excess capacity is underused plant and equipment.

Oligopoly: a very diverse market structure characterized by a small number of interdependent large firms, producing a standardized or differentiated product in a market with a barrier to entry.

Four-firm concentration ratio: a measure of industry market power. Sum the market share of the four largest firms and a ratio above 40 percent is a good indicator of oligopoly.

Non-collusive oligopoly: models where firms are competitive rivals seeking to gain at the expense of their rivals.

Prisoners' dilemma: a game where the two rivals achieve a less desirable outcome because they are unable to coordinate their strategies.

Dominant strategy: a strategy that is always the best strategy to pursue, regardless of what a rival is doing.

Collusive oligopoly: models where firms agree to mutually improve their situation.

Cartel: a group of firms that agree not to compete with each other on the basis of price, production, or other competitive dimensions. Cartel members operate as a monopolist to maximize their joint profits.

CHAPTER 10

Factor Markets

IN THIS CHAPTER

Summary: We have invested significant time reviewing the forces of supply and demand in the competitive market for goods and services. In addition, we have investigated the theory behind production and cost, but have not brought market forces to bear on those input, or factor, markets. We begin with the demand for inputs in a perfectly competitive input market, move then to the supply of inputs and construct a model of wage and employment. We then tweak the competitive model by allowing for some monopoly hiring behavior. How is the wage of college professors determined? Can we predict whether employment of steel workers is going to grow or decline? A study of input markets sheds some light on many important microeconomic issues that have critical macroeconomic implications.

Key Ideas
- ✪ Factor Demand
- ✪ Least-Cost Hiring of Inputs
- ✪ Factor Supply
- ✪ Equilibrium in Competitive Factor Markets
- ✪ Non-Competitive Factor Markets

10.1 Factor Demand

Main Topics: *Competitive Markets, Marginal Revenue Product, Profit Maximizing Employment, Derived Demand, Determinants of Resource Demand*

The theory of factor (or resource, or input) demand is applicable to any factor of production, but it is more intuitive if we focus on labor, the production input with which we are all most comfortable. Because we are most familiar with it, most examples below address labor and not some generic resource.

Competitive Factor Markets

To best see the theory of factor demand we assume the simplest market structure. First, we'll assume that the firms are price takers in the product (output) market. Second, we'll assume that they are price takers in the factor (input) market. This means that they cannot impact either the price of their product or the price they must pay to employ more of an input. In a competitive labor market, they can employ as much labor as they wish at the going market determined wage.

Marginal Revenue Product

Here's a difficult question for any employee to ask: What am I worth to my employer? Sure, I'm a snazzy dresser; I can tell a humorous joke and my personal hygiene is top notch. However, the bottom line to my employer is probably more important than these civilities. To build a model of factor demand, economists assert that the demand for a unit of labor is a function of two things important to employers. First, employers are very interested in the marginal productivity of the next unit of labor. If the next worker is going to greatly contribute to the firm's total production, he is likely to be a good hire for the firm. Second, the firm must then receive good value for the production. The value of this production to the firm is the additional, or marginal, revenue that it brings to the firm. Combining the necessary components of marginal productivity of labor and marginal revenue provides **marginal revenue product of labor (MRP$_L$)**, a measure of what the next unit of a resource, such as labor, brings to the firm. With the assumption of a perfectly competitive output market, the marginal revenue is simply the price of the product.

$$MRP = \frac{\text{Change in Total Revenue}}{\text{Change in Resource Quantity}} = MR * MP_L = P * MP_L$$

In our examples, we change the resource (labor) by a quantity of one. Table 10.1 revises the hourly production function for Molly's lemonade stand. Recall that in the short run she hires additional units of labor to a fixed level of capital. The competitive price of a cup of lemonade is 50 cents.

Table 10.1

LABOR INPUT (WORKERS PER HOUR)	TOTAL PRODUCT (TP$_L$) (CUPS PER HOUR)	MARGINAL PRODUCT (MP$_L$)	MARGINAL REVENUE (MR = P)	MARGINAL REVENUE PRODUCT (MRP$_L$ = MP$_L$ * MR)
0	0			
1	25	25	$.50	$12.50
2	45	20	$.50	$10.00
3	60	15	$.50	$7.50
4	70	10	$.50	$5.00

Table 10.1—cont'd

LABOR INPUT (WORKERS PER HOUR)	TOTAL PRODUCT (TP$_L$) (CUPS PER HOUR)	MARGINAL PRODUCT (MP$_L$)	MARGINAL REVENUE (MR = P)	MARGINAL REVENUE PRODUCT (MRP$_L$ = MP$_L$ * MR)
5	75	5	$.50	$2.50
6	70	−5	$.50	−$2.50
7	60	−10	$.50	−$5.00

Profit Maximizing Resource Employment

Yet again, we are faced with a decision that must be based upon marginal benefits and marginal costs. Our decision rule is, and has always been:

- If MB > MC, do more of it.
- If MB < MC, do less of it.
- If MB = MC, stop here.

In the case of resource hiring, the marginal benefit is **MRP**. The marginal cost of resource hiring is **marginal resource cost (MRC)**, a measure of how much cost the firm incurs from using an additional unit of an input. When the firm is hiring labor in a competitive labor market, MRC is equal to the wage (w).

$$MRC = \frac{\text{Change in Total Resource Cost}}{\text{Change in Resource Quantity}} = \text{Wage}$$

With this measure of marginal cost, the profit maximizing employer of labor would hire to the point where MRP$_L$ = MRC = wage. Table 10.2 adds a competitive $7.50 hourly wage to Molly's table of lemonade production. At this wage, Molly should employ three hourly workers to her fixed capital.

Table 10.2

TOTAL LABOR INPUT (WORKERS PER HOUR)	PRODUCT (TP$_L$) (CUPS PER HOUR)	MARGINAL PRODUCT (MP$_L$)	MARGINAL REVENUE (MR = P)	MARGINAL REVENUE PRODUCT (MRP$_L$ = MP$_L$*MR)	MARGINAL RESOURCE COST (MRC = WAGE)
0	0				
1	25	25	$.50	$12.50	$7.50
2	45	20	$.50	$10.00	$7.50
3	60	15	$.50	$7.50	$7.50
4	70	10	$.50	$5.00	$7.50
5	75	5	$.50	$2.50	$7.50
6	70	−5	$.50	−$2.50	$7.50
7	60	−10	$.50	−$5.00	$7.50

MRP as Demand for Labor

If the hourly wage were to rise to $10, Molly would reduce her employment to two workers per hour. If the wage decreases to $5 per hour, she would employ four workers. All else equal, as the price of labor increases, the employment falls and as the price of labor decreases, employment rises. This is the Law of Demand again! Figure 10.1 illustrates the MRP_L and Molly's hiring at three wages.

Molly's demand for labor is actually represented by the MRP_L. It is downward sloping, like any demand curve would be, because of the diminishing marginal productivity of labor in the short run. To move from Molly's demand for labor to the overall market demand for labor, we simply sum up all of the individual firms' MRP_L curves. Market $D_L = \Sigma MRP_L$.

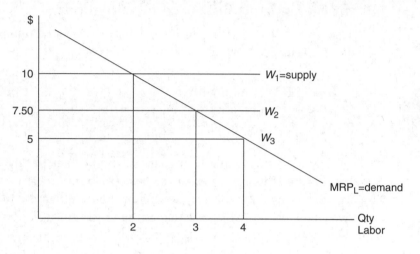

Figure 10.1

Market Wage as Supply of Labor

Under the assumptions of a perfectly competitive labor market, the supply of labor to the individual firm is perfectly elastic and equal to the wage. This means that the firm can employ all of the workers it desires at the going market wage.

- In competitive markets, MRP_L is the firm's labor demand curve.
- In competitive markets, wage is the firm's labor supply curve.

Derived Demand

Economists say that the demand for an input like labor is derived from the demand for the goods produced by the input. If the weather is hot and demand for lemonade rises, local economists might predict a stronger demand for production resources like lemonade workers, lemons, and sugar. An increase in the demand for a resource means that at any wage, the firm wishes to employ more of that resource. If the demand for lemonade increases and the price rises to $1 per cup, the MRP_L increases at all quantities of labor. This is seen in Figure 10.2.

- You are **very** likely to see the topic of derived demand on the AP exam. To avoid losing points on the free-response question, you *must* make the connection between the price of the product rising and the increased demand for the labor.
- ↑D for product, ↑ price of product, ↑MRP_L, ↑ hiring of labor at the current wage.

Determinants of Resource Demand

The demand for the goods themselves is an important determinant of resource demand, but not the only determinant.

> "Keep answers crisp, graphs labeled, and you are on your way to a 5."
> —Navin, AP Student

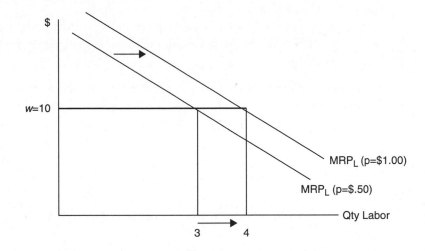

Figure 10.2

- *Product demand.* An increase in the demand for textiles, towels, for example, results in an increased price of those goods. The higher price increases the marginal revenue product of resources used in the production of textiles (i.e., textile workers) and this shifts the demand for those resources to the right. Of course this works in the opposite direction and is probably a more accurate story of what has happened to textile workers in the United States.
- *Productivity (output per resource unit).* If the productivity of the resource increases, the firm has a profit motive to take advantage of that heightened productivity and the demand for the resource should increase. Productivity of a resource is affected by a few different things.

  1. *Quantity of other resources.* Give workers more equipment to help production and labor's productivity can be increased. If Molly were to provide her workers with a larger workspace or more manual juicers or pitchers or stirring spoons or measuring cups, they might achieve increased output per worker.
  2. *Technical progress.* Better technology with which to work can increase labor's productivity. Rather than using manual lemon squeezers, Molly invests in electric squeezers that allow for a given number of employees to produce more lemonade every hour.
  3. *Quality of variable resources.* Fertile farmland in the Midwest is a huge productivity advantage over the same acreage of farmland in Nevada. A more educated and trained workforce is an improvement in the quality of the labor and therefore provides more productivity. Maybe Molly employs only those who have completed daylong training at the local community college.

- *Prices of other resources.* Employers hire several different resources so the demand for one (labor) often depends upon the prices of the others.

  1. *Substitute resources.* If the price of a substitute resource, machinery, for example, falls, it has two competing effects on the demand for labor.

     a. Substitution effect (SE). Because machinery is now relatively less expensive, the firm uses more machinery and decreases demand for labor. For Molly, a lower price of electric lemon squeezers would put pressure on her to decrease the demand for labor.

b. Output effect (OE). Lower machine prices lower production costs (a downward, or rightward shift in MC), which increases output for the firm and prompts an increased demand for labor. With the lower marginal cost of producing lemonade, Molly sees that she can actually produce more and would therefore need more labor.

c. The net effect of a lower price of capital depends upon the magnitude of each effect. If the SE > OE, demand for labor falls. If the OE > SE, the demand for labor increases.

2. *Complementary resources.* When labor and machine work together, a lower price of the machine makes it more affordable to purchase more machinery, but also increases the demand for labor. Interstate trucking companies need trucks, fuel, and drivers. When the price of fuel increases, this can have a negative impact on the demand for drivers. For Molly's firm, if the price of lemons falls, this more affordable complement to labor might increase the demand for labor.

Table 10.3 is a summary of the determinants of labor demand.

Table 10.3

LABOR DEMAND INCREASES IF . . .	LABOR DEMAND DECREASES IF . . .
Demand for the product increases, increasing the price.	Demand for the product decreases, decreasing the price.
The labor becomes more productive, either with more resources available, better technology, or a higher quality workforce.	The labor becomes less productive, either with fewer resources available, lessened technology, or a lower quality workforce.
The price of a substitute resource falls and the OE > SE.	The price of a substitute resource falls and the SE > OE.
The price of a substitute resource rises and the SE > OE.	The price of a substitute resource rises and the OE > SE.
The price of a complementary resource falls.	The price of a complementary resource rises.

10.2 Least-Cost Hiring of Multiple Inputs

Main Topic: *The Least-Cost Rule*

Finding the best way to cope with scarcity really excites economists. We found that consumers needed to find the best (utility maximizing) combination of two goods, given the prices and an income constraint. For producers, we would like to find the best (cost minimizing) combination of two inputs, given the prices and production constraint. To do this, we use the consumer's decision as a model for the producer's decision. The consumer's utility maximizing rule said to find the combination of good X and good Y so that $MU_x/P_x = MU_y/P_y$ while spending exactly his or her income, and paying prices P_x and P_y.

Least-Cost Hiring Rule

For a producer, we can express the constraint in two equivalent ways. Remember the bridge between production and cost?

1. You must produce Q^* units of output, now find the least-cost ($TC) way of doing so.

2. You can only spend $TC, now find the highest level of output (Q^*).

There is only one combination of two resources (we'll use labor and capital) that satisfies either of these two constraints and it is found by using this **least-cost rule**. The price of labor is P_L and the price of capital (K) is P_K.

$$MP_L/P_L = MP_K/P_K \text{ or equivalently, } MP_L/MP_K = P_L/P_K$$

Example:

If each of the inputs is hired at $1 per unit and at the current amount of labor and capital you have employed, the $MP_L = 100$ and the $MP_K = 10$. Clearly, the least-cost rule is not satisfied:

$$100 \text{ units}/\$1 > 10 \text{ units}/\$1$$

If you could spend $1 more on labor, you would see output increase by 100 units. That extra $1 would come from spending $1 less on capital, which would decrease output by 10 units. So you spend the same amount of money, but get 90 more units of output.

Great deal! In situations like this, where $MP_L/P_L > MP_K/P_K$, the firm is going to find it in its best interest to increase spending on L and decrease spending on K. The Law of Diminishing Marginal Returns predicts that as you increase L, MP_L falls. And as you decrease K, MP_K rises. The substitution of labor for capital ceases to be a great deal at the combination of L and K where the ratios of marginal product per dollar are equal again.

SITUATION	FIRM WILL . . .	WHICH CAUSES . . .	AND . . .	UNTIL
$MP_L/P_L > MP_K/P_K$	↑L and ↓K	↓MP_L	↑MP_K	$MP_L/P_L = MP_K/P_K$
$MP_L/P_L < MP_K/P_K$	↑K and ↓L	↓MP_K	↑MP_L	$MP_L/P_L = MP_K/P_K$

Example:

A producer of gadgets pays $5 for each hour of labor and $10 for each hour of capital employed. Table 10.4 describes the marginal products of each at various levels of employment. Told that you must produce $Q = 360$ gadgets, find the least-cost combination of labor and capital.

Table 10.4

# OF L EMPLOYED	MPL	# OF K EMPLOYED	MPK
1	50	1	100
2	40	2	90
3	30	3	80
4	20	4	60
5	10	5	45
6	5	6	30

Find all of the combinations of L and K where our rule is satisfied:

$$MP_L/P_L = MP_K/P_K$$
$$\text{or } MP_L/MP_K = \$5/\$10 = 1/2.$$

There are three possibilities where the MP_L is one-half the size of MP_K:

- L = 1, K = 1. Total Product = 50 + 100 = 150

- L = 2, K = 3. Total Product = (50 + 40) + (100 + 90 + 80) = 360
- L = 3, K = 4. Total Product = (50 + 40 + 30) + (100 + 90 + 80 + 60) = 450

The best way to produce 360 gadgets is to hire two units of labor and three units of capital at a total cost of TC = $5 * 2 + $10 * 3 = $40. The same problem could have been modified to use a cost constraint rather than an output constraint.

Told that you can only spend $40, find the combination of labor and capital that maximizes production. Of course the solution is again L = 2, K = 3 and output is 360 gadgets.

10.3 Factor Supply and Market Equilibrium

Main Topics: *Supply of Labor, Wage Determination*

If you have ever had a job, you have been a small part of the labor supply curve. We quickly investigate labor supply and combine it with labor demand to complete a labor market. It is in this competitive market that wage and employment are determined.

Supply of Labor

Economic theory predicts that as the price of good increases, suppliers of that good increase the quantity supplied. This is the **Law of Supply**. If the price of labor (wage) increases, more hours of labor should be supplied. For the most part, this is true, and the market labor supply curve slopes upward. If the hourly wage increased from $5 to $8, most people respond by working more hours, earning more income ($320 per 40 hour workweek) and consuming more goods.

Wage and Employment Determination

Assuming competitive output and input markets, the competitive wage is found at the intersection of labor demand and labor supply. Changing demand and supply influence this wage, and the equilibrium quantity of labor that accompanies it.

Example:

The aging population in the United States is giving a boost to the market for nurses. An increase in the demand for nurses increases both the wage and employment of nurses. This is seen in the Figure 10.3.

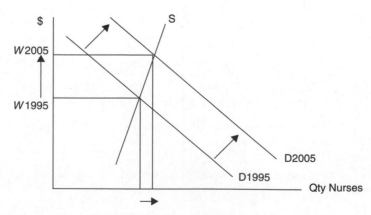

Figure 10.3

10.4 Imperfect Competition in Product and Factor Markets

Main Topics: *Market Power in Product Markets, Market Power in Resource Markets*

We saw in the previous chapter that perfectly competitive markets might not always exist. After all, the conditions for perfect competition are rather strict and not often observed in the "real world." In the sections below, we assume that the firm has some market power, first in the product market and then in the factor (labor) market. To no surprise, the outcome of wage and employment differs from the competitive outcome described above.

Market Power in Product Market

Perhaps the most important result seen from a firm that has the ability to be a price setter is that the price exceeds marginal revenue. Because MR < P with market power, this has an impact on the marginal revenue product function.

Under perfectly competitive price-taking conditions: $MRP_c = MR * MP_L = P * MP_L$

Under conditions of market power, MR < P: $MRP_m = MR * MP_L < MRP_c$

The result of a lower marginal revenue product function is that the optimal amount of employment falls at all wages. Figure 10.4 illustrates this. In other words, the monopolist hires lesser amounts of all resources, including labor. This should make sense if you recall that monopoly markets produce less output than the competitive market. If the market produces less output, it makes sense that the market would employ fewer resources.

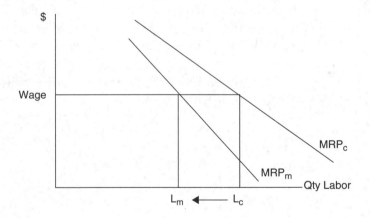

Figure 10.4

- Because MR < P, $MRP_m = MR * MP_L < MRP_c$.
- A monopoly market employs fewer workers than the competitive market.

Market Power in Factor Markets

When a producer has extreme market power in the product market, we label them a price-setting monopolist and the price of the product is set above marginal revenue. Let's turn this situation around to the factor market. If an employer has extreme market power in the factor market, we label them a wage-setting monopsonist and we observe the wage set below marginal factor cost.

In a competitive labor market, the firm could employ all it wanted at the market-determined wage. The key difference between **monopsony** and a perfectly competitive labor market is that the employer must increase the wage to increase the quantity of labor that is supplied. In other words, the labor supply to the firm is upward sloping, not horizontal. Marginal factor cost is now greater than the wage. Table 10.5 should illustrate how this happens.

Table 10.5

LABOR SUPPLIED TO THE FIRM (L_s)	NECESSARY HOURLY WAGE (W)	TOTAL WAGE BILL = L_s * W	MARGINAL FACTOR COST (MFC)
0		$0	
1	$4	$4	$4
2	$5	$10	$6
3	$6	$18	$8
4	$7	$28	$10
5	$8	$40	$12
6	$9	$54	$14

Example:

Molly's lemonade conglomerate can employ more workers but must increase the wage to do so. However, not only does she have to increase the wage for additional workers, but also to her current workers. This creates a situation where the MFC > W. See Figure 10.5. Molly still chooses to employ where MRP_L = MFC, but the wage is determined from the labor supply curve. Graphically the MFC curve lies above the labor supply curve, which means that labor is paid below their MRP_L.

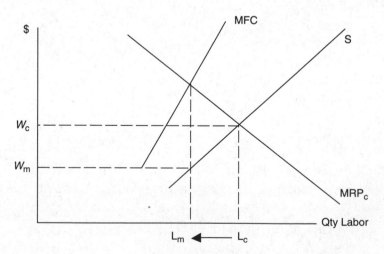

Figure 10.5

- Under monopsony, employers hire $L_m < L_c$.
- Monopsony firms pay $W_m < W_c = MRP_L$.

Remember that MRP_L measures the value of the last worker to the firm. The outcome that workers receive less than their value to the firm might be alarming. Does this happen?

If you doubt that an employer can get away with such rampant exploitation, I give you a four-letter response: N-C-A-A. A big time college star athlete might produce, over the course of a four-year career, millions of dollars in revenue to a university. Even if we include the value of four years of tuition, room and board, the star athlete is compensated well below his or her marginal revenue product. Is it so crazy that many talented college athletes make an early jump to a professional league, or in some cases skip college altogether?

› Review Questions

1. Your aunt runs a small firm from her home making apple pies. She hires some friends to help her. Which of the following situations would most likely increase her demand for labor?

   (A) The price of apple peelers/corers rises.
   (B) Your aunt's friends gossip all day, slowing their dough making process.
   (C) There is a sale on ovens.
   (D) A new study reveals that apples increase your risk of cancer.
   (E) The price of apples increases.

2. The price of labor is $2 and the price of capital is $1. The marginal product of labor is 200 and the marginal product of capital is 50. What should the firm do?

   (A) Increase capital and decrease labor so that the marginal product of capital falls and the marginal product of labor rises.
   (B) Increase capital and decrease labor so that the marginal product of capital rises and the marginal product of labor falls.
   (C) Decrease capital and increase labor so that the marginal product of capital rises and the marginal product of labor falls.
   (D) Decrease capital and increase labor so that the marginal product of capital falls and the marginal product of labor rises.
   (E) Increase both capital and labor until the ratio of marginal products per dollar is equal.

3. A competitive labor market is currently in equilibrium. Which of the following most likely increases the market wage?

   (A) More students graduate with the necessary skills for this labor market.
   (B) Demand for the good produced by this labor is stronger.

   (C) The price of a complementary resource increases.
   (D) The Labor Department removes the need for workers to pass an exam before they can work in this field.
   (E) Over time, one large employer grows to act as a monopsonist.

Use Table 10.6 to respond to questions 4 to 5.

Table 10.6

WAGE (W)	QUANTITY OF LABOR SUPPLIED	MARGINAL FACTOR COST OF LABOR (MFC)	MARGINAL REVENUE PRODUCT OF LABOR (MRP$_L$)
$3	0		
$4	10	$4	$10
$5	20	$6	$9
$6	30	$8	$8
$7	40	$10	$7

4. If a firm is hiring labor in the perfectly competitive labor market, the wage and employment are

   (A) $3 and zero.
   (B) $4 and 10.
   (C) $5 and 20.
   (D) $6 and 30.
   (E) $7 and 40.

5. If a firm hires labor in a monopsony labor market, the wage and employment are

   (A) $3 and zero.
   (B) $4 and 10.
   (C) $5 and 20.
   (D) $6 and 30.
   (E) $7 and 40.

❭ Answers and Explanations

1. **C**—Since ovens would be a less expensive complementary resource (with more ovens, they can bake more pies), your aunt needs more employees to go along with the extra ovens. Apple corers and peelers are complements, but even if you think they are substitutes, the impact on labor demand is uncertain because of the competing output and substitution effects.

2. **C**—Do a quick ratio of marginal product per dollar. When you see that the $MP_L/P_L > MP_K/P_K$, you notice that the firm is getting more "bang for the buck" with labor. Immediately rule out any choice that says they hire less labor. The only way that MP_L/P_L falls to equal MP_K/P_K is to decrease the capital and increase the labor, causing the MP_K to rise and the MP_L to fall. The firm does this until the marginal products divided by the prices are equal.

3. **B**—The equilibrium wage rises with stronger demand or lessened supply of labor. The stronger demand for the product increases the wage as the demand for labor increases. All other choices either increase the labor supply or decrease the demand, thus decreasing the wage. Emergence of monopsony decreases the wage below competitive levels.

4. **E**—In a competitive labor market, equilibrium is where $W = MRP_L$.

5. **D**—In a monopsony labor market, equilibrium is where $MFC = MRP_L$.

❭ Rapid Review

Marginal Revenue Product (MRP): measures the value of what the next unit of a resource (e.g., labor) brings to the firm. $MRP_L = MR * MP_L$. In a perfectly competitive product market, $MRP_L = P * MP_L$. In a monopoly product market, $MR < P$ so $MRP_m < MRP_c$.

Marginal Resource Cost (MRC): measures the cost the firm incurs from using an additional unit of an input. In a perfectly competitive labor market, $MRC = Wage$. In a monopsony labor market, the $MRC > Wage$.

Profit maximizing resource employment: the firm hires the profit maximizing amount of a resource at the point where $MRP = MRC$.

Demand for labor: labor demand for the firm is the MRP_L curve. The labor demand for the entire market $D_L = \Sigma MRP_L$ of all firms.

Derived demand: demand for a resource like labor is derived from the demand for the goods produced by the resource.

Determinants of labor demand: one of the external factors that influences labor demand. When these variables change, the entire demand curve shifts to the left or right.

Least-Cost Rule: The combination of labor and capital that minimizes total costs for a given production rate. Hire L and K so that: $MP_L/P_L = MP_K/P_K$ or $MP_L/MP_K = P_L/P_K$.

Monopsonist: a firm that has market power in the factor market, i.e., a wage-setter.

CHAPTER 11

Public Goods, Externalities, and the Role of Government

IN THIS CHAPTER

Summary: One of the recurring themes of the first half of this book is that the competitive marketplace provides the most efficient societal outcome where goods are produced at the point where MB = MC, or at the intersection of market supply and market demand. We have not, however, explored the possibility that the demand curve might not capture all of the benefits to society from the consumption of a good. There is also the possibility that the supply curve might not capture all of the costs to society from the production of the good. If these benefits and/or costs are indeed not reflected in the market equilibrium price and quantity, then we conclude that the market has failed to provide the efficient outcome. When this occurs, the government usually needs to step in.

Key Ideas
✪ Public and Private Goods
✪ Positive and Negative Externalities
✪ Income Distribution
✪ Tax Structures

11.1 Public Goods and Spillover Benefits

Main Topics: *Private and Public Goods, Spillover Benefits and Positive Externalities*

Private and Public Goods

So far, when discussing goods and services, we have focused on private goods and services. **Private goods** are goods that are both rival and excludable. A bag of potato chips and a cup of herbal tea are all private goods. These are rival in that only one person can consume the good, and so consumption by one consumer necessarily means another cannot. Private goods are excludable in that consumers who do not pay for the good are excluded from the consumption.

Public goods however, are special cases where the goods are both nonrival and nonexcludable. These characteristics mean that one person's consumption does not prevent another from also consuming the good. If a public good is provided to some, it is necessarily provided to all, even if they do not pay for the good. Common examples of public goods are national defense, local fire and police services, space exploration, and environmental protection.

Who Pays?

In the case of private goods, each individual decides whether he or she is going to pay the going price. If the marginal benefit to me is at least as high as the price, I might decide to purchase and consume the good. For private goods, those who want the good badly enough are the ones who pay.

Maybe you have confronted the difficulty in paying for a public good if you have been assigned a group project in school. If each group member receives the same grade, regardless of his or her level of effort, some members of the group might slack off and benefit from the hard work of the others. If this sounds familiar, you have experienced the **free-rider problem.** The free-rider problem pops up whenever some members of the community understand that they can consume the public good while others provide for it.

A small town has a community meeting to decide how to pay for local police protection. The mayor passes a collection plate around the room and we each make a voluntary donation toward this public good. There are some difficulties with paying for a public good in this way. How much do I use or value the next unit of police services in my protection? Is this more than, less than, or the same as my neighbor's use and value of police protection? It is impossible to answer this question and even if it were possible to determine how much my neighbor values police service, maybe he won't pay his fair share. After all, if police protection is going to be provided to the entire community, and this protection cannot be denied to anyone, some members of the community might become **free riders.** The free-rider problem and the nonexcludable nature of public goods require that the government collect taxes to pay for their provision.

Spillover Benefits

In graduate school I rented a small house on a dead-end street. On the other side of the street, two older ladies had an immaculately landscaped yard with gorgeous rosebushes. Riding my mountain bike home from campus I was happy to see, and smell, the results of their hard yard work. I'm sure that I was not the only neighbor who felt that way. When one person's consumption of a good provides utility to a third party who has not directly purchased the good, there exist **spillover benefits** that are not reflected in the market price of that good. In my case, my neighbors went to the trouble, expense, and effort, to beautify

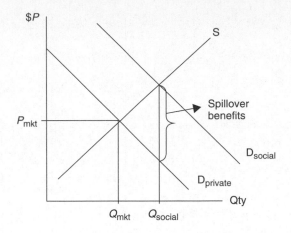

Figure 11.1

their yard. In the process, they beautified the neighborhood and provided benefits to those of us who received utility from the landscaping and the roses. This situation is described as a **positive externality** and is illustrated in Figure 11.1.

The market demand curve for roses captured the private benefits received by consumers of roses, but did not capture the additional benefits received by neighbors of those who consumed roses. Figure 11.1 incorporates the spillover benefits to the market for roses. The private demand curve, which does not include the spillover benefits, lies below the societal demand curve. The market produces only Q_{mkt} roses, but the optimal amount is greater at Q_{social}. Because the market produces less than the socially optimal amount, it is said that there is an underallocation of resources to rose production. In other words, society wants more than the market provides.

• The existence of spillover benefits in a market results in an underallocation of resources in that market. In other words, there is not enough of a good thing.

The older ladies who lived across the street from my house were essentially pro-viding a public good that we might call "community beautification" and the rest of us were free riding on their activity. How could we have contributed to the provision of the public good? Maybe we could have brought these ladies cash donations, or we could have volunteered our labor. Each of these gestures would have lessened their burden and freed up their private resources to provide even more landscaping for the neighborhood.

Subsidies

On a larger scale, this type of market failure can be remedied through government intervention. Our goal as economic policymakers is to move the equilibrium quantity from Q_{mkt} to Q_{social}. One solution might be to provide a subsidy to gardeners equal to the amount of the spillover benefit that their activity provides to the community. By sending a check (or voucher) to the ladies, they would have increased their demand for roses and other landscaping and shifted the private demand out to equal the social demand. This is seen in Figure 11.2. The price received by the firm has risen to P_{firm}, but when the consumer applies the voucher, the actual price to the consumer is lower at P_{cons}.

Another possibility is to provide a subsidy to producers of roses. This type of subsidy would result in an outward shift in the supply curve so that the equilibrium quantity of roses would be at Q_{social}. This policy is seen in Figure 11.3. The price to consumers, P_{cons}, is also lower in this case, while producers receive, with the subsidy, P_{firm}.

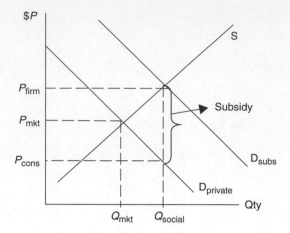

Figure 11.2

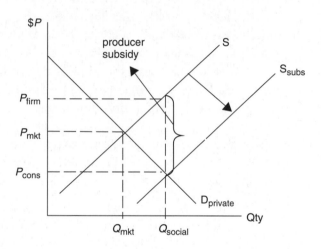

Figure 11.3

11.2 Pollution and Spillover Costs

Main Topics: *Spillover Costs and Negative Externalities*

Another kind of market failure occurs when there are additional costs associated with production of a good that are not reflected in the market price. Pollution of all kinds is a classic example.

Spillover Costs

Almost anyone who has dined at a restaurant has experienced secondhand smoke. Even a non-smoker sitting in the nonsmoking section expects to come home smelling like an ashtray. While the smoker has chosen to pay the market price of tobacco, the nonsmoker also pays a price for that choice, either in minor disutility or worsened health. When one person's consumption of a good imposes disutility on a third party who has not directly purchased the good, there exist **spillover costs** that are not reflected in the market price of that good. A situation in which polluters impose costs upon third parties is called a **negative externality**.

The existence of spillover costs from a negative externality means that not all of the costs of production are captured by the supply curve. In the Midwest, the burning of coal produces most electricity. The private cost of electricity production includes the coal, the labor, and capital at the plant. But the burning of coal imposes environmental costs in the form of air, water, and land pollution. These societal costs are not found in the market price (P_{mkt}) of booting up your PC or running the dishwasher. The difference between the private cost and the societal cost of producing electricity is seen in Figure 11.4. The private supply curve, which does not include the spillover costs, lies below the societal supply curve. The market produces Q_{mkt} units of electricity, but the optimal amount is less at Q_{social}. Because the market produces more than the socially optimal amount, it is said that there is an overallocation of resources to electricity production. In other words, society wants less than the market provides.

- The existence of spillover costs in a market results in an overallocation of resources in that market. In other words, there is too much of a bad thing.

So how could cigarette smokers alleviate the discomfort that they impose upon their nonsmoking citizens? The aim of any such policy is to try to move the spillover costs away from the third party victims and back upon those who produce the externality.

> "I was always told to make big graphs to keep things clear. It ended up saving me from many careless errors."
> — Ross, AP Student

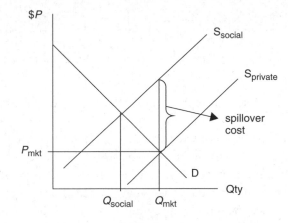

Figure 11.4

Pollution Taxes

Rather than allow the spillover costs to fall externally on members of society, the goal of pollution taxes is to internalize these costs by imposing a tax on the production or consumption of goods that create negative externalities. Our goal is to move the market equilibrium quantity closer to the socially optimal quantity of electricity. Suppose government imposes a tax, equal to the spillover cost, on every unit of coal that our power plant uses to produce electricity. This pollution tax results in an inward shift of the private supply curve so that it equals the social supply curve. See Figure 11.5. The price of using your PC has now increased, but now that price incorporates all of the costs of electricity, including the effects of pollution on the environment and human health.

In some cases, a tax may be imposed on consumers, if they are responsible for the negative externality. For example, in major metropolitan areas traffic is a serious problem and millions of commuters create significant amounts of pollution. We might increase the automobile registration tax, or create a system of toll highways so that the users of automobiles and the commuters themselves must pay an additional price for that behavior. We have seen that any time the price increases, quantity demanded (driving) must fall.

Be careful when designing a tax to remedy a negative externality. We must tax those who are imposing the spillover costs on society. Would you tax the nonsmoker to fix the problem of secondhand smoke? Hardly.

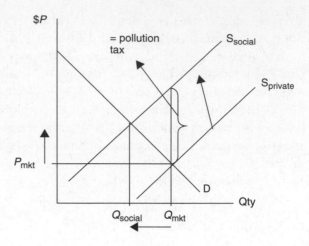

Figure 11.5

11.3 Income Distribution and Tax Structures

Main Topics: *Equity as a Goal, Marginal and Average Tax Rates, Progressive Taxes, Regressive Taxes, Proportional Taxes.*

In the case of pollution and other negative externalities, the marketplace fails to protect the victims of spillover costs. In the case of public goods or other positive externalities, the market fails to provide an adequate quantity to satisfy the needs of society. As we saw above, the government is called to action to move the market outcome closer to the societal efficient outcome. The government is also called to action to remedy issues of equity, or fairness. This section discusses equity, distribution of income, and tax structures to move closer to a more equitable outcome.

Equity as a Goal

While we tout the efficiency of competitive markets with a fervor that approaches deification, the one thing even the most efficient market does not do is provide equity, or fairness. Some consumers can afford a new Mercedes, some cannot; but I doubt that this is a good example of the unfairness of markets. But some consumers cannot afford pediatric services for their infant children. Even if these services are exchanged at the efficient quantity where the marginal social benefit is equal to the marginal social cost, even the most die-hard advocates of the free market can see that it is an outcome that should be remedied through some form of income redistribution.

An Equal Share?

There are some who propose that the economic resources should be equally divided amongst all members of society. This egalitarian, or equal share view, seems fair but has at least one serious criticism. **Egalitarianism** suffers from an issue of compensation that fails to match productivity. In other words, the incentives to work hard, take risks and seek a competitive advantage are greatly reduced. If you were guaranteed an equal share of the resources, how hard would you work?

> **Example:**
> All students in your class are assured of being compensated with a "B," regardless
> of the effort and productivity that might merit a B. C-level students lack the
> motivation to become more productive because they are guaranteed compensation

above their productivity. A-level students lack the motivation to produce A-level work because they know compensation falls below that. The high productivity students get disenchanted, disgruntled, and work even less.

Productivity Share?

If egalitarianism suffers from a lack of productivity incentives, maybe everyone's share of economic resources should be based upon individual productivity. In other words, this **marginal productivity theory** says your wage is a function of your marginal revenue product. If markets are competitive, this can be quite efficient. In theory, this could even be fair. The flaw in this method of income distribution is that not all citizens are given a fair shake at demonstrating to the labor market their true marginal revenue product. Think of all of the advantages, large or small, that you were lucky enough to be born with. Now imagine all of them being removed from your past and present. Productive individuals who have few advantages can overcome obstacles with hard work, but some societal barriers (e.g., discrimination, a disability) prevent them from ever receiving a compensation equal to their productivity.

How Do We Measure the Income Distribution?

There are a couple of common ways to see a nation's income distribution. Whether or not we think this is "fair" is another question entirely.

1. Quintiles

Economists sort households from the lowest incomes to the highest incomes and then divide that range into fifths, or **quintiles.** In each quintile lies 20 percent of all households. Table 11.1 illustrates the income distribution in 2001 as published by the Bureau of the Census. If income were perfectly distributed, each 20 percent of the families in the United States would have 20 percent of the total income.

Table 11.1

QUINTILE	% OF TOTAL INCOME	UPPER INCOME LIMITS
Lowest 20%	4.2%	$24,000
Second 20%	9.7%	$41,127
Third 20%	15.4%	$62,500
Fourth 20%	22.9%	$94,150
Highest 20%	*47.7%*	No limit
Total	100.0%	

2. Lorenz Curve and Gini Ratio

The above quintile distribution can be graphically illustrated with a **Lorenz curve** (see Figure 11.6). The farther the Lorenz curve lies below the hypothetical line of perfect equality, the more unequal the distribution of income. This distance of the actual distribution of income from the line of perfect equality is calculated by constructing a **Gini ratio,** the area of the gap between the perfect equality line and the Lorenz curve (A) as a ratio of the entire area (A + B). The closer the Gini ratio is to zero, the more equal the distribution. The closer to one, the more unequal the income distribution.

$$\text{Gini ratio} = \text{Area A}/(\text{Area A} + \text{Area B})$$

- The closer the Gini ratio gets to zero, the more equal the distribution of income.
- The closer the Gini ratio gets to one, the more unequal the distribution of income.

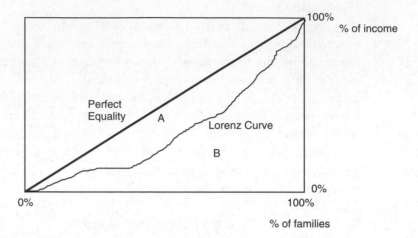

Figure 11.6

What Are the Sources of Inequality?

The market is not always a good mechanism for distributing income equally. There are some commonly accepted factors for income inequality.

- *Ability.* Because natural ability is not distributed equally, income is not distributed equally. This factor would explain why some quarterbacks or artists are more highly paid than other quarterbacks or artists.
- *Human capital.* Individuals augment their ability with education and training, resulting in higher income. Not everyone attains the same level of human capital, so income is not equally distributed.
- *Discrimination.* Despite social progress, discrimination is a hurdle that might not be surmountable even with high levels of ability and human capital.
- *Preferences.* Some individuals, even with high ability and human capital, prefer to maximize utility with more leisure and less labor.
- *Market power.* We learned that monopoly and monopsony markets are detrimental to consumers and workers. The more market power held in the hands of the few, the more unequal the distribution of income.
- *Luck and connections.* Some are born into prosperity and some are lucky enough to stumble upon the right connections.

Can Income Be Redistributed?

Our economic system emphasizes a productivity-based distribution of resources, but we know that this system does not overcome all of the equity issues that are theoretically solved by egalitarianism. We have decided that the government should have a role in income distribution. The idea behind redistribution of income is that the government collects taxes from one segment of society and transfers it to another. These transfers come in the form of social programs like government housing, Medicare, or public education. And while most agree that these programs are essentially good, how government decides to tax is a hotly debated issue along philosophical and political grounds. We summarize the nature of progressive, regressive, and proportional taxes, and use the marginal and average concepts again in this new context.

Marginal and Average Tax Rates

Marginal tax rate is the rate paid on the last dollar earned. This is found by taking the ratio of the change in taxes divided by the change in income.

$$\text{Marginal Tax Rate} = (\Delta \text{ taxes due})/(\Delta \text{ taxable income})$$

Example:

If my income rises by $100 and the taxes that I owe the government rise by $25, the marginal tax rate is 25 percent on those additional $100.

Average tax rate is the proportion of total income paid to taxes. It is calculated by dividing the total taxes owed by the total taxable income.

$$\text{Average Tax Rate} = (\text{total taxes due})/(\text{total taxable income})$$

Example:

If my monthly taxable income is $1000 and $200 is deducted for taxes, my average tax rate is 20 percent.

Progressive, Regressive, and Proportional

The way in which a redistributive tax works depends upon how the average tax rate changes as income changes.

A Progressive Tax

A progressive tax exists if as income increases, the average tax rates increase. The Federal income tax works this way. If your household income is above a certain minimum level but below a certain maximum level (a tax bracket) you might pay an average of 20 percent of your income in taxes. If your household income rises above that upper limit and falls into a higher tax bracket, your average tax rate might increase to 24 percent. A **tax bracket** is a range of income on which is applied a given marginal tax rate. This structure is designed so that the lowest incomes pay taxes at a much lower rate than the highest incomes.

A Regressive Tax

A tax is **regressive** if the average tax rate falls as income rises. A sales tax on consumption is a good example of a regressive tax.

Example:

Two unmarried consumers with no children both shop at the grocery store in a state with a 5 percent sales tax. One consumer, Bill, earns a modest $20,000 and spends $10,000 annually on food at the store. He pays $500 in sales tax. A second consumer, Mary, earns $200,000, or 10 times as much as Bill. Can we expect her to spend 10 times as much on food? Doubtful. Let's be generous and say that Mary spends $20,000 annually on food at the grocery store, and pays $1000 in sales tax. Everyone in the state pays 5 percent sales tax on his or her consumption spending, but as a percentage of income, Bill pays a much higher average tax rate.

Bill's average tax rate = $500/$20,000 = 2.5%

Mary's average tax rate = $1000/$200,000 = .5%

A Proportional Tax

A proportional tax exists if a constant tax rate is applied regardless of income. Many politicians, on the grounds of a more streamlined way of taxing the population, have proposed this kind of "flat tax." Corporate taxes are taxed at a flat rate of approximately 35 percent and are one of few examples of a proportional tax in the United States. Some U.S. states have adopted a proportional income tax rather than the more traditional progressive tax on income.

Example:
Bob and Nancy earn $30,000 and $60,000 respectively. A proportional tax of 10% would require that Bob pays $300 and Nancy pays $600 in taxes.

› Review Questions

1. In the figure below, X represents

   (A) spillover benefits.
   (B) a potential producer subsidy to eliminate an externality.
   (C) a potential consumer subsidy to eliminate an externality.
   (D) both A and C.
   (E) A, B, and C.

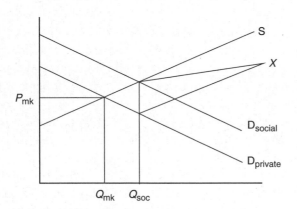

2. Which of the following scenarios best describes a negative externality?

   (A) A roommate subscribes to a monthly CD club and you share the same taste in music.
   (B) Your neighbor has a swimming pool and you have an open invitation to come on over for a pool party.
   (C) Your neighbor has a swimming pool and their six-year-old child has his first grade friends over every day for a pool party.
   (D) Your roommate's mom has decided that your apartment needs TiVo and pays for it.
   (E) Your dad has purchased a new sports coupe and has agreed that you can drive it to the prom.

3. Which of the following is the best example of a public good?

   (A) A lighthouse on a rocky coastline.
   (B) Tickets to the Super Bowl.
   (C) A granola bar.
   (D) A cup of coffee.
   (E) A magazine subscription.

4. Production of energy (i.e, electricity, natural gas, heating oil) creates a negative externality in the form of air pollution blown to communities downwind from the source of the pollution. Of the choices below, which is the most appropriate policy to remedy this negative externality?

   (A) a per unit tax on consumers of subway tickets and city bus passes.
   (B) a per unit tax on producers of energy.
   (C) a per unit subsidy for energy consumers.
   (D) a per unit tax on consumers of energy efficient light bulbs.
   (E) a per unit subsidy for energy producers.

5. Jason earns $1000 a week and pays a total of $200 in taxes. Jennifer earns $2000 a week and pays a total of $300 in taxes. We can conclude from this information that their income is taxed with a(n)

   (A) progressive tax.
   (B) proportional tax.
   (C) regressive tax.
   (D) tax bracket.
   (E) egalitarian tax.

6. You learn that one nation has a Gini ratio of .25 and another nation has a Gini ratio of .85. Based on this you might conclude:

   (A) the nation with the higher Gini ratio has a more equal distribution of wealth and income.

   (B) the nation with the higher Gini ratio has a more unequal distribution of citizens with college degrees.

   (C) the nation with the lower Gini ratio has more societal barriers like discrimination.

   (D) the nation with the higher Gini ratio has fewer societal barriers like discrimination.

   (E) the nation with the lower Gini ratio has more oligopolistic industries.

> Answers and Explanations

1. **E**—This vertical distance between society's demand curve and the market demand curve represents spillover benefits, or additional benefits to society not captured by market demand. However, it could also be the amount of a producer or consumer subsidy if the government chose to eliminate the externality.

2. **C**—A negative externality is a situation where a third party is harmed by the actions of consumers and/or producers. The first grade pool party is the best candidate for such a situation as all of the other choices are likely to benefit you, rather than impose cost upon you.

3. **A**—A public good is a good that is nonrival and nonexcludable. In other words, if one person consumes it, all others can still consume it.

4. **B**—The presence of the negative externality should rule out any choice that refers to a subsidy of either producers or consumers of energy. To reduce consumption and production, we must reduce the market quantity, not encourage more of it. Subsidies could be used to encourage more energy-efficient behavior, but choices A and D would actually inhibit this kind of action. The per unit tax on producers of the negative externality is the most appropriate choice as the tax shifts the market supply inward, making it closer to the socially optimal supply of energy.

5. **C**—Jennifer's weekly income is twice Jason's, yet she pays less than double his taxes. This is a regressive tax. A proportional tax would require Jennifer to pay $400 and a progressive tax would require that she pay more than $400 in weekly taxes.

6. **B**—The distribution of human capital is a factor in determining the distribution of income and wealth. A nation that has a more unequal distribution of educational attainment would therefore likely have a more unequal distribution of income.

> Rapid Review

Private goods: goods that are both rival and excludable. Only one person can consume the good at a time and consumers who do not pay for the good are excluded from the consumption. Examples: a tube of toothpaste, an airline ticket.

Public goods: goods that are both nonrival and nonexcludable. One person's consumption does not prevent another from also consuming the good and if it is provided to some, it is necessarily provided to all, even if they do not pay for the good. Examples: local police services, national defense.

Free-rider problem: in the case of a public good, some members of the community know that they can consume the public good while others provide for it. This results in a lack of private funding for the good and requires that the government provide it.

Spillover benefits: additional benefits to society, not captured by the market demand curve from the production of a good, result in a price that is too high and a market quantity that is too low. Resources are underallocated to the production of this good.

Positive externality: exists when the production of a good creates utility (the spillover benefits) for third parties not directly involved in the consumption or production of the good.

Spillover costs: additional costs to society, not captured by the market supply curve from the production of a good, result in a price that is too low and market quantity that is too high. Resources are overallocated to the production of this good.

Negative externality: exists when the production of a good imposes disutility (the spillover costs) upon third parties not directly involved in the consumption or production of the good.

Egalitarianism: the philosophy that all citizens should receive an equal share of the economic resources.

Marginal Productivity Theory: the philosophy that a citizen should receive a share of economic resources proportional to the marginal revenue product of his or her productivity.

Marginal tax rate: the rate paid on the last dollar earned. This is found by taking the ratio of the change in taxes divided by the change in income.

Average tax rate: the proportion of total income paid to taxes. It is calculated by dividing the total taxes owed by the total taxable income.

Progressive tax: the proportion of income paid in taxes rises as income rises. An example is the personal income tax.

Tax bracket: a range of income on which a given marginal tax rate is applied.

Regressive tax: the proportion of income paid in taxes decreases as income rises. An example is a sales tax.

Proportional tax: a constant proportion of income is paid in taxes no matter the level of income. An example is a "flat tax" or the corporate income tax.

CHAPTER 12

Macroeconomic Measures of Performance

Technically, this is the first chapter in the review of macroeconomics, but both AP Microeconomics and Macroeconomics courses begin with coverage of "Basic Economic Concepts," a section that includes the following topics:

- *Scarcity, choice and opportunity costs*
- *Production possibilities curve*
- *Comparative advantage, specialization, and exchange*
- *Demand, supply, and market equilibrium*

If you are reviewing only macroeconomics, or have decided to begin your review with macroeconomics, you should begin by working through Chapters 5 and 6 before returning to Chapter 12.

IN THIS CHAPTER

Summary: Should we raise or lower interest rates? Should we cut or increase taxes? The media is always buzzing about some macroeconomic policy intended to make our lives better. What does it mean to do better? How is "better" measured in something as large and complex as the macroeconomy? In general, macroeconomic policies share the goal of stabilizing and improving the economy, and they also share reliance upon statistical measures of economic performance. Though "statistics" might sound like a dirty word to you and your classmates, as AP Macroeconomics test takers, you need to understand how some important measures are, well, measured. Knowing how they are measured provides you with a much better way of responding to exam questions that ask you to use theoretical models to fix a macroeconomic problem. You cannot speak intelligently about growing the economy until you know how economic growth is measured. Likewise, if you want to perform better on the AP Economics exams, you might want to know exactly how those statistics (your grade) are compiled and study accordingly. This chapter introduces measurement of economic production and paves the way for models of the macroeconomy and policies intended to improve this economic performance.

Key Ideas:
- ✪ The Circular Flow Model
- ✪ Gross Domestic Product
- ✪ Real vs. Nominal
- ✪ Inflation and the Consumer Price Index
- ✪ Unemployment

12.1 The Circular Flow Model

Main Topic: *Circular Flow Model of a Closed Economy*

The Circular Flow Model

"What comes around goes around." If you remember nothing else about the circular flow model, remember this old phrase. **The circular flow of goods and services (or circular flow of economic activity)** is a model of an economy showing the interactions among households, firms, and government as they exchange goods and services and resources in markets. In other words, it is a game of "follow the dollars."

Figure 12.1 illustrates a model of a **closed economy**, where the foreign markets are not assumed (yet) to exist. Domestic households offer their resources to firms in the resource market so that those firms can produce goods and services. The households are paid competitive prices for those resources. They use that income to consume the very goods that were produced through the employment of their productive resources. Revenues from the sale of goods and services are then used to provide income to those households. In this simplified model, every dollar of income in the household ends up as revenue for the firm.

"What About the Government?"

Though not pictured in Figure 12.1 the government plays an important role in the circular flow model. The government is an employer of inputs and a producer of goods and services. The government collects taxes both from households and firms and uses the funds to pay for the inputs that they employ.

"How Much Economic Activity is Being Generated?"

We can add up all of the dollars earned as income by resource owners; or we can add up all of the spending done on goods and services; or we can add up the value of all of those goods and services.

"Where Does it Begin, Where Does it End?"

It doesn't matter; it's the counting of the dollars that is the important first step in measuring economic performance.

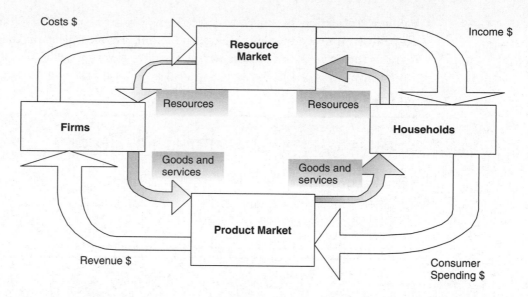

Figure 12.1

Macroeconomic Goals

Figure 12.1 implies that a steady flow of goods and dollars circulating throughout the economy is necessary or commerce ceases. The big issue is how we keep this flow strong, and how we know when it is weak. Measuring success is the focus of the sections that follow. Most modern societies maintain the fairly broad goal of keeping spending and production in the macroeconomy strong without drastically increasing prices.

12.2 Accounting for Output and Income

Main Topics: *Valuing Production, Gross Domestic Product (GDP), National Income Concepts, Real and Nominal GDP, The GDP Deflator, Business Cycles*

Valuing Production

The key here is to measure the value of the goods that are produced, not just the amount of goods that are produced. Remember the circular flow? If we need to follow the dollars to measure economic activity, we need to know prices of these goods.

Value of Production, Not Just Production

When you track the monthly production of a small coffee shop, you could sum up all of the cappuccinos, café lattes, and scones that were purchased. Table 12.1 represents the output in two recent months. At first glance, the two months produced the same amount (100) of goods, but clearly the mix of goods at the coffee shop is different.

Production

Table 12.1

JANUARY			FEBRUARY		
# of Cappuccinos	# of Café Lattes	# of Scones	# of Cappuccinos	# of Café Lattes	# of Scones
25	25	50	30	30	40

Valuing Production

To paint a more accurate picture of production, we need to incorporate the value of these items as shown in Table 12.2.

Table 12.2

JANUARY	QUANTITY	PRICES	VALUE OF PRODUCTION
Cappuccinos	25	$3.00	$75
Café Lattes	25	$2.50	$62.50
Scones	50	$1.50	$75
Totals	100		$212.50
FEBRUARY			
Cappuccinos	30	$3.00	$90
Café Lattes	30	$2.50	$75
Scones	40	$1.50	$60
Totals	100		$225

While the total production at the coffee shop remained the same from month to month, the value of that production has increased in February. There are now more dollars circulating.

- Don't just add up the quantities; multiply by prices and add up the values.

Gross Domestic Product (GDP)

Aggregation, not Aggravation

To move from valuing production of one firm to the entire town, to the state, or to the U.S. economy, we need to **aggregate**. Simply stated, we need to value all production of all firms and then add them up to get the value of production for the entire domestic economy. It is this aggregated measure of the total value of domestic production that allows us to calculate our first important macroeconomic statistic, **GDP**. GDP is the market value of the final goods and services produced within a nation in a year. If the good or service is produced within the borders of the United States, it counts toward U.S. GDP. It does not matter if the firm is headquartered in Indonesia; so long as it is producing in Indiana, it appears in the U.S. GDP.

What's In, What's Out

Final goods are those that are ready for consumption. A bottle of ketchup at the Piggly Wiggly is counted. **Intermediate goods** are those that require further processing before they are counted as a final good. When the tomatoes used to make ketchup are purchased from a grower, they are not counted toward the GDP. At least not until those tomatoes, and their value, find themselves in a bottle of ketchup and sold at the supermarket. A raw material like a tomato might be bought and sold several times before it appears as a final product. If we were to count the dollars at every stage of this process, we would be **double counting,** and this is to be avoided. Suppose the tomatoes go through three stages: harvest, processing, and retail sale as a bottle of ketchup. Along the way a pound of tomatoes is sold, bought, and altered. The pound of tomatoes was sold from the grower to the processor for 50 cents.

The bottle of ketchup was sold to a grocery store for $1.50 and eventually the ketchup was sold to a consumer for $3. If we added all of these transactions, we come up with $5, which overstates the value of the good in its final use. GDP only adds the final transaction as the value of the final good produced and consumed.

Second-hand sales are not counted. This falls under the "do not double count" rule. If you buy a new Xbox in 2002 at Circuit City, it would count in the GDP for 2002. If you resell it on eBay in 2004, it is not counted again. Final goods and services are only counted once, in the year in which they were produced.

Nonmarket transactions are not counted toward GDP. For example, if I have a clogged drain in my kitchen I have two choices: fix it myself, or call the plumber and pay to have it fixed. Doing it myself does not contribute to GDP, but paying a plumber to do it does. The same job is done, but only the latter ends up in the books. In a similar way, regular housework done at home by an unpaid member of the household is not counted, though it is very much a productive effort. This reality is sometimes cited as a criticism of GDP accounting: some valuable services are counted and others are not.

Underground economy transactions are not counted. For obvious reasons, the illegal sale of goods or services or paying someone cash "under the table" for work are not counted. Informal bartering between individuals is also not counted. You might help a friend study for economics while they help you study for biology, but this kind of bartering would not appear on any official ledger of production, even though it might be quite productive.

As a practical matter, official tabulation of GDP is never 100 percent accurate because the value of final goods and services is based upon a survey of representative firms, not a complete census of all firms throughout the nation. Despite this methodology, economists work very hard to get a fairly accurate picture of the value of a nation's production.

Aggregate Spending

Since GDP is measured by adding up the value of the final goods and services produced in a given year, we just need to figure out from where this spending is coming. Spending on output is done by four sectors of the macroeconomy.

Consumer Spending (*C*): The largest component of GDP is the spending done by consumers. Consumers purchase services, like tax preparation or a college degree. Consumers also consume nondurable goods, like food, which are those goods that are consumed in under a year. Durable goods, like a jet ski, are goods expected to last a year or more.

Investment Spending (*I*): Investment is defined as current spending in order to increase output or productivity later. There are three general types of investment that are included in GDP:

- *New capital machinery purchased by firms.* A fleet of delivery trucks produced for UPS, or a new air conditioning system at a Holiday Inn.
- *New construction for firms or consumers.* A new store built for the Gap is investment spending. New residential housing (apartments or homes) is considered investment spending since it is expected to provide housing services for years.
- *Market value of the change in unsold inventories.* If GM produces a new Cadillac in 2003 but it remains unsold on December 31, 2003, it would not be counted as consumer spending in 2003. It would appear in *I* as unsold inventory. Later, when it is eventually sold, it is added to *C* and deducted from *I*.

Government Spending (*G*): The government, at all levels, purchases final goods and services and invests in infrastructure. These include police cars, the services provided by social workers, computers for the Pentagon, or Humvees for the Marines. Infrastructure investments include highways, an airport, and a new county jail.

Note: Government transfer payments to citizens who qualify for government benefits (e.g., retired veterans) amount to sizeable government expenditures, but do not count toward GDP because these are not dollars spent on the production of goods and services.

Net Exports (*X − M*): We should add any domestically produced goods purchased by foreign consumers (exports = *X*) but subtract any spending by our citizens on purchases of goods made within other nations (imports = *M*). This way we include dollars flowing into our economy, and acknowledge that some dollars flow out and land in other economies.

Most macroeconomic policies, directly or indirectly, influence GDP. Knowing components of GDP is very useful when you are tested on policies.

Aggregate Spending (GDP) = *C* + *I* + *G* + *(X − M)*

National Income Concepts

The basic circular flow model tells us that if we add up all of the spending, it equals all of the income, and either measure provides us with GDP. This simplicity is a bit deceiving, because in practice there are several necessary accounting entries that complicate matters. We keep it simple enough for the AP exam and leave the accounting to those who wear the pocket protectors.

Aggregate Income

Calculating GDP from the income half of the circular flow (a.k.a. "The Income Approach") must begin with incomes that are paid to the suppliers of resources. These are the households and they supply labor, land, capital, and entrepreneurial talents. See Table 12.3. Payments to these resources are usually referred to as wages, rents, interest, and profits. With some accounting adjustments, the sum of all income sources is approximately equal to the sum of all spending sources, or GDP.

Table 12.3

RESOURCE SUPPLIED	INCOME RECEIVED
Labor	Wages
Land	Rent
Capital	Interest
Entrepreneurial Talent	Profits

K.I.S.S. Keep it Simple, Silly

National income accounting makes my head spin and studying it usually sends students off to their guidance counselors to investigate majoring in Scandinavian poetry. If we focus on the simplicities of the circular flow model, we can use the relationships between income and spending with some powerful results.

GDP = *C* + *I* + *G* + *(X − M)* = Aggregate Spending

= Aggregate Income (*Y*)

- The most recent AP Macroeconomics curriculum focuses on GDP, or total spending, as the nation's measure of economic output. Your study should therefore focus on the components of GDP.

Real and Nominal GDP

Remember that calculation of GDP requires that we take production of goods and services and apply the value of those items. But we know that prices change, so when we compare GDP from one year to the next, we have to account for changing prices. Reporting that GDP has risen without acknowledging that this is simply because prices have risen doesn't tell a very accurate story. We need a way to compare GDP over time by accounting for different prices over time.

Example:

Our small coffee shop, in 2002, sold 1000 café lattes at a price of $2 each. The total value of this production is $2000. In 2003, firms across town experienced a higher cost of living and so the coffee shop increased the price of a latte to $3 and still sold 1000. The total value of the production has shown an increase of $1000, but production didn't increase at all.

Nominal GDP: The value of current production at the current prices. Valuing 2003 production with 2003 prices creates nominal GDP in 2003. This is also known as current-dollar GDP or "money" GDP.

Real GDP: The value of current production, but using prices from a fixed point in time. Valuing 2003 production at 2002 prices creates real GDP in 2003 and allows us to compare it back to 2002. This is also known as constant-dollar or real GDP.

Keepin' it Real, an Espresso Example

Suppose GDP is made up of just one product, cups of latte. Table 12.4 shows how many lattes have been made in a four-year period, the prices, and a price index. We need a **price index** in order to calculate real GDP. This index is a measure of the price of a good in a given year, when compared to the price of that good in a **reference (or base) year.** Using 2000 as the base year, I'll create a latte index and use it to adjust nominal GDP to real GDP for this one good. First the latte price index, or LPI.

LPI in year t = 100 * (Price of a latte in year t)/(Price of a latte in base year)

Table 12.4

YEAR	# OF LATTES	PRICE PER CUP	NOMINAL GDP	PRICE INDEX	REAL GDP
2000	1000	$2	$2000	= 100*$2/$2 = 100	= $2000
2001	1200	$3	$3600	150	$2400
2002	1800	$4	$7200	200	$3600
2003	1600	$5	$8000	250	$3200

Notice that a price index always equals 100 in the base year. Even if you didn't know the actual price of a latte in 2000, by looking at the LPI, you can see that the price doubled by 2002 since the LPI is 200 compared to the base value of 100.

Deflating Nominal GDP

To deflate a nominal value, or adjust for inflation, you do a simple division:

$$\text{Real GDP} = 100 * (\text{Nominal GDP})/(\text{Price Index}) \text{ or you can think of it as}$$

$$\text{Real GDP} = (\text{Nominal GDP})/(\text{Price Index})(\text{in hundreds})$$

Making this adjustment provides the final column of the above table. While nominal GDP appears to be rapidly rising from 2000 to 2003, you can see that, in real terms, the value of latte production has risen more modestly from 2000 to 2002, but actually fell in 2003.

Using Percentages

Another way to look at the relationship between a price index, real GDP, and nominal GDP is to look at them in terms of percentage change.

$$\%\Delta \text{ Real GDP} = \%\Delta \text{ Nominal GDP} - \%\Delta \text{ Price Index}$$

Example:
If nominal GDP increased by 5 percent and the price index increased by 1 percent, we could say that real GDP increased by 4 percent.

The GDP Deflator

GDP is constructed by aggregating the consumption and production of thousands of goods and services. The prices of these many goods that comprise GDP are used to construct a price index informally called the **GDP price deflator.** Nominal GDP is deflated, with this price index, to create real GDP. Economists watch real GDP to look for signs of economic growth and recession. We see these changes in real GDP by looking at the business cycle.

Business Cycles

The **business cycle** is the periodic rise and fall in economic activity, and can be measured by changes in real GDP. Figure 12.2 is a simplification of a complete business cycle. In general, there are four phases of the cycle.

- **Expansion:** A period where real GDP is growing.
- **Peak:** The top of the cycle where an expansion has run its course and is about to turn down.

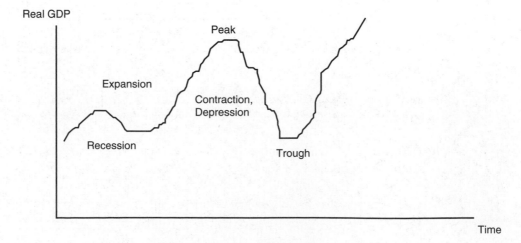

Figure 12.2

- **Contraction:** A period where real GDP is falling. A **recession** is generally described as two consecutive quarters of falling real GDP. If the contraction is prolonged or deep enough, it is called a **depression.**
- **Trough:** The bottom of the cycle where a contraction has stopped and is about to turn up.

- *Though it is an imperfect measure, GDP is used as a measure of economic prosperity and growth.*
- *You must focus on real GDP, not nominal.*
- *Nominal GDP is deflated to real GDP by dividing by the price index known as the GDP deflator.*

This chapter stressed that we need to know how economic activity is measured so that we can understand how and why policies can be used to strengthen the economy. Real GDP is one of these important economic indicators, and probably the most all-encompassing of macroeconomic measures of performance, but not the only one. The economic indicators of inflation and unemployment are also targets of economic policy and are widely covered by the media. Before getting to macroeconomic models and policy, the next two sections spend some time learning more about what these statistics do, and do not, tell us.

12.3 Inflation and the Consumer Price Index

Main Topics: *Consumer Price Index, Inflation, Is Inflation Bad, Measurement Issues*

My "Latte Price Index" illustrates that a price index can be constructed to measure changes in the price of anything. Another price index, the GDP price deflator, measures the increase in the price level of items that compose GDP. But not all goods that fall into GDP are goods that the everyday household shops for. If United Airlines buys a 767 from Boeing, it falls in GDP, but the price of a new 767 doesn't exactly fall within what we might call consumer spending. We need a statistic that focuses on consumer prices.

The Consumer Price Index (CPI)

To measure the average price level of items that consumers actually buy, use the **Consumer Price Index (CPI).** The Bureau of Labor Statistics (BLS) selects a base year and a **market basket** is compiled of approximately 400 consumer goods and services bought in that year. A monthly survey is conducted in 50 urban areas around the country, and based on the results of this survey, the average prices of the items in the base year market basket is factored into the CPI. Confused yet? Let's do a simple example of a price index for a typical consumer using Table 12.5.

Table 12.5

Items in the Basket	2000 (BASE PERIOD)			2001 (CURRENT PERIOD)	
	Quantity Purchased	Price	Spending	Price	Spending on 2000 Quantities
Chocolate Bars	12	$1.50	$18	$1.75	$21
Concert Tickets	4	$45	$180	$60	$240
Compact Disks	18	$16	$288	$15	$270
Total Spending			=$486		=$531

Price Index Current Year = 100 * (Spending Current Year)/(Spending Base Year)

2001 Price Index = 100 * (531)/(486) = 109.26

Inflation

In the above example, the price index increased from 100 in the base year to 109.26 in 2001. In other words, the average price level increased by 9.26 percent.

On a much larger scale, the official CPI is constructed and used to measure the increase in the average price level of consumer goods. The annual rate of **inflation** on goods consumed by the typical consumer is the percentage change in the CPI from one year to the next.

"So What Is the Difference Between the CPI and the GDP Deflator?"

"Know these things for multiple-choice especially."
—Lucas, AP Student

This can be confusing. The difference between these two price indices lies in the content of the market basket of goods. The CPI is based upon a market basket of goods that are bought by consumers, even those goods that are produced abroad. The GDP deflator includes all items that make up domestic production. Because GDP includes more than just consumer goods, the index is a broader measure of inflation, while the CPI is a measure of inflation of only consumer goods.

- *Consumer Inflation Rate = 100 * (CPI New − CPI Old)/CPI Old*
- *If you wished to calculate the rate of price inflation for all goods produced in a nation, you would use the GDP deflator and not the CPI.*

Nominal and Real Income

As a consumer, I am also a worker and an income earner. Rising consumer prices hurt my ability to purchase the items that make me happy. In other words, rising prices can cause a decrease in my purchasing power. Ideally, I would like to see my income rise at a faster rate than the price of consumer goods. One way to see if this is happening is to deflate nominal income by the CPI to calculate my real income. Real income is calculated in the same way that real GDP is calculated.

- **Real Income This Year = 8(Nominal Income This Year)/CPI (in hundredths)**

Example:

In 2002 Kelsey's nominal income is $40,000 and it increases to $41,000 in 2003. Curious about her purchasing power, she looks up the CPI in 2002 and finds that at the end of 2002 it was 181.6 and at the end of 2003 it was 185. This is compared to the base year value of 100 in 1984.

Real Income 2002 = $40,000/1.816 = $22,026

Real Income 2003 = $41,000/1.85 = $22,162

After accounting for inflation, real income increased by $136. Her nominal income increased at a rate slightly faster than the rate of inflation, and so her purchasing power has slightly increased.

Example:

What if Kelsey's wages were frozen and she did not receive that raise in 2003?

Real Income 2003 = $40,000/1.85 = $21,622,

or a $404 decrease in purchasing power

KEY IDEA

"Make sure you understand the difference between expected and unexpected inflation."
—AP Teacher

Is Inflation Bad?

The previous example illustrates that inflation erodes the purchasing power of consumers if nominal wages do not keep up with prices. In general, inflation impacts different groups in different ways. It can actually help some individuals! The main thing to keep in mind with inflation is that it is the unexpected or sudden inflation that creates winners and losers. If the inflation is predictable and expected, most groups can plan for it and adjust behavior and prices accordingly.

Expected Inflation

If my employer and I agree that the general price level is going to increase by 3 percent next year, then my salary can be adjusted by at least 3 percent so that my purchasing power does not fall. This **cost of living adjustment** doesn't hurt my employer so long as the prices of the firm's output and any other inputs also increase by 3 percent. Many unions and government employees have cost of living raises written into employment contracts to recognize predictable inflation over time.

Banks and other lenders acknowledge inflation by factoring expected inflation into interest rates. If they do not, savers and lenders can be hurt by rising prices. For this reason, the bank adds an inflation factor on the **real rate** of interest to create a **nominal rate** of interest that savers receive and borrowers pay.

TIP

Nominal Interest Rate = Real Interest Rate + Expected Inflation

Savings Example 1:

When I see the bank offering an interest rate of 1 percent for a savings account and I put $100 in the bank, I expect to have $101 worth of purchasing power a year from now. But if prices increase by 2 percent, my original deposit is only worth $98. So even when I receive my $1 of interest, I have lost purchasing power.

If you have a savings account, the real rate is the rate the bank pays you to borrow your money for a year. You must be compensated for this because you do not have $100 to spend if you put it into the bank. Look at my savings example again with an inflation expectation of 2 percent and a real interest rate of 1 percent.

Savings Example 2:

- January 1: The purchasing power of my $100 is $100 and the bank offers me a 3 percent nominal interest rate on a savings account.
- Throughout the year, inflation is indeed 2 percent.
- December 31: My bank balance says $103, but $2 of purchasing power has been lost to inflation, leaving me with $1 as payment from the bank for having my money for one year.

Borrowing Example:

If you are looking for a loan of $100, the real interest is the rate the bank will charge you for borrowing the bank's money for a year. After all, if the bank lends the money to you, it will not have those funds for some other profitable opportunity. Again, let's assume that the expected inflation is 2 percent but the real rate of interest is 3 percent.

- January 1: The purchasing power of the bank's $100 is $100 and the bank lends it to me with a 5 percent nominal interest rate.

- Throughout the year, inflation is indeed 2 percent.
- December 31: I pay the bank back $105, but $2 of the bank's purchasing power has been lost to inflation, leaving it with $3 as payment from me for having its money for one year.

- So long as the actual inflation is identical to the expected inflation, workers, employers, savers, lenders, and borrowers are not harmed by the inflation.

Unexpected Inflation

When price levels are unpredictable or increase by a much larger or much smaller amount than predicted, some sectors of the economy gain and others lose. Though not a comprehensive list, some of the groups that win and lose from unexpected inflation include the following.

- *Employees and Employers.* If the real income of workers is falling because of rapid inflation, it is possible that firms are benefiting at the expense of the workers. In a simple case, you work at a grocery store and the price of groceries unexpectedly rises by 10 percent a year, but your nominal wages rise by 8 percent. Your employer is clearly benefiting by selling goods at higher and higher prices but paying you wages that are rising more slowly.
- *Fixed Income Recipients.* A retiree receiving a pension can expect to see it slowly eroded by rising prices. Likewise a landlord who is locked into a long-term lease receives payments that slowly decline in purchasing power. If the minimum wage is not adjusted for inflation then minimum wage workers see a decline in their purchasing power.
- *Savers and Borrowers.* If I put my money in the bank and leave it for a year when inflation is higher than expected, and then withdraw it, the purchasing power is greatly diminished. On the other hand, if I borrow from the bank at the beginning of that year and pay it back after higher than expected inflation, I am giving back dollars that are not worth as much as they used to be. This benefits me and hurts the bank.

- Rapid unexpected inflation usually hurts employees if real wages are falling, fixed income recipients, savers, and lenders.
- Rapid unexpected inflation usually helps firms if real wages are falling, and borrowers. It might also increase the value of some assets like real estate or other properties.

Difficulties with the CPI

Like all statistical measures, we should be careful not to read too much into them and acknowledge that they all have some problematic issues.

- *Consumers substitute:* The market basket uses consumption patterns from the base year, which could be several years ago. As the price of goods begins to rise, we know that consumers seek substitutes. This substitution might make the base year market basket a poor representation of the current consumption pattern.
- *Goods evolve:* Imagine if the CPI market basket were using 1912 as a base year. The basket would include the price of buggy whips and stove pipe hats in the inflation rate. The emergence of new products (DVD players) and extinction of others (manual typewriters) is understood by firms and consumers, but the market basket must reflect this or it risks becoming irrelevant.
- *Quality differences:* Some price increases are the result of improvements in quality. As automakers improve safety features, luxury options, and mechanical sophistication,

we should expect the price to rise. Prices that increase because the product is fundamentally better are not an indication of overall inflation. Because the Bureau of Labor Statistics (BLS) has a difficult time telling the difference between quality improvements and actual inflation, the CPI can be overstated for this reason.

If the market basket is not altered to account for the above effects, the CPI is not very accurate. The BLS reviews the market basket from time to time and updates it if necessary. Comparisons over long periods of time are not very useful, but from month to month and year to year, the CPI is a fairly useful measure of how the average price level of consumer items is changing.

12.4 Unemployment

Main Topics: *Measuring Unemployment Rates, Types of Unemployment*

Whenever an economy has idle, or unemployed, resources, it is operating inside the production possibility frontier. Though unemployment can describe any idle resource, it is almost always applied to labor.

The Unemployment Rate

Is an infant unemployed? What about an 85-year-old retiree? A parent staying home with young children? Before we can calculate an unemployment rate, we must first define who is a candidate for employment. Once again, a monthly survey is conducted by the Bureau of Labor Statistics (BLS) and through a series of questions they classify all persons in a surveyed household above the age of 16 into one of three groups: "Employed" for pay at least one hour per week; "Unemployed" but looking for work; or "Out of the Labor Force." If a person is out of the labor force he has chosen to not seek employment. Our retiree and stay-at-home parent of young children would fall into this category. Many students, at least those who choose not to work, also fall in this latter category.

The **labor force** is the sum of all individuals 16 years and older who are either currently employed (E) or unemployed (U). To be counted as one of the unemployed, you must be actively searching for work.

$$LF = E + U$$

The **unemployment rate** is the ratio of unemployed to the total labor force.

$$UR = U/LF$$

Example:

Table 12.6 summarizes the 2002 and 2003 labor market in Smallville.

Table 12.6

	POPULATION	OUT OF THE LABOR FORCE	EMPLOYED	UNEMPLOYED	LABOR FORCE = E + U	UNEMPLOYMENT RATE = U/LF
2002	1800	800	900	100	1000	=10%
2003	1800	820	900	80	980	=8.2%

In 2002, 100 citizens are unemployed but are seeking work and the reported unemployment rate is 10 percent. After a year of searching, 20 of these unemployed citizens become tired of looking for work and move back home to live in the basement of their parent's home. These **discouraged workers** are not counted in the ranks of the unemployed and this results in an unemployment rate that falls to 8.2 percent. On the surface, the economy looks to be improving, but these 20 individuals have *not* found employment. The statistic hides their presence.

To give you an idea of the statistical impact that discouraged workers have on the official unemployment rate, we can look at labor force data from March 2007. The Bureau of Labor Statistics estimated a U.S. labor force of 152,979,000 people and of those, 6,724,000 were counted as unemployed. The March 2007 official unemployment rate was 4.4 percent. However, there were an estimated 381,000 people who were not in the labor force because they were discouraged over their job prospects. If you add these people to the ranks of the unemployed and also to the labor force, the adjusted unemployment rate increases to 4.6 percent.

- The presence of discouraged workers understates the true unemployment rate.

Types of Unemployment

"Be sure to give examples of each type."
—AP Teacher

People are unemployed for different reasons. Some of these reasons are predictable and relatively harmless and others can even be beneficial to the individual and the economy. Others reasons for lost jobs are quite damaging, however, and policies need to target these types of job loss.

Frictional Unemployment: This type of unemployment occurs when someone new enters the labor market or switches jobs. Frictional unemployment can happen voluntarily if a person is seeking a better match for his or her skills, or has just finished schooling, and is usually short lived. Employers who fire employees for poor work habits or sub-par performance also contribute to the level of frictional unemployment. The provision of unemployment insurance for six months allows for a cushion to these events and assists the person in finding a job compatible with his or her skills. Because frictional unemployment is typically a short-term phenomenon, it is considered the least troublesome for the economy as a whole.

Seasonal Unemployment: This type of unemployment emerges as the periodic and predictable job loss that follows the calendar. Agricultural jobs are gained and lost as crops are grown and harvested. Teens are employed during the summers and over the holidays, but most are not employed during the school year. Summer resorts close in the winter and winter ski lodges close in the spring. Workers and employers alike anticipate these changes in employment and plan accordingly, thus the damage is minimal. The BLS accounts for the seasonality of some employment, so such factors are not going to affect the published unemployment rate.

Structural Unemployment: This type of unemployment is caused by fundamental, underlying changes in the economy that can create job loss for skills that are no longer in demand. A worker who manually tightened bolts on the assembly line can be structurally replaced by robotics. In cases of technological unemployment like this, the job skills of the worker need to change to suit the new workplace. In some cases of structural employment, jobs are lost because the product is no longer in demand, probably because a better product has replaced it. This market evolution is inevitable, so the more flexible the skills of the workers, the less painful this kind of structural change. Government-provided job training and subsidized public universities help the structurally unemployed help themselves.

Cyclical Unemployment: Jobs are gained and lost as the business cycle improves and worsens. The unemployment rate rises when the economy is contracting, and the unemployment rate falls as the economy is expanding. This form of unemployment is usually felt throughout the economy rather than on certain subgroups and therefore policies are going to focus on stimulating job growth throughout the economy. Structural unemployment might be forever but cyclical unemployment only lasts as long as it takes to get through the recession.

Full Employment

Economists acknowledge that frictional and structural unemployment are always present. In fact, in a rapidly evolving economy, these are often beneficial in the long run. Because of these forms of unemployment, the unemployment rate can never be zero. Economists define **full employment** as the situation when there is no cyclical unemployment in the economy. The unemployment rate associated with full employment is called the **natural rate of unemployment** and in the United States this rate has traditionally been 5–6 percent. However, the recent prolonged economic expansion of the mid-1990s has caused some economists to revise this estimate to maybe 4 percent.

› Review Questions

1. Which of the following transactions would be counted in GDP?

   (A) The wage you receive from babysitting your neighbor's kids.
   (B) The sale of illegal drugs.
   (C) The sale of cucumbers to a pickle manufacturer.
   (D) The sale of a pound of tomatoes at a supermarket.
   (E) The resale of a sweater you received from your great aunt at Christmas that you never wore on eBay.

2. GDP is $10 million, consumer spending is $6 million, government spending is $3 million, exports are $2 million, and imports are $3 million. How much is spent for investments?

   (A) $0 million
   (B) $1 million
   (C) $2 million
   (D) $3 million
   (E) $4 million

3. If Real GDP = $200 billion and the price index = 200, Nominal GDP is

   (A) $4 billion.
   (B) $400 billion.
   (C) $200 billion.
   (D) $2 billion.
   (E) impossible to determine since the base year is not given.

For questions 4 to 5 use the information below for a small town.

Total Population:	2000
Total Employed Adults:	950
Total Unemployed Adults:	50

4. What is the size of the labor force?

   (A) 2000
   (B) 950
   (C) 900
   (D) 1000
   (E) 1950

5. What is the unemployment rate?

   (A) 5 percent
   (B) 2.5 percent
   (C) 5.5 percent
   (D) 7 percent
   (E) Unknown, as we do not know the number of discouraged workers.

6. You are working at a supermarket bagging groceries but you are unhappy about your wage so you quit and begin looking for a new job at a competing grocery store. What type of unemployment is this?

   (A) Cyclical
   (B) Structural
   (C) Seasonal
   (D) Frictional
   (E) Discouraged

› Answers and Explanations

1. **D**—The supermarket tomatoes are the only final good sale and are counted. Babysitting is a non-market, cash "under the table," service. The sale of illegal drugs is a part of an underground economy. The sale of the cucumbers is an intermediate good. The resale of the sweater, even though it was never worn, is a second-hand sale. When your great aunt originally purchased it at the mall, it was counted in GDP.

2. **C**—GDP = $C + I + G + (X − M)$. This would mean that $10 = 6 + I + 3 + (2 − 3)$ therefore $I = \$2$ million.

3. **B**—Nominal GDP/price index (in hundredths) = real GDP. Use this relationship to solve for Nominal GDP. $200 = $ (Nominal GDP)/2. Nominal GDP = $400 billion.

4. **D**—Labor force is the employed + the unemployed. LF = 950 + 50 = 1000. The remaining citizens are out of the labor force.

5. **A**—The unemployment rate is the ratio of unemployed to the total labor force. UR = U/LF = 50/1000 = 5%.

6. **D**—Frictional unemployment occurs when a person is in between jobs. This person has not been laid off due to a structural change in the demand for skills, or because of a cyclical economic downturn, or because of a new season. A low wage might be discouraging; a discouraged worker is a worker who has been unemployed for so long that he or she has ceased the search for work.

› Rapid Review

Circular flow of economic activity: a model that shows how households and firms circulate resources, goods, and incomes through the economy. This basic model is expanded to include the government and the foreign sector.

Closed economy: a model that assumes there is no foreign sector (imports and exports).

Aggregation: the process of summing the microeconomic activity of households and firms into a more macroeconomic measure of economic activity.

Gross Domestic Product (GDP): the market value of the final goods and services produced within a nation in a given period of time.

Final goods: goods that are ready for their final use by consumers and firms, e.g., a new Harley-Davidson motorcycle.

Intermediate goods: goods that require further modification before they are ready for final use, e.g., steel used to produce the new Harley.

Double counting: the mistake of including the value of intermediate stages of production in GDP on top of the value of the final good.

Second-hand sales: final goods and services that are resold. Even if they are resold many times, final goods and services are only counted once, in the year in which they were produced.

Nonmarket transactions: household work or do-it-yourself jobs are missed by GDP accounting. The same is true of government transfer payments and purely financial transactions like the purchase of a share of IBM stock.

Underground economy: these include unreported illegal activity, bartering, or informal exchange of cash.

Aggregate Spending (GDP): the sum of all spending from four sectors of the economy. GDP = $C + I + G + (X - M)$.

Aggregate Income (AI): the sum of all income earned by suppliers of resources in the economy. With some accounting adjustments, aggregate spending equals aggregate income.

Nominal GDP: the value of current production at the current prices. Valuing 2003 production with 2003 prices creates nominal GDP in 2003.

Real GDP: the value of current production, but using prices from a fixed point in time. Valuing 2003 production at 2002 prices creates real GDP in 2003 and allows us to compare it back to 2002.

Base year: the year that serves as a reference point for constructing a price index and comparing real values over time.

Price index: a measure of the average level of prices in a market basket for a given year, when compared to the prices in a reference (or base) year. You can interpret the price index as the current price level as a percentage of the level in the base year.

Market basket: a collection of goods and services used to represent what is consumed in the economy.

GDP price deflator: the price index that measures the average price level of the goods and services that make up GDP.

Real rate of interest: the percentage increase in purchasing power that a borrower pays a lender.

Expected (Anticipated) Inflation: the inflation expected in a future time period. This expected inflation is added to the real interest rate to compensate for lost purchasing power.

Nominal rate of interest: the percentage increase in money that the borrower pays the lender and is equal to the real rate plus the expected inflation.

Business cycle: the periodic rise and fall (in four phases) of economic activity.

Expansion: a period where real GDP is growing.

Peak: the top of a business cycle where an expansion has ended.

Contraction: a period where real GDP is falling.

Recession: two consecutive quarters of falling real GDP.

Trough: the bottom of the cycle where a contraction has stopped.

Depression: a prolonged, deep contraction in the business cycle.

Consumer Price Index (CPI): the price index that measures the average price level of the items in the base year market basket. This is the main measure of consumer inflation.

Inflation: the percentage change in the CPI from one period to the next.

Nominal income: today's income measured in today's dollars. These are dollars unadjusted by inflation.

Real income: today's income measured in base year dollars. These inflation-adjusted dollars can be compared from year to year to determine whether purchasing power has increased or decreased.

Employed: a person is employed if she has worked for pay at least one hour per week.

Unemployed: a person is unemployed if he is not currently working but is actively seeking work.

Labor force: the sum of all individuals 16 years and older who are either currently employed (E) or unemployed (U). LF = E + U.

Out of the labor force: a person is classified as out of the labor force if he has chosen to not seek employment.

Unemployment rate: the percentage of the labor force that falls into the unemployed category. Sometimes called the *jobless rate*. UR = 100*U/LF.

Discouraged workers: citizens who have been without work for so long that they become tired of looking for work and drop out of the labor force. Because these citizens are not counted in the ranks of the unemployed, the reported unemployment rate is understated.

Frictional unemployment: a type of unemployment that occurs when someone new enters the labor market or switches jobs. This is a relatively harmless form of unemployment and not expected to last long.

Seasonal unemployment: a type of unemployment that is periodic, predictable, and that follows the calendar. Workers and employers alike anticipate these changes in employment and plan accordingly, thus the damage is minimal.

Structural unemployment: a type of unemployment that is the result of fundamental, underlying changes in the economy such that some job skills are no longer in demand.

Cyclical unemployment: a type of unemployment that rises and falls with the business cycle. This form of unemployment is felt economy-wide, which makes it the focus of macroeconomic policy.

Full employment: exists when the economy is experiencing no cyclical unemployment.

Natural rate of unemployment: the unemployment rate associated with full employment, somewhere between 4–5 percent in the United States.

CHAPTER 13

Consumption, Saving, Investment, and the Multiplier

IN THIS CHAPTER

Summary: Having described GDP as the macroeconomic measure of a nation's output, we begin to build a model that helps to explain how and why GDP fluctuates. As the largest component of GDP, we spend some time on consumption. Investment is also a component of GDP, but because investment plays an important role in monetary policy, we investigate it as well. The market for loanable funds combines savings and investment and is a prelude to the interaction of interest rates and the role of financial institutions. This chapter begins to show how changes in spending affect output and employment through the multiplier process. Discussion of the spending multiplier previews how policy affects the macroeconomy and leads to the aggregate demand and supply model in the next chapter.

Key Ideas

✪ Consumption and Saving Functions
✪ Investment
✪ Market for Loanable Funds
✪ The Spending Multiplier, Tax Multiplier and Balanced-Budget Multiplier

13.1 Consumption and Saving

Main Topics: *Consumption and Saving Functions, Marginal Propensity to Consume and Save, Changes in Consumption Functions*

The circular flow model illustrates the importance of consumption in the production of goods and the employment of resources. A better understanding of consumption allows us to build a model of the macroeconomy and see the role of policy in affecting macroeconomic indicators like GDP, employment, and inflation.

Consumption and Saving Functions

Though not the only factor, the most important element affecting consumption (and savings) is disposable income. **Disposable income (DI)** is what consumers have left over to spend or save once they have paid out their net taxes.

$$\text{DI} = \textbf{Gross Income} - \textbf{Net Taxes} \text{ where net taxes}$$
$$= (\text{taxes paid} - \text{transfers received})$$

With no government transfers or taxation, DI = $C + S$. Though not all consumers save part of their income, typical consumers spend the majority of their disposable income and save whatever is left over. To see the relationship between disposable income and consumption we create a **consumption function**.

Consumption and Saving Schedules
The consumption and saving schedules are the direct relationships between disposable income and consumption and savings. As DI increases for a typical household, C and S both increase. Table 13.1 provides an example.

Table 13.1

DISPOSABLE INCOME (DI)	CONSUMPTION (C)	SAVINGS (S)
0	40	−40
100	120	−20
200	200	0
300	280	20
400	360	40
500	440	60

Consumption
Even with zero disposable income, households still consume as they liquidate wealth (sell assets), spend some savings, or borrow (dissavings). For every additional $100 of disposable income, consumers increase their spending by $80 and increase saving by $20. We can convert the above consumption schedule to a linear equation or **consumption function**:

$$C = 40 + .80(\text{DI})$$

The constant $40 is referred to as **autonomous consumption** because it does not change as DI changes. The slope of the consumption function is .80. This function is plotted in Figure 13.1.

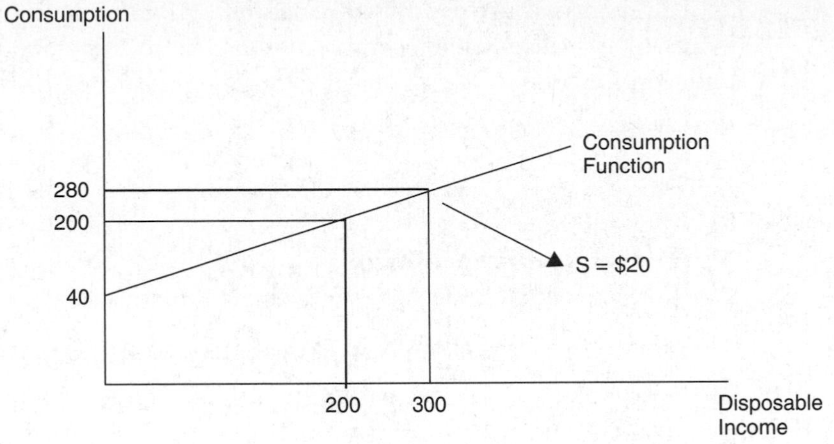

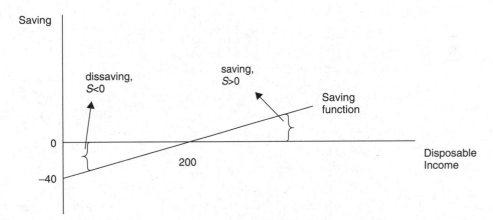

Figure 13.1

At every level of DI, the consumption function tells us how much is consumed. Both Table 13.1 and Figure.13.1 tell us that at incomes below $200, the consumer is consuming more than his income; as a result saving is negative and this is referred to as **dissaving**. But at incomes above $200, the consumer is spending less than his income; and so saving is positive.

Saving

The saving schedule above can also be converted into a linear equation, or **saving function**:

$$S = -40 + .20(DI)$$

Figure 13.2

The constant $ – 40 is referred to as **autonomous saving** because it does not change as DI changes. With zero disposable income, the household would need to borrow $40 to consume $40 worth of goods. The slope of the saving function is .20. This function is plotted in Figure 13.2

Marginal Propensity to Consume and Save

KEY IDEA

An important lesson from the study of microeconomics is the marginal concept. You can think of it in two equivalent ways. Marginal always means an incremental change caused by an external force, or it is always the slope of a "total" function. The same is true here.

The **marginal propensity to consume (MPC)** is the change in consumption caused by a change in disposable income. Another way to think about it is the slope of the consumption function.

$$MPC = \Delta C/\Delta DI = \text{slope of consumption function}$$

Using Table 13.1, we see that for every additional $100 of DI, C increases by $80 so the MPC = .80.

The **marginal propensity to save (MPS)** is the change in saving caused by a change in disposable income. Another way to think about it is the slope of the saving function.

$$MPS = \Delta S/\Delta DI = \text{slope of saving function}$$

Using Table 13.1, we can see that for every additional $100 of DI, S increases by $20 so the MPS = .20.

There is a nice relationship between the MPC and the MPS. For every additional dollar not consumed, it is saved. So if the consumer gains $100 in disposable income, he increases his consumption by $80 and increases saving by $20. In other words, MPC + MPS = 1. If you know one, you can find the other.

- MPC = $\Delta C/\Delta DI$ = constant slope of consumption function.
- MPS = $\Delta S/\Delta DI$ = constant slope of saving function.
- MPC + MPS = 1.

Changes in Consumption and Saving

A change in disposable income causes a movement along the consumption and savings functions. Economists typically recognize four external determinants of household consumption and saving that shift the functions upward or downward.

Determinants of Consumption and Saving

- *Wealth.* When the value of accumulated wealth increases, consumption functions shift upward, and the saving function shifts downward, because households can sell stock or other assets to consume more goods at their current level of disposable income.
- *Expectations.* Uncertainty or a low expectation about future income usually prompts a household to decrease consumption and increase saving. An expectation of a higher future price level spurs higher consumption right now and less saving.
- *Household Debt.* Households can increase consumption with borrowing, or debt. However, as households accumulate more and more debt, they need to use more and more disposable income to pay off the debt, and thus decrease consumption.
- *Taxes and Transfers.* A change in taxes impacts both consumption and saving in the same direction. If the government increases taxes, households see both consumption and saving decrease because more of their gross income is sent to the government. On the other hand, an increase in government transfer payments increases both consumption and saving functions. In the case of taxes and transfers, consumption and saving functions shift in the same way.

An upward shift in consumption tells us that at all levels of disposable income, consumption is greater (C_{High}). If consumption is greater at all levels of disposable income, saving must be lower (S_{Low}), and vice versa. The only exception is the case of taxes and transfers described above. Figures 13.3 and 13.4 illustrate these simultaneous shifts in the opposite directions.

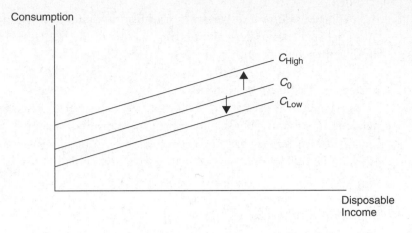

Figure 13.3

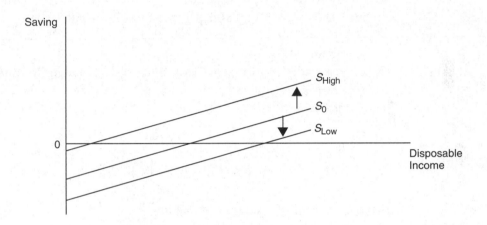

Figure 13.4

- With the exception of taxes and transfers, when the consumption function shifts upward, the saving function shifts downward.
- With the exception of taxes and transfers, when the consumption function shifts downward, the saving function shifts upward.
- When taxes increase (or transfers decrease), both consumption and saving functions shift downward.
- When taxes decrease (or transfers increase), both consumption and saving functions shift upward.

13.2 Investment

Main Topics: *The Decision to Invest, Investment Demand, Investment and GDP, Market for Loanable Funds*

Investment is the other source of private spending. We spend a little time examining why firms increase or decrease investment, build the investment demand curve and then introduce the market for loanable funds.

Decision to Invest

The decision of a firm to spend money on new machinery or construction is simply a decision based upon marginal benefits and marginal costs. The marginal benefit of an investment is the expected real rate of return (r) the firm anticipates receiving on the expenditure. The marginal cost of the investment is the real rate of interest (i), or the cost of borrowing. Let's look at this concept with examples.

Expected Real Rate of Return

A local pizza firm invests $10,000 in a new delivery car. The owner expects this to help to deliver more pizzas, increasing revenues and profits. The car lasts exactly one year and the increased real profits are anticipated to be $2000. This expected real rate of return is $2000/$10,000 = .20 or 20 percent. Of course an actual car lasts more than one year, but this decision to invest is shown for one year to keep it simple, while still making the point.

Real Rate of Interest

The owner goes to the bank and asks for a one-year loan to purchase the new delivery car. The bank offers a nominal rate of interest of 15 percent; this includes 5 percent for expected inflation and 10 percent as the real rate of borrowing the money for a year. At the end of the year, he spends $1000 as real interest on the $10,000 loan.

The Decision

Since the new delivery car provides $2000 in additional real profits ($r = 20\%$), and the loan costs $1000 in real interest ($i = 10\%$), this investment should be made. Another way to make this decision is with a comparison of interest rates.

- If $r\% \geq i\%$, make the investment.
- If $r\% < i\%$, do not make the investment.

Investment Demand

Like any demand curve, the quantity demanded increases as the price falls. The same is true for investment demand. The rational firm invests in all projects up to the point where the real rate of interest equals the expected real rate of return ($i = r$). Very few investment projects are available at extremely high rates of return and so those opportunities are taken first. As the real rate of return (r) falls, those very profitable opportunities are gone, but many less profitable investments remain. So as the expected real rate falls, the cumulative amount of investment dollars rises. Likewise, as the real cost of borrowing (i) falls, more and more projects become worthwhile, so dollars of investment rises. Either way, as interest rates fall, the total amount of investment rises. Figure 13.5 illustrates the **investment demand curve**, which shows the inverse relationship between the interest rate and the cumulative dollars invested. At an interest rate of 5 percent, $20 billion dollars might be invested.

Investment and GDP

In the simple model of private investment outlined in Figure 13.5, there is no mention of GDP or disposable income. With no government or foreign sector, GDP = DI. To keep the model simple, we assume that investment spending (I) is determined from the investment demand curve and is constant at all levels of GDP.

Example:

In Figure 13.5 if the interest rate was 5%, firms would invest $20 billion this year, regardless of the level of disposable income or GDP. This **autonomous investment** is illustrated in Figure 13.6 as a horizontal line with GDP on the x axis. If something happened to interest rates, or to investment demand, autonomous

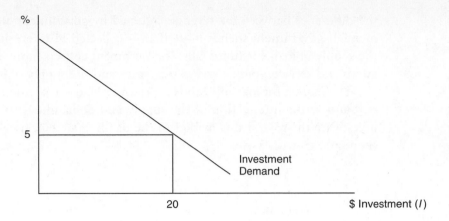

Figure 13.5

Figure 13.6

investment could increase or decrease, but at that new level, would once again be constant at any value of GDP.

Market for Loanable Funds

It is useful to see the relationship between saving and investment by looking at the **market for loanable funds.** When savers place their money in banks or buy bonds, those funds are available to be borrowed by firms for private investment.

Demand for Loanable Funds

The inverse relationship between investment and the real interest rate is fairly straightforward. As the real interest rate falls, borrowing becomes less costly, and large investment projects become more attractive to firms. This investment demand curve can also be thought of as a **demand for loanable funds**.

Supply of Loanable Funds

The **supply of loanable funds** comes from saving on the part of households **(private saving)** and government **(public saving).** If disposable income is greater than consumption, private saving exists, and is positively related to the real interest rate. Public saving is the difference between tax revenue collected by government and dollars spent by government. If government spends more than is collected in taxes, public saving is negative and the supply of loanable funds falls. If government collects more tax revenue than is spent on goods and services, public saving is positive and the supply of loanable funds rises.

The market for loanable funds is shown in Figure 13.7 and the equilibrium interest rate is found at the intersection of the supply and demand curves. In upcoming chapters we investigate the role of this market in the banking system, fiscal and monetary policy, and economic growth.

"Make the connections between concepts learned in a previous chapter to what you are learning now, because everything is cumulative."
—Caroline, AP Student

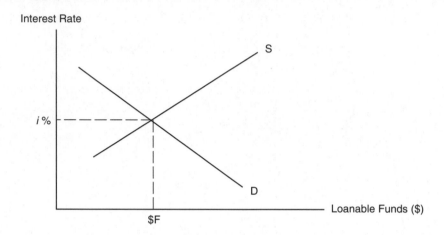

Figure 13.7

- The supply of loanable funds comes from saving.
- The demand for loanable funds comes from investment.
- Equilibrium is at the real interest rate where dollars saved equals dollars invested.

13.3 The Multiplier Effect

Main Topics: *The Multiplier Effect and Spending Multiplier, Public and Foreign Sectors, The Tax Multiplier, Balanced Budget Multiplier*

The most simple circular flow consists solely of consumers and firms; in other words, GDP = C + I. But the public sector (G) and foreign sector (X – M) are also important sources of domestic spending and income. Inclusion of these two sectors provides very little in the way of complications; they introduce the concept of the spending multiplier, the tax multiplier, and the balanced budget multiplier. This also paves the way for fiscal policy aimed at macroeconomic stability.

The Multiplier Effect and Spending Multiplier

When you buy an ear of corn at the farmer's market, those dollars serve as income to several people. The farmers use those dollars to pay employees, to run their farm equipment, and to buy their own food. Farm employees use those wages to buy bacon, pay the rent, and many other goods and services. The circular flow explains how the injection of a few dollars of spending creates many more dollars of spending. Follow the dollars for a few rounds to see how it works. With the marginal propensity to consume of .80, if households receive a $1 of new income they spend $.80 and save $.20.

Round 1:   Firms *increase* **investment spending by $10,** which acts as an injection of new money into the economy.

Round 2:   The **$10** acts as income to resource suppliers (households) and with an MPC = .80, **households spend $8** and save $2.

Round 3:   The **$8** of new consumption spending (*C*) is income for other households and they also spend 80 percent, or **$6.40** and save $1.60.

Round 4:   The **$6.40** of new *C* is income for other households and they spend 80 percent, or **$5.12**, and save $1.28.

This process repeats. Each time the dollars circulate through the economy, 80 percent is spent, and 20 percent is saved. After only four rounds, there has been $10 + 8 + 6.40 + 5.12 = **$29.52 of new GDP**. The process continues until households are trying to consume 80 percent of virtually nothing and the increase in new GDP comes to an eventual stop.

This is called the **multiplier effect**. A change in any component of autonomous spending creates a larger change in GDP. The discussion of the "rounds" of spending above implies that the marginal propensities to consume and save play a critical role in determining the magnitude of the multiplier. There are two equivalent ways to calculate the multiplier if you know the MPC or MPS. The magnitude of the **spending multiplier** is found by taking a ratio:

$$\text{Multiplier} = 1/(1 - \text{MPC}) = 1/(1 - .80) = 5.$$
$$\text{Since MPC} + \text{MPS} = 1,$$
$$\text{Multiplier} = 1/\text{MPS} = 1/.20 = 5.$$

The spending multiplier can be found by using one of the following equations:

- Multiplier = 1/MPS
- Multiplier = 1/(1−MPC)
- Multiplier = (Δ GDP)/(Δ Spending)

Some common autonomous multipliers are:

- MPC = .90, Multiplier = 1/.10 = 10.
- MPC = .80, Multiplier = 1/.20 = 5.
- MPC = .75, Multiplier = 1/.25 = 4.
- MPC = .50, Multiplier =   1/.5 = 2.

The Public and Foreign Sectors

The inclusion of government spending (*G*) and net exports (*X* – *M*) act in the very same way as the change in investment illustrated in the above example.

Government Spending (*G*)

With the MPC =.80, we have found the spending multiplier equal to 5. If autonomous government spending is incorporated into the circular flow model, the multiplier effect is again felt throughout the economy. If *G* = $20, we could expect those $20 to multiply to $100 in new GDP.

Net Exports (*X*– *M*)

The final sector of the macroeconomy is the foreign sector. The addition or subtraction (if imports exceed exports) of autonomous net exports is an increase (or decrease) of dollars in the circular flow. Using a spending multiplier of 5, if $(X - M) = \$10$, GDP would increase by $50.

The Tax Multiplier

The above discussion of the public sector shows that when the government injects money into the economy (G), it multiplies by a factor of the spending multiplier. But the government can also have an impact on aggregate expenditures and real GDP by changing taxes and/or transfers.

The Multiplier Effect

Recipients of a decrease in taxes treat it as an increase in disposable income. The typical household increases consumption by a factor of the MPC and increases saving by a factor of the MPS. It is important to keep in mind that less than 100 percent of this increase in disposable income circulates through the economy because most households save a proportion of it.

> **Example:**
> The MPC is equal to .90, and the government transfers back tax revenue to consumers by sending each taxpayer a $200 check. With an MPC = .90, $180 is consumed and $20 is saved. The multiplier process kicks in, but not on the entire $200, only on the consumed portion of $180. The multiplier being $1/.10 = 10$, GDP increases by $1800.
>
> In other words, a $200 change in tax policy (a tax rebate in this case) caused an $1800 change in real GDP. This tax multiplier of 9 measures the magnitude of the multiplier process when there is a change in taxes.

The Difference in Multipliers

"Remember that taxes will have a smaller multiplier than government spending!"
—Richard, AP Student

With an MPC = .90, the spending multiplier is 10, but the tax multiplier is smaller, Tm = 9. Why? The spending multiplier begins to work as soon as there is a change in autonomous spending $(C, I, G,$ net exports) but the tax multiplier must first go through a person's consumption function as disposable income. In that first "round" of spending, some of those injected dollars are leakages in the form of savings. In our example above, 10 percent of those injected dollars fail to be recirculated and therefore the final multiplier effect is smaller. The relationship between the spending multiplier and the tax multiplier (Tm) is:

$$Tm = MPC * (\text{Spending multiplier}) = .90 * (1/.10) = 9 \text{ in our example}$$

Be prepared to respond to a free-response question that asks you to explain why the tax multiplier is smaller than the spending multiplier.

> **Example:**
> The MPC = .80 and the government decides to impose a $50 increase in taxes. What happens to GDP?
>
> $$Tm = .80 * \text{Multiplier} = .80 * (1/.20) = 4$$
>
> Because the tax multiplier is equal to 4, we determine that GDP falls by $200. How do we know? Because taxes were *increased*, disposable income falls, consumption falls, causing GDP to fall, in this case by a factor of 4.

The tax multiplier is found by:

- Tm = (Δ GDP)/(Δ taxes)
- Tm = MPC * *M* = MPC/MPS

The Balanced-Budget Multiplier

The government both collects and spends tax revenue. In a simplified model, if the dollars spent equal the dollars collected, the budget is balanced. We have already discussed how the spending multiplier and tax multiplier are different. A quick example of a balanced budget policy illustrates what is called the **balanced-budget multiplier.**

Example:

The government wants to spend $100 on a federal program and pay for it by collecting $100 in additional taxes. The MPC = .90 in this example.

Spending Effect

The spending multiplier = 10 implies that the $100 of new spending (*G*) creates a $1000 *increase* in real GDP.

Taxation Effect

The tax multiplier Tm = 9 implies that a $100 increase in taxes *decreases* real GDP by $900.

Balanced Budget Effect

$$\text{Change in real GDP} = +\$1000 - \$900 = +\$100$$

So a $100 increase in spending, financed by a $100 increase in taxes, created only $100 in new GDP. *The balanced-budget multiplier is always equal to one, regardless of the MPC.*

- Balanced-Budget Multiplier = 1

› Review Questions

1. When disposable income increases by $X,

   (A) consumption increases by more than $X.
   (B) saving increases by less than $X.
   (C) saving increases by exactly $X.
   (D) saving remains constant.
   (E) saving decreases by more than $X.

2. Which of the following is true about the consumption function?

   (A) The slope is equal to the MPC.
   (B) The slope is equal to the MPS.
   (C) The slope is equal to MPC + MPS.
   (D) It shifts upward when consumers are more pessimistic about the future.
   (E) It shifts downward when consumer wealth increases in value.

3. Which of the following events most likely increases real GDP?

   (A) An increase in the real rate of interest.
   (B) An increase in taxes.
   (C) A decrease in net exports.
   (D) An increase in government spending.
   (E) A lower value of consumer wealth.

4. Which of the following choices is most likely to create the greatest decrease in real GDP?

   (A) The government decreases spending, matched with a decrease in taxes.
   (B) The government increases spending with no increase in taxes.
   (C) The government decreases spending with no change in taxes.
   (D) The government holds spending constant while increasing taxes.
   (E) The government increases spending, matched with an increase in taxes.

5. The tax multiplier increases in magnitude when

   (A) the MPS increases.
   (B) the spending multiplier falls.
   (C) the MPC increases.
   (D) government spending increases.
   (E) taxes increase.

6. Which of the following is the source of the supply of loanable funds?

   (A) The stock market.
   (B) Investors.
   (C) Net exports.
   (D) Banks and mutual funds.
   (E) Savers.

› Answers and Explanations

1. **B**—A $1 increase in DI increases consumption by a factor of the MPC and increases saving by a factor of the MPS. Because both MPC and MPS represent the fraction of new income that is consumed and saved, consumption and saving increase by less than the increase in DI.

2. **A**—The slope of the consumption function is the MPC. The slope of the saving function is the MPS.

3. **D**—An increase in GDP is the result of an increase in C, I, G, or $(X - M)$. All other choices represent less spending in some economic sector.

4. **C**—Look for choices that decrease GDP by the largest magnitude. Choices B and E actually improve the economy (and GDP) so they are eliminated. A decrease in spending lowers GDP by a magnitude equal to the spending multiplier, which is larger than the tax multiplier, which in turn is larger than the balanced budget multiplier. This question is a prelude to fiscal policy.

5. **C**—Knowing the relationship between the tax and spending multipliers allows you to make the right choice. Tm = MPC * Multiplier = MPC/MPS.

6. **E**—Banks help facilitate lending to investors, but the real supply of those loanable funds are the savers who choose to place some of their disposable income dollars in those banks as saving.

› Rapid Review

Disposable Income (DI): the income a consumer has left over to spend or save once they have paid out their net taxes. DI = $Y - T$.

Consumption and saving schedules: tables that show the direct relationships between disposable income and consumption and saving. As DI increases for a typical household, C and S both increase.

Consumption function: a linear relationship showing how increases in disposable income cause increases in consumption.

Autonomous consumption: the amount of consumption that occurs no matter the level of disposable income. In a linear consumption function, this shows up as a constant and graphically it appears as the y intercept.

Saving function: a linear relationship showing how increases in disposable income cause increases in saving.

Dissaving: another way of saying that saving is less than zero. This can occur at low levels of disposable income when the consumer must liquidate assets or borrow to maintain consumption.

Autonomous saving: the amount of saving that occurs no matter the level of disposable income. In a linear saving function, this shows up as a constant and graphically it appears as the y intercept.

Marginal Propensity to Consume (MPC): the change in consumption caused by a change in disposable income, or the slope of the consumption function. MPC = $\Delta C/\Delta \mathrm{DI}$.

Marginal Propensity to Save (MPS): the change in saving caused by a change in disposable income, or the slope of the saving function. MPS = $\Delta S/\Delta \mathrm{DI}$.

Determinants of Consumption and Saving: factors that shift the consumption and saving functions in the opposite direction are Wealth, Expectations, and Household Debt. The factors that change consumption and saving functions in the same direction are Taxes and Transfers.

Expected real rate of return (r): the rate of real profit the firm anticipates receiving on investment expenditures. This is the marginal benefit of an investment project.

Real rate of interest (i): the cost of borrowing to fund an investment. This can be thought of as the marginal cost of an investment project.

Decision to invest: a firm invests in projects so long as $r \geq i$.

Investment demand: the inverse relationship between the real interest rate and the cumulative dollars invested. Like any demand curve, this is drawn with a negative slope.

Autonomous investment: the level of investment determined by investment demand. It is autonomous because it is assumed to be constant at all levels of GDP.

Market for loanable funds: the market for dollars that are available to be borrowed for investment projects. Equilibrium in this market is determined at the real interest rate where the dollars saved (supply) is equal to the dollars borrowed (demand)

Demand for loanable funds: the negative relationship between the real interest rate and the dollars invested by firms.

Private saving: saving conducted by households and equal to the difference between disposable income and consumption.

Public saving: saving conducted by government and equal to the difference between tax revenue collected and spending on goods and services.

Supply of loanable funds: the positive relationship between the dollars saved and the real interest rate.

Multiplier effect: describes how a change in any component of aggregate expenditures creates a larger change in GDP.

Spending multiplier: the magnitude of the spending multiplier effect is calculated as = $(\Delta\text{GDP})/(\Delta\text{ spending})$ = $1/\text{MPS}$ = $1/(1 - \text{MPC})$.

Tax multiplier: the magnitude of the effect that a change in taxes has on real GDP. Tm = $(\Delta\text{GDP})/(\Delta\text{ taxes})$ = MPC * Multiplier = MPC/MPS.

Balanced-budget multiplier: when a change in government spending is offset by a change in lump sum taxes, real GDP changes by the amount of the change in G; the balanced-budget multiplier is thus equal to one.

CHAPTER 14

Aggregate Demand and Aggregate Supply

"This is the bulk of the Macro exam— very important!" —AP Teacher

IN THIS CHAPTER

Summary: Chapter 12 addressed three widely used measures of macroeconomic performance: real GDP, inflation, and unemployment. Economists have built upon the models of supply and demand for microeconomic markets to model an aggregate picture of the macro economy. The models of Aggregate Demand (AD) and Aggregate Supply (AS) have been extremely useful to predict how real GDP, employment and the average price level are affected by external factors and government policy. Before discussing macroeconomic policy, we first need to describe the AD/AS model.

Key Ideas

✪ Aggregate Demand (AD)
✪ Aggregate Supply (AS)
✪ Short-Run and Long-Run AS
✪ Macroeconomic Equilibrium
✪ The Inflation and Unemployment Trade-off

14.1 Aggregate Demand (AD)

Main Topics: *Aggregate Demand, Components of AD, Shape of AD, Changes in AD*

When we discussed microeconomic markets, we described the shape of any microeconomic demand curve with the Law of Demand, income and substitution effects.

Both effects work to change quantity demanded in the opposite direction of any price change. What tends to be the case for the demand of a microeconomic good is also the case for AD, but for different theoretical reasons.

What Is Aggregate Demand?

A microeconomic demand curve for peaches illustrates the relationship between the quantity of peaches demanded and the price of peaches. When economists aggregate all microeconomic markets to build AD, we include peaches and all other items that are domestically produced. **Aggregate Demand** is the relationship between all spending on domestic output and the average price level of that output.

Components of AD

Demand in the macroeconomy comes from four general sources and we have already seen these components when we described how total production is measured in the economy. In the previous chapter we defined real GDP as $= C + I + G + (X - M)$.

So AD measures the sum of consumption spending by households, investment spending by firms, government purchases of goods and services, and the net exports bought by foreign consumers.

The Shape of AD

When the price of peaches rises, consumers find another microeconomic good (with a lower relative price) to substitute for peaches and this helps to explain why the demand for peaches is downward sloping. But if the overall price level is rising, the price of peaches, pears, and apples might all be rising. It is important to remember that this average price level is not the same as the price of one good relative to another. Where are the substitutes when the "good" we are discussing is a unit of real GDP? Macroeconomists describe three general groups of substitutes for national output. They are:

- Goods and services produced in other nations (foreign sector substitution effect).
- Goods and services in the future (interest rate effect).
- Money and financial assets (wealth effect).

Foreign Sector Substitution Effect: When the average price of United States output (as measured by the CPI or some other price index) increases, consumers naturally begin to look for similar items produced elsewhere. A Japanese computer, French brie, and a Mexican textile all begin to look more attractive when inflation heats up in the United States. The resulting increase in imports pushes real GDP down at a higher price level.

Interest Rate Effect: Remember that consumers have two general choices with their disposable income; they can consume it or they can save it for future consumption. If the average price level rises, consumers might need to borrow more money for big-ticket items like autos or college tuition. When more and more households seek loans, the real interest rate begins to rise and this increases the cost of borrowing. Firms postpone their investment in plant and equipment, and households postpone their consumption of more expensive items for a future when their spending might go further and borrowing might be more affordable. This "wait and see" mentality reduces current consumption of domestic production as the price level rises and real GDP falls.

Wealth Effect: Wealth is the value of accumulated assets like stocks, bonds, savings, and especially cash on hand. As the average price level rises, the purchasing power of wealth and savings begins to fall. Higher prices therefore tend to reduce the quantity of domestic output purchased.

The combination of the foreign sector substitution, interest rate, and wealth effects predict a downward sloping AD curve. For all three reasons, as the overall price level rises, consumption of domestic output (real GDP) falls along the AD curve. This is seen as a movement from points *a* to *b* in Figure 14.1.

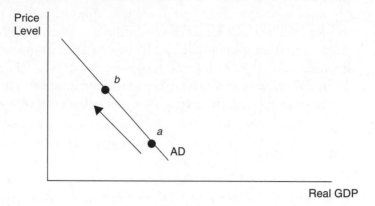

Figure 14.1

- Aggregate demand is not the vertical or horizontal summation of the demand curves for all microeconomic goods and services.
- AD is a model of how domestic production changes when the average price level changes.

Changes in AD

Since AD is the sum of the four components of domestic spending [*C, I, G,* (*X − M*)], if any of these components increases, holding the price level constant, AD increases, which increases real GDP. This is seen as a shift to the right of AD. If any of these components decreases, holding the price level constant, AD decreases, which decreases real GDP. This is seen as a shift to the left of AD. Figure 14.2 illustrates these shifts in AD.

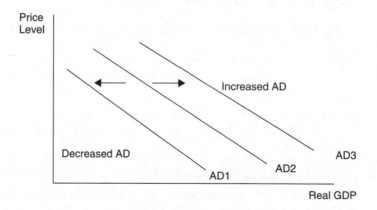

Figure 14.2

This is a preview for policy to manipulate the macroeconomy. If you want to stimulate real GDP and lower unemployment, you need to boost any or all of the components of AD. If you feel AD must slow down, you need to rein in the components of AD. Policies are tackled in more depth in the next chapter, but for now we take a quick look at some variables that can increase C, *I, G,* or (*X − M*).

Consumer Spending (*C*): If you put more money in the pockets of households, expect them to consume a great deal of it and save the rest. Consumers also increase their consumption if they are more optimistic about the future.

Investment Spending (*I*): Firms increase investment if they believe the investment will be profitable. This expected return on the investment is increased if investors are optimistic about the future profitability, or if the necessary borrowing can be done at a low rate of interest.

Government Spending (*G*): The government injects money into the economy by spending more on goods and services, or by reducing taxes or by increasing transfer payments.

a. *Government spending* on goods and services acts as a direct increase in AD.

b. *Taxes and Transfers.* Lowering taxes and increasing transfer payments increase AD through *C* by increasing DI.

Net Exports (*X − M*): When we sell more goods to foreign consumers and buy fewer goods from foreign producers, this component of AD increases.

a. *Foreign incomes.* Exports (*X*) increase with a strong Canadian, Mexican, or Brazilian economy. When foreign consumers have more disposable income, this increases the AD in the United States because those consumers spend some of that income on U.S.-made goods.

b. *Consumer tastes.* Consumer tastes and preferences, both foreign and domestic, are constantly changing. If American blue jeans become more popular in France, American AD increases. If French wines become more preferred by American consumers, AD in France increases.

c. *Exchange rates:* Imports (*M*) decrease when the exchange rate between the U.S. dollar and foreign currency falls. The model of foreign currency exchange is covered in a later chapter, but the idea is that foreign goods become relatively more expensive and so consumers buy fewer foreign-produced items.

14.2 Aggregate Supply (AS)

Main Topics: *Aggregate Supply, Short-Run and Long-Run Shape of AS, Changes in AS*

Again, there are parallels between our coverage of supply in micro markets, and aggregate supply. The Law of Supply describes the positive relationship between the micro price of a product and the quantity of that product that firms supply, and is explained in part by increasing marginal cost as output rises. What tends to be the case for the supply of a micro good is also the case for AS, but for different theoretical reasons.

What is Aggregate Supply?

A microeconomic supply curve for salt illustrates the relationship between the price of salt and the quantity of salt supplied. When economists aggregate all microeconomic markets to build AS, we include salt and all other items that are domestically supplied. **Aggregate Supply** is the relationship between the average price level of all domestic output and the level of domestic output produced.

Short-Run and Long-Run Shape of AS

The model of AS and the resulting shape of the AS curve depends upon whether the economy has fully adjusted to market forces and price changes.

Macroeconomic Short Run

In the **macroeconomic short run** period of time, the prices of goods and services are changing in their respective markets, but input prices have not yet adjusted to those product market changes. This lag between the increase in the output price, and the increase in input prices, gives us a shape of the short-run AS curve that is described in three stages. Figure 14.3 illustrates the stages of short-run AS.

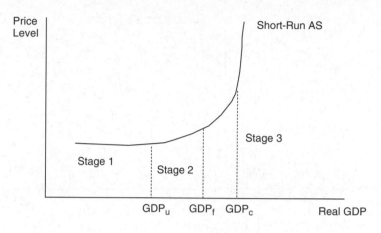

Figure 14.3

If the economy is in a recession with low production (GDP_u), there are many unemployed resources. Increasing output from this low level puts little pressure on input costs and subsequent minimal increase in the overall price level. The first stage of AS is drawn as almost horizontal. The "Keynesian School" of economics believes that the economy often resembles this recessionary situation, and so one of the cornerstones of Keynesian economics is a horizontal AS curve.

As real GDP increases in the second stage of AS and approaches full employment (GDP_f), available resources become more difficult to find, and so input costs begin to rise. If the price level for output rises at a faster rate than the rising costs, producers have a profit incentive to increase output. Most of the time the economy is operating in this upward sloping range of AS and so you see short-run AS commonly drawn with a positive slope.

If the economy grows and approaches the nation's productive capacity (GDP_c) firms cannot find unemployed inputs. Input costs and the price level rise much more sharply and so in this third stage of AS, the curve is almost vertical.

Macroeconomic Long Run

The period of time known as the **macroeconomic long run** is long enough for input prices to have fully adjusted to market forces. Now all product and input markets are in equilibrium and the economy is at full employment. In this long-run equilibrium, the AS curve is vertical at GDP_f. The "Classical School" of economics asserts that the economy always gravitates toward full employment; so a cornerstone of classical macroeconomics is a vertical AS curve. Figure 14.4 illustrates the long-run AS curve.

Shifts in Aggregate Supply

In the short run, AS may fluctuate without changing the level of full employment. There are some factors, however, that can cause a fundamental shift in the long-run AS curve because they can change the level of output at full employment.

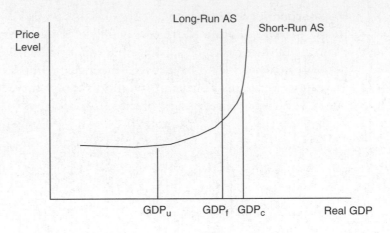

Figure 14.4

Short-Run Shifts

The most common factor that affects short-run AS is an economy-wide change in input prices. Taxes, government policy, and short-term political or natural events can change the short-term ability of a nation to supply goods and services.

- *Input prices.* If input prices fall, the short-run AS curve increases (shifting to the right) without changing the level of full employment.
- *Tax policy.* Some taxes are aimed at producers, rather than consumers. If these "supply-side taxes" are lowered, aggregate supply shifts to the right.
- *Deregulation.* In some cases the regulation of industries can restrict their ability to produce (for good reasons in many cases). If these regulations are lessened, the short-run AS likely increases.
- *Political or environmental phenomena.* For a nation as large as the United States, wars and natural disasters can decrease the short-run AS without permanently decreasing the level of full employment. For a smaller nation or a large nation hit by an epic disaster, this could be a permanent decrease in the ability to produce.

Long-Run Shifts

There are a few main factors that affect both long-run and short-run AS and fundamentally affect the level of full employment in a nation's macroeconomy.

- *Availability of resources.* A larger labor force, or larger stock of capital, or more widely available natural resources, can increase the level of full employment.
- *Technology and Productivity.* Better technology raises the productivity of both capital and labor. A more highly trained or educated populace increases the productivity of the labor force. These factors increase long-run AS over time.
- *Policy incentives.* Different national policies like unemployment insurance provide incentives for a nation's labor force to work. If policy provides large incentives to quickly find a job, full-employment real GDP rises. If government gives tax incentives to invest in capital or technology, GDP_f rises.

Example:

In the 1990s, the U.S. economy saw dramatic increases in technology and investment in the capital stock. This period produced a significant increase in the real GDP at full employment. This is illustrated in Figure 14.5.

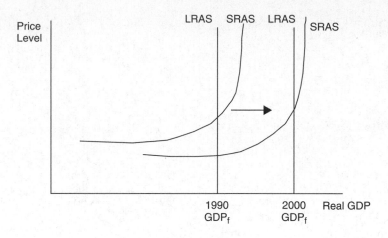

Figure 14.5

14.3 Macroeconomic Equilibrium

Main Topics: *Equilibrium Real GDP and Price Level, Recessionary and Inflationary Gaps, Shifting AD, The Multiplier Again, Shifting AS*

We use supply and demand models to predict changes in the prices and quantities of microeconomic goods and services. Now that we have built a model of aggregate demand and aggregate supply, we use similar analysis to predict changes in real GDP and the average price level.

Equilibrium Real GDP and Price Level

When the quantity of real output demanded is equal to the quantity of real output supplied, the macroeconomy is said to be in equilibrium. Figure 14.6 below illustrates **macroeconomic equilibrium** at full employment Q_f and price level PL_f at the intersection of AD and AS.

Recessionary and Inflationary Gaps

When the economy is in equilibrium, but not at the level of GDP that corresponds to full employment (GDP_f), the economy is experiencing either a recessionary or an inflationary gap.

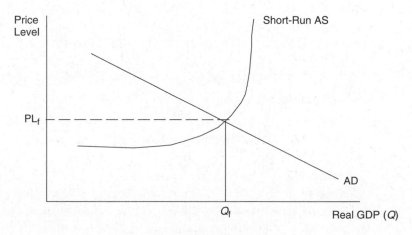

Figure 14.6

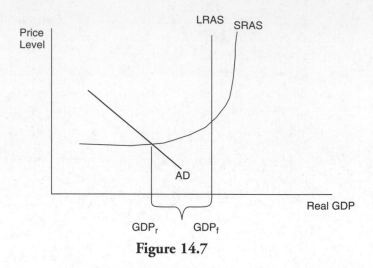

Figure 14.7

As the name implies, a **recessionary gap** exists when the economy is operating below Q_f and the economy is likely experiencing a high unemployment rate. In Figure14.7, the recessionary gap is the difference between GDP_f and GDP_r, or the amount that GDP must rise to reach GDP_f.

> *"Be able to locate these on a graph."*
> *—AP teacher*

An **inflationary gap** exists when the economy is operating above GDP_f. Because production is higher than GDP_f, a rising price level is the greatest danger to the economy. In Figure 14.8, the inflationary gap is the difference between GDP_i and GDP_f, or the amount that GDP must fall to reach GDP_f.

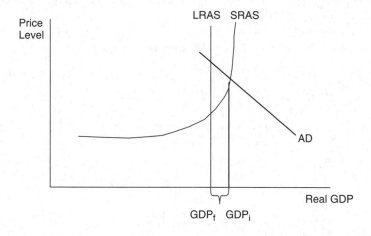

Figure 14.8

Shifting AD

Since you have mastered the microeconomic tools of supply and demand, you should have little trouble predicting how macroeconomic factors affect real GDP and the price level.

Shifts in AD

The economy is currently in equilibrium but at a very low recessionary level of real GDP. If AD increases from AD_0 to AD_1 in the nearly horizontal range of SRAS, the price level maybe only slightly increases, while real GDP significantly increases and the unemployment rate falls.

If AD continues to increase to AD_2 in the upward sloping range of SRAS, the price level begins to rise and inflation is felt in the economy. This **demand-pull inflation** is the result of rising consumption from all sectors of AD.

If AD increases much beyond full employment to AD_3, inflation is quite significant and real GDP experiences minimal increases. Figures 14.9, 14.10, and 14.11 illustrate how rising AD has different effects on the price level and real GDP in the three stages of short-run AS.

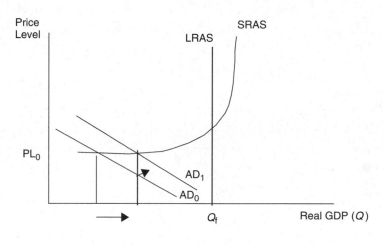

Figure 14.9

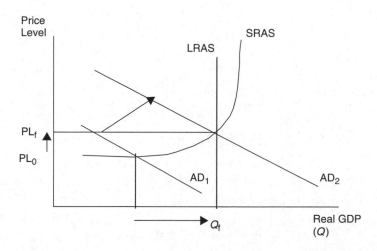

Figure 14.10

If aggregate demand weakens, we can expect the opposite effects on price level and real GDP. In fact, one of the most common causes of a recession is falling AD as it lowers real GDP and increases the unemployment rate. Inflation is not typically a problem with this kind of recession as we expect the price level to fall, or **deflation**, with falling AD. This is seen in Figure 14.12.

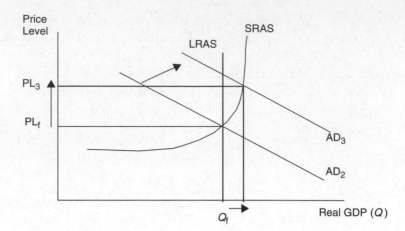

Figure 14.11

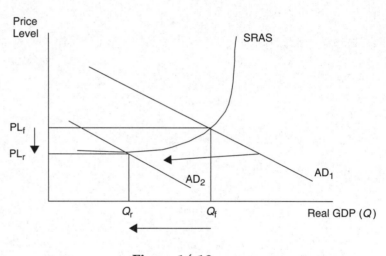

Figure 14.12

The Multiplier Again

One of the important topics of the previous chapter is the spending multiplier. When a component of autonomous spending increases by $1, real GDP increases by a magnitude of the multiplier. The full multiplier effect is only observed if the price level does not increase, and this only occurs if the economy is operating on the horizontal range of the SRAS curve. Figure 14.13 shows the full multiplier effect. (Note that the SRAS curve is likely a much smoother curve, but the multiplier effect can be illustrated more clearly with more linear segments.)

But what if the economy is operating in the upward sloping range of SRAS? Figure 14.14 shows an identical rightward shift in AD. If there were no increase in the price level, the new equilibrium GDP would be at GDP$_1$, but with a rising price level, it is somewhat smaller at GDP$_2$. This means that the full multiplier effect is not felt because the rising price level weakens the impact of increased spending in the macroeconomy.

- The multiplier effect of an increase in AD is greater if there is no increase in the price level.
- The multiplier effect of an increase in AD is smaller if there is a larger increase in the price level.

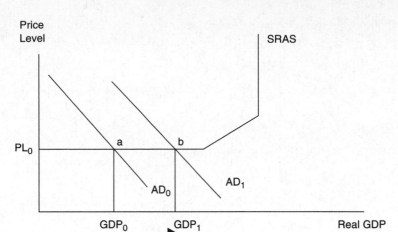

Figure 14.13

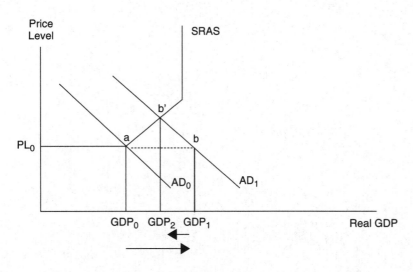

Figure 14.14

Shifting AS

The macroeconomy is currently in equilibrium at full employment. If input prices temporarily fall, the AS curve shifts outward as in Figure 14.15. If the AD curve stays constant, the price level falls, real GDP increases, and the unemployment rate falls. This kind of **supply-side boom** would seemingly be the best of all situations. If AS increases because of a more permanent factor like increased productivity or better technology, the LRAS curve and the level of full employment could move outward from Q_f to Q_1.

If an increase in AS is the best of possible macroeconomic situations, a decrease in AS is the worst. Figure 14.16 shows that a decrease, or leftward shift, in AS creates inflation, lowers real GDP, and increases the unemployment rate. This **cost-push inflation**, or **stagflation**, is the bane of economists, the general public, and politicians alike.

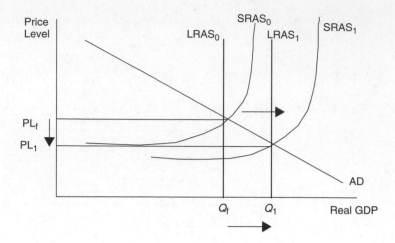

Figure 14.15

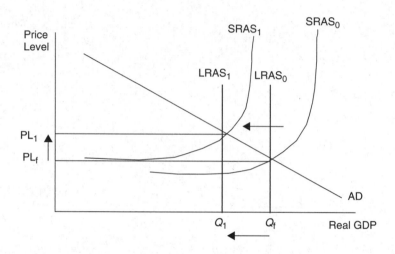

Figure 14.16

Supply Shocks

These shifts in AS are caused by events that are called **supply shocks**. A supply shock is an economy-wide phenomenon that affects the costs of firms, positively or negatively. Positive supply shocks might be the result of higher productivity or lower energy prices. Negative supply shocks usually occur when economy-wide input prices suddenly increase, like the OPEC oil embargoes of the 1970s or the Gulf War of 1990–1991. For small nations, natural catastrophes like drought or hurricane damage can have the same negative effect on AS.

- ↑ AD causes ↑ real GDP, ↓ unemployment and ↑ price level.
- ↓ AD causes ↓ real GDP, ↑ unemployment and ↓ price level.
- ↑ AS causes ↑ real GDP, ↓ unemployment and ↓ price level.
- ↓ AS causes ↓ real GDP, ↑ unemployment and ↑ price level.

14.4 The Trade-Off Between Inflation and Unemployment

Main Topics: *The Inflation and Unemployment Trade-off, The Short-Run Phillips curve, The Long-Run Phillips curve, Expectations*

Changes in AD and AS create changes in our main macroeconomic indicators of inflation and unemployment. Many economists have studied the relationship between inflation and unemployment and this section provides a very brief overview of one prominent theory, the Phillips curve. We also take another look at the effects of supply shocks and expectations.

Short-Run Changes in AD

In the upward sloping range of the AS curve, there is a positive relationship between the price level and output. If AD is rising, the price level and real GDP are both rising. Since rising real GDP creates jobs and lowers unemployment, we connect these points of equilibrium and show an inverse relationship between inflation and the unemployment rate. See Figure 14.17.

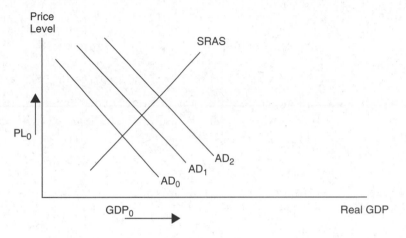

Figure 14.17

The Phillips Curve

The inverse relationship between inflation and the unemployment rate has come to be known as the Phillips curve and in the short-run is downward sloping. The short-run Phillips curve is drawn in Figure 14.18. Though Figure 14.18 does not show it, the possibility of deflation at extremely high unemployment rates means that the Phillips curve may actually continue falling below the x axis.

Supply Shocks and the Phillips Curve

We saw that when AS shifts to the right, holding AD constant, that both the price level and unemployment rate would fall. On the other hand, when AS shifts to the left, we get

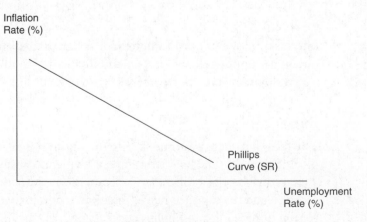

Figure 14.18

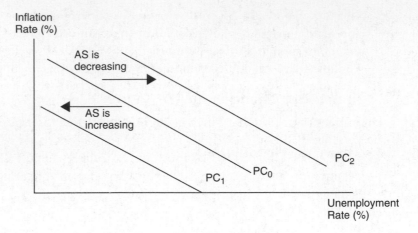

Figure 14.19

stagflation because inflation and unemployment rates are both rising. Figure 14.19 shows how supply shocks shift the Phillips curve inward when AS shifts to the right, and outward when AS shifts to the left.

The Long-Run Phillips Curve

The AD and AS model presumes that the long-run AS curve is vertical and located at full employment. As a result, the Phillips curve in the long run is also vertical at the natural

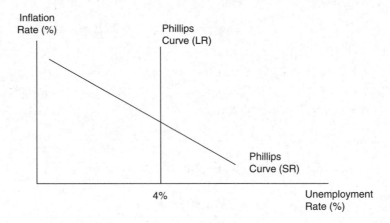

Figure 14.20

rate of employment. You might recall that the natural rate of employment is the unemployment rate where cyclical unemployment is zero. Suppose this occurs at a measured unemployment rate of 4 percent. Figure 14.20 illustrates the long-run Phillips curve.

Expectations

The idea that there is, in the short term, an inverse relationship between inflation and unemployment, and in the long term, unemployment is always at the natural rate can be confusing. The reason there is a difference is because sometimes there is a gap between the actual rate of inflation and the expected rate of inflation. Inflationary expectations play a role here in the derivation of the long-run Phillips curve. Figure 14.21 illustrates this concept with an example.

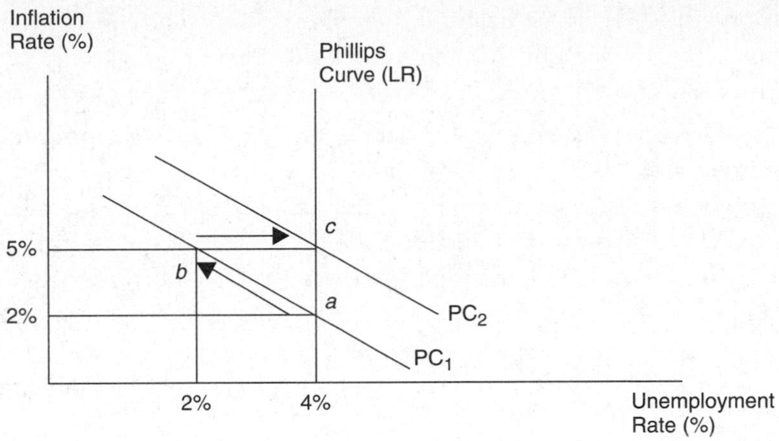

Figure 14.21

The expected inflation rate is 2 percent at a 4 percent natural rate of unemployment (point *a*). If AD unexpectedly rises, this drives up the rate of inflation to 5 percent and as a result, firms are earning higher profits. Firms respond with more hiring and this temporarily drops the unemployment rate to 2 percent (point *b*). This is seen as a movement along the short-run PC above from *a* to *b*.

The point at 5 percent inflation and 2 percent unemployment will not last. Workers realize that their real wages are falling and insist on a raise! As wages rise, the profits of firms begin to fall and so too does employment back to the natural rate of 4 percent (point *c*). At this point both actual and expected inflation is 5 percent. Another short-run Phillips curve runs through this point. Points *a* and *c* must lie on one long-run Phillips curve, and that curve must be vertical. The above process can repeat itself if AD continues to increase, or it can reverse itself if AD falls.

What happens if citizens and firms expect a higher rate of inflation than the actual rate? Expecting higher prices in the future, consumers and firms increase purchasing now and AD increases, which serves to increase the price level. The expectation in this case is really a self-fulfilling prophecy.

› Review Questions

1. Using the model of AD and AS, what happens to real GDP, the price level, and unemployment with more consumption spending (*C*)?

	REAL GDP	PRICE LEVEL	UNEMPLOYMENT
(A)	Increases	Decreases	Decreases
(B)	Decreases	Increases	Increases
(C)	Increases	Increases	Decreases
(D)	Decreases	Decreases	Decreases
(E)	Decreases	Decreases	Increases

2. Which is the best way to describe the AS curve in the long run?

   (A) Always vertical in the long run.
   (B) Always upward sloping because it follows the Law of Supply.
   (C) Always horizontal.
   (D) Always downward sloping.
   (E) Without more information we cannot predict how it looks in the long run.

3. Stagflation most likely results from

   (A) increasing AD with constant AS.
   (B) decreasing AS with constant AD.
   (C) decreasing AD with constant AS.
   (D) a decrease in both AD and AS.
   (E) an increase in both AD and AS.

4. Equilibrium real GDP is far below full employment and the government lowers household taxes. Which is the likely result?

(A) Unemployment falls with little inflation.
(B) Unemployment rises with little inflation.
(C) Unemployment falls with rampant inflation.
(D) Unemployment rises with rampant inflation.
(E) No change occurs in unemployment or inflation.

5. What is the main contrast between the short-run and long-run Phillips curve?

(A) In the short run there is a positive relationship between inflation and unemployment, and in the long run the relationship is negative.
(B) In the short run there is a positive relationship between inflation and unemployment, and in the long run the relationship is constant.
(C) In the short run there is a negative relationship between inflation and unemployment, and in the long run the relationship is positive.
(D) In the short run there is a negative relationship between inflation and unemployment, and in the long run the relationship is constant.
(E) In the short run there is a constant relationship between inflation and unemployment, and in the long run the relationship is negative.

6. The effect of the spending multiplier is lessened if

(A) the price level is constant with an increase in aggregate demand.
(B) the price level falls with an increase in aggregate supply.
(C) the price level is constant with an increase in long-run aggregate supply.
(D) the price level falls with an increase in both aggregate demand and aggregate supply.
(E) the price level rises with an increase in aggregate demand.

> Answers and Explanations

1. **C**—An increase in consumption spending increases, or shifts rightward, the AD curve, increasing the level of real GDP, the price level, and lowers the unemployment rate.

2. **A**—All resources are employed at full employment in the long run so firms cannot respond to an increase in the price level by increasing production. Thus any increase in prices cannot increase production in the long run, and so AS is assumed to be vertical. Any short-run discrepancy in GDP, above or below, full employment adjusts back to GDP$_f$ in the long run.

3. **B**—Stagflation is an increase in the price level and an increase in unemployment. This is most often the result of falling AS and a constant AD. Choice D is incorrect because a simultaneous decrease in AD puts downward pressure on the price level, which offsets the upward pressure from falling AS.

4. **A**—A deep recession describes macroeconomic equilibrium in the horizontal section of AS. Here, rising AD increases real GDP, lowers unemployment rates, with little inflation.

5. **D**—The short-run Phillips curve is downward sloping but vertical in the long run.

6. **E**—The full spending multiplier effect of an increase in AD is felt only if there is no rise in the price.

› Rapid Review

Aggregate Demand (AD): the inverse relationship between all spending on domestic output and the average price level of that output. AD measures the sum of consumption spending by households, investment spending by firms, government purchases of goods and services, and the net exports bought by foreign consumers.

Foreign sector substitution effect: when the average price of U.S. output increases, consumers naturally begin to look for similar items produced elsewhere.

Interest rate effect: if the average price level rises, consumers and firms might need to borrow more money for spending and capital investment, which increases the interest rate and delays current consumption. This postponement reduces current consumption of domestic production as the price level rises.

Wealth effect: as the average price level rises, the purchasing power of wealth and savings begins to fall. Higher prices therefore tend to reduce the quantity of domestic output purchased.

Determinants of AD: AD is a function of the four components of domestic spending (C, I, G $(X - M)$). If any of these components increases (decreases), holding the others constant, AD increases (decreases), or shifts to the right (left).

Aggregate Supply (AS): the positive relationship between the level of domestic output produced and the average price level of that output.

Macroeconomic short run: a period of time during which the prices of goods and services are changing in their respective markets, but the input prices have not yet adjusted to those changes in the product markets. During the short run, the AS curve has three stages—horizontal, upward sloping, and vertical.

Macroeconomic long run: a period of time long enough for input prices to have fully adjusted to market forces. In this period, all product and input markets are in a state of equilibrium and the economy is operating at full employment (GDP_f). Once all markets in the economy have adjusted and there exists this long-run equilibrium, the AS curve is vertical at GDP_f.

Determinants of AS: AS is a function of many factors that impact the production capacity of the nation. If these factors make it easier, or less costly, for a nation to produce, AS shifts to the right. If these factors make it more difficult, or more costly, for a nation to produce, AS shifts to the left.

Macroeconomic equilibrium: occurs when the quantity of real output demanded is equal to the quantity of real output supplied. Graphically this is at the intersection of AD and AS. Equilibrium can exist at, above, or below full employment.

Recessionary gap: The amount by which full-employment GDP exceeds equilibrium GDP.

Inflationary gap: The amount by which equilibrium GDP exceeds full-employment GDP.

Demand-pull inflation: this inflation is the result of stronger consumption from all sectors of AD as it continues to increase in the upward sloping range of AS. The price level begins to rise and inflation is felt in the economy.

Deflation: a sustained falling price level, usually due to weakened aggregate demand and a constant AS.

Recession: in the AD and AS model, a recession is described as falling AD with a constant AS curve. Real GDP falls far below full employment levels and the unemployment rate rises.

Supply-side boom: when the AS curve shifts outward and the AD curve stays constant, the price level falls, real GDP increases and the unemployment rate falls.

Stagflation: a situation in the macroeconomy when inflation and the unemployment rate are both increasing. This is most likely the cause of falling AS while AD stays constant.

Supply shocks: a supply shock is an economy-wide phenomenon that affects the costs of firms, and the position of the AS curve, either positively or negatively.

Phillips curve: A graphical device that shows the relationship between inflation and the unemployment rate. In the short run it is downward sloping and in the long run it is vertical at the natural rate of employment.

CHAPTER 15

Fiscal Policy, Economic Growth, and Productivity

IN THIS CHAPTER

Summary: The model of AD and AS is a useful mechanism for looking at how the macroeconomy can be deliberately expanded, or contracted, by the government. **Fiscal policy** measures include government spending and tax collection to affect economic output, unemployment, and the price level. We use graphical analysis to show how fiscal policy attempts to move the economy to full employment and also discuss some of the ways in which fiscal policy is less effective than predicted by theory. This chapter concludes with a discussion of economic growth and productivity, and how policy might affect growth.

Key Ideas

✪ Fiscal Policy
✪ Budget Deficits and Crowding Out
✪ Economic Growth
✪ Productivity and Supply-Side Policy

15.1 Expansionary and Contractionary Fiscal Policy

Main Topics: *Expansionary Fiscal Policy, Contractionary Fiscal Policy, Deficits and Surpluses, Automatic Stabilizers*

This section of the chapter uses AD and AS to illustrate how fiscal policy can work in theory. Fiscal policy stresses the importance of a hands-on role for government in manipulating AD to "fix" the economy. Difficulties in fiscal policy and the supply-side perspective are addressed in the following section.

Expansionary Fiscal Policy

When the economy is suffering a recession, real GDP is low and unemployment is high. In the AD and AS model, a recessionary equilibrium is located in the horizontal range of AS, as seen in Figure 15.1. If the government increases its spending or lowers net taxes, the AD curve increases. Net taxes, if you recall, are tax revenues minus transfer payments. In this range of AS, the economy should experience the full magnitude of the multiplier with very little inflation. Of course if the government is using tax cuts, rather than government spending, to expand the economy, the multiplier is smaller; so to get the same increase in real GDP, the size of the tax cut must be larger than an increase in government spending.

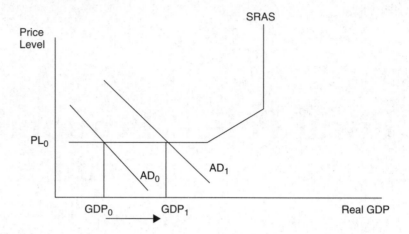

Figure 15.1

Contractionary Fiscal Policy

If the economy is operating beyond full employment, and inflation is becoming a problem, the government might need to contract the economy. This inflationary equilibrium is seen in the vertical range of the AS curve, as seen in Figure 15.2. This can be done by decreasing government spending or by increasing taxes, both of which cause a leftward shift in AD. In this range of AS, the economy might see very little decrease in real GDP, but ideally a substantial decrease in the rate of inflation.

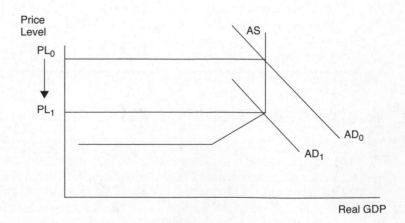

Figure 15.2

Are Prices Sticky?

Do prices fall, as Figure 15.2 seems to indicate? One of the points of contention is whether the price level can fall. Many economists (Keynesians) predict that prices are fairly inflexible, or "sticky" in the downward direction, so efforts to fight inflation are really efforts to slow inflation, not to actually lower the price level. Conversely, Classical School economists believe that the long-run economy naturally adjusts to full employment and so they see the AS curve as vertical. This argument implies that prices are flexible and can rise and fall as seen above.

Deficits and Surpluses

When the government starts to adjust spending and/or taxation, there is an effect on the budget. A **budget deficit** exists if government spending exceeds the revenue collected from taxes in a given period of time, usually a year. A **budget surplus** exists if the revenue collected from taxes exceeds government spending.

The Difference Between Deficit and Debt

An annual budget deficit occurs when, in one year, the government spends more than is collected in tax revenue. To pay for the deficit, the government must borrow funds. When deficits are an annual occurrence, a nation begins to accumulate a **national debt**. The national debt is therefore an accumulation of the borrowing needed to cover past annual deficits.

Expansionary Policy

If the economy is in a recession, the appropriate fiscal policy is to increase government spending or lower taxes. When the government spends more, or collects less tax revenue, budget deficits are likely. There are two ways to finance the deficit, and each has the potential to weaken the expansionary policy.

- *Borrowing*. If a household wants to spend beyond its means, it enters the market for loanable funds as a borrower. The borrowed funds provide a short-term ability to purchase goods and services, but must be paid back, with interest, when the loan is due. The same is true when the government borrows, but when an entity as large as the federal government is borrowing from the banking system or from the public in the form of Treasury securities (i.e., bonds), it decreases the supply of loanable funds available to private borrowers. A decrease in the supply of loanable funds tends to drive up the price, or real rate of interest. So what? Well, if the goal is to expand the macroeconomy, then borrowing to finance the deficit slows down the expansion by increasing interest rates. This **crowding out effect** is examined in the next section of this chapter.
- *Creating Money*. The creation of new money to fund a deficit can avoid the higher interest rates caused by borrowing. The primary disadvantage of creating more money is the risk of inflation, which can also lessen the effectiveness of expansionary fiscal policy. The effect that inflation has on the multiplier was illustrated in the previous chapter, and more detailed effects of expanding the money supply are looked at in the next chapter.

Contractionary Policy

If the economy is operating above full employment, the appropriate fiscal policy is to lower government spending or raise taxes. When the government spends less, or collects more tax revenue, a budget surplus can occur. The effectiveness of the contractionary fiscal policy depends upon what is done with the surplus.

- *Pay down debt*. If the government pays down debt and retires bonds ahead of schedule, the supply of loanable funds increases, decreasing interest rates. Lower interest rates stimulate investment and consumption, which counters the contractionary fiscal policy and lessens the downward effects on the price level.

- *Do nothing.* By making regularly scheduled payments on Treasury bonds and retiring them on schedule, idle surplus funds are removed from the economy. By not allowing these funds to be recirculated through the economy, the anti-inflationary fiscal policy can be more effective.

Automatic Stabilizers

An **automatic stabilizer** is anything that increases a deficit during a recessionary period and increases a budget surplus during an inflationary period, without any discretionary change on the part of the government. There are some mechanisms built into the tax system that automatically regulate, or stabilize, the macroeconomy as it moves through the business cycle by changing net taxes collected by the government.

Progressive Taxes and Transfers

When the economy is booming and GDP is increasing, more and more households and firms begin to fall into higher and higher tax brackets. This means that a larger percentage of income is taken as income tax, which slows down the consumption of both households and firms. In addition, a strong economy reduces the need for such transfer payments as unemployment insurance and welfare. Thus net taxes increase with GDP. Our progressive tax system is therefore contractionary when the economy is very strong. By automatically putting the brakes on spending, this reduces the threat of inflation and contributes to a budget surplus.

When the economy is suffering a recession and GDP is falling, households and firms find themselves in lower tax brackets. With a smaller percentage of income being taken as income tax, this provides a way for more consumption than would have been possible at the higher tax rate. Simultaneously, a weak economy increases the need for transfer payments like welfare payments. Thus net taxes decrease with GDP. When the economy is sluggish, the progressive tax system is expansionary in nature. The lower tax brackets soften the effect of a recession and contribute to a deficit.

Figure 15.3 shows how, for a given level of government spending, net taxes rise and fall with GDP. These automatically reduce the threat of inflation when the economy is strong (GDP_i), and reduce the negative effects of a recession when the economy is weak (GDP_r). Ideally, at full employment (GDP_f) the budget should be balanced.

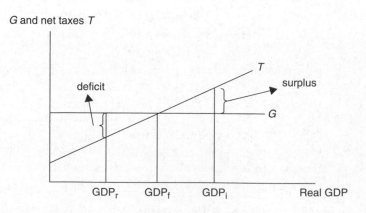

Figure 15.3

- Automatic stabilizers lessen, but do not eliminate, the business cycle swings.
- Automatic stabilizers lead to deficits during recession and surpluses during economic growth.

15.2 Difficulties of Fiscal Policy

Main Topics: *Crowding Out, Net Export Effects, State and Local Policies*

In theory, aggregate demand can be expanded or contracted, with government spending and/or taxes, to move the economy closer to full employment. In practice, there are some factors that lessen the effectiveness of fiscal policy. There are also some economists who disagree on fiscal policy targets.

Crowding Out

> "Crowding out is an important concept that may get asked more than once."
> —AP Teacher

If the government must borrow funds to pay for expansionary fiscal policy, the government has an effect on the market for loanable funds. The market for loanable funds was introduced earlier in this text and you might recall that public saving affects the supply of loanable funds. A government deficit, or negative public saving, is a reduction in total saving and decreases the supply of loanable funds available to the private borrowers. Figure 15.4 below shows how a decreased supply of loanable funds increases the interest rate and decreases the dollars that are borrowed for investment. Less investment spending on capital goods is likely to reduce a nation's growth rate, a topic we'll explore at the end of this chapter.

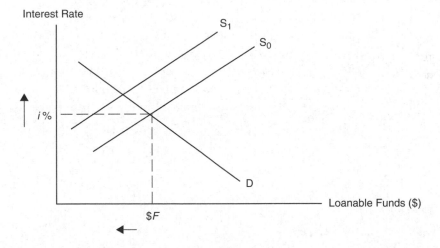

Figure 15.4

When the interest rate increases, households and firms are "**crowded out**" of the market for loanable funds. This decrease in C and I dampens the effect of expansionary fiscal policy. This is seen in Figure 15.5 as a movement from AD_1 to AD_2.

As we saw in Chapter 14, if increases in AD continue into the upward sloping range of AS, some of the multiplier effect of the fiscal policy is consumed by inflation and thus it is less effective.

When the government is fighting inflation with contractionary policy, we are likely to see the opposite of the crowding out problem. If a budget surplus is the result of the contractionary policy, and government debt is retired, the supply of loanable funds increases, interest rates fall, and investment increases ("crowding in" perhaps), thus lessening the impact of contractionary fiscal policy.

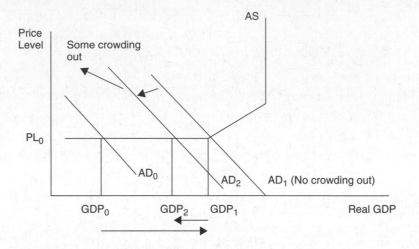

Figure 15.5

Net Export Effect

If the government is borrowing to conduct fiscal policy, the resulting increase in interest rates has a similar "crowding out" effect on net exports through foreign exchange rates. Again, this is a topic that is addressed in a later chapter, but the basics can be described here. If you are a German, a Malaysian, or a Brazilian and you see interest rates rising in the United States, this higher interest rate makes the United States an attractive place to invest your money and earn higher interest payments. However, you need dollars to purchase a U.S. security (e.g., a U.S. Treasury bond). The increased demand for dollars drives up the "price" of a dollar, which is measured in how many euros, ringgits, or pesos it takes to buy a dollar on the currency market. The market for U.S. dollars is illustrated in Figure 15.6, where the price is measured in the number of euros it takes to acquire one dollar.

"Don't try to figure it out in your head. Draw the graphs and read your answers from them."
—Nate,
AP Student

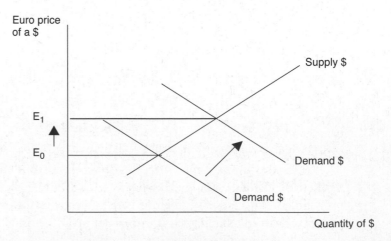

Figure 15.6

When the price of a dollar rises from E_0 to E_1, it now becomes more expensive for foreign citizens to buy goods made in the United States. All else equal, net exports in the

United States fall when the dollar appreciates in value. Falling net exports decreases AD, which lessens the impact of the expansionary fiscal policy. This would be seen in much the same way as in Figure 15.5.

If the government is using fiscal policy to fight inflation and interest rates begin to fall, the demand for dollars falls, depreciating the dollar and increasing net exports. This increase in net exports lessens the effectiveness of the contractionary fiscal policy.

- Expansionary fiscal policy is less effective if government borrowing crowds out private investment with higher interest rates.
- Expansionary fiscal policy is less effective if net exports fall because of an appreciating dollar.
- These effects also work in the opposite direction, making contractionary fiscal policy less effective when interest rates fall.

State and Local Policies

The U.S. Constitution does not require that the federal government balance the budget and most economists would agree that this is a good thing. After all, when the economy is in a recession, tax revenues are going to be low and deficits are likely to occur. Balancing the budget requires a combination of higher taxes and less spending, which only exacerbates the recession! Likewise, during a period of economic expansion, tax revenues are high and surpluses occur. Balancing the budget requires lower taxes or higher levels of spending to eliminate the surplus, which continues the expansion and risks higher inflation rates.

On the other hand, many state and local governments are required by law to balance their budgets. During recessions, tax revenue collected by these levels of government fall and elected officials are required to increase taxes and make difficult decisions on which state and local programs need to be cut.

So while the federal government is cutting taxes to increase your disposable income and spur economic growth, your state and local governments are increasing your taxes to make up for the budgetary shortfalls caused by the very recession the federal government is trying to fix. Argh! In this author's state of Indiana, since 2001 citizens have seen a 1 percent increase in the sales tax, increases in property taxes and, in the history of my county, the first ever county income tax. Meanwhile, programs like education, law enforcement, and transportation have seen cutbacks to help offset lost federal funds.

- State and local governments that are sometimes required by law to balance their budgets can thwart federal fiscal policy.

15.3 Economic Growth and Productivity

Main Topics: *Production Possibilities, Productivity, Supply-Side Policies*

Production Possibilities

Way back in Chapter 5, the topic of the PPF was introduced and that chapter illustrated how the frontier can move outward over time. This simple graphical technique can be extremely useful and adaptable to seeing how growth can be impacted by government policy. Before moving to policy, here is a quick refresher course in economic growth and productivity.

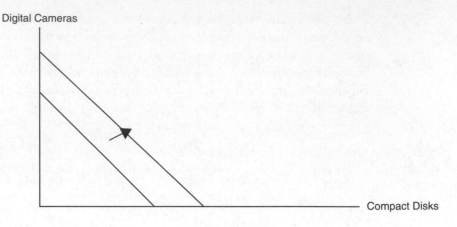

Figure 15.7

Figure 15.7 shows that this nation's production possibilities in CDs and digital cameras can grow over time if:
a. the quantity of economic resources increases.
b. the quality of those resources improves.
c. and/or the nation's technology improves.

Productivity

The factors that shift a PPF outward over time make a lot of sense, but what they all have in common is that each has the potential to represent increased **productivity**. Productivity is typically described as measuring the quantity of output that can be produced per worker in a given amount of time. If a nation's labor force can produce more output from one year to the next, we say that productivity has increased and the nation's PPF has shifted outward.

Determinants of Productivity

The determinants of productivity help to explain why some nations have grown at faster rates than other nations. This short list of determinants provides policy makers with a list of targets that can help to focus policy on factors that increase a nation's growth rate.

Stock of Physical Capital

Workers are more productive when they have tools at their disposal. Try painting a house without a brush, digging a hole without a shovel, or writing a term paper without a personal computer and you know how important tools can be to your productivity. The nice thing about increasing the quantity of physical capital in an economy is that, in many cases, the capital helps to increase the quantity of more capital. There should be policies that provide incentives to invest in physical capital. The supply-side policies described below are examples of policies that can increase investment in physical capital.

Human Capital

Labor is a much more productive resource when it has more **human capital**. Human capital is the amount of knowledge and skills that labor can apply to the work that they do. An accountant who takes extra courses so that she can earn her stockbroker's license has increased her human capital. A nurse who studies to become a physician's assistant is increasing her human capital and becoming more productive. Human capital also includes the general health of the nation's labor force. A labor force that has been vaccinated against debilitating disease can bring more productivity to the nation's workplace than the labor force of a nation that has not received these vaccinations. There should be national policies that provide incentives to invest in human capital. How about subsidies to public education to decrease the price to households? Or low-interest Federal student loans to help fund college? Or government agencies to research and promote the general physical and psychological health of the population?

Natural Resources

Productive resources provided by nature are called natural resources. A nation's stocks of minerals, fertile soil, timber, or navigable waterways contribute to productivity. **Non-renewable** resources, such as oil and coal, have a finite supply and cannot replenish themselves. **Renewable** resources, such as timber and salmon, have the ability to repopulate themselves. Environmental protection laws are designed to maintain the quality of natural resources so the productivity does not rapidly depreciate.

Technology

Technology is thought of as a nation's knowledge of how to produce goods in the best possible way. Imagine the technological leap that was made when humankind created fire, or the wheel, or the radio, or the assembly line, or the pizza crust with cheese in the middle. Amazing stuff! There should be policies that provide incentives to increase the rate of technological progress. The government's provision of research grants to university professors and laboratories helps to further our state of technology.

"What Do All of These Productivity Determinants Have in Common?"

They all require an investment, and funds for investment come from **saving**. Firms invest in physical capital and individuals invest in human capital. Nations invest in the conservation of their natural resources, and entrepreneurs invest in technological research. Productivity "friendly" policies should make it easier to invest, easier to save, or both. Some economists believe that supply-side policies have the potential to increase productivity, and therefore economic growth.

Supply-Side Policies

So far the discussion of fiscal policy is centered on changing government spending and/or taxing to stimulate or contract AD as a way to move the economy closer to full employment. Other economists believe that the government's fiscal policy should not be so proactive in manipulation of AD. These economists advocate a government that is more hands-off when it comes to fiscal policy. These economists believe that the economy generally moves to full employment without government intervention, but if the government does get involved, fiscal policy should focus on, or at least strongly consider, the AS half of the equation by providing incentives to increase saving and investment. The main idea behind **supply-side** fiscal policy is that tax reductions targeted to AS increase AS so that real GDP increases with very little inflation. This was our "best of all possible macroeconomic situations" from the previous chapter.

Saving and Investment

Supply-side proponents would suggest policies that lower, or remove, taxes on income earned from savings. This would encourage saving and increase the supply of loanable funds, decrease the real interest rate, and increase the amount of money that firms invest. Figure 15.8 shows an increase in the supply of loanable funds. These economists would also propose an **investment tax credit**, which reduces a firm's taxes if it invests in physical capital.

Lower income taxes increase disposable income for households, increase both consumption and savings from households, and increase the profitability of investment for firms. This increase in saving and investment allows for an increase in the productive capacity of a nation because more capital stock is accumulated. Ideally, this increase in investment increases the long-run AS curve. The increase in long-run AS is illustrated in Figure 15.9. Tax incentives to increase saving and investment on the supply side are likely to also increase AD. (Note: The price level is shown to remain constant, but this does not have to be, depending upon the magnitudes of the two curves' shifts.)

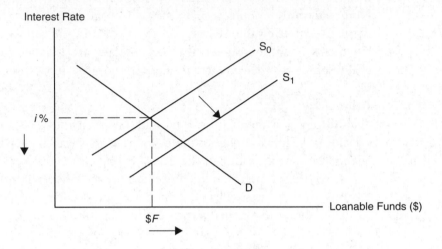

Figure 15.8

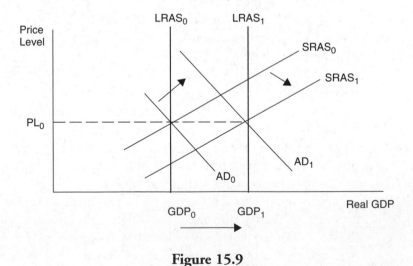

Figure 15.9

Though not all economists completely agree with their effectiveness, "supply-side" econo-mists typically advocate other explanations for how lower taxes can increase AS as well as AD.

- *Productivity Incentives.* Lower taxes mean workers take more of their pay home, which might prompt wage earners to work harder, take less time off, and be more productive. How hard would you work if 90 percent of your pay were lost to the taxman? People not currently in the workforce seek employment at lower tax rates. If the government has a large role in social programs, citizens learn to rely on the government and do less on their own.

- *Risk Taking.* Entrepreneurs take big risks to start businesses and invest in new capital. Lowering the tax rate on profits increases the expected rate of return and encourages more investment.

› Review Questions

1. Which of the following would NOT be an example of contractionary fiscal policy?

   (A) Decreasing money spent on social programs.
   (B) Increasing income taxes.
   (C) Canceling the annual cost of living adjustments to the salaries of government employees.
   (D) Increasing money spent to pay for government projects.
   (E) Doing nothing with a temporary budget surplus.

2. In a long period of economic expansion the tax revenue collected _____ and the amount spent on welfare programs _____ , creating a budget _____ .

   (A) increases, decreases, surplus
   (B) increases, decreases, deficit
   (C) decreases, decreases, surplus
   (D) decreases, increases, deficit
   (E) increases, increases, surplus

3. The "crowding out" effect from government borrowing is best described as

   (A) the rightward shift in AD in response to the decreasing interest rates from contractionary fiscal policy.
   (B) the leftward shift in AD in response to the rising interest rates from expansionary fiscal policy.
   (C) the effect of the President increasing the money supply, which decreases real interest rates, and increases AD.
   (D) the effect on the economy of hearing the chairperson of the central bank say that he/she believes that the economy is in a recession.
   (E) the lower exports due to an appreciating dollar versus other currencies.

4. Which of the following fiscal policies is likely to be most effective when the economy is experiencing an inflationary gap?

   (A) The government decreases taxes and keeps spending unchanged.
   (B) The government increases spending and keeps taxes unchanged.
   (C) The government increases spending matched with an increase in taxes.
   (D) The government decreases spending and keeps taxes unchanged.
   (E) The government increases taxes and decreases spending.

5. Which of the following would likely slow a nation's economic growth?

   (A) Guaranteed low-interest loans for college students.
   (B) Removal of a tax on income earned on saving.
   (C) Removal of the investment tax credit.
   (D) More research grants given to medical schools.
   (E) Conservation policies to manage the renewable harvest of timber.

6. The U.S. economy currently suffers a recessionary gap. Which of the following choices best describes the appropriate fiscal policy, the impact on the market for loanable funds, the interest rate, and the market for the U.S. dollar?

	FISCAL POLICY	LOANABLE FUNDS	INTEREST RATE	MARKET FOR $
(A)	Tax Increase	Demand Rises	Falling	Demand Falls
(B)	Tax Cut	Supply Rises	Rising	Demand Rises
(C)	Tax Cut	Supply Falls	Rising	Demand Rises
(D)	Tax Increase	Supply Falls	Falling	Demand Rises
(E)	Tax Cut	Supply Falls	Rising	Demand Falls

› Answers and Explanations

1. **D**—This is expansionary policy and the others either contract the economy or do nothing.

2. **A**—In an expansion, households should earn more income, which increases the taxes paid to the government. At the same time, people who needed welfare, or other government assistance, do not need it now because the unemployment level is low and wages are high. In this time of prosperity, the government should run a budget surplus.

3. **B**—If the government borrows to expand the economy, interest rates rise, thus crowding out private investors. This shifts AD leftward, weakening the fiscal policy impact.

4. **E**—Real GDP is at a level above full employment so AD must be shifted leftward. Choice D shifts AD to the left and lessens the inflationary gap, but choice E couples higher taxes with lower spending and therefore is the most effective remedy. All other choices increase AD and worsen the inflationary gap.

5. **C**—An investment tax credit rewards firms that invest in physical assets. Removal of this tax credit slows investment, productivity and growth. All other policies would increase the productivity of resources or increase technological innovation.

6. **C**—When facing a recessionary gap, the appropriate fiscal policy is to cut taxes and run a budget deficit. The borrowing necessary to pay for a budget deficit decreases the supply of loanable funds and increases the interest rate. Rising interest rates create a stronger demand for the U.S. dollar because U.S. Treasury bondholders are receiving more interest income. Knowing that the economy is in a recession allows you to quickly eliminate all tax increases.

› Rapid Review

Fiscal policy: deliberate changes in government spending and net tax collection to affect economic output, unemployment, and the price level. Fiscal policy is typically designed to manipulate AD to "fix" the economy.

Expansionary fiscal policy: increases in government spending or lower net taxes meant to shift the aggregate expenditure function upward and shift AD to the right.

Contractionary fiscal policy: decreases in government spending or higher net taxes meant to shift the aggregate expenditure function downward and shift AD to the left.

Sticky prices: if price levels do not change, especially downward, with changes in AD, then prices are thought of as sticky or inflexible. Keynesians believe the price level does not usually fall with contractionary policy.

Budget deficit: exists when government spending exceeds the revenue collected from taxes.

Budget surplus: exists when the revenue collected from taxes exceeds government spending.

Automatic stabilizers: mechanisms built into the tax system that automatically regulate, or stabilize, the macroeconomy as it moves through the business cycle by changing net taxes collected by the government. These stabilizers increase a deficit during a recessionary period and increase a budget surplus during an inflationary period, without any discretionary change on the part of the government.

Crowding out effect: when the government borrows funds to cover a deficit, the interest rate increases and households and firms are "crowded out" of the market for loanable funds. The resulting decrease in C and I dampens the effect of expansionary fiscal policy.

Net export effect: a rising interest rate increases foreign demand for U.S. dollars. The dollar then appreciates in value, causing net exports from the United States to fall. Falling net exports decreases AD, which lessens the impact of the expansionary fiscal policy. This is a variation of crowding out.

Productivity: the quantity of output that can be produced per worker in a given amount of time.

Human capital: the amount of knowledge and skills that labor can apply to the work that they do and the general level of health that the labor force enjoys.

Non-renewable resources: natural resources that cannot replenish themselves. Coal is a good example.

Renewable resources: natural resources that can replenish themselves if they are not over-harvested. Lobster is a good example.

Technology: a nation's knowledge of how to produce goods in the best possible way.

Investment tax credit: a reduction in taxes for firms that invest in new capital like a factory or piece of equipment.

Supply-side fiscal policy: fiscal policy centered on tax reductions targeted to AS so that real GDP increases with very little inflation. The main justification is that lower taxes on individuals and firms increase incentives to work, save, invest, and take risks.

CHAPTER 16

Money, Banking, and Monetary Policy

IN THIS CHAPTER

Summary: People often think that economics is the study of money. While you have already discovered that, strictly speaking, this is not the case, there is no denying the critical role of money in any economic system in the exchange of goods and services, employment of resources, and macroeconomic stability. This chapter first briefly defines money, the functions that it serves, and the market for it. Following a brief overview of the fractional reserve banking system, we discuss money creation. We then focus on the tools of monetary policy that the Federal Reserve uses to influence the macroeconomy. The chapter concludes with a discussion of fiscal and monetary policy coordination and how one school of economic thought sees the role of monetary policy.

Key Ideas

✪ Money as an Asset
✪ The Money Market
✪ The Money Multiplier
✪ Monetary Policy

16.1 Money and Financial Assets

Main Topics: *Financial Assets, Functions of Money, Money Supply, Money Demand, The Money Market, Changes in Money Supply*

In general, money is anything that is used to facilitate exchange of goods between buyers and sellers. Human history has seen many things used as money, from shells and tobacco to gold and spices. These different forms of money have all performed certain functions.

Financial Assets

We have already discussed investment in physical (or capital) assets like machinery or new construction as components of GDP. The firm invests in a physical asset if the expected rate of return is at least as high as the real interest rate. Sometimes firms and households seek other forms of assets as a place for their money. Financial investments also yield a rate of return. We spend much more time discussing money as a short-term financial asset, but quickly address other financial assets like stocks and bonds.

Stocks

A share of stock represents a claim on the ownership of the firm and is exchanged in a stock market. Firms that wish to raise money for capital investment can issue, and sell, these partial shares of ownership. This form of **equity financing** avoids debt, but relinquishes a small degree of control over the management, and profits, of the firm.

Bonds

A bond is a certificate of indebtedness. When a firm wants to raise money by borrowing, they can issue corporate bonds that promise the bondholders the principle amount, plus a specified rate of interest, with repayment on a specific maturity date. This form of **debt financing** commits the corporation to interest payments, but does not relinquish shares of ownership. Like stocks, bonds can be bought and sold in a secondary market. We shall see how the central bank can intervene in this market in a way that has profound effects on the economy.

Functions of Money

Today's paper and coin money is called **fiat money** because it has no intrinsic value (like gold) and no value as a commodity (like tobacco). It serves as money because the government declares it to be legal tender, and in doing so, the government assures us that it performs three general functions.

- *Medium of Exchange.* Your employer exchanges dollars for an hour of your labor. You exchange those dollars for a grocer's pound of apples. The grocer exchanges those dollars for an orchard's apple crop, and on and on. If it weren't for money, we would still be engaging in the barter system, an extremely inconvenient way to exchange goods and services. If I were a cheese maker and I wanted apples, I would need to find an orchard that also needed cheese, and this would be a supremely difficult way to do my shopping.
- *Unit of Account.* Units of currency (dollars, euro, yen, etc.) measure the relative worth of goods and services just as inches and meters measure relative distance between two points. Again, this is an improvement over the barter system where all goods are measured in terms of many other goods. The value of a pound of cheese in a barter economy is measured in a dozen eggs, or a half pound of sausage, or three pints of ale. With money, the value of cheese, and all other goods and services, is measured in terms of a monetary unit like dollars.
- *Store of Value.* So long as prices are not rapidly increasing, money is a decent way to store value. You can put money under your mattress or in a checking account and it is still useful, with essentially the same value, a week or a month later. If I were the town cheese maker, I must quickly find merchants with whom to exchange my cheese, because if I wait too long, moldy cheese loses its value.

Time Value of Money

Money may serve as a store of value, but money does lose its value over time. Most of us prefer to receive money income as early as possible (the sooner we can begin to consume stuff) and pay our debts as late as possible. If you lend your best friend $100, would you rather be paid back tomorrow, or five years from tomorrow? If you are not going to charge your best friend any interest on this loan, then you probably prefer your money as soon as possible. If your best friend paid you back in five years without interest, your $100 would have certainly lost value over time. After all, not having $100 for such a long period of time means that you were unable to consume $100 worth of goods! Delaying your consumption of goods that would give you utility must surely come at a cost. The idea of a **time value of money** is perhaps the most important reason for paying interest on savings and charging interest on borrowing.

Present Value and Future Value

Many decisions in life involve paying upfront costs today with the promise of a payoff tomorrow or even years from now. Many of you are familiar with this trade-off because you were told by a parent that, "If you finish eating your vegetables, you can watch TV before bedtime"; or "If you wash the car, you can go to the movie with your friends." As you consider attending college, the same principle applies. The costs (tuition, books, etc.) are paid today; but the payoffs (marketable skills, useful knowledge, etc.) are received years from today. As the previous section illustrates, dollars today are worth more than future dollars; so there must be a way to convert present and future dollars to the same time period so that wise decisions can be made. The interest rate is the key.

Let's again assume that you are going to lend your friend $100, and that he is going to pay you back in one year. We'll also assume that there is no inflation, so a 10 percent nominal interest rate is equal to the real interest rate. The opportunity cost of lending your friend $100 is the interest you could have earned—$10, after a year had passed. So the interest rate measures the cost to you of forgoing the use of that $100. After all, you could have spent $100 on clothing right now that would have provided immediate benefit to you. To see the relationship between dollars today (present value, or PV) and dollars one year from now (future value, or FV), a simple equation is applied:

$$FV = PV*(1 + r) \text{ or, using our example,}$$
$$FV = \$100*(1.10) = \$110$$

In other words, one year into the future, that $100 will be worth $110.
We can also rearrange our equation and solve for the present value PV:

$$PV = FV/(1 + r) \text{ and, using our example again,}$$
$$PV = \$110/(1.10) = \$100$$

This tells us that $110 a year from now is worth only $100 in today's dollars.
If you were lending the money for a period of two years,

$$FV = PV(1 + r)^2 = \$100(1.10)*(1.10) = \$121$$

What does this all mean? It means that your friend, as a borrower, must pay you $21 to compensate you for the fact that he has your $100 for a period of two years. It also says that had you, as a saver, put the $100 in the bank today, two years from now you would have $121 to spend on goods and services. This implies that you would be completely indifferent to having $100 in your hand today or $121 two years from today. The differing sums are equivalent units of purchasing power, just measured at two different points in time; and it is the interest rate that equates the two.

- Money today is more valuable than the same amount of money in the future.
- The present value of $1 received one year from now is $1/(1 + r)$.
- The future value of $1 invested today is $1*(1+r)$.

- Interest paid on savings and interest charged on borrowing is designed to equate the value of dollars today with the value of future dollars.

Supply of Money

At the core of monetary policy is regulation of the supply of money. Because our paper money is not backed by precious metals or crown jewels, we trust the government to keep the value of our money as stable as possible. This value is guaranteed by stabilizing the **money supply**, which is measured by the central bank as **M1, M2 and M3**, each of which is more broadly defined and less liquid than the previous one. **Liquidity** refers to how easily an asset can be converted to cash. A five-dollar bill, already being cash, is as liquid as it gets. A Van Gogh hidden in your attic is also an asset, but not a very liquid one.

"There are a couple of questions on this. Know what is included in each category."
—Kristy,
AP Student

- $M1$ = cash + coins + checking deposits + traveler's checks. $M1$ is the most liquid of money definitions.
- $M2 = M1$ + savings deposits + small (i.e., under $100,000 certificates of deposit) time deposits + money market deposits + money market mutual funds. $M2$ is slightly less liquid because the holders of these assets would likely incur a penalty if they wished to immediately convert the asset to cash.
- $M3 = M2$ + large (over $100,000) time deposits. $M3$ is even less liquid than $M2$ because the asset holder would have to wait longer to liquidate a CD or pay a large penalty.

At any given point in time, the supply of money is a constant. This implies that the current money supply curve is vertical. Because other measures of money supply are based upon the most liquid $M1$, when we discuss the money supply, we focus on $M1$. Insight gained from studying the expansion and contraction of $M1$ can be applied to $M2$ and $M3$.

Demand for Money

People demand goods like cheese because cheese helps satisfy wants. People demand money because it facilitates the purchase of cheese and other goods. In addition to this transaction demand for money, people also demand money as an asset, just as a government bond or a share of Intel stock is an asset. We quickly look at demand for money as the sum of money demand for transactions and money demand as an asset.

Transaction Demand. As nominal GDP increases, consumers demand more money to buy goods and services. For a given price level, if output increases, more money is demanded. Or for a given level of output, if the price level rises, more money is demanded. If nominal GDP is $1000 and each dollar is spent an average of four times each year, money demand for transactions would be $1000/4 = $250. If nominal GDP increases to $1200, money demand for transactions increases to $1200/4 = $300. We assume that the nominal rate of interest does not affect transaction demand for money, so when plotted on a graph with the nominal interest rate on the y axis, it is a constant.

Asset Demand. Money can be held as an asset at very little risk. If you put money under your mattress, there is the advantage of knowing that a crashing stock market or real estate market does not diminish the value of this asset. The main disadvantage of putting this asset under your mattress is that it cannot earn you any interest. As the interest rate on bonds rises, the opportunity cost of holding money under your mattress begins to rise and so you are more likely to lessen your asset demand for money. At a lower interest rate on bonds, you are more likely to increase your asset demand for money.

Total Demand. Plotted against the nominal interest rate, the transaction demand for money is a constant MD_t. Adding this constant amount of money needed to make transactions to a downward sloping asset demand for money (MD_a) provides us with the total money demand curve. This is seen in Figure 16.1.

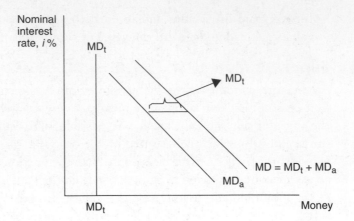

Figure 16.1

The Money Market

The central bank, having established a given level of money supply circulating in the economy, allows us to incorporate a vertical money supply (MS) curve with a downward sloping money demand curve to complete the money market. John Maynard Keynes developed the *theory of liquidity preference*, which postulates that the equilibrium "price" of money is the interest rate where money supply intersects money demand. Just like any market, if the price is below equilibrium (a shortage) the price must rise, and if the price is above equilibrium (a surplus) the price must fall. Money demand can increase if more transactions are being made, but the real focus of the rest of this chapter is on changes in money supply. Equilibrium is shown in Figure 16.2.

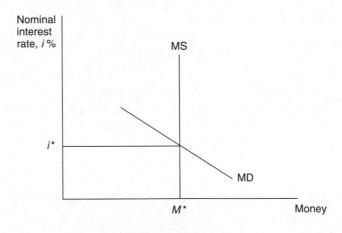

Figure 16.2

"How Is the Money Market Different from the Market for Loanable Funds?"

Tough question, we'll take it in two and a half parts. I'm sure the first is much more helpful, the second much more esoteric and the half is going to earn you the graphing points.

1. *Breadth of scope*

*"This is an important question. Know the difference."
—AP Teacher*

   The supply of loanable funds, which varies directly with the interest rate, comes from national saving. The supply of money is more inclusive than just saving; it includes currency and checking deposits. A $100 bill in your wallet would fall into the money supply curve, but not into the supply of loanable funds. The demand for loanable funds comes from investment demand. The demand for money includes the money used for investment, but also for consumption (transaction demand) and for holding as an asset (asset demand). So basically the money market, both on the supply and the demand side, is broader, and more inclusive, than the market for loanable funds. The price (a.k.a. the interest rate) appears to be the same in both markets, and is the result of . . .

2. *Different philosophies*

We don't want to delve too much into the Keynesian versus Classical philosophical debates because they are quite unlikely to appear on your AP Macroeconomics exam. It can seem a little confusing to show the interest rate as the "price" in both the market for loanable funds and the market for money. The reason that both markets are presented here, and in your textbook, is that they represent fundamental differences in macroeconomic philosophies.

• Classical economists believe that the price level is flexible and long-run GDP adjusts to the natural rate of employment. For any level of GDP, the interest rate adjusts to balance the supply and demand for loanable funds and the price level adjusts to keep the money market in equilibrium.

• Keynesian economists believe that the price level is sticky. For any price level, the interest rate adjusts to balance the supply and demand for money and this interest rate influences aggregate demand and thus the short-run level of GDP.

• Bottom line here: the two different ways of looking at the interest rate are the result of two different ways of looking at the overall economy and the difference in the long-run (Classical) and short-run (Keynesian) views of the economy.

. . . and ½. *Graphing*

While it *appears* that the same interest rate is graphed on the vertical axis of both the loanable funds and money market graphs, they are not in fact the same. It is correct to label the vertical axis of the money market with a nominal interest rate and the vertical axis of the loanable funds market with the real interest rate. Changes in the money market can be viewed as short-term changes and therefore the role of expected inflation is negligible. For long-term decisions like investment and saving, the price of investment, or return on saving, does depend upon expected inflation and so it makes sense to focus on the real rate of interest when making long-term plans. Here's a way to keep it straight: "Loanable funds are REAL-ly fun."

Changes in Money Supply

When we talk about monetary policy, we are really talking about money supply policy. The tools used to expand or contract the money supply are discussed later in this chapter, but it's useful to see what is happening in the money market when the money supply increases or decreases.

An Increase in the Money Supply

Like the market for any commodity, when the supply increases, there exists a temporary surplus at the original equilibrium price. The money market is no different. At the original interest rate of 10 percent, the supply of money is $1000. Now the Fed increases the money supply to $1500. In Figure 16.3, you can see that at 10 percent, there is now a surplus of money.

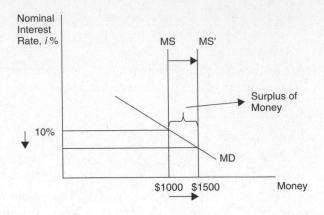

Figure 16.3

With surplus money on their hands, people find other assets, like bonds, as places to put the extra money. As more people increase the demand for bonds, the bond price rises, and this lowers the effective interest rate paid on the bonds.

How does this work?

A bond is selling at a price of $100 and promises to pay $10 in interest. The interest rate = $10/$100 = 10 percent. But if the price of the bond is driven up to $125, the same $10 of interest actually yields only $10/$125 = 8.0 percent. With lower interest rates available in the bond market, the opportunity cost of holding cash falls and the quantity of money demanded increases until MD = $1500. An increase in the money supply therefore decreases the interest rate.

A Decrease in the Money Supply

If the Fed decides to decrease the supply of money from $1000 to $500, there is a shortage of money at the 10 percent interest rate. A shortage of money sends some bondholders to sell their bonds so that they have money for transactions. An increase in the supply of bonds in the bond market decreases the price and increases the rate of interest earned on those assets.

How does this work?

If the original price of the bond is $100, promising to pay $10 in interest, the interest rate is 10 percent. If the price falls to $90, the same $10 of interest now yields $10/$90 = 11.1 percent. Higher interest rates on bonds increase the opportunity cost of holding cash and so the quantity of money demanded falls until the interest rate rises to the point where MD = $500. This adjustment is seen in Figure 16.4.

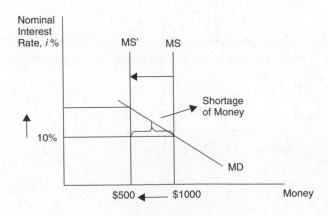

Figure 16.4

- Increasing the money supply lowers interest rates as surplus money moves into the bond market, increasing bond prices.
- Decreasing the money supply increases interest rates as a shortage of money creates a sell-off of bonds, decreasing bond prices.

16.2 Fractional Reserve Banking and Money Creation

Main Topics: *Fractional Reserve Banking, Money Creation, The Money Multiplier*

If you asked 10 bank tellers in your hometown, "do you create money here?" I'm guessing that 9 or 10 of them would reply, "no way." They're wrong. The fractional reserve system of banking, plus the bank's profit motive, creates money and opens the door for the Fed to promote or inhibit such money creation.

Fractional Reserve Banking

Fractional reserve banking is a system in which only a fraction of the total money supply is held in reserve as currency. The short story that follows illustrates how fractional reserve banking might have evolved.

Eli's Community Bank (ECB) opens its doors and is now accepting deposits from citizens who want a safe place to put their money. Eli promises to always keep 100 percent of their money on hand so that if a person needs to buy groceries, he or she can simply withdraw some money and take it to the store.

One day, a citizen came up to the bank asking to borrow some money to start a lemonade stand, but Eli had to turn her down because if any of his customers came to withdraw money for groceries, and found that it was not in the vault, they would be extremely irritated. After a month or so, Eli observes that on any given day, there are very few withdrawals and most of the time the deposited money just sits there in the vault, doing nothing.

Eli decides, just to be safe, to hold a small percentage of his total deposits in the vault to cover any daily withdrawals, and earn some interest income by lending out the rest to households or small businesses. He even realizes that he must offer a small rate of interest to his depositors to compensate them for that "whole time value of money thing." The fraction of total deposits kept on reserve is called the **reserve ratio**. Each time he receives a deposit, he puts that fraction in the vault and lends the rest. This process is the foundation for money creation and the Fed's ability to conduct monetary policy.

Money Creation

A specific example of how the fractional reserve system can multiply one new bank deposit into new created money illustrates the process of money creation.

The reserve ratio is 10 percent. In other words,

Reserve ratio (rr) = required reserves/total deposits = .10

One way to see how checking deposits turn into loans, and how loans turn into new money is to create a basic T-account, or **balance sheet**. The idea of a balance sheet is to show the assets and liabilities of a bank. In our example, total assets must equal total liabilities.

Asset. Anything owned by the bank or owed to the bank is an asset of the bank. Cash on reserve is an asset and so are loans made to citizens.

Liability. Anything owned by depositors or lenders to the bank is a liability. Checking deposits of citizens or loans made to the bank are liabilities to the bank.

Step 1. Katie takes $1000 from under her mattress, deposits it at ECB, and opens a checking account. ECB must put $100 in required reserves, but the remaining $900 are excess reserves and can be either kept on reserve or lent.

Balance Sheet ECB (Step 1)

ASSETS		LIABILITIES	
Required Reserves	$ 100	Checking Deposits	$1000
Excess Reserves	$ 900		
Total Assets	$ 1000	Total Liabilities	$1000

Step 2. ECB lends all $900 in excess reserves to Bob, a local farmer. This loan does not yet count as newly created money.

Balance Sheet ECB (Step 2)

ASSETS		LIABILITIES	
Required Reserves	$ 100	Checking Deposits	$1000
Excess Reserves	$ 0		
Loans	$ 900		
Total Assets	$ 1000	Total Liabilities	$1000

Step 3. Bob uses his $900 at Tractor Supply, which has a checking account with ECB. Checking deposits have now increased by $900 and this is new money. ECB must keep $90 as required reserves and there are now $810 of excess reserves.

Balance Sheet ECB (Step 3)

ASSETS		LIABILITIES	
Required Reserves	$ 190	Checking Deposits	$1900
Excess Reserves	$ 810		
Loans	$ 900		
Total Assets	$1900	Total Liabilities	$1900

Step 4. ECB makes an $810 loan to Brent, who is looking to buy some furniture. Brent spends $810 at Furniture Factory, which also banks with ECB, increasing checking deposits by $810. ECB must keep $81 in required reserves and there are now $729 in excess reserves.

Balance Sheet ECB (Step 4)

ASSETS		LIABILITIES	
Required Reserves	$ 271	Checking Deposits	$2710
Excess Reserves	$ 729		
Loans	$ 1710		
Total Assets	$ 2710	Total Liabilities	$2710

The Money Multiplier

An initial deposit of $1000 creates, after only two loans are made and redeposited, $2710 of checking deposits. This process could continue until there are no more excess reserves to be loaned, ultimately creating $10,000 of deposits. Of this $10,000 of deposits, $1000 was already in the money supply (cash under Katie's mattress) but $9000 has been created as new money, seemingly out of thin air. This process is known as the money multiplier, which measures the maximum amount of new checking deposits that can be created by a single dollar of excess reserves. The idea of the money multiplier, not to mention the mathematics, is identical to our coverage of the spending multiplier.

$$M = 1/(\text{reserve ratio}) = 1/rr \; (= 1/.10 = 10 \text{ in our example})$$

We had $900 in initial excess reserves and this would have multiplied into a maximum of $9000 if (a) at every stage the banks kept only the required dollars in reserve, (b) at every stage borrowers redeposit funds into the bank and keep none as cash, and (c) borrowers are willing to take out excess reserves as loans.

- The maximum, or simple, money multiplier $M = 1/rr$.
- An initial amount of excess reserves multiplies by, at most, a factor of M.

This process works in reverse if, instead of an initial deposit, Katie makes a $1000 withdrawal. Rather than money creation, this could be called money destruction.

16.3 Monetary Policy

Main Topics: *Expansionary Policy, Contractionary Policy, Open Market Operations, The Discount Rate, The Reserve Ratio, Fiscal and Monetary Coordination, Quantity Theory of Money*

The Federal Reserve, the central bank of the United States, has three general tools of monetary policy at their disposal. The Fed can engage in open market operations, can change the discount rate, and can change the reserve ratio. Each of these can be used to expand or contract the money supply to stabilize prices and move the economy to full employment. We first look at the intended effects of expansionary and contractionary monetary policy and then investigate each of the tools in more detail.

Expansionary Monetary Policy

Unlike fiscal policy, which has a rather direct impact on real GDP, unemployment, and the price level, monetary policy takes a longer path to impact. Expansionary monetary policy is designed to fix a recession and increase aggregate demand, lower the unemployment rate, and increase real GDP. By increasing the money supply, the interest rate is lowered. A lower rate of interest increases private consumption and investment, which shifts the aggregate demand curve to the right. This process is illustrated in Figures 16.5 and 16.6.

Contractionary Monetary Policy

As you might imagine, contractionary monetary policy has the opposite effect as expansionary and is designed to avoid inflation by decreasing aggregate demand, which lowers the price level and decreases real GDP back to the full employment level. By decreasing the money supply, the interest rate is increased. A higher rate of interest decreases private consumption and investment, which shifts the aggregate demand to the left. This process is illustrated in Figures 16.7 and 16.8.

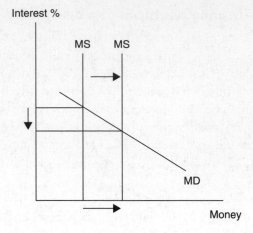

Figure 16.5

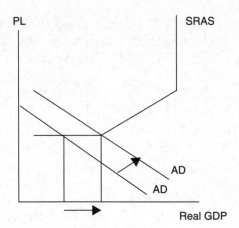

Figure 16.6

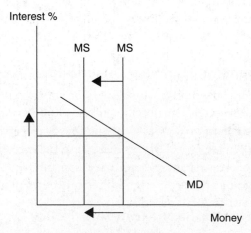

Figure 16.7

The chain of events for expansionary and contractionary monetary policy is described below.

- *Unemployment is too high* →↑MS, ↓*i*%, ↑*I*, ↑AD, ↑real GDP, ↓unemployment
- *Inflation is too high* →↓MS, ↑*i*%, ↓*I*, ↓AD, ↓real GDP, ↓price level

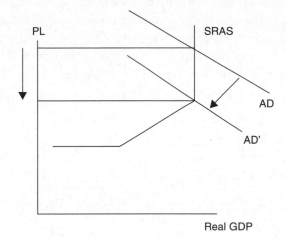

Figure 16.8

Open Market Operations

Just like individuals and firms, the Federal Reserve, through the Federal Open Market Committee (FOMC), can buy and sell securities on the open market. Such an **open market** operation (OMO) typically involves the buying (or selling) of Treasury bonds from (or to) commercial banks and the general public. Of the three tools of monetary policy, conducting OMOs is by far the approach most frequently taken by the Fed.

Buying Securities. Commercial banks hold Treasury bonds as an asset rather than excess cash reserves. If the Fed offers to buy some of those securities, the banks would receive excess cash reserves and the Fed would get the bonds. When banks have excess reserves, the money creation process begins. The money supply increases and the interest rate falls.

"This is a great way to remember this!"
—AP Teacher

- When the Fed buys securities, the money supply expands. If it helps to remember, use this: "**B**"uying "**B**"onds = "**B**"igger "**B**"ucks (money supply).

Selling Securities. Commercial banks might be in the market to buy Treasury bonds as an asset rather than excess cash reserves. If the Fed offers to sell some of their securities, the banks would get the bonds and their excess cash reserves would fall. When banks have fewer excess reserves, the money destruction process begins. The money supply decreases and the interest rate rises.

- When the Fed sells securities, the money supply contracts. If it helps to remember, use this: "**S**"elling "**B**"onds = "**S**"maller "**B**"ucks (money supply).

The Federal Funds Rate

The discussion of OMOs seems to indicate that the buying and selling of securities is the main policy tool. If the FOMC wants to lower the interest rate, they buy bonds. If the FOMC wants to increase the interest rate, they sell bonds. In reality, the federal funds rate is set as a target interest rate and the FOMC then proceeds to engage in OMOs to hit that target rate. The federal funds rate is the interest rate that banks charge other banks for short-term loans. One bank might need to borrow funds from other banks, primarily to cover an unexpected dip in reserves. The important thing to remember is that our analysis of monetary policy is the same whether we talk about changes in the money supply or changes in the target federal funds interest rate.

Changing the Discount Rate

There are times when commercial banks need a short-term loan from the Fed. When they borrow from the Fed, they pay an interest rate called the **discount rate**. When the Fed lowers the discount rate, it makes it more affordable for commercial banks to increase excess reserves by borrowing from the Fed. The entire amount of the loan goes into excess reserves and can be borrowed by customers of the bank, increasing the money supply. As a practical matter, the Fed tends to change the discount rate in lockstep with the federal funds target rate.

- Lowering the discount rate (or federal funds rate) increases excess reserves in commercial banks and expands the money supply.
- Raising the discount rate (or federal funds rate) decreases excess reserves in commercial banks and contracts the money supply.

Changing the Required Reserve Ratio

Though rarely used, if the Fed wants to increase excess reserves, and expand the money supply, it could change the fraction of deposits that must be kept as required reserves. If the reserve ratio is .50, half of all deposits must be kept in the vault, leaving half to be loaned as excess reserves. The money multiplier in this case is two. But if the required reserve ratio were lowered to .10, 90 percent of all deposits could be lent as excess reserves. The money multiplier increases to 10.

- Lowering the reserve ratio increases excess reserves in commercial banks and expands the money supply.
- Increasing the reserve ratio decreases excess reserves in commercial banks and contracts the money supply.

Table 16.1 summarizes how various tools of monetary policy can be used to target high unemployment or high inflation.

Table 16.1

	PROBLEM: HIGH UNEMPLOYMENT	PROBLEM: HIGH INFLATION
Monetary tool could be . . .	Buy bonds in an OMO	Sell bonds in an OMO
Or . . .	Lower the discount rate	Raise the discount rate
Or . . .	Lower the reserve ratio	Raise the reserve ratio
Effect would be . . .	$\uparrow$MS, $\downarrow i$%, $\uparrow I$, $\uparrow$AD, $\uparrow$real GDP, $\downarrow$unemployment	$\downarrow$MS, $\uparrow i$%, $\downarrow I$, $\downarrow$AD, $\downarrow$real GDP, $\downarrow$price level

Coordination of Fiscal and Monetary Policy

Congress and the President develop fiscal policy through the annual process of approving a spending budget and tax law. Chapter 15 showed how fiscal policy can be used to move the economy closer to full employment, but that it has some weakness, especially in the case when private investment is crowded out by government borrowing.

> *"Monetary policy does not affect government spending."*
> *—Elliot, AP Student*

The central bank develops monetary policy and is independent of Congress and the President. This independence of monetary policy is believed to be a critical balance to fiscal policy that can be heavily politicized. After all, the creators of fiscal policy are elected by their constituents and might let an upcoming election taint the policy-making process. The central bank, free of election pressures, can develop monetary policy without this conflict of interest and perhaps work to counterbalance the downsides to fiscal policy. Let's look at three different scenarios where monetary and fiscal policy might be coordinated in Table 16.2.

Table 16.2

THE PROBLEM:	FISCAL POLICY SOLUTION	BUDGET IMPACT	POTENTIAL CONSEQUENCE	MONETARY POLICY COMPLEMENT	KEEP AN EYE ON . . .
Deep recessionary gap and high unemployment	Tax cuts *and* increased spending to rapidly increase AD and real GDP.	Large Deficit	Higher interest rates, crowding out private investment, lower net exports and even weaker AD.	Expand MS to keep interest rates from rising. Increases AD to assist fiscal policy.	Higher Inflation
Mild recessionary gap and moderate unemployment	Tax cuts *or* increased spending to gradually increase AD and real GDP.	Moderate Deficit	Rising prices. Mild crowding out and lower net exports, weakening AD.	Contract MS to keep inflation from rising. Decreases AD, offsetting fiscal policy.	Rising Interest Rates
Inflationary gap	Tax hikes *and/or* decreased spending to rapidly decrease AD and real GDP.	Surplus	Lower interest rates "crowding in" private investment, higher net exports and even stronger AD.	Contract MS to keep interest rates from falling. Decreases AD to assist fiscal policy.	Higher Unemployment

- In a deep recessionary gap, expansionary monetary policy could be used to assist expansionary fiscal policy to quickly move to full employment. The risk then becomes a burst of inflation.
- In a mild recessionary gap, contractionary monetary policy could be used to offset expansionary fiscal policy to gradually move to full employment. The risk then becomes rising interest rates.
- In an inflationary gap, contractionary monetary policy could be used to assist contractionary fiscal policy to put downward pressure on the price level. The risk then becomes a rising unemployment rate.

Quantity Theory of Money

Fiscal policy directly puts money into, or takes money out of, the pockets of households and firms, but monetary policy depends upon several cause-and-effect relationships. The critical link between monetary policy and real GDP is the relationship between changes in money supply, the real interest rate, and the level of private investment. After all, if the money supply increases and there is no increase in investment, expansionary monetary policy would have no effect on real GDP. Some economists, called monetarists, have become proponents of the **quantity theory of money**, which postulates that increasing the money supply has no effect on real GDP, but only serves to increase the price level.

One way to view this theory is to use the **equation of exchange**. The equation says that nominal GDP ($P * Q$) is equal to the quantity of money (M) multiplied by the number of times each dollar is spent in a year (V), the **velocity of money**. For example, if in a given year the money supply is $100 and nominal GDP is $1000, then each dollar must be spent 10 times; $V = 10$.

$$MV = PQ, \text{ or } V = PQ/M$$

If the money supply (M) increases, this increase must be reflected in the other three variables. To accommodate an increase in money supply, the velocity of money must fall, the price level must rise, or the economy's output of goods and services must increase.

Historically the velocity of money in the United States has been fairly constant and stable, so the increase in M must result in changes in either P or Q. Economists believe that the quantity of output produced in a given year is a function of technology and the supply of resources, rather than the quantity of money circulating in the economy. Therefore the increased money supply is going to only create a higher price level—inflation.

- The quantity theory of money predicts that any increase in the money supply only causes an increase in the price level.

❯ Review Questions

1. Which function of money best defines $1.25 as the price of a 20 oz. bottle of pop?

   (A) Medium of exchange.
   (B) Unit of account.
   (C) Store of value.
   (D) Transfer of ownership.
   (E) Fiat money.

2. If a bank has $500 in checking deposits and the bank is required to reserve $50, what is the reserve ratio? How much does the bank have in excess reserves?

   (A) 10 percent, $450 in excess reserves.
   (B) 90 percent, $50 in excess reserves.
   (C) 90 percent, $450 in excess reserves.
   (D) 10 percent, $50 in excess reserves.
   (E) 10 percent, $500 in excess reserves.

3. Which is NOT a way that the Fed can affect the money supply?

   (A) A change in discount rate.
   (B) An open market operation.
   (C) A change in reserve ratio.
   (D) A change in tax rates.
   (E) Buying Treasury securities from commercial banks.

4. If the money supply increases, what happens in the money market? (Assuming money demand is downward sloping)

   (A) The nominal interest rates rises.
   (B) The nominal interest rates falls.
   (C) The nominal interest rate does not change.
   (D) Transaction demand for money falls.
   (E) Transaction demand for money rises.

5. To move the economy closer to full employment, the central bank decides that the federal funds rate must be increased. The appropriate open market operation is to _____, which _____ the money supply, _____ aggregate demand, and fight _____.

	OMO	MONEY SUPPLY	AD	TO FIGHT
(A)	Buy bonds	Increases	Increase	Unemployment
(B)	Buy bonds	Increases	Increase	Inflation
(C)	Sell bonds	Decreases	Decrease	Unemployment
(D)	Sell bonds	Decreases	Increase	Inflation
(E)	Sell bonds	Decreases	Decrease	Inflation

6. Which of the following is a predictable advantage of expansionary monetary policy in a recession?

   (A) Decreases aggregate demand so that the price level falls.
   (B) Increases aggregate demand, which increases real GDP and increases employment.
   (C) Increases unemployment, but low prices negate this effect.
   (D) It keeps interest rates high, which attracts foreign investment.
   (E) It boosts the value of the dollar in foreign currency markets.

› Answers and Explanations

1. **B**—The price in this case measures the relative price (value) of the pop.

2. **A**—The reserve ratio = Required reserves/checking deposits = .1 = 10%. Excess reserves = (checking deposits – required reserves) = ($500 – $50) = $450.

3. **D**—The Fed has no control of tax rates, which are an example of fiscal policy. All of the other choices are tools of monetary policy.

4. **B**—If the demand for money is downward sloping, the nominal interest rate falls because the money supply curve has shifted rightward.

5. **E**—If the central bank has decided that moving to full employment requires an increase in the federal funds rate, it must sell bonds to decrease the money supply. The resulting increase in interest rates decreases AD and puts downward pressure on the price level.

6. **B**—Expansionary monetary policies decrease the interest rate causing AD to increase, which increases GDP at equilibrium and increases employment.

› Rapid Review

Stock: a certificate that represents a claim to, or share of, the ownership of a firm.

Equity financing: the firm's method of raising funds for investment by issuing shares of stock to the public.

Bond: a certificate of indebtedness from the issuer to the bond holder.

Debt financing: a firm's way of raising investment funds by issuing bonds to the public.

Fiat money: paper and coin money used to make transactions because the government declares it to be legal tender. Because it has no intrinsic value, it is backed by the public's trust that the government maintains its value.

Functions of money: money serves three functions. It serves as a medium of exchange, a unit of account, and a store of value.

Money supply: the quantity of money in circulation as measured by the Federal Reserve (the Fed) as $M1$, $M2$, and $M3$. Assumed to be fixed at a given point in time.

$M1$; the most liquid of money definitions and the basis for all other more broadly defined measures of money. $M1$ = cash + coins + checking deposits + traveler's checks.

Liquidity: a measure of how easily an asset can be converted to cash. The more easily it can be converted to cash, the more liquid the asset.

Transaction demand: the amount of money held in order to make transactions. This is not related to the interest rate, but increases as nominal GDP increases.

Asset demand: the amount of money demanded as an asset. As nominal interest rates rise, the opportunity cost of holding money begins to rise and you are more likely to lessen your asset demand for money.

Money demand: the demand for money is the sum of money demanded for transactions and money demanded as an asset. It is inversely related to the nominal interest rate.

Theory of Liquidity Preference: Keynes' theory that the interest rate adjusts to bring the money market into equilibrium.

Fractional reserve banking: a system in which only a fraction of the total money deposited in banks is held in reserve as currency.

Reserve ratio: the fraction of total deposits that must be kept on reserve. rr = (required reserves)/(total deposits).

Required reserves: the portion of a deposit that must be held at the bank for withdrawals. Required Reserves = Reserve ratio * Total Deposits.

Excess reserves: the portion of a deposit that may be borrowed by customers. Excess Reserves = (1–rr) * Total Deposits.

Balance sheet or T-account: a tabular way to show the assets and liabilities of a bank. Total assets must equal liabilities.

Asset of a bank: anything owned by the bank or owed to the bank is an asset of the bank. Cash on reserve is an asset and so are loans made to citizens.

Liability of a bank: anything owned by depositors or lenders is a liability to the bank. Checking deposits of citizens or loans made to the bank are liabilities to the bank.

Money multiplier: this measures the maximum amount of new checking deposits that can be created by a single dollar of excess reserves. $M = 1/($reserve ratio$) = 1/$rr. The money multiplier is smaller if (a) at any stage the banks keep more than the required dollars in reserve, (b) at any stage borrowers do not redeposit funds into the bank and keep some as cash, and (c) customers are willing to borrow.

Expansionary monetary policy: designed to fix a recession and increase aggregate demand, lower the unemployment rate, and increase real GDP, which may increase the price level.

Contractionary monetary policy: designed to avoid inflation by decreasing aggregate demand, which lowers the price level and decreases real GDP back to full employment.

Open Market Operations (OMOs): a tool of monetary policy, it involves the Fed's buying (or selling) of securities from (or to) commercial banks and the general public.

Federal funds rate: the interest rate paid on short-term loans made from one bank to another. When this rate is a target for an OMO, bonds are bought or sold accordingly until the interest rate target has been met.

Discount rate: the interest rate commercial banks pay on short-term loans from the Fed.

Quantity Theory of Money: a theory that asserts that the quantity of money determines the price level and that the growth rate of money determines the rate of inflation.

Equation of Exchange: the equation says that nominal GDP ($P * Q$) is equal to the quantity of money (M) multiplied by the number of times each dollar is spent in a year (V). $MV = PQ$.

Velocity of money: the average number of times that a dollar is spent in a year. V is defined as PQ/M.

CHAPTER 17

International Trade

IN THIS CHAPTER

Summary: Economists agree on few things, but one of the few unifying themes in economics is that free trade between two nations is mutually beneficial. Chapter 17 begins by reviewing the concept of comparative advantage and gains from trade, and the difference between the domestic and world price of a good. This chapter also revisits the currency exchange markets to illustrate how trade between nations requires the trade of currency and the connection of monetary policy to foreign exchange rates. Lastly we look at the economic impact of trade barriers.

Key Ideas

- ✪ Absolute and Comparative Advantage
- ✪ Specialization and Gains From Trade
- ✪ Balance of Payments
- ✪ Foreign Exchange
- ✪ Trade Barriers

17.1 Comparative Advantage and Gains from Trade

Main Topics: *Comparative and Absolute Advantage, Gains from Trade, Exports, Imports and the World Price*

Chapter 5 of this book introduces, albeit from the microeconomic perspective, the concept of production possibility frontiers (PPFs). Comparative advantage and specialization at the microeconomic level explains why brain surgeons do not fly 747s and pilots do not analyze CAT scans. At the macroeconomic level, the **Law of Comparative Advantage** says that nations can mutually benefit from trade so long as the relative production costs differ.

Comparative and Absolute Advantage

Our discussion of production possibilities illustrated the Law of Increasing Costs. The more an economy produces of any one good, the more costly it becomes to produce the next unit. Rising costs of production lead to a search for less costly ways to produce and consume those goods. In many cases, this search leads to a potential trading partner who has **comparative advantage** in the production of a good. If Nation ABC can produce a good at lower opportunity cost than can Nation XYZ, it is said that Nation ABC has comparative advantage. An example can illustrate how this works between two states, but the same principle works between two nations.

Example:

Climate and topography have blessed Indiana with land extremely suitable for the cultivation of soybeans, but with very little harvestable timber. Oregon's timber production is unmatched, but farmers find it difficult to produce a self-sustaining soybean crop. Table 17.1 summarizes the production possibilities of these two isolated economies. Because Oregon can produce more timber than Indiana, Oregon is said to have an **absolute advantage** over Indiana in timber production. Indiana has an absolute advantage over Oregon in soybean production. Trade does not rely on absolute advantages, but on comparative advantages.

Table 17.1

INDIANA		OREGON	
Soybeans (tons)	Timber (tons)	Soybeans (tons)	Timber (tons)
0	6	0	10
9	3	5	5
18	0	10	0

Comparative Advantage and Specialization

In isolation, both states can produce soybeans and timber along their production possibility frontiers, which are constrained by available technology and resources. Suppose that without trade, they enjoy consuming at the midpoint of the frontier. But if there are differences in production costs, they can each gain from specialization and trade. The opportunity costs of each good can be found from the table and can be illustrated in a production possibility frontier for each state.

Oregon:
Opportunity cost of timber is 1 soybean.
Opportunity cost of soybeans is 1 timber.

Indiana:
Opportunity cost of timber is 3 soybeans.
Opportunity cost of soybeans is 1/3 timber.

Since Indiana can produce soybeans at a cost that is lower than Oregon's cost of soybeans, Indiana has a comparative advantage in soybeans. Oregon can produce timber at a lower cost than Indiana's cost of timber, so Oregon has a comparative advantage in timber production. With these differences in cost, Indiana should specialize in soybean production (zero timber) while Oregon should specialize in timber production (zero soybeans), then trade. These specialization points are labeled in Figure 17.1.

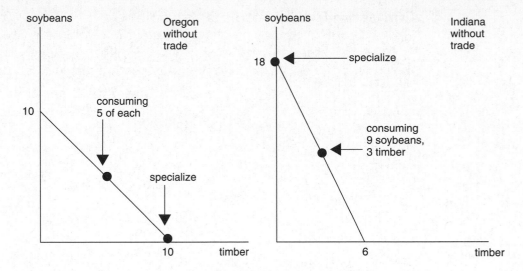

Figure 17.1

Gains from Trade

After each state specializes, suppose that each decides to keep half of their production and send the other half to the other state. See Figure 17.2.

Oregon:

Produce 10 timbers and send 5 to Indiana in exchange for 9 soybeans. Cost of a soybean before trade was 1 timber. Now I'm getting 9 soybeans, but only giving up 5. The cost now is 5/9, which is less than 1 timber. Great deal!

Indiana:

Produce 18 soybeans, and send 9 to Oregon in exchange for 5 timbers. Cost of a timber before trade was 3 soybeans. Now I'm getting 5 timbers and only giving up 9 soybeans. The cost now is 9/5, which is less than 3 soybeans. Great deal!

Another look at the production possibility frontiers after the trade shows that each state has actually moved *beyond* the constraints of their technology and resources.

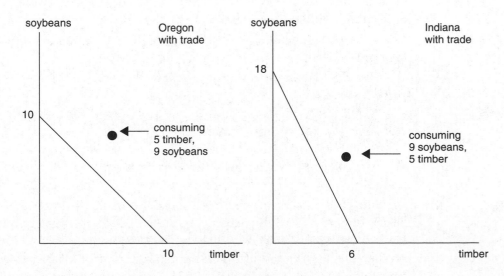

Figure 17.2

Consumption Frontier

There are many such trade possibilities. Figure 17.3 overlaps the two production possibility frontiers. The line that connects Indiana's specialization of soybeans to Oregon's specialization of timber is called the **consumption possibility frontier** because with trade, each state can consume along this line; without trade, these points are impossible to attain.

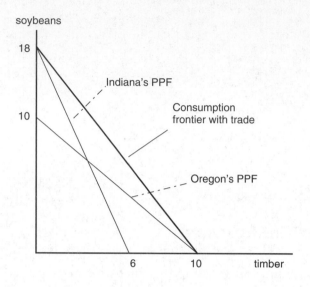

Figure 17.3

- If the opportunity costs of production are different, two economies find it mutually beneficial to specialize and trade.
- If you have comparative advantage in production of a good, specialize in production of that good and trade for the other.
- Specialization and trade allow nations to consume beyond the PPF.
- Free trade (i.e., without trade barriers) based on comparative advantage allows for a more efficient allocation of resources and greater prosperity for the trading partners than can be achieved without free trade.

Exports, Imports, and the World Price

In the market for a commodity like soybeans, many nations are both producers of soybeans and traders of soybeans. Whether or not a nation is a net exporter or a net importer of soybeans depends upon the difference between the **world price** with trade, and the **domestic price** without trade.

Domestic Market Without Trade

Figure 17.4 illustrates the competitive U.S. market for soybeans without trade. The competitive price of $10 per bushel is found at the intersection of domestic demand and supply. At this point six million bushels are produced.

World Market With Trade

If the United States begins to trade soybeans with other nations, the world price may rise above, or fall below, $10 per bushel. If the world price falls to $8, there exists a shortage of soybeans in the U.S. market. Domestic producers supply only four million bushels, but domestic consumers demand eight million bushels. The United States must then import the difference of four million bushels. If the world price rises to $12, there exists a four million bushel surplus in the U.S. market and the United States exports this surplus.

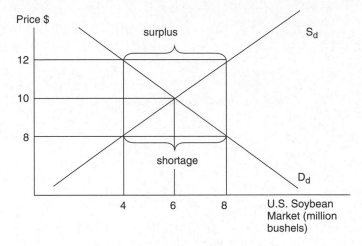

Figure 17.4

- If the world price of a good is above the domestic price, the nation becomes an exporter of that good.
- If the world price of a good is below the domestic price, the nation becomes an importer of that good.

17.2 Balance of Payments

Main Topic: *Balance of Payments Accounts*

If Japanese citizens wish to purchase U.S. soybeans, the Japanese must pay in dollars. If U.S. citizens wish to buy Spanish olives, the Americans must pay in euros. Before goods can be exchanged between foreign trading partners, the currency of the importing nation must first be converted to the currency of the exporting nation.

Balance of Payments Accounts

When American citizens and firms exchange goods and services with foreign consumers and firms, payments are sent back and forth through major banks around the world. The Bureau of Economic Analysis tracks the flow of goods and currency in the **balance of payments statement**. This statement summarizes the payments received by the United States from foreign countries and the payments sent by the United States to foreign countries. Table 17.2 summarizes the main components of a hypothetical balance of trade for 2005.

Current Account

The current account shows current import and export payments of both goods and services. It also reflects investment income sent to foreign investors and investment income received by U.S. citizens who invest abroad. For example, if a Canadian is receiving dividends from an American corporation or interest from a U.S. Treasury bill, these dollars would be sent out of the country. After accounting for all of the payments sent to foreign countries and payments received from foreign countries, the balance on the current account in 2005 was –$26. A deficit balance such as this tells us that the United States sent more American dollars abroad than foreign currency received in current transactions.

Table 17.2

U.S. BALANCE OF PAYMENTS (HYPOTHETICAL)			
Current Account			
Goods exports	$30		
Goods imports	−$50		
Balance on goods (merchandise)		*−$20*	
Service exports	$18		
Service imports	−$12		
Balance on services		*$6*	
Balance on goods and service		*−$14*	Note: This negative balance indicates a trade deficit in goods and services.
Net investment income	−$5		
Net transfers	−$7		
Balance on current account		*−$26*	
Capital (or Financial) Account			
Inflow of foreign assets to U.S.	$35		
Outflow of U.S. assets abroad	−$20		
Balance on capital account		*$15*	
Official Reserves Account			
Official reserves		*$11*	
		$0	

Capital (or Financial) Account

When a nation buys a foreign firm, or real estate or financial assets of another nation, it appears in the capital account. For example, if a Swedish firm buys a manufacturing facility in Idaho, or if a Mexican citizen buys a U.S. Treasury bond, it is recorded as an inflow of foreign capital assets into the United States. If an American firm buys a ship-building company in Turkey, it would be an outflow of assets to foreign nations. A surplus balance of $11 tells us that there was more foreign capital investment in the United States than there was U.S. investment abroad.

Official Reserves Account

The Federal Reserve holds quantities of foreign currency called **official reserves**. When adding the current account and the capital account, if the United States has sent more dollars out than foreign currency has come in, as in the hypothetical example above, there exists a **balance of payments deficit**. In this case the Fed credits the account so that it balances. This is similar to taking money from your savings account to make up for an over-drafted checking account. If the current and capital account balances are positive, more foreign currency was coming into the United States than American dollars flowed abroad.

With this **balance of payments surplus**, the Fed transfers the surplus currency back into official reserves.

A Circular Flow of Dollars

With the exception of some statistical discrepancies, the U.S. dollars that Americans send to foreigners are equal to the U.S. dollars that foreigners send to Americans. It is helpful to think of the global circulation of dollars as another example of the circular-flow model. When you buy an imported jacket made in Honduras, this appears in the U.S. current account as a negative entry, because those dollars are leaving the country. However, what will a Honduran jacket producer do with those dollars? American dollars in Honduras are not very useful unless they are being spent on either American-made goods and services or American assets. One way or another, either through the purchase of an American good (like a Ford) or the purchase of an American financial asset (like a share of Ford stock), those dollars will return as a positive entry in either the current or capital account. And while the Federal Reserve will make short-term adjustments to the official reserves account to balance the difference between the current account balance and the capital account balance, in the long-term, dollars that leave the U.S. will eventually circle back into the U.S. Thus, with all else equal, if Americans import more goods and services from abroad, the current account will move in the deficit direction but the capital/financial account will move in the surplus direction as those dollars return.

- U.S. imports require a demand for foreign currency and a supply of U.S. dollars.
- U.S. exports require a supply of foreign currency and a demand for U.S. dollars.
- If current account balance + capital account balance < 0, there is a balance of payments deficit.
- If current account balance + capital account balance > 0, there is a balance of payments surplus.

17.3 Foreign Exchange Rates

Main Topics: *The Currency Market, Depreciation and Appreciation, Changes in Exchange Rates, Connection to Monetary Policy*

The previous section of the chapter discussed accounting for the flow of goods and services and currency between trading partners. The foreign exchange market, the topic of the following section, facilitates the importing and exporting of goods around the world.

Currency Markets

When nations trade goods and services, they are implicitly trading currency. The rate of exchange between two currencies is determined in the foreign currency market. Some nations fix their exchange rates while others are allowed to "float" with the forces of demand and supply. For example, in the flexible exchange market for euros pictured in Figure 17.5, the equilibrium $2 dollar price of a euro is at the intersection of the supply of euros and the demand. Likewise, in the market for dollars seen in Figure 17.6 the equilibrium euro price of one dollar is .50 euros. This floating exchange rate has an impact on the balance of payments of both the United States and the European Union.

- The **exchange rate** between two currencies tells you how much of one currency you must give up to get one unit of the second currency.
- For example, if $2 = 1 euro, $1 = .5 euro.
- For example, if $1 = 10 pesos, $.10 = 1 peso.

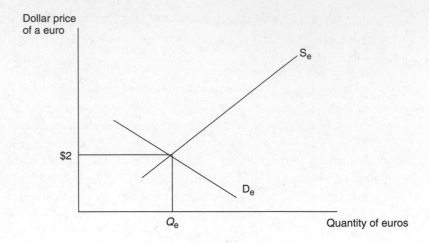

Figure 17.5

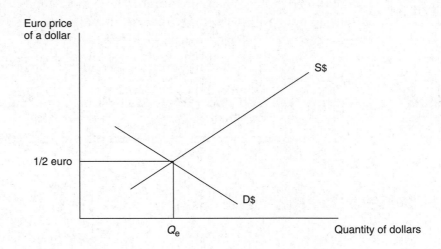

Figure 17.6

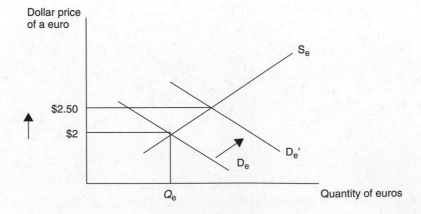

Figure 17.7

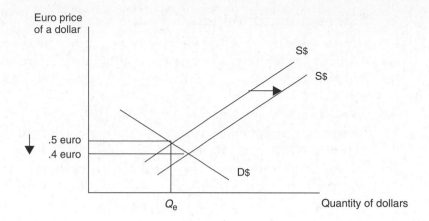

Figure 17.8

Appreciating and Depreciating Currency

If the U.S. economy is strong, Americans increase their demand for European goods and services. As American consumers increase their demand for the euro, they increase the supply of dollars in the foreign exchange market; the dollar price of a euro rises, and the euro price of a dollar falls. The euro as an asset is **appreciating** in value and the dollar as an asset is **depreciating** in value. The changing value of euros and dollars is seen in Figures 17.7 and 17.8.

- When the price of a currency is rising, it is said to be appreciating or "stronger". More dollars are needed to buy a euro.
- When the price of a currency is falling, it is said to be depreciating or "weaker". Fewer euros are needed to buy a dollar.

Changes in Exchange Rates

The above example illustrates that market forces and changing macroeconomic variables have an impact in the rate of exchange between the dollar and the euro. There are several determinants that affect currency appreciation and depreciation.

Consumer Tastes. When domestic consumers build a stronger preference for foreign-produced goods and services, the demand for those currencies increases and the dollar depreciates. On the other hand, if foreign consumers increase their demand for U.S.-made goods, the dollar appreciates.

Relative Incomes. When one nation's macroeconomy is strong and incomes are rising, all else equal, they increase their demand for all goods, including those produced abroad. So if Europeans are enjoying economic growth and the United States is in a recession, the relative buying power of European citizens is growing. They increase their consumption of both domestic and U.S.-made goods, increasing demand for the dollar and appreciating its value.

Relative Inflation. If one nation's price level is rising faster than another nation, consumers seek the goods that are relatively less expensive. If European inflation is higher than inflation in the United States, American-made goods are a relative bargain to German consumers and the dollar appreciates. This is another good reason for the Fed to keep inflationary pressure low.

Speculation. Because foreign currencies can be traded as assets, there are investors who seek to profit from buying currency at a low rate and selling it at a higher rate. For example, if it appears that future interest rates will fall in the United States relative to interest rates in Japan, the yen is looking like a good investment. Speculators would then increase their demand for Japanese assets, thus appreciating the yen and depreciating the dollar.

Connection to Monetary Policy

A final variable that affects the price of one currency relative to another is a difference in relative interest rates between nations. When the Fed increases the money supply, the interest rates on American financial assets begin to fall. If the interest rate is relatively lower in the United States, people around the world see U.S. financial assets as less attractive places to put their money. Demand for the dollar falls, and the dollar depreciates relative to other foreign currencies. A depreciating dollar makes goods in the United States less expensive to foreign consumers, so American net exports increase, which shifts the AD to the right.

Likewise, if the Fed decreases the money supply, American interest rates begin to rise and the dollar appreciates relative to foreign currencies. An appreciating dollar makes American goods more expensive to foreign consumers, decreasing American net exports, shifting AD to the left.

Be careful! When interest rates rise, we see a decrease in capital investments (machinery and other equipment) because it becomes more costly to borrow for those projects. But, when interest rates rise, we see an increase in financial investments (bonds) because income earned on those bonds is rising.

- If the Fed $\uparrow$ MS, $\downarrow i\%$, $\downarrow$D\$, Depreciates the \$, $\uparrow$ U.S. Net Exports, $\uparrow$ AD.
- If the Fed $\downarrow$ MS, $\uparrow i\%$, $\uparrow$D\$, Appreciates the \$, $\downarrow$ U.S. Net Exports, $\downarrow$ AD.

Pay attention to the relationship between relative interest rates and exchange rates because it has made an appearance on several recent AP Macroeconomics exams.

All else equal, demand for the U.S. dollar increases and the dollar appreciates relative to the euro if:

- European taste for American-made goods is stronger.
- European relatives incomes are rising, increasing demand for U.S. goods.
- The U.S. relative price level is falling, making U.S. goods relatively less expensive.
- Speculators are betting on the dollar to rise in value.
- The U.S. relative interest rate is higher, making the United States a relatively more attractive place for financial investments (i.e., bonds).

17.4 Trade Barriers

Main Topics: *Tariffs, Quotas*

The issue of free trade is hotly politicized. Proponents usually argue that free trade raises the standard of living in **both nations**, and most economists agree. Detractors argue that free trade, especially with nations that pay lower wages than those paid to domestic workers, costs domestic jobs in higher-wage nations. The evidence shows that in some industries, job losses have certainly occurred as free trade has become more prevalent. To protect domestic jobs, nations can impose trade barriers. Tariffs and quotas are among the most common of barriers.

Tariffs

In general, there are two types of tariffs. A **revenue tariff** is an excise tax levied on goods that are not produced in the domestic market. For example, the United States does not produce bananas. If a revenue tariff were levied on bananas, it would not be a serious impediment to trade, and it would raise a little revenue for the government. A **protective tariff** is an excise tax levied on a good that is produced in the domestic market.

Though this tariff also raises revenue, the purpose of this tariff, as the name suggests, is to protect the domestic industry from global competition by increasing the price of foreign products.

Example:

The domestic supply and demand for steel is pictured in Figure 17.9. The domestic price is $100 per ton and the equilibrium quantity of domestic steel is 10 million tons. Maybe other nations can produce steel at lower cost. As a result, in the competitive world market, the price is $80 per ton. At that price, the United States would demand 12 million tons, but only produce eight million tons and so four million tons are **imported**. It is important to see that in the competitive (free-trade) world market, consumer surplus is maximized and no dead weight loss exists. You can see the consumer surplus as the triangle below the demand curve and above the $80 world price.

If the steel industry is successful in getting a protective tariff passed through Congress, the world price rises by $10, increasing the quantity of domestic steel supplied, reducing the amount of steel imported from four million to two million tons. A higher price and lower consumption reduces the area of consumer surplus and creates dead weight loss.

Economic Effects of the Tariff

- *Consumers pay higher prices and consume less steel.* If you are building airplanes or door hinges, you have seen an increase in your costs.
- *Consumer surplus has been lost.*
- *Domestic producers increase output.* Domestic steel firms are not subject to the tariff, so they can sell more steel at the price of $90 than they could at $80.
- *Declining imports.* Fewer tons of imported steel arrive in the United States.
- *Tariff revenue.* The government collects $10*2 million = $20 million in tariff revenue as seen in the shaded box in Figure 17.10 This is a transfer from consumers of steel to the government, not an increase in the total well being of the nation.
- *Inefficiency.* There was a reason the world price was lower than the domestic price. It was more efficient to produce steel abroad and export it to the United States. By taxing this efficiency, the United States promotes the inefficient domestic industry and stunts the efficient foreign sector. As a result, resources are diverted from the efficient to the inefficient sector.
- *Dead weight loss now exists.*

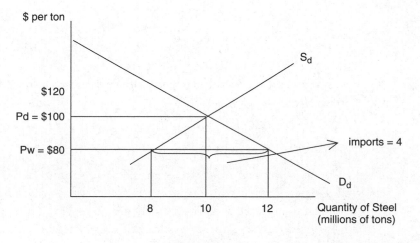

Figure 17.9

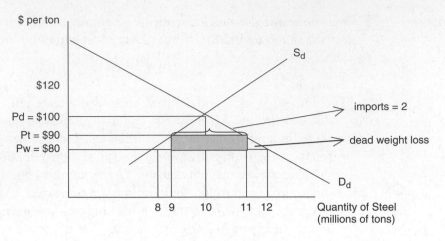

Figure 17.10

Quotas

Quotas work in much the same way as a tariff. An **import quota** is a maximum amount of a good that can be imported into the domestic market. With a quota, the government only allows two million tons to be imported. Figure 17.11 looks much like Figure 17.10, only

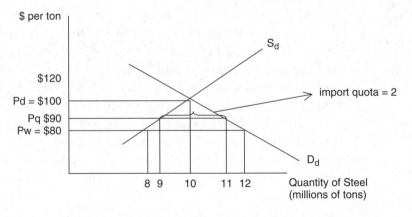

Figure 17.11

> "It is important to know the differences between tariffs and quotas"
> —Lucas, AP Student

without revenue collected by government. So the impact of the quota, with the exception of the revenue, is the same: higher consumer price and inefficient resource allocation.

Tariffs and quotas share many of the same economic effects.

- Both hurt consumers with artificially high prices and lower consumer surplus.
- Both protect inefficient domestic producers at the expense of efficient foreign firms, creating dead weight loss.
- Both reallocate economic resources toward inefficient producers.
- Tariffs collect revenue for the government, while quotas do not.

› Review Questions

1. The united states produces rice in a competitive market. With free trade, the world price is lower than the domestic price. What must be true?

   (A) The United States begins to import rice to make up for a domestic shortage.
   (B) The United States begins to export rice to make up for a domestic shortage.
   (C) The United States begins to import rice to eliminate a domestic surplus.
   (D) The United States begins to export rice to eliminate a domestic surplus.
   (E) There is no incentive to import or export rice.

2. If the U.S. dollar and Chinese yuan are traded in flexible currency markets, which of the following causes an appreciation of the dollar relative to the Chinese yuan?

   (A) Lower interest rates in the United States relative to China.
   (B) Lower price levels in China relative to the United States.
   (C) Growing American preference to consume more Chinese-made goods.
   (D) Rising per capita GDP in China, increasing imports from the United States.
   (E) Speculation that the Chinese will decrease the money supply.

3. You hear that the United States has a negative balance in the current account. With this information we conclude that

   (A) there is a trade deficit.
   (B) there is a capital account deficit.
   (C) there is a capital account surplus.
   (D) more U.S. dollars are being sent abroad than foreign currencies are being sent to the United States.
   (E) there is a trade surplus.

4. Which of the following is a consequence of a protective tariff on imported steel?

   (A) Net exports fall.
   (B) Income is transferred from steel consumers to steel producers.
   (C) Allocative efficiency is improved.
   (D) Income is transferred from domestic steel to foreign steel producers.
   (E) Aggregate supply increases.

5. If the Japanese economy suffers a deep, prolonged recession, in what ways would U.S. net exports and the values of the dollar and yen change?

	U.S. NET EXPORTS	VALUE OF DOLLAR	VALUE OF YEN
(A)	Decrease	Increase	Increase
(B)	Decrease	Decrease	Decrease
(C)	Decrease	Decrease	Increase
(D)	Increase	Decrease	Increase
(E)	Increase	Increase	Increase

6. When the United States places an import quota on imported sugar, we expect which of the following effects?

   (A) Consumers seek substitutes for sugar and products that use sugar.
   (B) Consumers consume more sugar and products that use sugar.
   (C) The supply of sugar increases.
   (D) Net exports in the United States fall.
   (E) The government collects revenue on every ton of imported sugar.

❯ Answers and Explanations

1. **A**—If the world price is below the domestic price, a shortage exists in the domestic market. The importation of foreign rice fills this shortage.

2. **D**—Higher per capita income in trading nations increases demand for imported goods. The Chinese consumer increases demand for U.S. goods and services and for dollars.

3. **D**—The trade of goods and services is not the only component of the current account. A negative balance in the current account does not always mean there is a trade deficit. For current transactions, more U.S. dollars were sent abroad than foreign currencies sent to the United States.

4. **B**—Protective tariffs increase the price of steel above the free-trade equilibrium. This higher price is a transfer of money from consumers to domestic producers of steel.

5. **C**—When the Japanese economy is suffering, demand for U.S. goods falls, decreasing U.S. net exports and demand for dollars. The dollar depreciates and the yen appreciates.

6. **A**—A quota increases the price of sugar so consumers seek substitutes. We may see rising demand for sugar-free gum or falling demand for rich desserts.

❯ Rapid Review

Domestic price: the equilibrium price of a good in a nation without trade.

World price: the global equilibrium price of a good when nations engage in trade.

Balance of Payments Statement: a summary of the payments received by the United States from foreign countries and the payments sent by the United States to foreign countries.

Current account: this account shows current import and export payments of both goods and services and investment income sent to foreign investors of United States and investment income received by U.S. citizens who invest abroad.

Capital (or financial) account: this account shows the flow of investment on real or financial assets between a nation and foreigners.

Official reserves account: the Fed's adjustment of a deficit or surplus in the current and capital account by the addition or subtraction of foreign currencies so that the balance of payments is zero.

Exchange rate: the price of one currency in terms of a second currency.

Appreciating (depreciating) currency: when the value of a currency is rising (falling) relative to another currency, it is said to be appreciating (depreciating).

Determinants of exchange rates: external factors that increase the price of one currency relative to another.

Revenue tariff: an excise tax levied on goods not produced in the domestic market.

Protective tariff: an excise tax levied on a good that is produced in the domestic market so that it may be protected from foreign competition.

Import quota: a limitation on the amount of a good that can be imported into the domestic market.

STEP 5

Build Your Test-Taking Confidence

AP Microeconomics Practice Exam 1 for Multiple-Choice Questions

ANSWER SHEET

1 Ⓐ Ⓑ Ⓒ Ⓓ Ⓔ	21 Ⓐ Ⓑ Ⓒ Ⓓ Ⓔ	41 Ⓐ Ⓑ Ⓒ Ⓓ Ⓔ
2 Ⓐ Ⓑ Ⓒ Ⓓ Ⓔ	22 Ⓐ Ⓑ Ⓒ Ⓓ Ⓔ	42 Ⓐ Ⓑ Ⓒ Ⓓ Ⓔ
3 Ⓐ Ⓑ Ⓒ Ⓓ Ⓔ	23 Ⓐ Ⓑ Ⓒ Ⓓ Ⓔ	43 Ⓐ Ⓑ Ⓒ Ⓓ Ⓔ
4 Ⓐ Ⓑ Ⓒ Ⓓ Ⓔ	24 Ⓐ Ⓑ Ⓒ Ⓓ Ⓔ	44 Ⓐ Ⓑ Ⓒ Ⓓ Ⓔ
5 Ⓐ Ⓑ Ⓒ Ⓓ Ⓔ	25 Ⓐ Ⓑ Ⓒ Ⓓ Ⓔ	45 Ⓐ Ⓑ Ⓒ Ⓓ Ⓔ
6 Ⓐ Ⓑ Ⓒ Ⓓ Ⓔ	26 Ⓐ Ⓑ Ⓒ Ⓓ Ⓔ	46 Ⓐ Ⓑ Ⓒ Ⓓ Ⓔ
7 Ⓐ Ⓑ Ⓒ Ⓓ Ⓔ	27 Ⓐ Ⓑ Ⓒ Ⓓ Ⓔ	47 Ⓐ Ⓑ Ⓒ Ⓓ Ⓔ
8 Ⓐ Ⓑ Ⓒ Ⓓ Ⓔ	28 Ⓐ Ⓑ Ⓒ Ⓓ Ⓔ	48 Ⓐ Ⓑ Ⓒ Ⓓ Ⓔ
9 Ⓐ Ⓑ Ⓒ Ⓓ Ⓔ	29 Ⓐ Ⓑ Ⓒ Ⓓ Ⓔ	49 Ⓐ Ⓑ Ⓒ Ⓓ Ⓔ
10 Ⓐ Ⓑ Ⓒ Ⓓ Ⓔ	30 Ⓐ Ⓑ Ⓒ Ⓓ Ⓔ	50 Ⓐ Ⓑ Ⓒ Ⓓ Ⓔ
11 Ⓐ Ⓑ Ⓒ Ⓓ Ⓔ	31 Ⓐ Ⓑ Ⓒ Ⓓ Ⓔ	51 Ⓐ Ⓑ Ⓒ Ⓓ Ⓔ
12 Ⓐ Ⓑ Ⓒ Ⓓ Ⓔ	32 Ⓐ Ⓑ Ⓒ Ⓓ Ⓔ	52 Ⓐ Ⓑ Ⓒ Ⓓ Ⓔ
13 Ⓐ Ⓑ Ⓒ Ⓓ Ⓔ	33 Ⓐ Ⓑ Ⓒ Ⓓ Ⓔ	53 Ⓐ Ⓑ Ⓒ Ⓓ Ⓔ
14 Ⓐ Ⓑ Ⓒ Ⓓ Ⓔ	34 Ⓐ Ⓑ Ⓒ Ⓓ Ⓔ	54 Ⓐ Ⓑ Ⓒ Ⓓ Ⓔ
15 Ⓐ Ⓑ Ⓒ Ⓓ Ⓔ	35 Ⓐ Ⓑ Ⓒ Ⓓ Ⓔ	55 Ⓐ Ⓑ Ⓒ Ⓓ Ⓔ
16 Ⓐ Ⓑ Ⓒ Ⓓ Ⓔ	36 Ⓐ Ⓑ Ⓒ Ⓓ Ⓔ	56 Ⓐ Ⓑ Ⓒ Ⓓ Ⓔ
17 Ⓐ Ⓑ Ⓒ Ⓓ Ⓔ	37 Ⓐ Ⓑ Ⓒ Ⓓ Ⓔ	57 Ⓐ Ⓑ Ⓒ Ⓓ Ⓔ
18 Ⓐ Ⓑ Ⓒ Ⓓ Ⓔ	38 Ⓐ Ⓑ Ⓒ Ⓓ Ⓔ	58 Ⓐ Ⓑ Ⓒ Ⓓ Ⓔ
19 Ⓐ Ⓑ Ⓒ Ⓓ Ⓔ	39 Ⓐ Ⓑ Ⓒ Ⓓ Ⓔ	59 Ⓐ Ⓑ Ⓒ Ⓓ Ⓔ
20 Ⓐ Ⓑ Ⓒ Ⓓ Ⓔ	40 Ⓐ Ⓑ Ⓒ Ⓓ Ⓔ	60 Ⓐ Ⓑ Ⓒ Ⓓ Ⓔ

AP Microeconomics Practice Exam 1

Multiple-Choice Questions

Time—1 hour and 10 minutes

60 questions

For the multiple-choice questions that follow, select the best answer and fill in the appropriate letter on the answer sheet.

1. At the birthday party of your best friend, you see Skylar help himself to a second piece of cake. For this individual, it must be the case that

   (A) the marginal benefit of the second piece of cake is less than the marginal cost.
   (B) the total benefit received from eating cake is falling.
   (C) the ratio of marginal benefit over marginal cost is less than one.
   (D) the marginal benefit of the second piece of cake is greater than the marginal cost.
   (E) Skylar is irrationally consuming too much cake.

2. Nancy has the choice to spend one hour studying for an exam, mowing the lawn for one hour at a wage of $6, or babysitting her niece for one hour at a wage of $8. If we know that Nancy has chosen to study for the exam, which of the following is true?

   (A) The benefit received from studying is greater than the opportunity cost of $8.
   (B) The opportunity cost of studying is $14, which is less than the benefit received from studying.
   (C) Nancy is indifferent between studying and mowing the lawn.
   (D) Nancy's behavior is irrational since babysitting was clearly superior to all other options.
   (E) Nancy is indifferent between babysitting and mowing the lawn.

3. Suppose the market for roses is currently in equilibrium. If the supply of roses falls, while at the same time the demand for roses rises, what can you say about the price and quantity of roses in the market?

   (A) Price and quantity both rise.
   (B) Price rises, but the change in quantity is ambiguous.
   (C) Price and quantity both fall.
   (D) Quantity rises, but the change in price is ambiguous.
   (E) Neither price nor quantity change as these shifts offset one another.

4. The United States is trading salmon to Peru in exchange for anchovies. If these nations are trading based upon relative opportunity costs, what must be the case?

   (A) The United States has comparative advantage in anchovy production and Peru has comparative advantage in salmon production.
   (B) The United States has comparative advantage in salmon production and Peru has comparative advantage in anchovy production.
   (C) The United States has absolute advantage in anchovy production and Peru has absolute advantage in salmon production.
   (D) The United States has absolute advantage in salmon production and Peru has absolute advantage in anchovy production.
   (E) The United States has comparative advantage in salmon production and Peru has absolute advantage in anchovy production.

5. Which of the following is the best example of a public good?

   (A) Private violin lessons
   (B) The volunteer fire department in your community
   (C) A ticket for admission to a museum
   (D) A bag of potato chips
   (E) A history textbook

6. Which of the following statements are true of a capitalist market economy?

   I. Economic resources are publicly owned.
   II. Freedom of enterprise is critical.
   III. The price system allocates resources in the most efficient way.

   (A) I only
   (B) II only
   (C) III only
   (D) I and II only
   (E) II and III only

Questions 7–9 refer to the graph below.

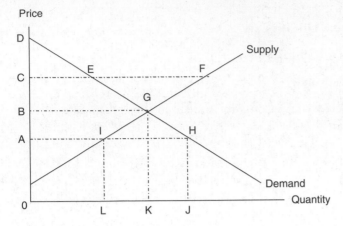

7. Assuming no government involvement in this market, if the current price were at the level of 0A, we would expect

(A) a surplus in the market to be eliminated by rising prices.
(B) a shortage in the market to be eliminated by falling prices.
(C) a surplus in the market to be eliminated by falling prices.
(D) a shortage in the market to be eliminated by rising prices.
(E) a decrease in quantity supplied and an increase in quantity demanded as the price rises.

8. If the market is initially in equilibrium, which of the following would create a new equilibrium at point H?

(A) A decrease in consumer income if this good is normal.
(B) An increase in the price of a substitute for this good.
(C) A decrease in the cost of a production input for this good.
(D) An increase in the number of consumers of this good.
(E) An increase in consumer income if this good is normal.

9. If the price were to rise from 0B to 0C,

(A) dollars spent on this good would increase if demand for the good were price elastic.
(B) dollars spent on this good would decrease if demand for the good were price inelastic.
(C) dollars spent on this good would increase if demand for the good were price inelastic.
(D) dollars spent on this good would increase if demand for the good were unitary price elastic.
(E) dollars spent on this good would decrease if demand for the good were unitary price elastic.

10. Every day Molly spends her lunch money consuming apples, at $1 each, and oranges, at $2 each. At her current level of consumption, Molly's marginal utility of apples is 12 and her marginal utility of oranges is 18. If she has already spent all of her lunch money, how should Molly change her consumption decision to maximize utility?

(A) She should make no changes; she is consuming the utility maximizing combination of apples and oranges.
(B) She should increase her apple consumption and decrease her orange consumption until the marginal utility per dollar is equal for both.
(C) She should decrease her apple consumption and increase her orange consumption until the marginal utility per dollar is equal for both.
(D) She should increase her apple consumption and decrease her orange consumption until the marginal utility is equal for both.
(E) She should decrease her apple consumption and increase her orange consumption until the marginal utility is equal for both.

11. When the production or consumption of a good creates a positive externality, it is deemed a market failure because at the market quantity

(A) the marginal social benefit exceeds the marginal social cost.
(B) the marginal social cost exceeds the marginal social benefit.
(C) society produces too much of the good.
(D) the private benefits from consuming the good exceed the social benefits.
(E) a surplus of the good always exists without government intervention.

12. Which of the following would best complete a short definition of economics? "Economics is the study of . . ."

(A) how unlimited resources are allocated between scarce wants.
(B) how money is circulated through the economy.
(C) how corporations maximize the share price of their stock.
(D) how nations trade goods and services in a global marketplace.
(E) how scarce resources are allocated to satisfy unlimited wants.

13. Suppose the price elasticity of demand for cigarettes is less than one. When an excise tax is imposed on cigarette production, it changes the price, quantity, and consumer spending in which of the following ways?

	PRICE	QUANTITY	SPENDING
(A)	Decrease	Increase	Increase
(B)	Decrease	Decrease	Decrease
(C)	Increase	Decrease	Decrease
(D)	Increase	Decrease	Increase
(E)	Increase	Increase	Increase

14. Which of the following is true of a price floor?

(A) The price floor shifts the demand curve to the left.
(B) An effective floor creates a shortage of the good.
(C) The price floor shifts the supply curve of the good to the right.
(D) To be an effective floor, it must be set above the equilibrium price.
(E) The government sets the price floor to assist consumers who are exploited at the equilibrium price.

15. You are told that the income elasticity for CDs is + 1.5. This means that

(A) a 10 percent increase in income produces a 15 percent increase in consumption of CDs. CDs are a normal luxury good.
(B) a 10 percent increase in income produces a 15 percent increase in consumption of CDs. CDs are an inferior good.
(C) a 10 percent increase in income produces a 15 percent decrease in consumption of CDs. CDs are an inferior good.
(D) a 10 percent increase in the price of CDs produces a 15 percent decrease in consumption of CDs. CDs are a price elastic good.
(E) a 10 percent increase in the price of CDs produces a 15 percent decrease in consumption of CDs. CDs are a price inelastic good.

16. Which of the following causes the supply curve of paper to shift to the left?

(A) Paper producers expect lower paper prices in the months ahead.
(B) The price of pencils, a complement to paper, increases.
(C) Improvements in the technology used to produce paper.
(D) Household income falls.
(E) Environmental concerns reduce the yearly amount of timber that can be harvested.

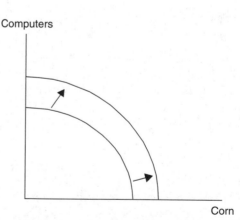

Computers

Corn

17. Using the diagram above, which of the following might have caused the outward movement of the production possibility frontier?

(A) A decrease in the availability of fertile farmland.
(B) A plague of destructive grasshoppers.
(C) An increase in the productivity of the labor force.
(D) A severe and long-lasting drought.
(E) A decline in the rate of technological improvements.

18. Suppose the county government sends each parent a coupon that can be used to subsidize the cost of sending each child to daycare. What would you expect to occur in the market for daycare services?

    (A) The demand for daycare falls, lowering the price.
    (B) The demand for daycare rises, increasing the price.
    (C) The supply of daycare rises, lowering the price.
    (D) The supply of daycare falls, increasing the price.
    (E) A permanent shortage of daycare services exists.

19. Monopoly dead weight loss is the result of

    (A) setting the price above marginal cost.
    (B) setting the price above average total cost.
    (C) monopoly output being greater than the competitive output.
    (D) long-run normal profits.
    (E) marginal revenue equaling marginal cost.

20. The market for Cincinnati Reds baseball tickets is currently in equilibrium. Which of the following events would most likely increase the consumer surplus received by Reds fans?

    (A) The Reds offer discounted parking for all home games.
    (B) The Reds increase hot dog prices to reflect a higher cost of buns.
    (C) The city of Cincinnati is undertaking a huge highway construction project that strands fans in pregame traffic jams for hours.
    (D) The Reds must increase ticket prices to afford the most talented players.
    (E) Fans must pay a steep service charge in order to purchase tickets online or over the phone.

21. If Matt's total utility from consuming bratwurst increased at a constant rate, no matter how many bratwurst Matt consumed, what would Matt's demand curve for bratwurst look like?

    (A) Vertical
    (B) Horizontal
    (C) Downward sloping
    (D) Upward sloping
    (E) First upward, but eventually downward sloping

22. When a firm is earning a normal profit from the production of a good, it is true that

    (A) total revenues from production are equal to explicit costs.
    (B) explicit costs are equal to implicit costs.
    (C) total revenues from production are equal to implicit costs.
    (D) total revenues from production are equal to the sum of explicit and implicit costs.
    (E) implicit costs are greater than explicit costs.

23. You are told that the cross-price elasticity between goods X and Y is +2.0. This means that

    (A) goods X and Y are normal goods.
    (B) goods X and Y are inferior goods.
    (C) goods X and Y are complementary goods.
    (D) goods X and Y are substitute goods.
    (E) good X is twice as elastic as good Y.

24. Which of the following is an example of a long-run adjustment for the owners of a small café?

    (A) The owners switch from whole wheat to sourdough bread.
    (B) The owners hire several part-time workers to cover the dinner shifts.
    (C) The owners work overtime on a busy weekend.
    (D) The owners install more energy-efficient light bulbs in all of the light fixtures.
    (E) The owners buy the office next door and this doubles the customer seating.

25. If total product of labor is rising at an increasing rate,

    (A) marginal product of labor is rising.
    (B) marginal product of labor is at its minimum.
    (C) marginal product of labor is at its maximum.
    (D) marginal cost is rising.
    (E) average product of labor is at its minimum.

26. The demand curve for a perfectly competitive firm's product is

    (A) downward sloping and equal to the market demand curve.
    (B) perfectly elastic.
    (C) perfectly inelastic.
    (D) "kinked" at the going market price.
    (E) the same as the firm's marginal cost curve.

27. Which of the following is true in the long run in perfect competition?

(A) $P = MR = MC = ATC$
(B) $P = MR = MC > ATC$
(C) $P > MR = MC = ATC$
(D) $P = MR > MC = ATC$
(E) $P > MR = MC > ATC$

28. If the market price is above the perfectly competitive firm's average total cost curve, we expect that in the long run,

(A) the industry contracts as firms exit the market.
(B) the industry expands as firms exit the market.
(C) the industry contracts as firms enter the market.
(D) the industry expands as firms enter the market.
(E) the government seeks to regulate the market to insure efficient outcomes.

29. If a market is organized by a cartel, we can expect

(A) normal profits for all cartel firms.
(B) an incentive for cartel firms to cheat on the cartel agreement.
(C) profit maximization by individual firms in the cartel.
(D) allocative efficiency.
(E) perfectly competitive prices.

30. Jason cleans swimming pools in a perfectly competitive local market. A profit-maximizer, he can charge $10 per pool to clean 9 pools per day, incurring total variable costs of $80 and total fixed costs of $20. Which of the following is true?

(A) Jason should shut down in the short run, with economic losses of $20.
(B) Jason should shut down in the short run, with economic losses of $10.
(C) Jason should clean 9 pools per day, with economic losses of $20.
(D) Jason should clean 9 pools per day, with economic losses of $10.
(E) Jason should clean 9 pools per day, with economic profits of $10.

31. Which of the following might explain how a price decrease might cause a decrease in quantity demanded and an upward sloping demand curve?

(A) The good is inferior and the income effect is stronger than the substitution effect.
(B) The good is normal and the income effect is stronger than the substitution effect.
(C) The good is normal and the income effect is weaker than the substitution effect.
(D) The good is inferior and a luxury.
(E) The good is highly subsidized, creating a large increase in marginal utility per dollar.

32. For the perfectly competitive firm, the profit maximizing decision to shut down is made when the price

(A) falls below minimum average total cost.
(B) is greater than minimum average variable cost, but lower than minimum average total cost.
(C) falls below minimum average variable cost.
(D) is equal to minimum average total cost.
(E) is equal to average fixed cost.

33. Declining populations of tuna in the Atlantic Ocean have likely had which of the following impacts on the wages of tuna fishermen, the employment of tuna fishermen, and real estate prices in New England fishing towns?

	FISHERMAN WAGES	EMPLOYMENT OF FISHERMEN	REAL ESTATE PRICES
(A)	Decrease	Increase	Increase
(B)	Decrease	Decrease	Decrease
(C)	Decrease	Decrease	Increase
(D)	Increase	Decrease	Decrease
(E)	Increase	Increase	Increase

34. Which of the following is true of monopoly markets?

(A) Dead weight loss exists in the short run, but not in the long run.
(B) A homogenous product allows for long-run entry of competing firms.
(C) Collusion between close rivals creates pricing above marginal cost.
(D) Barriers to entry allow for the power to set prices above marginal cost.
(E) Allocative efficiency is guaranteed because marginal revenue equals marginal cost.

Questions 35–36 refer to the graph below.

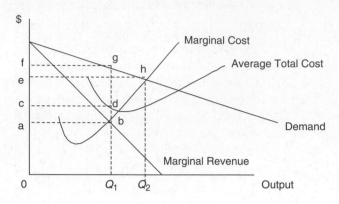

35. If this firm were a profit-maximizing monopolist, the price and output would be which of the following?

(A) 0a and Q_1
(B) 0c and Q_1
(C) 0e and Q_1
(D) 0e and Q_2
(E) 0f and Q_1

36. Dead weight loss is equal to which of the following areas?

(A) abcd
(B) cdfg
(C) 0abQ_1
(D) $Q_1 Q_2$gh
(E) bdgh

Two competing firms are deciding whether to enter a new market or maintain the status quo. Use the following profit matrix to respond to question 37.

FIRM Y		FIRM X	
		ENTER MARKET	STATUS QUO
	Enter Market	X: $3 million Y: $3 million	X: $1 million Y: $6 million
	Status Quo	X: $6 million Y: $1 million	X: $5 million Y: $5 million

37. If these firms do not collude, the outcome will be

(A) Both firms maintain the status quo.
(B) Both firms enter the market.
(C) Firm X enters the market and Firm Y maintains the status quo.
(D) Firm Y enters the market and Firm X maintains the status quo.
(E) Both firms alternate between entering the market and maintaining the status quo.

38. When the marginal product of labor is equal to the average product of labor,

(A) marginal product of labor is at its maximum.
(B) marginal cost of production is at its minimum.
(C) marginal cost is equal to minimum average variable cost.
(D) average total cost is at its minimum.
(E) total product of labor is at its maximum.

Questions 39–41 refer to the graph below.

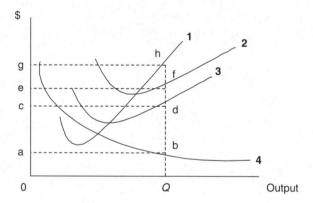

39. The area 0ab$Q$ is equal to

(A) total cost.
(B) total variable cost.
(C) total fixed cost.
(D) marginal cost.
(E) average product of labor.

40. The curve labeled **1** represents which of the following?

(A) Marginal cost
(B) Marginal product of labor
(C) Average total cost
(D) Average variable cost
(E) Average fixed cost

41. If this firm was operating in a perfectly competitive market, and the price was equal to 0g, economic profit would be equal to which of the following areas?

    (A) abcd
    (B) cdgh
    (C) cdef
    (D) efgh
    (E) abgh

42. Which is true of monopolistic competition?

    (A) Firms earn long-run economic profits.
    (B) $P = MR = MC = ATC$.
    (C) Firms spend money to differentiate and advertise their products.
    (D) In the long run the market is allocatively efficient.
    (E) Excess capacity is eliminated in the long run.

43. If firms are entering an industry that is monopolistically competitive, we would expect

    (A) the demand for existing firms to shift rightward.
    (B) the market price of the product to increase.
    (C) the demand for existing firms to become more inelastic.
    (D) economic profits to rise for all firms.
    (E) the demand for existing firms to shift leftward.

44. Monopolistic competition is said to be productively inefficient because

    (A) the long-run price is above minimum average total cost.
    (B) long-run profits are positive.
    (C) firms engage in collusive behavior.
    (D) there exist no barriers to entry.
    (E) there exist diseconomies of scale.

45. One of the reasons that the government discourages and regulates monopolies is that

    (A) producer surplus is lost and consumer surplus is gained.
    (B) monopoly prices insure productive efficiency, but cost society allocative efficiency.
    (C) monopoly firms do not engage in significant research and development.
    (D) consumer surplus is lost with higher prices and lower levels of output.
    (E) lower prices and higher levels of output create dead weight loss.

46. What is one reason why the government discourages collusion between large firms in the same industry?

    (A) Collusive output levels tend to increase, driving the price above competitive levels.
    (B) Consumer surplus falls as the price is driven downward.
    (C) Collusive output levels tend to decrease, driving the price down to competitive levels.
    (D) Joint profit maximization drives profits downward, forcing colluding firms to exit the industry.
    (E) Joint profit maximization costs society consumer surplus as the price rises above competitive levels.

47. In a competitive labor market for housepainters, which of the following would increase the demand for housepainters?

    (A) An effective minimum wage imposed on this labor market.
    (B) An increase in the price of gallons of paint.
    (C) An increase in the construction of new houses.
    (D) An increase in the price of mechanical painters so long as the output effect exceeds the substitution effect.
    (E) An increase in home mortgage interest rates.

48. If a monopsony labor market suddenly were transformed into a perfectly competitive labor market, how would the wage and employment change?

    (A) Both would increase.
    (B) Both would decrease.
    (C) The wage would remain constant, but employment would increase.
    (D) The wage would fall, but employment would increase.
    (E) The wage would rise, but employment would decrease.

49. Which of the following is most likely to be true in the long run for a monopoly firm?

    (A) $P = MR = MC = ATC$
    (B) $P = MR = MC > ATC$
    (C) $P > MR = MC = ATC$
    (D) $P = MR > MC = ATC$
    (E) $P > ATC > MR = MC$

Questions 50–51 refer to the table below, which describes employment and production of a firm.

UNITS OF LABOR	TOTAL PRODUCT	PRICE OF OUTPUT
0	0	$2
1	8	$2
2	20	$2
3	30	$2
4	38	$2
5	44	$2

50. The marginal revenue product of the fourth unit of labor is equal to

(A) $19
(B) $16
(C) $8
(D) $20
(E) $2

51. If the wage paid to all units of labor is $20, how many units of labor are employed?

(A) 1
(B) 2
(C) 3
(D) 4
(E) 5

52. An industry described as an oligopoly would most likely have

(A) normal profits in the long run.
(B) no opportunities for collusive behavior.
(C) significant barriers to entry.
(D) price-taking behavior.
(E) one firm with no close rivals.

53. A minimum wage in the market for fast food workers is likely to produce

(A) an increase in the demand for fast food workers.
(B) a decrease in the supply of fast food workers.
(C) a shortage of fast food workers.
(D) a lower price of fast food products.
(E) a surplus of fast food workers.

54. In order to hire the least-cost combination of labor and capital, the firm must do which of the following?

(A) Find the combination of labor and capital where the marginal product of labor is equal to the marginal product of capital.
(B) Find the combination of labor and capital where the ratio of the marginal product of labor to the marginal product of capital is equal to one.
(C) Find the combination of labor and capital where the marginal product of labor divided by the price of labor is equal to the marginal product of capital divided by the price of capital.
(D) Find the combination of labor and capital where the price of labor is equal to the price of capital.
(E) Find the combination of labor and capital where the marginal revenue product of labor is equal to the marginal revenue product of capital.

55. More college students are graduating with BA degrees in economics. Given this trend, we would expect the wage of BA economists, the employment of BA economists, and the demand for economics textbooks to change in which of the following ways?

	BA ECONOMIST WAGES	EMPLOYMENT OF ECONOMISTS	DEMAND FOR ECONOMICS TEXTBOOKS
(A)	Decrease	Increase	Increase
(B)	Decrease	Decrease	Decrease
(C)	Increase	Decrease	Decrease
(D)	Increase	Decrease	Increase
(E)	Increase	Increase	Increase

56. Which of the following is the best example of a negative externality and the appropriate plan for eliminating it?

    (A) Air pollution from a factory blows downwind and harms children in a small community. Tax the citizens of the community.
    (B) Your neighbor plants a fragrant blooming cherry tree in her front yard. Give a tree subsidy to your neighbor.
    (C) The waste from a hog farm pollutes a neighbor's drinking water. Give a subsidy to the hog farmer.
    (D) A cigarette smoker suffers multiple health problems from using tobacco. Tax the cigarettes that he is smoking.
    (E) Air pollution from a power plant is blowing downwind and harming the trees in your community. Tax the production of electricity.

57. A perfectly competitive employer hires labor up to the point where

    (A) wage = marginal factor cost.
    (B) wage = marginal product of labor.
    (C) wage = marginal revenue.
    (D) wage = marginal revenue product of labor.
    (E) wage = price of the good produced by the labor.

58. The sales tax that you pay at the grocery store is commonly labeled a

    (A) progressive tax.
    (B) regressive tax.
    (C) proportional tax.
    (D) excise tax.
    (E) tax bracket.

59. Which of the following is the best example of the free-rider effect?

    (A) You and a friend take a road trip to Florida in your friend's car. You pay for the gas.
    (B) In exchange for tutoring your friend in economics, she helps you with your geometry assignment.
    (C) You have ordered a big college football game on pay-per-view and several of your buddies show up unannounced to watch it at your place.
    (D) You buy your date dinner, but your date insists on leaving a tip for the server.
    (E) A local Girl Scout troop is giving a "free" carwash. You give them a $5 donation.

Question 60 refers to the graph below.

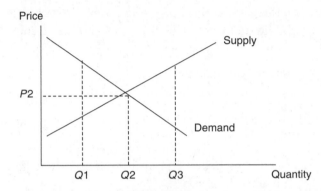

60. If the market for this good was in equilibrium at Q2, but the socially optimal output was Q1, the government could best remedy this _____ of resources by legislating a _____on _____of the good.

    (A) underallocation, per unit tax, consumers
    (B) overallocation, per unit subsidy, consumers
    (C) underallocation, per unit tax, producers
    (D) overallocation, per unit subsidy, producers
    (E) overallocation, per unit tax, producers

› Answers and Explanations

1. **D**—You have to assume that Skylar evaluated the marginal benefits and marginal costs of the second piece of cake and decided that he should consume it.

2. **A**—The opportunity cost is the value of the most attractive alternative; in this case, the babysitting wage.

3. **B**—If demand increases and supply decreases, the price definitely rises. The quantity is ambiguous and depends upon which effect is stronger. Draw these shifting curves in the margin of your exam book.

4. **B**—Trading nations specialize in the good in which they have lower opportunity costs. A nation trades this good to the other, in exchange for the good for which they do not have comparative advantage.

5. **B**—Public goods like police and fire protection are received by all citizens, even if they do not pay.

6. **E**—The citizens privately own resources in capitalist systems.

7. **D**—Prices below equilibrium create shortages, but they do not last.

8. **C**—A rightward shift in supply would move the market to point H and lower input prices would do just that.

9. **C**—If $E_d < 1$, a given % increase in the price outweighs the % decrease in quantity demanded, thus increasing total dollars spent on the good.

10. **B**—The utility maximizing rule requires that MU/P is equal for both goods. Now the MU/P is greater for apples than for oranges. Molly consumes more apples and fewer oranges, which lowers MU of apples and increases the MU of oranges.

11. **A**—Market equilibrium occurs where marginal private benefit equals marginal cost to society. With a positive externality, the MSB > MPB at the market quantity.

12. **E**—This is the definition of economics!

13. **D**—Excise taxes shift a supply curve leftward, increase price, and decrease quantity. If $E_d < 1$ cigarette consumers spend more on cigarettes.

14. **D**—Price floors are legal minimum prices so they are set above equilibrium. A surplus results.

15. **A**—When $E_I > 0$, it is a normal good. When $E_I > 1$, it is a luxury good.

16. **E**—Restricting the supply of a raw material to paper would increase the price of the production input and decrease the supply of paper.

17. **C**—Economic growth is the result of better, or more economic resources or more technological progress. A more productive labor force increases the PPF for both goods.

18. **B**—A subsidy given to consumers acts as an increase in income. Demand for day care rises, raising the price of day care.

19. **A**—If $P = MC$, the market is allocatively efficient and there is no dead weight loss. If the monopoly $P > MC$, DWL emerges.

20. **A**—Anything that effectively lowers the price of attending the Reds game increases CS.

21. **B**—Downward sloping demand is the result of diminishing marginal utility. This consumer's MU is constant, so the demand curve for bratwurst is horizontal.

22. **D**—Normal profits are also thought of as breakeven economic profits.

23. **D**—If $E_{xy} > 0$, goods are substitutes.

24. **E**—Long-run adjustments change the production capacity of a firm.

25. **A**—MP_L tells you how TP_L is changing when more labor is hired. If more labor is increasing TP_L at a faster and faster rate, MP_L is rising.

26. **B**—Perfectly competitive firms are price takers so demand for each firm's product is horizontal, $E_d = \infty$.

27. **A**—A defining outcome of long-run equilibrium in perfect competition.

28. **D**—If $P > ATC$, positive short-run economic profits exist. Long-run entry expands the market.

29. **B**—Cartels are illegal collusive agreements to lower output, raise the price, and maximize joint profits. Each member has an incentive to cheat by producing a little more.

30. **D**—TR > TVC so Jason does not shut down. Subtracting all costs from TR, he is losing $10 per day.

31. **A**—Income and substitution effects work in opposite directions for inferior goods. A lower price prompts a substitution effect, increasing quantity demanded of the good. A lower price increases purchasing power, and for an inferior good, decreases consumption. If the income effect outweighs the substitution effect, we can see an upward sloping demand curve.

32. **C**—This is the shutdown point.

33. **B**—Decreased labor demand lowers wage and employment. Lower incomes and higher unemployment decrease real estate prices.

34. **D**—Barriers to entry are the key to monopoly pricing power.

35. **E**—Find the output where MR = MC and the price is found vertically at the demand curve.

36. **E**—DWL is the area above MC and below the demand curve, between the monopoly output and the perfectly competitive output.

37. **B**—Entering is a dominant strategy for both firms.

38. **C**—MC and AVC are inverses of MP_L and AP_L. Because $MP_L = AP_L$ at the maximum of AP_L, MC = AVC at the minimum of AVC.

39. **C**—Familiarity with cost curves identifies curve 4 as AFC. The area of this rectangle is $Q * AFC = TFC$.

40. **A**—Quickly recognize this as MC.

41. **D**—The profit rectangle is the quantity multiplied by the vertical distance between price and ATC.

42. **C**—With product differentiation, monopolistically competitive firms spend money to promote their product as different from the others.

43. **E**—Entry of new firms takes market share from existing firms so demand curves begin to shift to the left.

44. **A**—Profits are normal and $P = ATC$, but unlike perfect competition $P >$ minimum ATC and so the industry is not productively efficient.

45. **D**—Lost CS is a big reason why government keeps an eye on the monopoly power of firms.

46. **E**—Colluding members of an oligopoly act as a monopolist, restraining competition, restricting output, and increasing the price.

47. **C**—This is the idea of derived demand.

48. **A**—Monopsony lowers both wage and employment when compared to the competitive labor market.

49. **E**—Like the competitive firm, the monopolist produces where MR = MC, but the $P >$ ATC which is most likely even further above MR = MC.

50. **B**—MRP = MP * P. Calculate MP by looking at the difference in TP as one more unit of labor is hired.

51. **C**—Labor is hired to the point where $W =$ MRP so quickly find the point in the table where MP = 10, which when multiplied by $P = \$2$, gives you MRP = $20.

52. **C**—This is a main identifier of oligopoly.

53. **E**—Minimum wages are price floors in a labor market. A surplus results.

54. **C**—This choice describes the least-cost rule for hiring inputs.

55. **A**—Increased labor supply lowers the wage, increases employment, and increases demand for goods that are "tools of the trade."

56. **E**—The appropriate fix to a negative externality is to tax either the producers or consumers of electricity. The health problems of the smoker are not a negative externality as the smoker is not a third party. The non-smoking spouse of the smoker whose health is impaired is a negative externality.

57. **D**—This describes the choice that is made by employers in competitive labor markets.

58. **B**—Sales taxes are typical examples of regressive taxes.

59. **C**—Free riders receive the benefit of a public good without contributing to its production.

60. **E**—If equilibrium output exceeds the socially desirable output, resources are overallocated to production of this good. This negative externality can be fixed with a tax on producers or sometimes on consumers.

AP Microeconomics Practice Exam 1

Free-Response Questions

Planning time—10 minutes

Writing time—50 minutes

At the conclusion of the planning time, you have 50 minutes to respond to the following three questions. Approximately half of your time should be given to the first question and the second half should be divided evenly between the remaining two questions. Be careful to clearly explain your reasoning and to provide clear labels to all graph axes and curves.

1. Bob's Beans is a perfectly competitive soybean producer. The short-run price of soybeans is currently below average total cost, but above Bob's shut-down point.

   (A) Using two correctly labeled graphs, show the soybean market side-by-side with Bob's Beans. Clearly indicate which graph represents the market and which represents Bob's Beans. In your graphs, identify:

      i. Price and quantity in the soybean market.
      ii. Price and quantity for Bob's Beans.
      iii. The area of economic profit or loss for Bob's Beans.

   (B) In a new set of side-by-side graphs for both the market and Bob's Beans, show the long-run adjustment in each of the following:

      i. Price and quantity in the soybean market.
      ii. Price and quantity for Bob's Beans.

   (C) Suppose now that Bob's Beans is a monopoly producer of soybeans. In a correctly labeled graph, show a profit-maximizing monopolist and indicate each of the following:

      i. Price
      ii. Output
      iii. The area of economic profit or loss for Bob's Beans.

2. Molly's lemonade stand employs only labor and lemons to produce lemonade. The table below shows how total production changes at different combinations of labor and lemons. Lemonade sells in a competitive market at $1 per cup.

HOURS OF LABOR	TOTAL PRODUCTION	POUNDS OF LEMONS	TOTAL PRODUCTION
0	0	0	0
1	12	1	9
2	22	2	17
3	30	3	23
4	36	4	27
5	39	5	29
6	40	6	30

   (A) In competitive input markets, each hour of labor costs $6 to employ and each pound of lemons costs $2 to employ. If Molly has a $14 budget for hiring inputs, identify the least-cost combination of labor and lemons. Explain your reasoning.

   (B) At the least-cost combination of labor and lemons, identify each of the following:

      i. The output produced.
      ii. The economic profit earned.

   (C) Identify the profit-maximizing quantities of labor and lemons. At the profit-maximizing quantities of labor and lemons, identify each of the following:

      i. The output produced.
      ii. The economic profit earned.

3. The production of pork on large corporate hog farms generates pollution that seeps into the ground and can pollute the local well-water supply.

(A) From society's perspective, use marginal analysis to explain how the competitive market creates a misallocation of resources in the market for pork.

(B) In a correctly labeled graph, illustrate the market for pork and identify:
    i. The market equilibrium price and quantity of pork.
    ii. The socially optimal price and quantity of pork.

(C) Recommend an appropriate policy that would correct for the misallocation of resources in the pork industry.

› Free-Response Grading Rubric

Note: Based on my experience, these point allocations roughly approximate the weighting on similar questions on the AP examinations. I have also tried to provide you with notation on where points would likely be deducted for responses that were not acceptable enough for full credit. However, be aware that every year the point allocations change and partial credit is awarded differently.

Question 1 (13 points)

Part (A): 5 points
These points are graphing points. 1 point for the correctly drawn soybean market.

    i. 1 point: Price and quantity correctly labeled in the market.
    ii. 2 points: The price is shown as horizontal and the quantity is found at $P = MR = MC$.

You cannot have a downward sloping MR curve here.

    iii. 1 point: The correctly labeled loss rectangle.

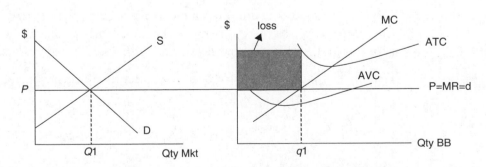

TIP 1: On graphing problems, you can lose a point for not indicating which variables lie on each graphical axis. In this case, it would be as simple as a $ and a Q.

TIP 2: When asked to identify equilibrium price and quantity, do these in some way. Dashed lines from the intersection to the axes are enough, or label the intersection E1.

TIP 3: Draw your graphs large enough for you to clearly identify the area of profit/loss. If your graph is the size of a postage stamp, it becomes more difficult for you to identify all relevant parts. It is also very tough for the reader to find all of the points.

When completing graphs, label everything and indicate direction of change and you will lose fewer points.

Part (B): 4 points
i. 1 point: Showing the leftward shift in market supply due to exit of firms.
    1 point: Showing how the decreased supply increases the market price and decreases market quantity.

TIP: You can lose points if you do not indicate, somehow, that the supply curve has shifted leftward. Do this with arrows or with a clear numbering system like S1 and S2.

ii. 1 point: Upward shift in the $P = $ MR curve for Bob's Beans.
     1 point: Showing Bob producing at the point where ATC is minimized.

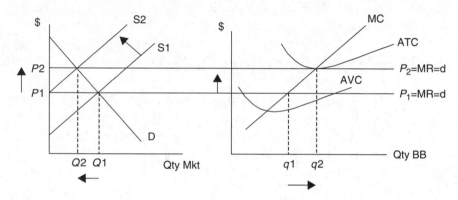

Question: OK, so what if I screwed up part (A)? Am I doomed in part (B)?

Answer: Maybe not, but you don't want to risk your "5" on generous partial credit.

Suppose in part (A), that you drew a graph that showed Bob earning positive profits, rather than losses. This is incorrect and so the 5th point in part (A) cannot be given to you. But . . . and here is where the partial credit may differ from year to year. If in part (B) you correctly described the long-run adjustment to profits, you may (and I stress *may*) receive some or all of the 4 points in part (B).

Part (B): alternative scoring to an incorrect presumption of profits in part (A).
1 point: Because positive economic profits were being made in part (A), firms enter the soybean industry, shifting the supply to the right.

1 point: The higher supply for beans decreases the price and increases the market quantity.

1 point: Downward shift in the $P = $ MR curve for Bob's Beans.

1 point: Showing Bob producing at the point where ATC is minimized.

Part (C): 4 points
1 point for a correctly labeled graph with a downward sloping market demand curve and a downward sloping MR curve that lies below demand.

i.   1 point: Showing the quantity where MR = MC.
ii. 1 point: Showing the price from the demand curve.
iii. 1 point: Identifying the area of profit.

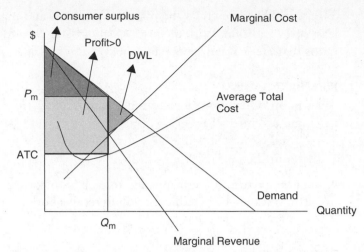

Note: I've also shaded the areas of consumer surplus and deadweight loss, which were not required in this practice problem. Because a more thorough analysis of monopoly has been asked in the past, be sure that you can identify monopoly profit, dead weight loss, and consumer surplus.

Question: So I've messed up the monopoly quantity, have I lost all points in part (C)?

Answer: Again, maybe not, but the rest of your response must be consistent with the incorrectly labeled output. In the figure below I have tried to replicate one possible incorrectly identified output, but consistent price and profit.

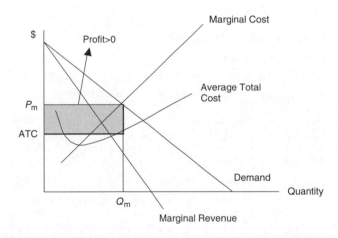

An Alternative Scoring for part (C).

This graph shows output where demand intersects MC, not where MR = MC. This response cannot be given the point for a correct level of output. However, you would likely get a point for a correctly drawn monopoly figure, a price P_m that is consistent with the Q_m in this figure, and a profit area that is also consistent with Q_m and P_m.

Question 2 (7 points)

Part (A): 2 points

1 point: Labor = 1, Lemons = 4

1 point: This is the least cost combination of inputs because the ratio of marginal product per dollar are equal for both inputs and Molly stays within her budget of $14.

$$MP_{labor}/P_{labor} = MP_{lemons}/P_{lemons}$$

TIP: Quickly write down the marginal products and highlight the options that satisfy the least cost condition. With the price of labor being $6 and the price of lemons $2, find those ratios that are 3:1 and ignore all other possibilities.

Part (B): 2 points
i.   1 point: Output = 39 (12 from 1 labor and 27 from 4 lemons)
ii. Total revenue = $1 * 39 = $39
     – Total Cost = $6 * 1 + $2 * 4 = $14
     1 point: Economic Profit = $25

Note: Once again, if you happened to pick an incorrect combination of labor and lemons in part (A) it may be possible for you to receive both points in part (B) if you find the consistent level of output and profit.

Part (C): 3 points
1 point: The profit-maximizing amount of labor is 4 (find MRP = input price = $6).

The profit-maximizing amount of lemons is 5 (find MRP = input price = $2).

i.   1 point: Output = 65 (36 from 4 labor and 29 from 5 lemons)
ii. Total revenue = $1 * 65 = $65
     – Total Cost = $6 * 4 + $2 * 5 = $34
     1 point: Economic Profit = $31

Note: Once again, if you happened to pick an incorrect combination of labor and lemons in the first part of (C) it may be possible for you to receive the last two points in part (C) if you find the consistent level of output and profit.

Question 3 (5 points)
Part (A): 2 points
1 point for explaining that a negative externality creates a situation where the marginal social cost exceeds the marginal social benefit.

1 point for explaining how this market failure results in an overallocation of resources to pork production. Too much pork is being produced.

Part (B): 2 points
i.   1 point: the market price and quantity identified at the intersection of marginal social benefit and marginal private costs.
ii. 1 point: the socially optimal price and quantity are identified at the intersection of marginal social benefit and marginal social costs. Quantity must be less than the market quantity and price must be higher than the market price.

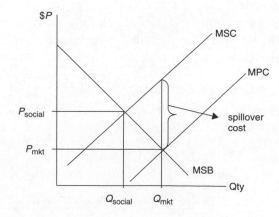

Part (C): 1 point
An appropriate policy for this kind of negative externality would be to levy a tax on pork production to shift the MPC upward and closer to the MSC.

Remember, too much pork is being produced at a price that is too low, so you do not want to advocate a policy that would increase pork production or lower the price of pork.

Scoring and Interpretation

AP Microeconomics Practice Exam 1

Multiple-Choice Questions:

Number of correct answers: _____
Number of incorrect answers: _____
Number of blank answers: _____
Did you complete this part of the test in the allotted time? Yes/No

Free-Response Questions:

1. _____/13
2. _____/7
3. _____/5

Did you complete this part of the test in the allotted time? Yes/No

Calculate Your Score:

Multiple-Choice Questions:

$$\underline{\hspace{3cm}} - \underline{\hspace{3cm}} = \underline{\hspace{3cm}}$$
$$\text{(\# right)} \qquad (.25 * \text{\# wrong}) \qquad \text{MC raw score}$$

Free-Response Questions:

Free-Response Raw Score = (1.1538 * Score #1) + (1.0714 * Score #2)
+ (1.50 * Score #3) = _____

Add the raw scores from the multiple choice and free-response sections to obtain your total raw score for the practice exam. Use the table below to determine your grade, remembering these are rough estimates using questions that are not actually from AP exams, so do not read too much into this conversion from raw score to AP score.

MICROECONOMICS #1	
RAW SCORE	APPROXIMATE AP GRADE
73–90	5
58–72	4
45–57	3
33–44	2
0–32	1

AP Macroeconomics Practice Exam 1
for Multiple-Choice Questions

ANSWER SHEET

1 (A) (B) (C) (D) (E)	21 (A) (B) (C) (D) (E)	41 (A) (B) (C) (D) (E)
2 (A) (B) (C) (D) (E)	22 (A) (B) (C) (D) (E)	42 (A) (B) (C) (D) (E)
3 (A) (B) (C) (D) (E)	23 (A) (B) (C) (D) (E)	43 (A) (B) (C) (D) (E)
4 (A) (B) (C) (D) (E)	24 (A) (B) (C) (D) (E)	44 (A) (B) (C) (D) (E)
5 (A) (B) (C) (D) (E)	25 (A) (B) (C) (D) (E)	45 (A) (B) (C) (D) (E)
6 (A) (B) (C) (D) (E)	26 (A) (B) (C) (D) (E)	46 (A) (B) (C) (D) (E)
7 (A) (B) (C) (D) (E)	27 (A) (B) (C) (D) (E)	47 (A) (B) (C) (D) (E)
8 (A) (B) (C) (D) (E)	28 (A) (B) (C) (D) (E)	48 (A) (B) (C) (D) (E)
9 (A) (B) (C) (D) (E)	29 (A) (B) (C) (D) (E)	49 (A) (B) (C) (D) (E)
10 (A) (B) (C) (D) (E)	30 (A) (B) (C) (D) (E)	50 (A) (B) (C) (D) (E)
11 (A) (B) (C) (D) (E)	31 (A) (B) (C) (D) (E)	51 (A) (B) (C) (D) (E)
12 (A) (B) (C) (D) (E)	32 (A) (B) (C) (D) (E)	52 (A) (B) (C) (D) (E)
13 (A) (B) (C) (D) (E)	33 (A) (B) (C) (D) (E)	53 (A) (B) (C) (D) (E)
14 (A) (B) (C) (D) (E)	34 (A) (B) (C) (D) (E)	54 (A) (B) (C) (D) (E)
15 (A) (B) (C) (D) (E)	35 (A) (B) (C) (D) (E)	55 (A) (B) (C) (D) (E)
16 (A) (B) (C) (D) (E)	36 (A) (B) (C) (D) (E)	56 (A) (B) (C) (D) (E)
17 (A) (B) (C) (D) (E)	37 (A) (B) (C) (D) (E)	57 (A) (B) (C) (D) (E)
18 (A) (B) (C) (D) (E)	38 (A) (B) (C) (D) (E)	58 (A) (B) (C) (D) (E)
19 (A) (B) (C) (D) (E)	39 (A) (B) (C) (D) (E)	59 (A) (B) (C) (D) (E)
20 (A) (B) (C) (D) (E)	40 (A) (B) (C) (D) (E)	60 (A) (B) (C) (D) (E)

AP Macroeconomics Practice Exam 1

Multiple-Choice Questions

Time—1 hour and 10 minutes

60 questions

For the multiple-choice questions that follow, select the best answer and fill in the appropriate letter on the answer sheet.

1. Which of the following statements are true of production possibility frontiers and trade between nations?

    I. Nations specialize and trade based on comparative advantage in production.
    II. Free trade allows each nation to consume beyond the production possibility frontier.
    III. The flow of goods and services is based on the principle of absolute advantage.
    IV. Nations can consume at points beyond the production possibility frontier by protecting domestic industries from free trade.

    (A) I and II only
    (B) II and III only
    (C) III and IV only
    (D) I, II, and III only
    (E) I, II, III, and IV

2. A nation is producing at a point inside of its production possibility frontier. Which of the following is a possible explanation for this outcome?

    (A) This nation has experienced a permanent decrease in its production capacity.
    (B) This nation has experienced slower than usual technological progress.
    (C) This nation has avoided free trade between other nations.
    (D) This nation is experiencing an economic recession.
    (E) This nation's economy is centrally planned.

3. How would fiscal and monetary policymakers combine spending, tax, and monetary policy to fight a recessionary gap, while avoiding large budget deficits?

	SPENDING POLICY	TAX POLICY	MONETARY POLICY
(A)	Higher spending	Lower taxes	Sell Treasury securities
(B)	Lower spending	Higher taxes	Buy Treasury securities
(C)	Lower spending	Lower taxes	Increasing the reserve ratio
(D)	Higher spending	Higher taxes	Lowering the discount rate
(E)	Higher spending	Higher taxes	Sell Treasury securities

4. Corn is exchanged in a competitive market. Which of the following definitely increases the equilibrium price of corn?

    (A) Both supply and demand shift rightward.
    (B) Both supply and demand shift leftward.
    (C) Supply shifts to the right; demand shifts to the left.
    (D) Supply shifts to the left; demand shifts to the right.
    (E) The government imposes an effective price ceiling in the corn market.

5. An increase in the Consumer Price Index is commonly referred to as

    (A) economic growth.
    (B) inflation.
    (C) unemployment.
    (D) discouraged workers.
    (E) deflation.

6. Which of the following is characteristic of a centrally planned economic system?

    (A) Resources are allocated based on relative prices.
    (B) The circular flow of goods and services minimizes the role of the federal government.
    (C) Private ownership of resources is fundamental to economic growth.
    (D) Government planners decide how best to produce goods and services.
    (E) Efficiency is superior to the market economic system.

7. The government has just lowered personal income taxes. Which of the following best describes the effects that this policy has on the economy?

    (A) Higher disposable income, higher consumption, higher real GDP, lower unemployment.
    (B) Higher disposable income, lower consumption, higher real GDP, lower unemployment.
    (C) Lower disposable income, higher consumption, higher real GDP, lower unemployment.
    (D) Lower disposable income, lower consumption, lower real GDP, higher unemployment.
    (E) Higher disposable income, higher consumption, higher real GDP, higher unemployment.

8. Which of the following are harmed by unexpectedly high rates of inflation?

    I. Borrowers repaying a long-term loan at a fixed interest rate.
    II. Savers who have put their money in long-term assets that pay a fixed interest rate.
    III. Workers who have negotiated cost-of-living raises into their contracts.
    IV. Persons living on fixed incomes.

    (A) I and III only
    (B) II and III only
    (C) II and IV only
    (D) I, II, and IV only
    (E) II, III, and IV only

9. Which of the following statements are true?

    I. The velocity of money is equal to real GDP divided by the money supply.
    II. Dollars earned today have more purchasing power than dollars earned a year from today.
    III. The supply of loanable funds consists of investors.

    (A) I only
    (B) II only
    (C) III only
    (D) I and II only
    (E) I, II, and III

10. If your nominal income rises 4 percent and your real income falls 1 percent, by how much did the price level change?

    (A) 5 percent decrease
    (B) ¼ percent increase
    (C) 3 percent increase
    (D) 3 percent decrease
    (E) 5 percent increase

11. Which of the following best measures changes in the price level of national product?

    (A) The consumer price index.
    (B) The real interest rate.
    (C) The unemployment rate.
    (D) The producer price index.
    (E) The GDP deflator.

12. Which of the following lessens the impact of expansionary fiscal policy?

    (A) An increase in the marginal propensity to consume.
    (B) Lower interest rates that cause a decrease in net exports.
    (C) Higher interest rates that cause an increase in net exports.
    (D) Higher interest rates that decrease private investment.
    (E) Falling price levels.

13. Suppose that the unemployment rate falls from 6 percent to 5 percent and the inflation rate falls from 3 percent to 2 percent. Which of the following best explains these trends?

(A) An increase in aggregate demand.
(B) A decrease in both aggregate demand and aggregate supply.
(C) An increase in both aggregate demand and aggregate supply.
(D) An increase in aggregate supply.
(E) An increase in aggregate demand and a decrease in aggregate supply.

14. Which of the following scenarios best describes the concepts of scarcity and opportunity cost?

(A) As a birthday present, your cousin sends you a $20 bill.
(B) Your state government, in order to increase support for higher education, must increase the sales tax to keep the budget balanced.
(C) Your state government, in order to increase support for higher education, must cut spending for environmental protection to keep the budget balanced.
(D) The local fire department conducts a raffle to raise funds for new equipment.
(E) Smoke from a forest fire impairs air quality in a small mountain town.

15. Some economists believe that when aggregate demand declines, prices are inflexible or "sticky" in the downward direction. This implies that the aggregate supply curve is

(A) upward sloping at full employment.
(B) horizontal below full employment.
(C) vertical at full employment.
(D) vertical below full employment.
(E) vertical above full employment.

16. Which of the following policies best describes supply-side fiscal policy?

(A) An increase in the money supply.
(B) Increased government spending.
(C) Lower taxes on research and development of new technology.
(D) Lower taxes on household income.
(E) More extensive government social welfare programs.

17. A likely cause of falling Treasury bond prices might be

(A) expansionary monetary policy.
(B) contractionary monetary policy.
(C) a depreciating dollar.
(D) fiscal policy designed to reduce the budget deficit.
(E) a decrease in the money demand.

18. The economy is currently operating at full employment. Assuming flexible wages and prices, how would a decline in aggregate demand affect GDP and the price level in the short run, and GDP and the price level in the long run?

	SHORT-RUN GDP	SHORT-RUN PRICE LEVEL	LONG-RUN GDP	LONG-RUN PRICE LEVEL
(A)	Falls	Falls	No change	Falls
(B)	Falls	Falls	Falls	Falls
(C)	No change	Falls	No change	No change
(D)	Falls	Falls	No change	No change
(E)	Falls	Falls	Falls	Falls

19. In the long run, aggregate supply is

(A) upward sloping at full employment.
(B) horizontal below full employment.
(C) vertical at full employment.
(D) vertical below full employment.
(E) vertical above full employment.

20. What does the presence of discouraged workers do to the measurement of the unemployment rate?

(A) Discouraged workers are counted as "out of the labor force," thus understating the unemployment rate, making the economy look stronger than it is.
(B) Discouraged workers are counted as "out of the labor force," thus overstating the unemployment rate, making the economy look weaker than it is.
(C) Discouraged workers are not surveyed so there is no impact on the unemployment rate.
(D) Discouraged workers are counted as "unemployed," thus understating the unemployment rate, making the economy look stronger than it is.
(E) Discouraged workers are counted as "unemployed," thus overstating the unemployment rate, making the economy look weaker than it is.

21. Which of the following is true of the complete circular flow model of an open economy?

    (A) All goods and services flow through the government in exchange for resource payments.
    (B) There is no role for the foreign sector.
    (C) Households supply resources to producers in exchange for goods and services.
    (D) Producers provide goods and services to households in exchange for the costs of production.
    (E) The government collects taxes from firms and households in exchange for goods and services.

22. Which of the following most likely increases aggregate demand in the United States.?

    (A) An American entrepreneur founds and locates a software company in London.
    (B) The U.S. military relocates a military base from San Diego to Seattle.
    (C) The Chinese government makes it increasingly difficult for American firms to export goods to China.
    (D) A Mexican entrepreneur founds and locates a software company in St. Louis.
    (E) The Canadian government cancels an order for airliners from a firm located in Seattle.

23. When both aggregate supply and aggregate demand increase, which of the following can be said for certain?

    (A) The price level rises, but real GDP falls.
    (B) Both the price level and real GDP rise.
    (C) The price level rises, but the change in real GDP is uncertain.
    (D) The price level falls, but real GDP rise.
    (E) Real GDP rises, but the change in the price level is uncertain.

24. When nominal GDP is rising, we would expect money demand to

    (A) increase as consumers demand more money as a financial asset, increasing the interest rate.
    (B) increase as consumers demand more money for transactions, increasing the interest rate.
    (C) decrease as the purchasing power of the dollar is falling, decreasing the interest rate.
    (D) decrease as consumers demand more money for transactions, increasing the interest rate.
    (E) increase as consumers demand more money as a financial asset, decreasing the interest rate.

25. Which of the following tends to increase the spending multiplier?

    (A) An increase in the marginal propensity to consume.
    (B) A decreased velocity of money.
    (C) An increase in the marginal propensity to save.
    (D) An increase in the real interest rate.
    (E) An increase in the price level.

26. Households demand more money as an asset when

    (A) nominal GDP falls.
    (B) the nominal interest rate falls.
    (C) bond prices fall.
    (D) the supply of money falls.
    (E) nominal GDP increases.

27. Which of the following represents a combination of contractionary fiscal and expansionary monetary policy?

	FISCAL POLICY	MONETARY POLICY
(A)	Higher taxes	Selling Treasury securities
(B)	Lower taxes	Buying Treasury securities
(C)	Lower government spending	Increasing the reserve ratio
(D)	Lower government spending	Increasing the discount rate
(E)	Higher taxes	Buying Treasury securities

28. Higher levels of consumer wealth and optimism would likely have which of the following changes in the market for loanable funds?

	MARKET FOR LOANABLE FUNDS	INTEREST RATE
(A)	Increase in supply	Rising
(B)	Increase in demand	Rising
(C)	Decrease in demand	Falling
(D)	Decrease in supply	Falling
(E)	Decrease in supply	Rising

29. Investment demand most likely increases when

(A) real GDP increases.
(B) the cost of acquiring and maintaining capital equipment rises.
(C) investor optimism improves.
(D) the real rate of interest rises.
(E) taxes on business investment rise.

30. At the peak of a typical business cycle, which of the following is likely the greatest threat to the macroeconomy?

(A) Unemployment
(B) Bankruptcy
(C) Declining labor productivity
(D) Falling real household income
(E) Inflation

31. Suppose that households increase the demand for U.S. Treasury bonds as financial assets. Which of the following accurately describes changes in the money market, the interest rate, and the value of the dollar in foreign currency markets?

	MONEY MARKET	INTEREST RATE	DOLLAR
(A)	Increased supply	Rising	Appreciates
(B)	Increased demand	Rising	Appreciates
(C)	Decreased demand	Falling	Appreciates
(D)	Decreased supply	Falling	Depreciates
(E)	Decreased demand	Falling	Depreciates

32. If households are more optimistic about the future, how would the consumption function be affected?

(A) The marginal propensity to consume would increase, increasing the slope of the consumption function.
(B) The entire consumption function would shift downward.
(C) The entire consumption function would shift upward.
(D) The marginal propensity to consume would decrease, increasing the slope of the consumption function.
(E) The marginal propensity to consume would increase, decreasing the slope of the consumption function.

33. U.S. real GDP most likely falls when

(A) tariffs and quotas are removed.
(B) investment in human capital is high.
(C) the money supply is increased.
(D) there is a trade surplus in goods and services.
(E) the value of the dollar, relative to foreign currencies, is high.

34. If current real GDP is $5000, and full employment real GDP is at $4000, which of the following combinations of policies might have brought the economy to this point?

(A) A decrease in taxes and a lower discount rate.
(B) An increase in government spending and an increase in taxes.
(C) A decrease in taxes and selling bonds in an open market operation.
(D) An increase in government spending and an increase in the discount rate.
(E) A decrease in taxes and a decrease in government spending.

35. If a nation is operating at full employment, and the central bank engages in contractionary monetary policy, the nation can expect the interest rate, the purchases of new homes, and the unemployment rate to change in which of the following ways?

	INTEREST RATES	NEW HOMES	UNEMPLOYMENT RATE
(A)	Decrease	Increase	Increase
(B)	Decrease	Decrease	Decrease
(C)	Increase	Decrease	Decrease
(D)	Increase	Decrease	Increase
(E)	Increase	Increase	Increase

36. Expansionary monetary policy is designed to

    (A) lower the interest rate, increase private investment, increase aggregate demand, and increase domestic output.
    (B) lower the interest rate, increase private investment, increase aggregate demand, and increase the unemployment rate.
    (C) increase the interest rate, increase private investment, increase aggregate demand, and increase domestic output.
    (D) increase the interest rate, decrease private investment, increase aggregate demand, and increase domestic output.
    (E) increase the interest rate, decrease private investment, decrease aggregate demand, and decrease the price level.

37. If the economy is experiencing an inflationary gap, which of the following is most likely to worsen the problem?

    (A) An increase in government spending matched by an equal increase in taxes.
    (B) An increase in government spending with no change in taxes.
    (C) A decrease in government spending and a matching increase in taxes.
    (D) A decrease in taxes with no change in government spending.
    (E) A decrease in government spending matched by an equal decrease in taxes.

38. Which of the following is a component of the $M1$ measure of money supply?

    (A) Savings deposits
    (B) Gold bullion
    (C) Cash and coins
    (D) 30-year Treasury certificates
    (E) 18-month certificates of deposits

39. Assuming that households save a proportion of disposable income, which of the following relationships between multipliers is correct?

    (A) Tax multiplier > Spending multiplier > Balanced budget multiplier.
    (B) Spending multiplier = Tax multiplier > Balanced budget multiplier.
    (C) Spending multiplier > Tax multiplier = Balanced budget multiplier.
    (D) Spending multiplier > Tax multiplier > Balanced budget multiplier.
    (E) Tax multiplier > Spending multiplier = Balanced budget multiplier.

40. The fractional reserve banking system's ability to create money is lessened if

    (A) households that borrow redeposit the entire loan amounts back into the banks.
    (B) banks hold excess reserves.
    (C) banks loan all excess reserves to borrowing customers.
    (D) households increase checking deposits in banks.
    (E) the Federal Reserve lowers the reserve ratio.

41. All else equal, when the United States exports more goods and services,

    (A) the value of the dollar falls as the supply of dollars increases.
    (B) the value of the dollar rises as demand for dollars increases.
    (C) the value of the dollar falls as demand for dollars decreases.
    (D) the value of the dollar rises as the supply of dollars increases.
    (E) the value of the dollar falls as demand for dollars increases.

42. If the reserve ratio is 10 percent and a new customer deposits $500, what is the maximum amount of money created?

    (A) $500
    (B) $4500
    (C) $5000
    (D) $50
    (E) $5500

43. Suppose today's headline is that private investment has decreased as a result of an action by the Federal Reserve. Which of the following choices is the most likely cause?

    (A) Selling Treasury securities to commercial banks.
    (B) Lowering of the discount rate.
    (C) Decreasing the reserve ratio.
    (D) Elimination of a corporate tax credit on investment.
    (E) A stronger stock market has increased investor optimism.

44. If $1000 is deposited into a checking account and excess reserves increase by $700, the reserve ratio must be:

    (A) 70%
    (B) 30%
    (C) 40%
    (D) 90%
    (E) 75%

45. Suppose a nation is experiencing an annual budget surplus and uses some of this surplus to pay down part of the national debt. One potential side effect of this policy would be

    (A) increase interest rates and throw the economy into a recession.
    (B) increase interest rates and depreciate the nation's currency.
    (C) decrease interest rates and risk an inflationary period.
    (D) decrease interest rates and throw the economy into a recession.
    (E) decrease interest rates and appreciate the nation's currency.

46. Which of the following best describes a key difference between the short-run and long-run aggregate supply curve?

    (A) Short-run aggregate supply is upward sloping as nominal wages quickly respond to price level changes.
    (B) Long-run aggregate supply is upward sloping as nominal wages quickly respond to price level changes.
    (C) Short-run aggregate supply is vertical as nominal wages quickly respond to price level changes.
    (D) Short-run aggregate supply is upward sloping as nominal wages do not quickly respond to price level changes.
    (E) Long-run aggregate supply is vertical as nominal wages do not quickly respond to price level changes.

47. The "crowding out" effect refers to which of the following?

    (A) Lower interest rates that result from borrowing to conduct expansionary monetary policy.
    (B) Higher interest rates that result from borrowing to conduct contractionary fiscal policy.
    (C) Higher interest rates that result from borrowing to conduct expansionary fiscal policy.
    (D) Higher interest rates due to borrowing to conduct contractionary monetary policy.
    (E) Lower interest rates due to borrowing to conduct expansionary fiscal policy.

48. Which of the following is a predictable consequence of import quotas?

    (A) Increased competition and lower consumer prices.
    (B) Increased government tax revenue from imported goods.
    (C) Rising net exports and a rightward shift in aggregate supply.
    (D) An improved allocation of resources away from inefficient producers and lower consumer prices.
    (E) Higher consumer prices and a misallocation of resources away from efficient producers.

49. If the Federal Reserve was concerned about the "crowding out" effect, they could engage in

    (A) expansionary monetary policy by lowering the discount rate.
    (B) expansionary monetary policy by selling Treasury securities.
    (C) contractionary monetary policy by raising the discount rate.
    (D) contractionary monetary policy by lowering the discount rate.
    (E) expansionary monetary policy by raising the reserve ratio.

50. Which of the following would likely contribute to faster rates of economic growth?

    (A) A more restrictive immigration policy.
    (B) Negative net investment.
    (C) Higher taxes on households and firms.
    (D) Higher government funding of research on clean energy supplies.
    (E) Protective trade policies.

51. A nation that must consistently borrow to cover annual budget deficits risks

    (A) a depreciation of the nation's currency as foreigners increase investment in the nation.
    (B) a decline in net exports as the nation's goods become more expensive to foreign consumers.
    (C) lower interest rates that discourage foreign investment in the nation.
    (D) an appreciation of the nation's currency as foreigners decrease investment in the nation.
    (E) lower interest rates that reduce private investment in productive capital.

52. Economic growth is best described as

    (A) an increase in the production possibility frontier and an increase in the natural rate of unemployment.
    (B) an increase in the production possibility frontier and a leftward shift in long-run aggregate supply.
    (C) a decrease in the production possibility frontier and a rightward shift in long-run aggregate supply.
    (D) a decrease in the production possibility frontier and a leftward shift in long-run aggregate supply.
    (E) an increase in the production possibility frontier and a rightward shift in long-run aggregate supply.

53. Which of the following is true of automatic fiscal policy stabilizers?

    (A) For a given level of government spending, they produce a deficit during a recession and a surplus during an expansion.
    (B) They serve to prolong recessionary and inflationary periods.
    (C) The regressive tax system is a fundamental component of automatic stabilizers.
    (D) For a given level of government spending, they produce a surplus during a recession and a surplus during an expansion.
    (E) They lengthen the business cycle.

54. Which of the following is an example of expansionary monetary policy for the Federal Reserve?

    (A) Increasing the discount rate.
    (B) Increasing the reserve ratio.
    (C) Buying Treasury securities from commercial banks.
    (D) Lowering income taxes.
    (E) Removal of import quotas.

55. Labor productivity and economic growth increase if

    (A) a nation subsidizes education for all citizens.
    (B) a nation imposes tariffs and quotas on imported goods.
    (C) a nation removes penalties for firms that pollute natural resources.
    (D) a nation ignores societal barriers like discrimination.
    (E) a nation taxes income from interest on saving.

56. The short-run Phillips curve depicts the _____ relationship between _____ and _____.

    (A) positive, price level, interest rate
    (B) negative, interest rate, private investment
    (C) negative, the inflation rate, the unemployment rate
    (D) positive, price level, real GDP
    (E) negative, interest rate, money demand

57. A negative, or contractionary, supply shock will

    (A) shift the Phillips curve to the left.
    (B) shift the investment demand curve to the right.
    (C) shift the money demand curve to the right.
    (D) shift the money supply curve to the left.
    (E) shift the Phillips curve to the right.

58. When a nation is operating at the natural rate of employment,

   (A) there is no cyclical unemployment.
   (B) the inflation rate is zero.
   (C) there is no structural unemployment.
   (D) the nation is experiencing a recession.
   (E) the unemployment rate is zero.

59. Which of the following likely results in a permanent increase in a nation's productive capacity?

   (A) A decline in the birth rate.
   (B) Declining adult literacy rates.
   (C) Widespread relocation of manufacturing firms to low-wage nations.
   (D) National program of child immunization.
   (E) A global increase in the price of crude oil.

60. Lower interest rates in the United States cause the value of the dollar and exports to change in which of the following ways?

	VALUE OF THE DOLLAR	U.S. EXPORTS
(A)	Increasing	Increasing
(B)	Increasing	Decreasing
(C)	Decreasing	Increasing
(D)	Decreasing	Unchanged
(E)	Increasing	Increasing

› Answers and Explanations

1. **A**—The gains from free trade are based upon the principles of comparative advantage and specialization. Free trade allows nations to consume at points beyond their own PPF. In this way, free trade improves the economic well being of trading nations.

2. **D**—Points within the PPF imply unemployed resources and this is indicative of a recession.

3. **D**—Balanced budget fiscal policy to eliminate a recession could increase spending and pay for that spending with higher taxes. Coordination of monetary policy requires some expansion of the money supply.

4. **D**—Combining a leftward supply shift with a rightward demand shift unambiguously raises the price.

5. **B**—Computing the change in the CPI is the most common way to measure price inflation.

6. **D**—A centrally planned economy decides which goods are needed and how best to provide them to the population. Resources are allocated and goods are distributed by the government, not the price system.

7. **A**—Lower taxes increase disposable income. Consumers spend most of this disposable income, which increases real GDP and lowers the unemployment rate.

8. **C**—Savers receive interest payments in "cheap" dollars and fixed income recipients lose purchasing power of their pensions due to rapid inflation.

9. **B**—Choice I is incorrect because the equation of exchange defines the velocity of money as nominal GDP divided by money supply. The supply of loanable funds includes savers, not investors.

10. **E**—The %Δ in real income is equal to the %Δ in nominal income less the rate of inflation.

11. **E**—The GDP deflator is a price index for all goods and services that go into national product. It is more inclusive than the CPI (consumer goods) and the PPI (producer inputs).

12. **D**—Expansionary fiscal policy can be weakened if government borrowing drives up interest rates and diminishes private investment.

13. **D**—If the unemployment rate and inflation rate are both falling, they are likely the result of an increase in AS.

14. **C**—Scarce resources require that difficult decisions be made. Something may be gained, but at the cost of something that was given up and this scenario illustrates the opportunity cost of increased funding for higher education.

15. **B**—If AD is falling and prices are not also falling, the AS curve must be horizontal. Keynesians believe that prices are sticky in the downward direction, but Classical economists believe prices are flexible. It is no surprise that the classical AS curve is vertical.

16. **C**—Supply-side fiscal policy tries to boost investment and productivity to increase AS and foster economic growth over time.

17. **B**—Falling bond prices correspond to rising interest rates so look for the choice that increases interest rates. Lower money demand, one financial asset, creates rising demand for bonds, an alternative financial asset. Choice E therefore increases bond prices and lowers interest rates.

18. **A**—If prices and wages are flexible, the long-run economy readjusts to full employment. Falling AD lowers the price level and real GDP in the short run, but eventually lower wages shift the short-run AS curve to the right, further lowering the price level and moving long-run production back to full employment.

19. **C**—The short-run AS curve is upward sloping, the long-run AS is vertical at full employment.

20. **A**—The BLS only counts a worker as "unemployed" if he is actively seeking work. A discouraged worker is, by definition, not seeking work and so his omission from the unemployment rate understates this measure of economic health, making the economy look better than it is.

21. **E**—In the full circular flow model, the role of government is to collect taxes from firms and households in exchange for goods and services. Choice C is tempting, but households supply resources in exchange for wages, which they then use to purchase goods and services.

22. **D**—All production done in the United States is counted in U.S. GDP, regardless of the nationality of the entrepreneur.

23. **E**—Increased AS lowers the price level, but increased AD increases the price level. The change in the price level is uncertain, but real GDP rises.

24. **B**—The transaction demand for money rises with higher levels of nominal GDP. With a fixed supply of money, increased demand for money increases the interest rate as consumers sell financial assets (e.g., bonds), lowering the bond price and increasing the interest rate.

25. **A**—The spending multiplier $M = 1/(1-MPC) = 1/MPS$ so an increase in the marginal propensity to consume increases the multiplier.

26. **B**—Asset demand for money is negatively related to the interest rate. Lower interest rates decrease the opportunity cost of holding money.

27. **E**—This is the only choice that combines contractionary fiscal and expansionary monetary policy.

28. **E**—Increased consumer wealth shifts the saving function downward. Less saving decreases the supply of loanable funds, raising the interest rate.

29. **C**—Increased optimism shifts investment demand to the right.

30. **E**—At the peak of the business cycle, the economy is very strong. Real GDP and incomes are high, unemployment is low, and the threat is a rapid increase in the price level.

31. **E**—An increase in demand for bonds as a financial asset decreases the demand for money and lowers the interest rate. A lower interest rate in the U.S. money market makes the United States a less attractive place for foreign investors to place their money. This decreased demand for dollars depreciates the value of the dollar relative to foreign currencies.

32. **C**—Greater optimism shifts the consumption function upward. The MPC is unchanged.

33. **E**—If the value of the dollar is high, it makes American goods more expensive to foreign consumers. This decreases net exports and lowers U.S. real GDP. All other choices likely increase real GDP.

34. **A**—With the economy operating beyond full employment, look for a combination of expansionary policies. All of the other choices include a contractionary policy with an expansionary policy, thus making A the most likely culprit.

35. **D**—Contractionary monetary policy increases interest rates. Higher interest rates decrease new home demand, investment spending, and AD, and increase the unemployment rate.

36. **A**—Expanding the money supply decreases the interest rate, increases investment, and stimulates AD.

37. **B**—Because the spending multiplier is larger than the tax multiplier, AD shifts further to the right when spending is increased with no change in taxes. This greatly exacerbates an already inflationary situation.

38. **C**—Because $M1$ is the most liquid measure of money, it begins with cash and coins.

39. **D**—For a given MPC, the spending multiplier exceeds the tax multiplier, which exceeds the balanced budget multiplier, which is always 1.

40. **B**—Money creation slows if banks do not loan all excess reserves.

41. **B**—More exports means an increased demand for the dollar. Stronger demand for the dollar increases the value of the dollar.

42. **B**—The money multiplier is $1/rr = 10$. So a $500 deposit creates $450 of new excess reserves, which can multiply to $4500 of newly created money.

43. **A**—Lower levels of investment are the result of higher interest rates so look for the choice that describes a decrease in the money supply.

44. **B**—If $700 of a $1000 deposit is in excess reserves, $300 or 30 percent must have been reserved.

45. **C**—Reducing debt lowers interest rates, which increases private investment and risks inflation. Lower interest rates decrease foreign investment in the United States. Weaker demand for dollars depreciates the value of the dollar.

46. **D**—The short-run AS curve is upward sloping because when AD increases, the prices of goods and services rise faster than wages. This results in a profit opportunity for producers to increase output. In the long run, wages have time to fully respond to changes in the price level.

47. **C**—High levels of government borrowing increase the interest rate and squeeze private investors out of the investment market.

48. **E**—Quotas do not raise money for the domestic government, but they do increase prices and protect inefficient domestic producers, drawing resources away from efficient foreign producers.

49. **A**—To avoid crowding out, the Fed should increase the money supply and a lower discount rate does that.

50. **D**—Long-term investment in human capital and new technologies increases economic growth rates. Protection of a nation's natural resources and health of the citizens increases labor productivity.

51. **B**—Extensive borrowing increases the interest rate on U.S. securities. Foreign investors seek to buy dollars so that they can invest in these securities, but when the dollar appreciates, American exports become more expensive to foreign consumers and so net exports fall.

52. **E**—When a nation's productive capacity increases, the PPF and long-run AS curves both shift rightward.

53. **A**—This choice describes exactly what automatic stabilizers do. By providing automatic fiscal stimulus during a recession, they also lessen the impact of a recession by shortening the business cycle.

54. **C**—Buying securities from commercial banks puts excess reserves in the banks, which begins the money creation process.

55. **A**—Subsidized public education is an investment in human capital and greatly increases labor productivity over time. This is one of the determinants of economic growth.

56. **C**—This choice describes the negative sloping Phillips curve with the inflation rate on the *y* axis and the unemployment rate on the *x* axis.

57. **E**—If AS shifts to the left, both inflation and unemployment rise, and results in a Phillips curve that is further to the right than before the supply shock.

58. **A**—At the natural rate of unemployment, there is frictional and structural unemployment, but no cyclical job loss.

59. **D**—If more children are immunized against disease, the size of the adult workforce increases and higher levels of human capital and productivity are seen over time.

60. **C**—Lower interest rates decrease the demand for the dollar, which makes U.S.-made goods more affordable to foreign consumers so exports from the United States increase.

AP Macroeconomics Practice Exam 1

Free-Response Questions

Planning time—10 minutes

Writing time—50 minutes

At the conclusion of the planning time, you have 50 minutes to respond to the following three questions. Approximately half of your time should be given to the first question and the second half should be divided evenly between the remaining two questions. Be careful to clearly explain your reasoning and to provide clear labels to all graph axes and curves.

1. It is January 1, 2010, and the U.S. economy is operating at the level of real GDP that corresponds to full employment. The U.S. government is operating with a balanced budget and net exports are equal to zero.

   (A) Using a correctly labeled aggregate demand and aggregate supply graph, identify each of the following:
      i.   The current level of real GDP.
      ii. The current price level.
   (B) Suppose that by the end of 2010 Americans are importing more goods and services from other nations than they are exporting to other nations (a trade deficit) and there exists a deficit balance in the current account.
      i.   How will this affect the balance of the capital/financial account? Explain.
      ii. In the AD/AS graph above, show how the trade deficit will affect the U.S. economy, the level of real GDP, and the equilibrium price level.
   (C) Consider again the deficit balance in the current account.
      i.   How will the deficit balance in the current account affect the demand for the dollar in the market for dollars?
      ii. Will the dollar appreciate or depreciate against other major foreign currencies?
   (D) Given your response to (B)(ii), how could the U.S. government engage in discretionary fiscal policy to return the economy to full employment GDP? Explain.

2. Suppose that political upheaval in Argentina has sparked rampant inflation.

   (A) Explain how this unexpected inflation would impact the following groups:
      i.   Retirees living on fixed monthly pensions.
      ii. Banks with many outstanding loans that are being repaid at fixed interest rates.
   (B) Assume that the central bank of Argentina has the same tools of monetary policy as the Fed in the United States. Explain one monetary policy that the central bank could use to lessen the inflation.
   (C) Explain one fiscal policy that the government could use to lessen the inflation.
   (D) Suppose that the inflation in Argentina is still a problem in the long run. Using a correctly labeled graph, show how the inflation would affect the value of the Argentine peso in the foreign exchange markets.

3. Assume that the United States economy is currently operating at the full employment level of real gross domestic product.

   (A) Based on this scenario, draw a correctly labeled AD/AS graph.
   (B) Suppose that full employment occurs at an unemployment rate of 4 percent, and an annual inflation rate of 3 percent.
      i.   Based upon this new information, draw correctly labeled short-run and long-run Phillips curves in a new graph.
   (C) Assume that rising global demand for oil, coal, and other nonrenewable sources of energy creates a permanent increase in the price of energy.

   i.   Show this impact on your graph in part (A). Identify changes to the equilibrium price level and real GDP.
   (D) Now assume the United States economy is back at full employment, with an unemployment rate of 4 percent and an annual inflation rate of 3 percent. The government decides to increase personal income taxes.
      i.   Identify how this will impact the United States economy, the equilibrium price level and real GDP.
      ii. Show the impact of this increase in personal income taxes on your graph in part B.

› Free-Response Grading Rubric

Note: Based on my experience, these point allocations roughly approximate the weighting on similar questions on the AP examinations. Be aware that every year the point allocations differ and partial credit is awarded differently.

Question 1 (11 points)

Part (A): 3 points

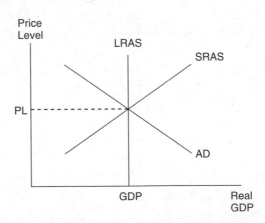

1 point is given for a downward sloping AD, an upward sloping SRAS, and a vertical LRAS all intersecting at the same point.

   i.   1 point is given for labeling real GDP on the horizontal axis at the intersection of all three curves.
   ii. 1 point is given for labeling the price level on the vertical axis at the intersection of all three curves.

Note: Keep in mind my tips regarding graphs and the ways in which you can avoid losing points.

Part (B): 4 points

i. 2 points. 1 point is given for identifying "surplus" or "moves toward surplus" and 1 point for explaining that the existence of excess dollars from trade deficit in the hands of foreign citizens leads to an increase in the purchase of U.S. financial assets by foreigners.

ii. 2 points. 1 point is given for a leftward shift in the AD curve and 1 point for showing the new intersection with SRAS and indicating the decreased level of real GDP and the decreased price level.

Part (C): 2 points

i. 1 point is given for stating that there will be a decrease in the demand for dollars.

ii. 1 point for indicating the dollar will depreciate in value relative to other foreign currencies.

Part (D): 2 points

1 point is given for stating either that the government could decrease taxes or increase government spending. 1 point is given for indicating that this policy would shift AD to the right, increasing real GDP.

What About Partial Credit?

Partial credit differs from year to year, so you do not want to bet your perfect 5 on the generosity of unknown readers. However, it is possible that you might receive some points for being consistent with an incorrect response. For example, suppose in (C)(i) you said that the demand for the dollar would increase. You would not receive the first point. However, if you said that the dollar would then appreciate, you could receive the second point for being consistent. Another opportunity for partial credit exists in (D). Suppose that in (B)(ii) you had shown the AD curve shift to the right. You would not receive any points in (B)(ii). However, in (D) you could describe a contractionary fiscal policy such as increasing taxes or decreasing government spending and you could receive both points in (D).

Question 2 (6 points)

Part (A): 2 points

i.   1 point: High unexpected inflation decreases the purchasing power of pensioners.
ii. 1 point: Banks collect loan repayments that have lost value with high inflation.

Part (B): 1 point

1 point is given for contractionary monetary policy. Either raising the discount rate, raising the reserve ratio or selling securities in an open market operation.

Part (C): 1 point

1 point given for contractionary fiscal policy. Raise taxes or lower government spending.

Part (D): 1 point

This is a graphing point. High rates of inflation decrease demand, depreciating the Argentine peso in relation to other currencies (e.g., the dollar).

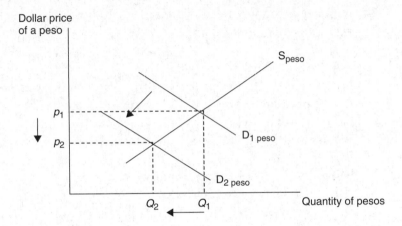

Question 3 (7 points)

Part (A): 2 points

These are graphing points so everything must be clearly and correctly labeled.

1 point: Real GDP and price level are clearly identified at the intersection of a downward sloping AD and upward sloping SRAS.

1 point: LRAS is drawn vertically at the intersection of AD and SRAS.

Note: you can also draw SRAS with the three stages as seen earlier in this text.

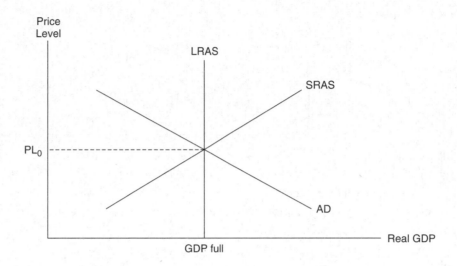

Part (B): 2 points

These are also graphing points but to get both points you would need to explicitly incorporate this new information in the Phillips curve graph.

1 point: Downward sloping SRPC intersecting vertical LRPC.

1 point: Identify on the horizontal axis an unemployment rate of 4 percent and on the vertical axis an inflation rate of 3 percent.

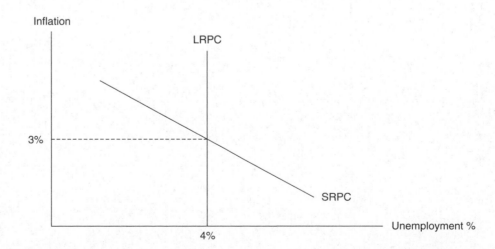

Part (C): 1 point

Show both the SRAS and LRAS shifting to the left in the graph from part A. Show that the equilibrium price level has risen and real GDP has fallen.

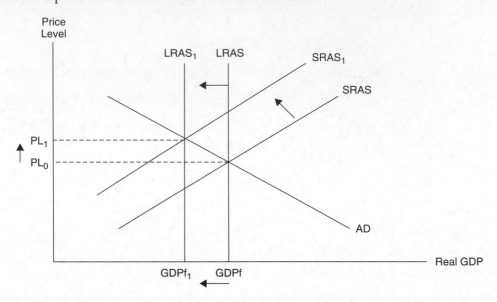

Part (D): 2 points

i. 1 point. A short sentence would suffice so long as you identify that higher income taxes will decrease AD, decrease real GDP and decrease the price level.

ii. 1 point. A change in AD does not shift either Phillips curve, it causes a movement along the SRPC. The reason is that shifting AD does not cause the level of full employment, and thus the natural rate of unemployment, to change. Because unemployment is rising and the price level is falling, you would show a movement downward and to the right on the SRPC.

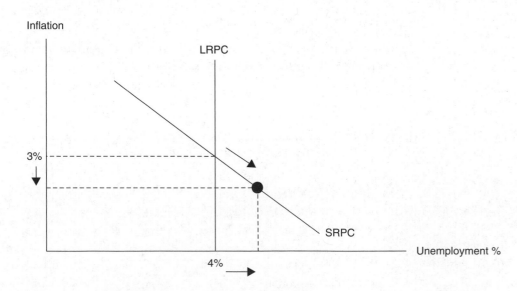

Scoring and Interpretation

AP Macroeconomics Practice Exam 1

Multiple-Choice Questions:

Number of correct answers: _____
Number of incorrect answers: _____
Number of blank answers: _____
Did you complete this part of the test in the allotted time? <u>Yes/No</u>

Free-Response Questions:

1. ____/11
2. ____/6
3. ____/7

Did you complete this part of the test in the allotted time? <u>Yes/No</u>

Calculate Your Score:

Multiple-Choice Questions:

$$\underset{\text{(\# right)}}{\rule{3cm}{0.4pt}} - \underset{(.25 * \text{\# wrong})}{\rule{3cm}{0.4pt}} = \underset{\text{MC raw score}}{\rule{3cm}{0.4pt}}$$

Free-Response Questions:

Free-Response Raw Score = $(1.3636 *$ Score #1$) + (1.25 *$ Score #2$)$
$ + (1.0714 *$ Score #3$) = $ _____

Add the raw scores from the multiple-choice and free-response sections to obtain your total raw score for the practice exam. Use the table below to determine your grade, remembering these are rough estimates using questions that are not actually from AP exams, so do not read too much into this conversion from raw score to AP score.

MACROECONOMICS #1	
RAW SCORE	APPROXIMATE AP GRADE
71–90	5
53–70	4
43–52	3
31–42	2
0–30	1

AP Microeconomics Practice Exam 2
for Multiple-Choice Questions

ANSWER SHEET

1 Ⓐ Ⓑ Ⓒ Ⓓ Ⓔ	21 Ⓐ Ⓑ Ⓒ Ⓓ Ⓔ	41 Ⓐ Ⓑ Ⓒ Ⓓ Ⓔ
2 Ⓐ Ⓑ Ⓒ Ⓓ Ⓔ	22 Ⓐ Ⓑ Ⓒ Ⓓ Ⓔ	42 Ⓐ Ⓑ Ⓒ Ⓓ Ⓔ
3 Ⓐ Ⓑ Ⓒ Ⓓ Ⓔ	23 Ⓐ Ⓑ Ⓒ Ⓓ Ⓔ	43 Ⓐ Ⓑ Ⓒ Ⓓ Ⓔ
4 Ⓐ Ⓑ Ⓒ Ⓓ Ⓔ	24 Ⓐ Ⓑ Ⓒ Ⓓ Ⓔ	44 Ⓐ Ⓑ Ⓒ Ⓓ Ⓔ
5 Ⓐ Ⓑ Ⓒ Ⓓ Ⓔ	25 Ⓐ Ⓑ Ⓒ Ⓓ Ⓔ	45 Ⓐ Ⓑ Ⓒ Ⓓ Ⓔ
6 Ⓐ Ⓑ Ⓒ Ⓓ Ⓔ	26 Ⓐ Ⓑ Ⓒ Ⓓ Ⓔ	46 Ⓐ Ⓑ Ⓒ Ⓓ Ⓔ
7 Ⓐ Ⓑ Ⓒ Ⓓ Ⓔ	27 Ⓐ Ⓑ Ⓒ Ⓓ Ⓔ	47 Ⓐ Ⓑ Ⓒ Ⓓ Ⓔ
8 Ⓐ Ⓑ Ⓒ Ⓓ Ⓔ	28 Ⓐ Ⓑ Ⓒ Ⓓ Ⓔ	48 Ⓐ Ⓑ Ⓒ Ⓓ Ⓔ
9 Ⓐ Ⓑ Ⓒ Ⓓ Ⓔ	29 Ⓐ Ⓑ Ⓒ Ⓓ Ⓔ	49 Ⓐ Ⓑ Ⓒ Ⓓ Ⓔ
10 Ⓐ Ⓑ Ⓒ Ⓓ Ⓔ	30 Ⓐ Ⓑ Ⓒ Ⓓ Ⓔ	50 Ⓐ Ⓑ Ⓒ Ⓓ Ⓔ
11 Ⓐ Ⓑ Ⓒ Ⓓ Ⓔ	31 Ⓐ Ⓑ Ⓒ Ⓓ Ⓔ	51 Ⓐ Ⓑ Ⓒ Ⓓ Ⓔ
12 Ⓐ Ⓑ Ⓒ Ⓓ Ⓔ	32 Ⓐ Ⓑ Ⓒ Ⓓ Ⓔ	52 Ⓐ Ⓑ Ⓒ Ⓓ Ⓔ
13 Ⓐ Ⓑ Ⓒ Ⓓ Ⓔ	33 Ⓐ Ⓑ Ⓒ Ⓓ Ⓔ	53 Ⓐ Ⓑ Ⓒ Ⓓ Ⓔ
14 Ⓐ Ⓑ Ⓒ Ⓓ Ⓔ	34 Ⓐ Ⓑ Ⓒ Ⓓ Ⓔ	54 Ⓐ Ⓑ Ⓒ Ⓓ Ⓔ
15 Ⓐ Ⓑ Ⓒ Ⓓ Ⓔ	35 Ⓐ Ⓑ Ⓒ Ⓓ Ⓔ	55 Ⓐ Ⓑ Ⓒ Ⓓ Ⓔ
16 Ⓐ Ⓑ Ⓒ Ⓓ Ⓔ	36 Ⓐ Ⓑ Ⓒ Ⓓ Ⓔ	56 Ⓐ Ⓑ Ⓒ Ⓓ Ⓔ
17 Ⓐ Ⓑ Ⓒ Ⓓ Ⓔ	37 Ⓐ Ⓑ Ⓒ Ⓓ Ⓔ	57 Ⓐ Ⓑ Ⓒ Ⓓ Ⓔ
18 Ⓐ Ⓑ Ⓒ Ⓓ Ⓔ	38 Ⓐ Ⓑ Ⓒ Ⓓ Ⓔ	58 Ⓐ Ⓑ Ⓒ Ⓓ Ⓔ
19 Ⓐ Ⓑ Ⓒ Ⓓ Ⓔ	39 Ⓐ Ⓑ Ⓒ Ⓓ Ⓔ	59 Ⓐ Ⓑ Ⓒ Ⓓ Ⓔ
20 Ⓐ Ⓑ Ⓒ Ⓓ Ⓔ	40 Ⓐ Ⓑ Ⓒ Ⓓ Ⓔ	60 Ⓐ Ⓑ Ⓒ Ⓓ Ⓔ

AP Microeconomics Practice Exam 2

Multiple-Choice

Time—1 hour and 10 minutes

60 questions

For the multiple-choice questions that follow, select the best answer and fill in the appropriate letter on the answer sheet.

1. Land, labor, capital and entrepreneurial talent are often referred to as

   (A) production possibilities.
   (B) goods and services.
   (C) unlimited human wants.
   (D) opportunity costs.
   (E) scarce economic resources.

2. The law of increasing costs is useful in describing

   (A) a demand curve.
   (B) a marginal benefit curve.
   (C) a linear production possibility frontier.
   (D) a concave production possibility frontier.
   (E) a total fixed costs curve.

3. Which of the following is likely to have a demand curve that is the least elastic?

   (A) Demand for the perfectly competitive firm's output.
   (B) Demand for the oligopoly firm's output with a homogenous product.
   (C) Demand for the oligopoly firm's output with a differentiated product.
   (D) Demand for the monopolistically competitive firm's output.
   (E) Demand for the monopoly firm's output.

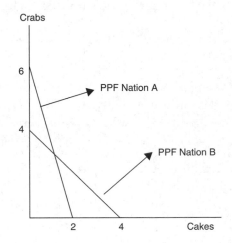

4. The figure above shows the production possibility frontiers (PPFs) for two nations that produce crabs and cakes. If these nations specialize and trade based on the principle of comparative advantage, which of the following trade agreements benefit both nations?

   (A) Nation A trades three crabs to Nation B in exchange for two cakes.
   (B) Nation A trades three cakes to Nation B in exchange for three crabs.
   (C) Nation A trades one cake to Nation B in exchange for two crabs.
   (D) Nation A trades one crab to Nation B in exchange for two cakes.
   (E) Nation A trades four crabs to Nation B in exchange for six cakes.

5. Which of the following scenarios would increase a nation's production possibility frontier (PPF)?

   (A) The nation's system of higher education slowly declines in quality.
   (B) The nation invests in research and development of new technology.
   (C) The nation's infant mortality rate increases.
   (D) Environmental pollution severely damages the health of the population.
   (E) Mineral reserves are exhausted.

6. A rational consumer who is eating Girl Scout cookies stops eating when

   (A) the total benefit equals the total cost of eating cookies.
   (B) the marginal benefit equals the marginal cost of the next cookie.
   (C) the marginal cost of eating cookies is maximized.
   (D) the marginal benefit of eating cookies is minimized.
   (E) the price of the cookie equals the marginal benefit of the next cookie.

7. A competitive market for coffee, a normal good, is currently in equilibrium. Which of the following would most likely result in an increase in the demand for coffee?

   (A) Consumer income falls.
   (B) The price of tea rises.
   (C) The wage of coffee plantation workers falls.
   (D) Technology in the harvesting of coffee beans improves.
   (E) The price of coffee brewing machines rises.

8. Which of the following certainly lowers the equilibrium price of a good exchanged in a competitive market?

   (A) The demand curve shifts to the right.
   (B) The supply curve shifts to the left.
   (C) The demand curve shifts to the left and the supply curve shifts to the right.
   (D) The demand curve shifts to the right and the supply curve shifts to the left.
   (E) Both the demand and supply curves shift to the left.

9. An effective price ceiling in the market for good X likely results in

   (A) a persistent surplus of good X.
   (B) a persistent shortage of good X.
   (C) an increase in the demand for good Y, a substitute for good X.
   (D) a decrease in the demand for good Z, a complement with good X.
   (E) a rightward shift in the supply curve of good X.

10. Which of the following goods is likely to have the most elastic demand curve?

    (A) Demand for white Ford minivans.
    (B) Demand for automobiles.
    (C) Demand for Ford automobiles.
    (D) Demand for American-made automobiles.
    (E) Demand for a Ford minivan.

11. Which of the following is a fundamental aspect of the free market system?

    (A) A high degree of government involvement.
    (B) Public ownership of resources.
    (C) Private property.
    (D) Central planners set wages and prices.
    (E) Employers consult government agencies for guidance in hiring workers with appropriate job skills.

12. The elasticity of supply is typically greater when

    (A) producers have fewer alternative goods to produce.
    (B) producers have less time to respond to price changes.
    (C) producers are operating near the limits to their production.
    (D) producers have less access to raw materials necessary for production.
    (E) producers have more time to respond to price changes.

13. Good X is exchanged in a competitive market. Which of the following is true if an excise tax is now imposed on the production of good X?

    (A) If the demand curve is perfectly elastic, the price rises by the amount of the tax.
    (B) The consumer's burden of the tax rises, as the demand curve is more elastic.
    (C) Consumer surplus rises as a result of the tax.
    (D) The consumer's burden of the tax rises, as the demand curve is less elastic.
    (E) If the demand curve is perfectly inelastic, the price does not rise as a result of the tax.

14. Which of the following is an implicit cost for the owner of a small store in your hometown?

   (A) The wage that is paid to the assistant manager.
   (B) The cost of purchasing canned goods from a wholesale food distributor.
   (C) The value placed on the owner's skills in an alternative career.
   (D) The cost of cooling the refrigerated meat display.
   (E) The price of placing an advertisement in the local newspaper.

15. Suppose a price floor is installed in the market for coffee. One result of this policy would be

   (A) a decrease in the demand for coffee-brewing machines.
   (B) a persistent shortage of coffee in the market.
   (C) an increase in consumer surplus due to lower coffee prices.
   (D) an increase in the demand for coffee.
   (E) a decrease in the profits for the owners of coffee plantations.

Questions 16–17 refer to the table below, which describes employment and production of a firm that hires labor and produces output in competitive markets. The competitive price of the product is $.50.

UNITS OF LABOR	TOTAL PRODUCT
0	0
1	11
2	20
3	27
4	32
5	35

16. Which unit of labor has marginal revenue product equal to $1.50?

   (A) 1st
   (B) 2nd
   (C) 3rd
   (D) 4th
   (E) 5th

17. If the wage paid to all units of labor is $4.50, how many units of labor are hired?

   (A) 1
   (B) 2
   (C) 3
   (D) 4
   (E) 5

18. Which of the following is true of the perfectly competitive firm in the short run?

   (A) The firm earns a normal profit.
   (B) The firm shuts down if the price falls below average total cost.
   (C) The firm earns positive economic profit.
   (D) The firm maximizes profit by producing where the price equals marginal revenue.
   (E) The firm may earn positive, negative, or normal profits.

Questions 19–21 refer to the figure below.

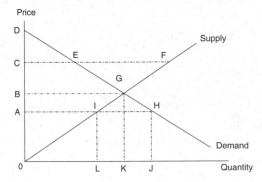

19. If the current price is 0B, we would expect

   (A) a surplus in the market to be eliminated by rising prices.
   (B) a shortage in the market to be eliminated by falling prices.
   (C) a surplus in the market to be eliminated by falling prices.
   (D) quantity demanded to be equal to quantity supplied as the market is in equilibrium.
   (E) a shortage in the market to be eliminated by rising prices.

20. If the price were to fall from 0C to 0A, which of the following would be true?

   (A) Dollars spent on this good would increase if demand for the good were price inelastic.
   (B) Dollars spent on this good would decrease if demand for the good were price elastic.
   (C) Dollars spent on this good would increase if demand for the good were price elastic.
   (D) Dollars spent on this good would increase if demand for the good were unitary price elastic.
   (E) Dollars spent on this good would decrease if demand for the good were unitary price elastic.

21. If the market is in equilibrium, which of the following areas corresponds to producer surplus?

(A) BGD
(B) 0AHJ
(C) 0DGK
(D) 0BG
(E) 0BGK

22. The downward sloping demand curve is partially explained by which of the following?

(A) Substitution effects and income effects.
(B) The Law of Increasing Marginal Costs.
(C) The principle of comparative advantage.
(D) The Law of Diminishing Marginal Returns to production.
(E) The least-cost principle.

23. Dorothy has daily income of $20, each cup of coffee costs $P_c = \$1$ and each scone costs $P_s = \$4$. The table below provides us with Dorothy's marginal utility (MU) received in the consumption of each good. As a utility-maximizing consumer, which combination of coffee and scones should Dorothy consume each day?

CUPS OF COFFEE	MU OF COFFEE	# OF SCONES	MU OF SCONES
1	10	1	30
2	8	2	24
3	6	3	20
4	4	4	16
5	2	5	14
6	1	6	8

(A) 2 coffee and 2 scones
(B) 5 coffee and 6 scones
(C) 3 coffee and 2 scones
(D) 4 coffee and 4 scones
(E) 4 coffee and 16 scones

24. You are told that the Gini coefficient of income inequality has risen from .35 to .85. Which of the following is a likely cause of this change?

(A) Market power in the factor and output markets has increased.
(B) Labor market discrimination has been eliminated.
(C) The distribution of wealth and property has become more equitable.
(D) The vast majority of adults have achieved at least a college degree.
(E) The tax system has become even more progressive.

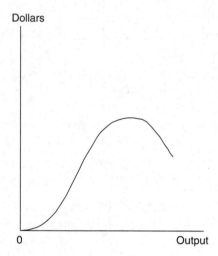

25. The figure above best represents which of the following functions?

(A) Total product of labor
(B) Total revenue
(C) Total cost
(D) Total utility
(E) Total short-run economic profits

26. If it is true that bacon and eggs are complementary goods, then

(A) the income elasticity of bacon is positive and the income elasticity for eggs is negative.
(B) the price elasticity for eggs is greater than the price elasticity for bacon.
(C) the cross-price elasticity between bacon and eggs is negative.
(D) the income elasticity of bacon is negative and the income elasticity for eggs is positive.
(E) the cross-price elasticity between bacon and eggs is positive.

27. A firm employs variable amounts of labor to a fixed amount of capital to produce output. If the daily wage paid to labor increases, how does this affect the firm's costs?

	TOTAL VARIABLE COST	TOTAL FIXED COST	TOTAL COST
(A)	Decrease	No change	Decrease
(B)	Decrease	Decrease	Decrease
(C)	Increase	Decrease	No change
(D)	Increase	No change	Increase
(E)	Increase	Increase	Increase

28. Diminishing marginal returns to short-run production begin when

(A) the average product of labor begins to fall.
(B) the total product of labor begins to fall.
(C) marginal product of labor becomes negative.
(D) average variable cost begins to rise.
(E) marginal product of labor begins to fall.

29. Which of the following is a characteristic of perfect competition?

(A) Firms produce a homogeneous product.
(B) Barriers to entry exist.
(C) Firms are price-setting profit maximizers.
(D) The government regulates the price so that dead weight loss is eliminated.
(E) Long-run positive profits are available.

UNITS OF LABOR	TOTAL PRODUCT (TP$_L$)
0	0 cups
1	5
2	15
3	30
4	40
5	45
6	40
7	30

30. The table above shows how hiring increasing amounts of labor to a fixed amount of capital affects the hourly output of Molly's lemonade stand. Based on this table of production data, which of the following can be said?

(A) Diminishing marginal returns begins with the first worker hired.
(B) Marginal cost begins to rise at the 6th worker hired.
(C) Total product is maximized at the 3rd worker hired.
(D) Average product begins to decline with the first worker hired.
(E) Diminishing marginal returns begins with the 4th worker hired.

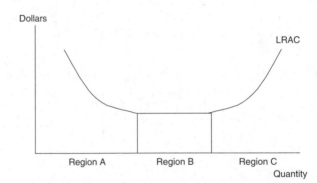

31. The figure above shows the long-run average cost curve of a competitive firm. Which of the following choices best describes Region B in the diagram?

(A) Economies of scale
(B) Diseconomies of scale
(C) Constant returns to scale
(D) Diminishing returns to scale
(E) Increasing returns to scale

32. The market for good X is currently in equilibrium. Which of the following choices would NOT cause both a decrease in the equilibrium price of good X and a decrease in the equilibrium quantity of good X?

(A) A decrease in consumer income and good X is a normal good.
(B) An increase in consumer income and good X is an inferior good.
(C) An increase in the price of good Y, a complement for good X.
(D) A decrease in the price of good Y, a substitute for good X.
(E) An increase in the number of consumers in the market for good X.

Questions 33–34 refer to the figure below, which shows cost curves for a competitive firm.

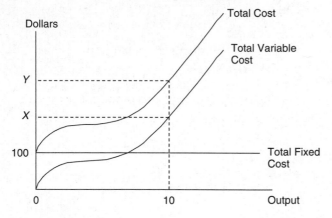

33. If average variable cost at a quantity of 10 is $25, what is the value of Y in the figure above?

(A) $250
(B) $25
(C) $35
(D) $1000
(E) $350

34. At a quantity of 10, what is the value of $(Y-X)$?

(A) $100
(B) $25
(C) $10
(D) $35
(E) $350

35. The demand for labor falls if

(A) labor productivity falls.
(B) price of the good produced by labor rises.
(C) the price of a complementary input falls.
(D) demand for the good produced by labor rises.
(E) a minimum wage is removed from the labor market.

Questions 36–37 refer to the graph below.

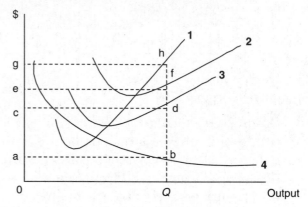

36. The curve labeled 4 represents which of the following?

(A) Marginal cost
(B) Marginal product of labor
(C) Average total cost
(D) Average fixed cost
(E) Average variable cost

37. Where is the shut down point for this perfectly competitive firm?

(A) Any price below curve 4.
(B) Any price below 0c.
(C) Any price below curve 3.
(D) Any price below curve 2.
(E) Any quantity less than Q.

38. If a market for a good is producing a negative externality,

    (A) at the market output the marginal costs to society exceed the private marginal costs of production.
    (B) at the market output the marginal benefits to society exceed the private marginal costs of production.
    (C) at the market output the marginal costs to society exceed the total benefits to society.
    (D) at the market output the private marginal costs of production exceed the marginal costs to society.
    (E) at the market output the marginal benefits to society exceed the marginal costs to society.

39. Which of the following is a characteristic of a monopoly market?

    (A) Firms produce a homogeneous product.
    (B) Barriers to entry exist.
    (C) Firms are price-taking profit maximizers.
    (D) Dead weight loss is eliminated through entry of competing firms in the long run.
    (E) In the long run the firm earns normal profits.

40. A monopolist may be able to maintain long-run positive profit due to

    (A) dead weight loss.
    (B) economies of scale in production.
    (C) a price that is set equal to average total cost.
    (D) perfectly elastic demand for the product.
    (E) entry of new firms that keep the price high.

Questions 41–42 refer to the graph below.

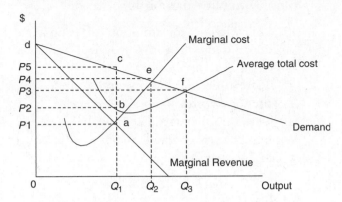

41. If this firm were a profit-maximizing monopolist, the price, output and profit would be

	PRICE	OUTPUT	PROFIT
(A)	$P5$	$Q1$	$Q1 * (c–b)$
(B)	$P5$	$Q1$	$Q1 * P1$
(C)	$P4$	$Q2$	$Q2 * (P4–P1)$
(D)	$P1$	$Q1$	$Q1 * (P5–P1)$
(E)	$P3$	$Q3$	$Q3 * P3$

42. Consumer surplus in the monopolist market is equal to the area:

    (A) abce.
    (B) abcf.
    (C) $P5$cd.
    (D) $0Q1aP1$.
    (E) $P1P5$ca.

43. The top six firms in an oligopolistic industry have market shares of 25%, 25%, 15%, 10%, 6%, and 3%. Many smaller firms split the rest of the market. What is the value of the four-firm concentration ratio?

    (A) 65%
    (B) 54%
    (C) 75%
    (D) 34%
    (E) 50%

44. Which of the following statements are true of consumer utility-maximizing behavior?

    I. Utility from consumption of good X is maximized when the marginal utility is equal to zero.
    II. Total utility from consumption of good X rises at a decreasing rate.
    III. The consumer spends limited income until the quantity of good X consumed is equal to the quantity of good Y.

    (A) I only
    (B) II only
    (C) III only
    (D) I and II only
    (E) II and III only

45. Oligopoly has at times been the subject of government antitrust regulation. Which of the following is a reason for this government regulation?

    (A) Price is approximately equal to marginal cost.
    (B) Price is approximately equal to average total cost.
    (C) Dead weight loss lessens over time.
    (D) Consumer surplus is lost as market power increases.
    (E) Market efficiency is maximized.

46. The production of chicken often results in offending odors that are picked up by the wind and blown over rural communities. This is an example of a _____externality, the result of which are spillover ____and an _____of resources to chicken production.

    (A) negative, costs, underallocation.
    (B) negative, benefits, overallocation.
    (C) negative, benefits, underallocation
    (D) positive, costs, overallocation
    (E) negative, costs, overallocation

47. Which of the following are shared by perfectly competitive firms and monopolistically competitive firms?

    I. Barriers to entry
    II. Normal profits in the long run
    III. Excess capacity
    IV. A homogenous product

    (A) I only
    (B) II only
    (C) III only
    (D) II and IV only
    (E) I, II, and III only

48. The monopolistically competitive price is above marginal revenue because

    (A) firms have differentiated products.
    (B) firms are price takers.
    (C) firms produce a homogenous product.
    (D) the market is allocatively efficient.
    (E) profits are normal in the long run.

49. Dead weight loss in industries with market power is a result of

    (A) profit-maximizing output occurs where price equals marginal revenue.
    (B) profit-maximizing output occurs where price exceeds marginal cost.
    (C) profit-maximizing output occurs where price equals marginal cost.
    (D) profit-maximizing output occurs where price exceeds average total cost.
    (E) profit-maximizing output occurs where price equals average total cost.

50. If the government wishes to regulate a natural monopoly so that it earns a normal profit, it sets

    (A) Price = Marginal Cost.
    (B) Marginal Revenue = Marginal Cost.
    (C) Price = Average Total Cost.
    (D) Price = Marginal Revenue.
    (E) Marginal Revenue = Average Total Cost.

51. Which of the following would improve the efficiency of a monopoly market?

    (A) The government regulates the monopolist to produce the output where marginal revenue equals marginal cost.
    (B) The government provides additional legal barriers to entry.
    (C) The government subsidizes the monopolist so that they achieve even greater economies of scale.
    (D) The government eliminates trade barriers on potential foreign producers.
    (E) The government regulates the monopolist to produce the output where monopoly profits are maximized.

52. Which of the following increases the demand for interstate truck drivers?

    (A) An increase in the wage of truck drivers.
    (B) An increase in the supply of truck drivers.
    (C) An increase in the price of diesel fuel, which is used to power semitrucks.
    (D) A decrease in the demand for interstate shipping.
    (E) A decrease in the price of semitrucks.

53. A monopsony employer hires labor up to the point where

    (A) Wage = Marginal Factor Cost.
    (B) Marginal Factor Cost = Marginal Product of Labor.
    (C) Marginal Factor Cost = Marginal Revenue Product of Labor.
    (D) Wage = Marginal Revenue Product of Labor.
    (E) Wage = Price of the good produced by the labor.

54. The price of labor is $5 and the price of capital is $10 per unit. Using the table below, what is the least cost combination of labor and capital that should be hired to produce 18 units of output?

UNITS OF LABOR	MARGINAL PRODUCT OF LABOR	UNITS OF CAPITAL	MARGINAL PRODUCT OF CAPITAL
1	6	1	8
2	4	2	6
3	3	3	5
4	2	4	4
5	1	5	2

    (A) 1 Labor and 2 Capital
    (B) 4 Labor and 8 Capital
    (C) 2 Labor and 1 Capital
    (D) 5 Labor and 5 Capital
    (E) 3 Labor and 2 Capital

55. A cartel is often the result of

    (A) perfectly competitive firms that agree to produce a homogenous product.
    (B) oligopoly competitors that agree to restrict output to maximize joint profits.
    (C) a monopoly that has been regulated by the government.
    (D) a natural monopoly that has evolved into a perfectly competitive industry.
    (E) monopolistically competitive firms that have agreed to earn normal profits in the long run.

56. Suppose the state requires hairdressers and manicurists to pass a series of exams to be certified cosmetologists. How does this policy change the supply of cosmetologists, the equilibrium wage, and the price of a manicure?

	SUPPLY OF COSMETOLOGISTS	WAGE	PRICE OF MANICURES
(A)	Decrease	Increase	Increase
(B)	Decrease	Decrease	Decrease
(C)	Increase	Decrease	Decrease
(D)	Increase	Decrease	Increase
(E)	Increase	Increase	Increase

57. The local market for bankers is currently in equilibrium. Which of the following increases the local wage paid to bankers?

    (A) Internet banking at home is becoming more popular.
    (B) More college students are majoring in finance and economics, majors that make them attractive as bank employees.
    (C) The price of banking software, a complementary resource to bankers, rises.
    (D) Several banks in the local market merge and consolidate many operations.
    (E) The price of automatic teller machines, a substitute for bankers, decreases and the output effect is greater than the substitution effect.

58. The U.S. government collects tax revenue, buys military equipment from many private firms, and uses this equipment to provide national defense to all Americans. This is a good example of

    (A) a natural monopoly.
    (B) an excise tax on military equipment.
    (C) a regressive tax.
    (D) a public good.
    (E) dead weight loss.

59. Which of the following scenarios is the best example of a positive externality?

    (A) Your neighbor has a swimming pool and throws loud late-night parties.
    (B) Your neighbor has a swimming pool and allows you free access.
    (C) Your neighbor has a swimming pool and the powerful chlorine odor blows into your open dining room window.
    (D) Your neighbor has a swimming pool and allows you to use it in exchange for letting his kids use your swing.
    (E) Your neighbor has a swimming pool that is conducive for the breeding of mosquitoes.

60. Because of the free-rider effect, the private marketplace tends to

    (A) provide the allocatively efficient amount of a public good.
    (B) produce too much of a public good, requiring the government to intervene and tax the production of it.
    (C) produce a public good in the amount where the marginal benefit to society equals the marginal cost to society.
    (D) produce too little of the public good, requiring the government to intervene and provide it for all.
    (E) produce too little of the public good, requiring the government to intervene and ban it.

› Answers and Explanations

1. **E**—Know the four scarce economic resources.

2. **D**—A concave PPF exhibits the Law of Increasing Costs. As more of a good is produced, opportunity costs rise. This is because resources are not perfectly substitutable between the production of different goods.

3. **E**—Demand is more elastic if there are more substitute goods. A monopolist has no close substitutes so is likely the least elastic demand.

4. **A**—Nation A has comparative advantage in crab production and Nation B has comparative advantage in cake production. Nation A specializes in crabs, Nation B specializes in cakes, so avoid any option suggesting the opposite. Choice A is the only one that allows both to consume beyond the PPF.

5. **B**—Nations that invest in research and technology expect the PPF to expand; the key to economic growth.

6. **B**—Rational decision makers consume right up to the point where the MB of the next cookie is exactly equal to the MC of the next cookie.

7. **B**—Tea is a coffee substitute. Higher tea prices increase coffee demand.

8. **C**—Leftward demand shifts, coupled with rightward supply shifts put downward pressure on prices.

9. **B**—Price ceilings are legal maximum prices set below the equilibrium price. A shortage results.

10. **A**—The more narrowly a good is defined, the more elastic demand.

11. **C**—Private property is fundamental to the free market economy.

12. **E**—The supply curve is more elastic as more time elapses.

13. **D**—If the demand curve is more inelastic (more vertical) a greater burden of an excise tax falls upon consumers and less upon producers.

14. **C**—The opportunity cost of starting a small store is the salary given up in the next best alternative for the entrepreneur's skills.

15. **A**—A price floor is a legal minimum price set above the equilibrium price. Higher coffee prices decrease the demand for complementary goods like coffee machines.

16. **E**—$P * MP_L = MRP_L$.

17. **B**—At the second worker, wage = MRP_L.

18. **E**—In perfect competition, short-run profits may be positive or negative, or normal, but long-run profits are always normal.

19. **D**—This is the equilibrium price.

20. **C**—When the price falls and quantity demanded rises, consumer spending on the good ($P * Q$) can change in two directions. If $E_d > 0$, a percent decrease in price increases quantity demanded by a greater percent, increasing spending on the good.

21. **D**—PS is the area under the price and above supply.

22. **A**—Substitution and income effects explain the Law of Demand.

23. **D**—Using the utility maximizing rule, set $MU_c/\$1 = MU_s/\$4$. There are three options where the MU_c is four times the MU_s, and only one of those options uses exactly \$20 of daily income.

24. **A**—The Gini coefficient measures income inequality. The closer it gets to one, the more unequal the income distribution. One explanation for inequality is more market power in product and input markets. This redistributes CS to monopoly producers and/or employers.

25. **B**—Quickly look at the graph to eliminate some possibilities. With dollars on the y axis, this curve cannot represent TP_L (output on the y axis) or total utility (utility on the y axis). The other key is that this curve has a value of zero dollars at an output of zero. TC = TFC at zero output and short-run economic losses equal TFC at zero output.

26. **C**—If the price of eggs rises, demand for bacon falls if they are complementary; $E_{xy} < 0$.

27. **D**—Labor is a variable cost so there is no change in TFC, but an increase in TVC and TC.

28. **E**—This defines diminishing marginal returns and is often missed by students, who make the mistake of identifying falling TP_L, rather than falling MP_L, with diminishing returns.

29. **A**—Know the characteristics of all market structures.

30. **E**—The 4th worker is the first to have lower MP_L than the worker before.

31. **C**—Constant returns exist when a larger firm has constant LRAC.

32. **E**—All other choices *would* produce a decrease in the demand for good X and would therefore decrease both the price and quantity. You are looking for the only choice that would NOT. More consumers for good X would increase demand and increase both the price and quantity

33. **E**—Since you know that AVC is $25 at $Q = 10$, TVC is $250. Adding this to the given $100 of TFC produces $350 of total cost at $Q = 10$.

34. **A**—The vertical distance between TC and TVC is TFC.

35. **A**—Demand for labor is the MRP_L curve. Higher labor productivity increases labor demand.

36. **D**—AFC declines as output rises.

37. **C**—The shutdown point is at $P < AVC$.

38. **A**—With no externality, MSB = MSC. With a negative externality MSC > MPC = MSB for the good.

39. **B**—Barriers to entry are a defining characteristic of monopoly.

40. **B**—Economies of scale are a common barrier to entry; a key to maintaining long-run positive profits.

41. **A**—Find the output level where MR = MC and locate the price from the demand curve. Profit is equal to $Q * (P–ATC)$ at that output.

42. **C**—CS is the area above price and under demand.

43. **C**—A four-firm concentration ratio is the sum of the market share of the four largest firms in an industry.

44. **D**—Utility-maximizing consumers do not equate the units of two goods, they equate MU/P for each good.

45. **D**—As industries approach monopoly, prices rise, lowering CS.

46. **E**—Negative externalities, like "fowl" odors, impose spillover costs upon third parties. These costs, ignored by the market, reflect an over-allocation of resources to chicken production.

47. **B**—Know the characteristics of all market structures.

48. **A**—Product differentiation results in a small degree of price-setting ability, and downward sloping demand curves for the firms. P = ATC and profits are normal in the long run, this output level does not occur where ATC is minimized. This defines excess capacity.

49. **B**—DWL emerges when output is moved away from where P = MC.

50. **C**—If P = ATC, economic profit is zero, or normal.

51. **D**—Allowing more foreign competition lessens market power of a monopolist and improves efficiency as the price falls closer to MC.

52. **E**—Semitrucks are a complementary resource to the truck drivers. If the price falls, demand for the labor rises.

53. **C**—The monopsony hiring decision.

54. **C**—Use the least-cost rule of $MP_L/\$5 = MP_K/\$10$ to find the optimal combination of labor and capital. There are three combinations of labor and capital where the MP_K is twice the MP_L but only one choice produces 18 units of output. Remember that adding the marginal products provides the total product.

55. **B**—This describes a cartel.

56. **A**—Certification exams decrease labor supply and raise the wage in the market. A higher wage increases the MC of producing the good, which raises the price of the good.

57. **E**—If the price of a substitute resource falls, labor demand can increase if the output effect is greater than the substitution effect.

58. **D**—Know your public goods.

59. **B**—You are the recipient of a spillover benefit from your neighbor's purchase of a pool.

60. **D**—The private marketplace underprovides for a public good because free riders benefit from the good without paying for it. Government must provide the public good.

AP Microeconomics Practice Exam 2

Free-Response Questions

Planning time—10 minutes

Writing time—50 minutes

At the conclusion of the planning time, you have 50 minutes to respond to the following three questions. Approximately half of your time should be given to the first question and the second half should be divided evenly between the remaining two questions. Be careful to clearly explain your reasoning and to provide clear labels to all graph axes and curves.

1. Salmon and tuna are substitutes in perfectly competitive markets that are experiencing long-run equilibrium.

   (A) Suppose that an unforeseen change in the weather patterns of the Pacific Ocean dramatically reduces the salmon population while leaving the tuna populations unaffected. In a correctly labeled graph, show how this weather pattern initially affects:

      i. Equilibrium price and quantity in the market for salmon.

   (B) Charlie owns a perfectly competitive tuna fishing boat. Explain how changes in the market for salmon affect each of the following:

      i.   Price of tuna in the market.
      ii. Quantity of tuna produced in the market.
      iii. Quantity of tuna produced by Charlie's firm.
      iv. Economic profit or loss for Charlie's firm.

   (C) Describe how the situation in the tuna market described in part (B) adjusts in the long run. Be sure to predict how the following changes in the long run:

      i.   Price of tuna in the market.
      ii. Quantity of tuna produced in the market.
      iii. Quantity of tuna produced by Charlie's firm.
      iv. Economic profit or loss for Charlie's firm.

2. Assume the following about the market for cigarettes.

   • Cigarettes are sold in a competitive market.
   • Cigarettes have no close substitute.
   • The demand for cigarettes is price inelastic.

   Suppose now that the government imposes a per unit excise tax on producers of cigarettes.

   (A) Using a correctly labeled graph, show the impact of the excise tax on each of the following in the cigarette market:

      i.   Price.
      ii. Output.
      iii. The area of tax revenue collected by the government.
      iv. Dead weight loss from the tax.

   (B) Given that demand for cigarettes is price inelastic, will consumer spending on cigarettes increase, decrease, or remain constant? How do you know?

3. Two rival firms operate in an oligopoly and, once a year, choose an advertising strategy. The firms can choose between an expensive television and radio advertising campaign (costly ads) or an inexpensive direct mail advertising campaign (cheap ads). Television and radio cost more, but reach more potential customers. Each firm decides their advertising strategy independently on January 1, 2007 and, once chosen, cannot alter the decision until January 1, 2008. The table below summarizes the profits each firm would earn given their own, and their rival's strategy. Use this matrix to answer the following questions.

		FIRM2	
		Costly Ads	Cheap Ads
FIRM 1	Costly Ads	Firm 1: $100 Firm 2: $100	Firm 1: $250 Firm 2: $75
	Cheap Ads	Firm 1: $75 Firm 2: $250	Firm 1: $200 Firm 2: $200

(A) Suppose Firm 1 chooses *Costly Ads* and Firm 2 chooses *Cheap Ads*.

  i. Identify the profit for Firm 1.
  ii. Identify the profit for Firm 2.

(B) It is now January 1, 2007 and each firm must independently make the advertising strategy decision. Is there a dominant strategy in this game? Explain how you know.

(C) If each firm chooses the advertising strategy independently without collusion, what is the outcome of this game?

(D) Is the outcome of this game an example of a "prisoners' dilemma"? Explain your answer.

› Free-Response Grading Rubric

Note: Based on my experience, these point allocations roughly approximate the weighting on similar questions on the AP examinations. Be aware that every year the point allocations differ and partial credit is awarded differently.

Question 1 (12 points)

Part (A): 2 points
These points are graphing points. A perfect response shows the salmon supply curve shifting to the left, increasing the price, and decreasing equilibrium quantity in the market. These prices and quantities must be labeled.

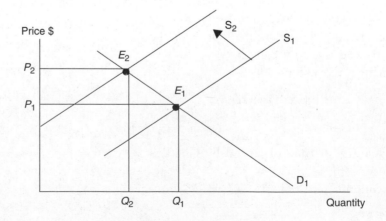

Part (B): 5 points
This part of the question asks you to explain something, which means a graph is not required. However, a graph may assist your explanations.

1 point: Explain that higher salmon prices increase the demand for tuna, a substitute.

   i. 1 point: The higher demand for tuna increases the price of tuna.
   ii. 1 point: Increased demand increases the market quantity.
  iii. 1 point: Charlie increases his production as the price rises.
  iv. 1 point: The price is now above average total cost so Charlie's economic profit is greater than zero.

Part (C): 5 points

1 point: Because positive economic profits were being made in part (B), firms enter the tuna fishing industry.

   i. 1 point: The higher supply for tuna decreases the price of tuna.
   ii. 1 point: Increased supply increases the market quantity.
  iii. 1 point: Charlie decreases his production as the price falls.
  iv. 1 point: In the long run $P = ATC$ so Charlie's economic profit is equal to zero. You can also say that he earns normal profits.

Question: OK, so what if I screwed up part (B)? Am I doomed in part (C)?

Answer: Maybe not, but you cannot bank your hopes for a 5 on generous partial credit.

Suppose in part (B) (iv), that you said Charlie would suffer economic losses because the price is below ATC. This is incorrect and so the last point in part (B) cannot be given.

    But . . . and here is where the partial credit may differ from year to year. If in part (C) you correctly described the long-run adjustment to losses, you may (and I stress *may*) receive some or all of the five points in part C.

Part (C): alternative scoring to an incorrect presumption of losses in part (B)

1 point: Because negative economic losses were being made in part (B), firms exit the tuna fishing industry.

   i. 1 point: The lessened supply for tuna increases the price of tuna.
   ii. 1 point: Decreased supply decreases the market quantity.
  iii. 1 point: Charlie increases his production as the price rises.
  iv. 1 point: In the long run $P = ATC$ so Charlie's economic profit is equal to zero. You can also say that he earns normal profits.

Question 2 (7 points)

Part (A): 5 points

These are all graphing points so to get all five points, all curves, axes, and directional shifts must be perfectly identified.

1 point: A correctly labeled graph showing the supply curve shifting upward by the amount of a tax.

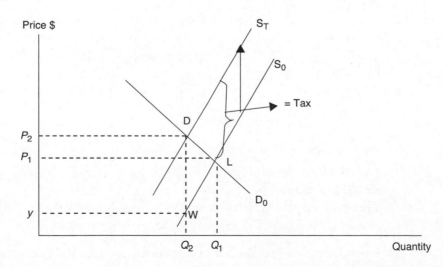

    i. 1 point: Showing that the price increases after the tax.
   ii. 1 point: Showing that the quantity decreases after the tax.
  iii. 1 point: Tax revenue is the area of the rectangle yP_2DW.
  iv. 1 point: Dead weight loss is the area of the triangle DWL shown above.

TIP: In a question like this, there are very little partial credit possibilities. You either get the graphing points or you do not.

Part (B): 2 points

1 point: Consumer spending increases.

1 point: Because the percent increase in the price is greater than the percent decrease in quantity. It is also accurate to refer to proportional changes.

TIP: The last point is the more difficult of the two and serves to differentiate students. In the past you might have also received credit for saying "a *large* increase in the price out-weighs a *small* decrease in quantity." It is much more accurate to refer to proportional or percentage changes and in future years the rubric might be more stringent on this point.

Question 3: (7 points)

Part (A): 2 points
These are points for just being able to read the payoff matrix in this game. Since we know that Firm 1 is choosing *Costly Ads*, then you must focus on the top half of the matrix. If Firm 2 is choosing *Cheap Ads*, then the game ends in the top right square.

   i. 1 point: $250
  ii. 1 point: $75

Part (B): 2 points
The key here is obviously to know what it means to have a dominant strategy. A dominant strategy is one that is always superior to the other option, no matter what the rival firm is doing. For example, if Firm 2 plays *Costly Ads*, Firm 1 should do the same because $100 (*Costly Ads*) beats $75 (*Cheap Ads*). If Firm 2 were to play *Cheap Ads*, Firm 1 would play *Costly Ads* because $250 (*Costly Ads*) beats $200 (*Cheap Ads*). So Firm 1 would always play *Costly Ads*. The same is true of Firm 2.

   i. 1 point: Yes, playing *Costly Ads* is a dominant strategy for both firms.
  ii. 1 point: Because, no matter what the rival firm is doing, this strategy always beats *Cheap Ads*.

Part (C): 1 point
The outcome is that both firms earn $100 because, without collusion, both will play the dominant strategy, *Costly Ads*.

Part (D): 2 points
A prisoners' dilemma is a situation where playing the dominant strategy produces an out-come that, in hindsight, could have been better for both if the firms could have colluded and coordinated their strategies.

1 point: Yes, it is an example of a prisoners' dilemma.

1 point: Both firms could have improved profits ($200 each vs. $100 each) by colluding with a selection of *Cheap Ads*.

Scoring and Interpretation

AP Microeconomics Practice Exam 2

Multiple-Choice Questions:

Number of correct answers: _____

Number of incorrect answers: _____

Number of blank answers: _____

Did you complete this part of the test in the allotted time? Yes/No

Free-Response Questions:

1. _____/12
2. _____/7
3. _____/7

Did you complete this part of the test in the allotted time? Yes/No

Calculate Your Score:

Multiple-Choice Questions:

$$\underline{\hspace{3cm}} - \underline{\hspace{3cm}} = \underline{\hspace{3cm}}$$

(\# right)   (.25 * \# wrong)   MC raw score

Free-Response Questions:

Free-Response Raw Score = (1.25 * Score \#1) + (1.0714 * Score \#2)
+ (1.0714 * Score \#3) = _____

Add the raw scores from the multiple-choice and free-response sections to obtain your total raw score for the practice exam. Use the table below to determine your grade, remembering these are rough estimates using questions that are not actually from AP exams, so do not read too much into this conversion from raw score to AP score.

MICROECONOMICS #2	
RAW SCORE	APPROXIMATE AP GRADE
73–90	5
58–72	4
45–57	3
33–44	2
0–32	1

AP Macroeconomics Practice Exam 2
for Multiple-Choice Questions

ANSWER SHEET

1 (A) (B) (C) (D) (E)	21 (A) (B) (C) (D) (E)	41 (A) (B) (C) (D) (E)
2 (A) (B) (C) (D) (E)	22 (A) (B) (C) (D) (E)	42 (A) (B) (C) (D) (E)
3 (A) (B) (C) (D) (E)	23 (A) (B) (C) (D) (E)	43 (A) (B) (C) (D) (E)
4 (A) (B) (C) (D) (E)	24 (A) (B) (C) (D) (E)	44 (A) (B) (C) (D) (E)
5 (A) (B) (C) (D) (E)	25 (A) (B) (C) (D) (E)	45 (A) (B) (C) (D) (E)
6 (A) (B) (C) (D) (E)	26 (A) (B) (C) (D) (E)	46 (A) (B) (C) (D) (E)
7 (A) (B) (C) (D) (E)	27 (A) (B) (C) (D) (E)	47 (A) (B) (C) (D) (E)
8 (A) (B) (C) (D) (E)	28 (A) (B) (C) (D) (E)	48 (A) (B) (C) (D) (E)
9 (A) (B) (C) (D) (E)	29 (A) (B) (C) (D) (E)	49 (A) (B) (C) (D) (E)
10 (A) (B) (C) (D) (E)	30 (A) (B) (C) (D) (E)	50 (A) (B) (C) (D) (E)
11 (A) (B) (C) (D) (E)	31 (A) (B) (C) (D) (E)	51 (A) (B) (C) (D) (E)
12 (A) (B) (C) (D) (E)	32 (A) (B) (C) (D) (E)	52 (A) (B) (C) (D) (E)
13 (A) (B) (C) (D) (E)	33 (A) (B) (C) (D) (E)	53 (A) (B) (C) (D) (E)
14 (A) (B) (C) (D) (E)	34 (A) (B) (C) (D) (E)	54 (A) (B) (C) (D) (E)
15 (A) (B) (C) (D) (E)	35 (A) (B) (C) (D) (E)	55 (A) (B) (C) (D) (E)
16 (A) (B) (C) (D) (E)	36 (A) (B) (C) (D) (E)	56 (A) (B) (C) (D) (E)
17 (A) (B) (C) (D) (E)	37 (A) (B) (C) (D) (E)	57 (A) (B) (C) (D) (E)
18 (A) (B) (C) (D) (E)	38 (A) (B) (C) (D) (E)	58 (A) (B) (C) (D) (E)
19 (A) (B) (C) (D) (E)	39 (A) (B) (C) (D) (E)	59 (A) (B) (C) (D) (E)
20 (A) (B) (C) (D) (E)	40 (A) (B) (C) (D) (E)	60 (A) (B) (C) (D) (E)

AP Macroeconomics Practice Exam 2

Multiple-Choice Questions

Time—1 hour and 10 minutes

60 questions

For the multiple-choice questions that follow, select the best answer and fill in the appropriate letter on the answer sheet.

Questions 1–2 refer to the figure below.

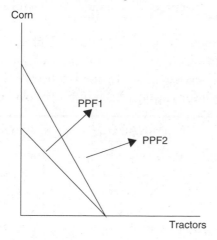

1. Suppose that the production possibility frontier (PPF) of this nation moves from PPF1 to PPF2. Which of the following could be the cause of this movement?

   (A) Technological improvements in the production of tractors.
   (B) A long-lasting and destructive drought.
   (C) A more efficient use of steel, an important raw material in the production of tractors.
   (D) An economy-wide improvement in the productivity of the labor force.
   (E) More effective pesticides used to protect crops from insect damage.

2. Now that the economy is operating on PPF2, what has happened to the opportunity cost of producing these goods?

   (A) The opportunity cost of producing tractors has decreased, while the opportunity cost of producing corn has increased.
   (B) The opportunity cost of producing tractors has increased, while the opportunity cost of producing corn has decreased.
   (C) The opportunity costs of producing tractors and corn have both decreased.
   (D) There has been no change in the opportunity cost of producing tractors and corn.
   (E) The opportunity costs of producing tractors and corn have both increased.

3. The price of gasoline has recently increased, while at the same time gasoline consumption has also increased. What is happening in the gasoline market?

   (A) This is evidence that contradicts the Law of Demand.
   (B) The price of crude oil has fallen, shifting the supply of gasoline to the right.
   (C) A price ceiling has been imposed in the market for gasoline.
   (D) The price of automobiles has increased, shifting the demand for gasoline to the left.
   (E) Consumers prefer larger automobiles, shifting the demand for gasoline to the right.

4. If Nation A can produce a good at lower opportunity cost than Nation B can produce the same good, it is said that

   (A) Nation A has comparative advantage in the production of that good.
   (B) Nation B has comparative advantage in the production of that good.
   (C) Nation A has absolute advantage in the production of that good.
   (D) Nation B has absolute advantage in the production of that good.
   (E) Nation A has economic growth in the production of that good.

5. Which of the following is a consequence of removal of a protective tariff on imported steel?

   (A) Imports fall.
   (B) Income is transferred from steel consumers to domestic steel producers.
   (C) Income is transferred from foreign steel producers to domestic steel producers.
   (D) Allocative efficiency is improved.
   (E) Aggregate supply is decreased.

6. In recent years, firms that produce cameras have begun to produce fewer 35-mm cameras and more digital cameras. This trend is an example of

   (A) how central planners dictate which goods are produced.
   (B) the market system answering the question of "how" cameras should be produced.
   (C) the market system answering the question of "what" cameras should be produced.
   (D) the market system answering the question of "who" should consume the cameras that are produced.
   (E) how firms fail to respond to improvements in technology and changes in consumer tastes.

7. Which of the following transactions would be included in the computation of Gross Domestic Product?

   (A) Josh buys a new pair of running shoes.
   (B) Nancy offers to babysit her granddaughter.
   (C) Katie buys her dad's used car.
   (D) Eli cannot go to a concert so he resells his ticket to a friend.
   (E) Molly rakes the leaves in her own yard.

8. Brent loses his job at the public swimming pool when the pool closes for the winter. This is an example of

   (A) cyclical unemployment.
   (B) discouraged worker.
   (C) seasonal unemployment.
   (D) frictional unemployment.
   (E) structural unemployment.

9. Which of the following is not a scarce economic resource?

   (A) Labor
   (B) Capital
   (C) Human wants
   (D) Land
   (E) Natural resources

10. How does an increasing national debt impact the market for U.S. dollars and the value of the dollar with respect to other currencies?

	MARKET FOR THE DOLLAR	VALUE OF THE DOLLAR
(A)	Increased demand	Appreciating
(B)	Increased supply	Appreciating
(C)	Decreased supply	Depreciating
(D)	Decreased demand	Depreciating
(E)	Increased demand	Depreciating

11. Suppose the price level in the United States has risen in the past year, but production of goods and services has remained constant. Based on this information, which of the following is true?

	NOMINAL GDP	REAL GDP
(A)	Increased	Increased
(B)	No change	Decreased
(C)	Decreased	Decreased
(D)	Increased	Decreased
(E)	Decreased	Increased

12. Which of the following is not included in national income?

   (A) Wages
   (B) Salaries
   (C) Interest
   (D) Depreciation
   (E) Profits

13. Which choice produces a faster rate of economic growth for the United States?

   (A) Institution of higher tariffs on imported goods.
   (B) More investment in capital infrastructure and less consumption of nondurable goods and services.
   (C) Elimination of mandatory school attendance laws.
   (D) Annual limits on the number of foreigners immigrating into the United States.
   (E) More investment in the military and less investment in higher education.

YEAR	ADULT POPULATION	EMPLOYED	UN-EMPLOYED
2003	1000	600	200
2004	1200	800	200

14. The table above summarizes the local labor market. Based on this information, which of the following is an accurate statement?

(A) The number of discouraged workers has fallen from 2003 to 2004.

(B) Although the population has grown, the labor force has remained constant from 2003 to 2004.

(C) The unemployment rate fell from 33 percent in 2003 to 25 percent in 2004.

(D) The economic recession in 2003 worsened in 2004.

(E) The unemployment rate fell from 25 percent in 2003 to 20 percent in 2004.

15. Which of the following is true of money and financial markets?

(A) As the demand for bonds increases, the interest rate increases.

(B) For a given money supply, if nominal GDP increases, the velocity of money decreases.

(C) When demand for stocks and bonds increases, the asset demand for money falls.

(D) A macroeconomic recession increases the demand for loanable funds.

(E) Equilibrium in the money market occurs where transaction demand for money equals the supply of money.

16. Which of the following would increase the aggregate demand function?

(A) Higher levels of imported goods.

(B) Lower levels of consumer wealth.

(C) A higher real interest rate.

(D) Lower taxes on personal income.

(E) Lower levels of exported goods.

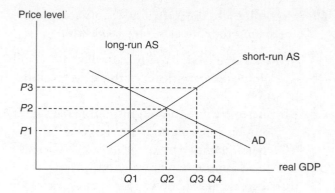

17. The figure above shows aggregate demand (AD) and supply (AS) for the economy. Assuming that aggregate demand remains constant, which of the following best predicts the short-run price level, the long-run price level, and the long-run level of output?

	SHORT-RUN PRICE LEVEL	LONG-RUN PRICE LEVEL	LONG-RUN OUTPUT
(A)	$P2$	$P1$	$Q4$
(B)	$P2$	$P2$	$Q1$
(C)	$P2$	$P3$	$Q1$
(D)	$P1$	$P2$	$Q3$
(E)	$P3$	$P2$	$Q2$

18. Which of the following is not included in the U.S. GDP?

(A) The U.S. military opens a new base in a foreign country with 1000 U.S. personnel.

(B) Japanese consumers buy thousands of CDs produced in the United States.

(C) An American pop singer performs a sold-out concert in Paris.

(D) A French theatrical production tours dozens of American cities.

(E) American construction companies build thousands of new homes all across the United States and Canada.

19. A policy supported by supply-side economists would be

(A) higher taxes on corporate profits.

(B) lower tax rates on interest earned from savings.

(C) removal of investment tax credits.

(D) a longer duration of unemployment benefits.

(E) higher marginal income tax rates to fund social welfare programs.

20. According to the quantity theory of money, increasing the money supply serves to

    (A) stimulate short-run production and employment with very little long-run inflation.
    (B) increase short-run output, but is the source of long-run inflation.
    (C) lower the unemployment rate while also lowering the rate of inflation.
    (D) increase the nation's long-run capacity to produce.
    (E) decrease short-run real GDP, but increase real GDP in the long run.

21. Of the following choices, the most direct exchange in the circular flow model of a private closed economy is when

    (A) households provide goods to firms in exchange for wage payments.
    (B) households provide resources to firms in exchange for goods.
    (C) households provide revenues to firms in exchange for wage payments.
    (D) firms supply goods to households in exchange for revenues.
    (E) firms supply resources to households in exchange for costs of production.

22. Suppose that the federal government reclassified the purchase of a new home as consumption spending rather than investment spending. This decision would

    (A) increase aggregate demand and decrease real GDP.
    (B) decrease aggregate demand and decrease real GDP.
    (C) decrease aggregate demand and increase real GDP.
    (D) increase aggregate demand and increase real GDP.
    (E) have no impact on aggregate demand and real GDP.

23. Suppose that current disposable income is $10,000 and consumption spending is $8000. For every $100 increase in disposable income, saving increases $10. Given this information,

    (A) the marginal propensity to consume is .80.
    (B) the marginal propensity to save is .20.
    (C) the marginal propensity to save is .10.
    (D) the marginal propensity to save is .90.
    (E) the marginal propensity to consume is .10.

24. When we observe an unplanned decrease in inventories, we can expect

    (A) prices to begin to fall.
    (B) output to begin to rise.
    (C) saving to begin to fall.
    (D) output to begin to fall.
    (E) planned investment to begin to rise.

25. Stagflation is the result of

    (A) a leftward shift in the aggregate supply curve.
    (B) a leftward shift in the aggregate demand curve.
    (C) a leftward shift in both the aggregate supply and aggregate demand curves.
    (D) a rightward shift in the aggregate supply curve.
    (E) a rightward shift in the aggregate demand curve.

26. If the short-run aggregate supply curve is horizontal, it is because

    (A) there exist many unemployed resources so that output can be increased without increasing wages and prices.
    (B) any increase in output requires a corresponding increase in wages and prices.
    (C) increases in output cause prices to increase, but wages adjust much less quickly.
    (D) falling interest rates increase the demand for goods and services, putting upward pressure on prices.
    (E) resources are fully employed so that output can be increased but only if the price level also increases.

27. In a private closed economy, which of the following statements are true?

   I. When unplanned changes in inventories are considered, saving and investment are always equal, no matter the level of GDP.
   II. Real GDP equals real spending in equilibrium.
   III. Households saving can never be negative.
   IV. Saving is equal to zero when consumption equals disposable income.

   (A) I and II only
   (B) II and III only
   (C) III and IV only
   (D) I, II, and IV only
   (E) II, III, and IV only

28. Which of the following is true of a typical contraction of the business cycle?

   (A) Consumption is falling, but household wealth is rising.
   (B) Consumption is increasing.
   (C) Private investment is rising.
   (D) Employment and inflation are low.
   (E) Private saving rates are rising.

29. Which of the following is most likely to produce stronger economic growth over time?

   (A) More rapid consumption of natural resources.
   (B) Higher adult illiteracy rates.
   (C) A falling stock of capital goods.
   (D) Investment tax credits.
   (E) Higher taxes on foreign capital investment.

30. If $100 of new autonomous private investment were added to an economy with a marginal propensity to consume of .90, by how much would aggregate demand shift to the right?

   (A) $190
   (B) $900
   (C) $1000
   (D) $1900
   (E) $90

31. Which of the following is true about the relationship between the $M1$, $M2$, and $M3$ measures of money?

   (A) $M1 + M2 = M3$
   (B) $M1$ includes checking deposits, while $M2$ includes checking and saving deposits.
   (C) $M2$ includes coin and paper money, but $M1$ does not.
   (D) $M2$ is more liquid than $M1$.
   (E) $M1$ is greater than $M2$.

32. Which of the following increases the size of the tax multiplier?

   (A) An increase in the marginal propensity to consume.
   (B) An increase in the reserve ratio.
   (C) An increase in the marginal propensity to save.
   (D) A decrease in the spending multiplier.
   (E) A decrease in the velocity of money.

33. Which of the following might worsen a nation's trade deficit?

   (A) Lower wages relative to other nations.
   (B) Lower taxes on corporate profits relative to other nations.
   (C) A higher interest rate on financial assets relative to other nations.
   (D) A higher rate of inflation relative to other nations.
   (E) Other nations remove tariffs and quotas on foreign imports.

34. If the economy is suffering from extremely high rates of inflation, which of the following fiscal policies would be an appropriate strategy for the economy?

   (A) Increase government spending and decrease taxes.
   (B) Decrease government spending and increase taxes.
   (C) Increase government spending with no change in taxes.
   (D) The Federal Reserve increases the discount rate.
   (E) Decrease taxes with no change in government spending.

35. Which of the following is an example of an expansionary supply shock?

    (A) Rapid increasing wages
    (B) A greatly depreciated currency
    (C) Declining labor productivity
    (D) Lower than expected agricultural harvests
    (E) Lower input prices in major industries

36. Which of the following fiscal policy combinations would be most likely to slowly increase real GDP without putting tremendous pressure on the price level?

    (A) Increase government spending with a matching decrease in taxes.
    (B) Decrease government spending with a matching increase in taxes.
    (C) Increase government spending with no change in taxes.
    (D) The Federal Reserve lowers the reserve ratio.
    (E) Increase taxes with a matching increase in government spending.

37. Which of the following is an example of contractionary monetary policy?

    (A) The Fed lowers the reserve ratio.
    (B) The Fed lowers the discount rate.
    (C) The Fed increases taxes on household income.
    (D) The Fed decreases spending on welfare programs.
    (E) The Fed sells Treasury securities to commercial banks.

38. The economy is in a deep recession. Given this economic situation, which of the following statements about monetary policy are accurate?

    I. Expansionary policy would only worsen the recession.
    II. Contractionary policy is the appropriate stimulus for investment and consumption.
    III. Expansionary policy greatly increases aggregate demand if investment is sensitive to changes in the interest rate.
    IV. If the demand for money is perfectly elastic, expansionary monetary policy might be quite effective.

    (A) I and II only
    (B) III only
    (C) III and IV only
    (D) IV only
    (E) II, III, and IV only

39. Daddy Morebucks withdraws $1 million from his savings account and puts the cash in his refrigerator. This affects M1, M2, and M3 in which of the following ways?

	M1	M2	M3
(A)	Rises	Rises	Rises
(B)	No change	No change	No change
(C)	Falls	Falls	Falls
(D)	Rises	Falls	No change
(E)	Rises	No change	No change

40. What is the main difference between the short-run and long-run Phillips curve?

    (A) The short-run Phillips curve is downward sloping and the long-run Phillips curve is upward sloping.
    (B) The short-run Phillips curve is upward sloping and the long-run Phillips curve is vertical.
    (C) The short-run Phillips curve is horizontal and the long-run Phillips curve is upward sloping.
    (D) The short-run Phillips curve is downward sloping and the long-run Phillips curve is vertical.
    (E) The short-run Phillips curve is vertical and the long-run Phillips curve is upward sloping.

41. Which of the following insures the value of the U.S. dollar?

    (A) The euro and other foreign currencies held by the Federal Reserve.
    (B) Gold bars in Fort Knox.
    (C) The promise of the U.S. government to maintain its value.
    (D) The value of the paper on which it is printed.
    (E) An equal amount of physical capital, land, and natural resources.

42. The reserve ratio is .10 and Daddy Morebucks withdraws $1 million from his checking account and keeps it as cash in his refrigerator. How does this withdrawal potentially impact money in circulation?

    (A) Decreases by $9 million.
    (B) Decreases by $1 million.
    (C) Decreases by $100,000.
    (D) Increases by $1 million.
    (E) Decreases by $10 million.

43. If the economy were experiencing a recessionary gap, choose the option below that would be an appropriate fiscal policy to eliminate the gap, and the predicted impact of the policy on real GDP and unemployment.

	FISCAL POLICY	REAL GDP	UN-EMPLOYMENT
(A)	Increase taxes	Increase	Decrease
(B)	Decrease spending	Decrease	Increase
(C)	Decrease taxes	Increase	Increase
(D)	Increase money supply	Increase	Decrease
(E)	Decrease taxes	Increase	Decrease

44. Monetary tools of the Federal Reserve do *not* include which of the following choices?

(A) Buying Treasury securities from commercial banks.
(B) Changing tariffs and quotas on imported goods.
(C) Changing the reserve ratio.
(D) Changing the discount rate.
(E) Selling Treasury securities to commercial banks.

45. Of the following choices, which combination of fiscal and monetary policy would most likely reduce a recessionary gap?

	FISCAL POLICY	MONETARY POLICY
(A)	Increase taxes	Increase the reserve ratio
(B)	Decrease spending	Sell Treasury securities
(C)	Decrease taxes	Buy Treasury securities
(D)	Increase spending	Increase the reserve ratio
(E)	Decrease taxes	Increase the discount rate

46. For a given level of government spending, the federal government usually experiences a budget____during economic____and a budget _____during economic_____.

(A) deficit, recession, surplus, expansion
(B) surplus, recession, deficit, expansion
(C) deficit, expansion, surplus, recession
(D) surplus, recession, surplus, expansion
(E) deficit, recession, deficit, expansion

47. Suppose that Congress and the Fed agreed to combine fiscal and monetary policies to lessen the threat of inflation. Which of the following combinations would likely accomplish this goal?

	FISCAL POLICY	MONETARY POLICY
(A)	Decrease taxes	Increase the reserve ratio
(B)	Decrease spending	Buy Treasury securities
(C)	Decrease taxes	Sell Treasury securities
(D)	Decrease spending	Decrease the reserve ratio
(E)	Increase taxes	Increase the discount rate.

48. Congress has embarked on another round of expansionary fiscal policy to boost employment and get reelected. As chair of the Fed, how would you reduce the "crowding out" effect and what macroeconomic problem might your policy exacerbate?

(A) Increase the reserve ratio, risking the devaluation of the dollar.
(B) Sell Treasury securities, risking inflation.
(C) Buy Treasury securities, risking a recessionary gap.
(D) Lower the discount rate, risking inflation.
(E) Lower the discount rate, risking cyclical unemployment.

49. Which of the following is likely to shift the long-run aggregate supply curve to the right?

(A) A nation that devotes more resources to nondurable consumption goods, rather than durable capital goods.
(B) Research that improves the productivity of labor and capital.
(C) More restrictive trade policies.
(D) Annual limits to immigration of foreign citizens.
(E) A permanent increase in the price of energy.

50. Holding all else equal, which of the following Fed monetary policies would be used to boost U.S. exports?

(A) Increasing the discount rate.
(B) Increasing the reserve ratio.
(C) Buying Treasury securities.
(D) Lowering tariffs.
(E) Removing import quotas.

51. Which of the following could limit the ability of the Fed to conduct expansionary monetary policy?

    (A) Money demand is nearly perfectly elastic.
    (B) Investment demand is nearly perfectly elastic.
    (C) Banks make loans with all excess reserves.
    (D) Households carry very little cash, holding their money in checking and saving deposits.
    (E) Money supply is nearly perfectly inelastic.

52. Which of the following is a predictable advantage of expansionary monetary policy in a recession?

    (A) It decreases aggregate demand so that the price level falls, which increases demand for the dollar.
    (B) It increases investment, which increases aggregate demand and increases employment.
    (C) It increases aggregate demand, which increases real GDP and increases the unemployment rate.
    (D) It keeps interest rates high, which attracts foreign investment.
    (E) It decreases the interest rate, which attracts foreign investment in U.S. financial assets.

53. Suppose the economy is in long-run equilibrium when temporary expansionary supply shock is felt in the economy. This changes the short-run Phillips curve, the short-run unemployment rate, and the long-run unemployment rate in which of the following ways?

	PHILLIPS CURVE	SHORT-RUN UN-EMPLOYMENT	LONG-RUN UN-EMPLOYMENT
(A)	Shifts left	Falls	Rises
(B)	Shifts right	Rises	Falls
(C)	Shifts left	Falls	Falls
(D)	Shifts right	Rises	Rises
(E)	Shifts left	Rises	Falls

54. As the Japanese economy expands, in what ways do U.S. net exports, the values of the dollar, and yen change?

	U.S. NET EXPORTS	VALUE OF DOLLAR	VALUE OF YEN
(A)	Decrease	Increase	Increase
(B)	Increase	Decrease	Increase
(C)	Decrease	Decrease	Increase
(D)	Increase	Increase	Decrease
(E)	Increase	Increase	Increase

55. Suppose the President plans to cut taxes for consumers and also plans to increase spending on the military. How does this affect real GDP and the price level?

    (A) GDP increases and the price level decreases.
    (B) GDP decreases and the price level increases.
    (C) GDP stays the same and the price level increases.
    (D) GDP decreases and the price level decreases.
    (E) GDP increases and the price level increases.

56. U.S. dollars and the European Union's (EU) euro are exchanged in global currency markets. Which of the following are true?

    I. If inflation is high in the EU and the price level in the United States is stable, the value of the dollar appreciates.
    II. If the Fed increases the money supply, the value of the dollar depreciates.
    III. If EU consumers are less inclined to purchase American goods, the dollar appreciates.
    IV. If U.S. income levels are rising relative to incomes in the EU, the euro depreciates.

    (A) I and II only
    (B) III only
    (C) II and IV only
    (D) I, II, and IV only
    (E) I and IV only

57. If in a given year the government collects more money in net taxes than it spends, there would exist

(A) a current account deficit.
(B) a budget surplus.
(C) a trade surplus.
(D) a budget deficit.
(E) a trade deficit.

58. Which component of a nation's balance of payments recognizes the purchase and sale of real and financial assets between nations?

(A) The capital account.
(B) The official reserves account.
(C) The current account.
(D) The trade deficit account.
(E) The trade surplus account.

59. An import quota on foreign automobiles is expected to

(A) increase domestic efficiency, and protect domestic producers at the expense of foreign producers.
(B) decrease the price of automobiles, and protect domestic consumers at the expense of foreign producers.
(C) increase the price of automobiles, and protect domestic producers at the expense of consumers.
(D) increase the price of automobiles, and protect domestic consumers at the expense of domestic producers.
(E) decrease domestic efficiency, and protect domestic producers at the expense of domestic autoworkers.

60. When a large increase in aggregate demand has an even greater increase in real GDP, economists refer to this as

(A) the balanced budget multiplier.
(B) the money multiplier.
(C) the foreign substitution effect.
(D) the wealth effect.
(E) the spending multiplier.

› Answers and Explanations

1. **E**—The capacity to produce corn has increased, but the capacity for tractor production is the same. More effective pesticides do not improve the ability to produce tractors, but improve the ability to harvest corn.

2. **B**—When the slope of the PPF increases, the opportunity cost of producing the *X*-axis good rises.

3. **E**—Rising prices and rising quantities does not disprove the Law of Demand, it simply reflects a rightward shift in demand, with a constant supply curve.

4. **A**—Defines comparative advantage.

5. **D**—Tariffs create inefficiency in the world steel market.

6. **C**—The free market responds to changes in consumer tastes, technology, and prices to produce "what" is most wanted by society.

7. **A**—Household production is not included in GDP calculations. Second-hand sales are counted the first time the good was produced.

8. **C**—Know the difference between types of unemployment.

9. **C**—Human wants are neither scarce nor are they economic resources.

10. **A**—Rising national debt increases interest rates and attracts foreign investment in U.S. financial assets. Greater demand for dollars appreciates the dollar.

11. **D**—Nominal GDP rises with the price level. If output increases at a slower rate than an increases in the price level, real GDP falls.

12. **D**—National income includes all sources of income and depreciation is not a source of income.

13. **B**—Know the factors critical to long-term economic growth.

14. **E**—UR = U/LF and LF = (E + U).

15. **C**—Stocks, bonds and money are all financial assets. All else equal, rising demand for stocks and bonds lowers the asset demand for money.

16. **D**—Lower taxes on personal income increase consumption and AD.

17. **C**—Short-run equilibrium is where short-run AS intersects AD, in this case, above full employment. In the long run, wages increase, shifting AS leftward until settling at full employment Q_1 and higher price P_3.

18. **C**—GDP includes all production done in the United States, regardless of nationality. A singer's production of a concert is counted in French GDP.

19. **B**—Supply-side economists prefer lower taxes on saving to encourage saving. More saving increases investment and increases AS.

20. **B**—The equation of exchange says MV = PQ and it is assumed that Q and V are fairly constant. Any increase in money supply (*M*) might initially boost output, but eventually results in a higher price level (*P*).

21. **D**—Know the circular flow model.

22. **E**—This reclassification would not affect AD or tabulation of GDP.

23. **C**—If income increases $100 and saving increases by $10, the MPS = .10 and the MPC = .90.

24. **B**—If inventories unexpectedly fall, consumption exceeds production so expect production to begin rising.

25. **A**—Stagflation is inflation with high unemployment and this occurs when AS shifts to the left.

26. **A**—The horizontal range of AS occurs when resources are unemployed. If output rises, wages do not rise and prices are constant.

27. **D**—Household savings can be negative if households consume more than their income.

28. **D**—Weak AD (contraction) causes job loss and low inflation rates.

29. **D**—Investment tax credits provide incentives for firms to invest in capital equipment and new factory construction. This policy stimulates economic growth and productivity.

30. **C**—With an MPC = .90, M = 10 so increased investment shifts AD $1000 to the right.

31. **B**—Don't let choice A fool you. $M3$ includes $M2$, which includes $M1$. If you added $M1$ and $M2$, you would be adding $M1$ twice.

32. **A**—Tm = M * MPC. A larger MPC increases the size of Tm.

33. **D**—Higher inflation relative to other nations causes goods to be more expensive relative to those produced abroad causing a drop in net exports.

34. **B**—High inflation rates require a decrease in AD and this is the only contractionary fiscal policy. Fed policy is not fiscal, it is monetary.

35. **E**—Lower input prices in major industries increase AS.

36. **E**—This balanced budget policy increases real GDP at a slower rate than the other expansionary options.

37. **E**—Selling securities pulls excess reserves out of the banking system, decreasing the money supply.

38. **B**—Expansionary policy lowers interest rates and is more effective if investment increases greatly. If money demand is perfectly elastic, increased money supply does not lower interest rates, thus failing to stimulate investment.

39. **E**—Moving money from savings to cash increases $M1$, but both savings and cash are already included in $M2$ and $M3$, so it has no effect on these two larger measures of money.

40. **D**—The short-run Phillips curve portrays the inverse relationship between inflation and unemployment rates. In the long run, it is vertical at the natural rate of unemployment.

41. **C**—The U.S. dollar is not "backed" by any physical asset or commodity.

42. **A**—The money multiplier is 10, so withdrawing $1 million leads you to conclude that money in circulation falls by $10 million, but the original $1 million is still in circulation so money falls by $9 million.

43. **E**—Know how fiscal policy affects real GDP and unemployment.

44. **B**—The Fed does not make changes in tariff and quota policy.

45. **C**—Have a strong knowledge of fiscal and monetary policies.

46. **A**—Budget deficits emerge during recessions because net taxes fall when incomes fall. The trend is reversed during expansion.

47. **E**—Know all combinations of fiscal and monetary policy.

48. **D**—The Fed wants to increase the money supply to lower interest rates. Combine the expansionary fiscal with the expansionary monetary policy and the Fed risks inflation.

49. **B**—Long-run AS rises if the productive capacity of the economy rises and more productive labor and capital resources have this effect.

50. **C**—Lower interest rates decrease foreign demand for U.S. securities, depreciating the dollar. "Cheap" dollars make U.S. exports more affordable to foreigners, increasing exports.

51. **A**—A horizontal money demand curve implies that increasing the money supply does not lower the interest rate. Investment is constant and AD does not increase.

52. **B**—Know how monetary policy affects investment, AD, and employment.

53. **A**—If short-run AS shifts rightward, the short-run Phillips curve shifts leftward. The short-run unemployment rate falls below the natural rate, but eventually rises back to the natural rate and a lower rate of inflation, as expectations readjust to the new AS.

54. **D**—Higher Japanese incomes increase net exports in the United States, increasing the value of the dollar versus the yen, decreasing the value of the yen versus the dollar.

55. **E**—Know how fiscal policy affects AD, real GDP, and the price level.

56. **A**—These first two statements are accurate. They predict how changes in relative prices and interest rates affect the exchange rate between the dollar and the euro. The second two statements are inaccurate. A stronger desire for U.S. goods appreciates the dollar and rising U.S. incomes appreciates the euro.

57. **B**—This defines a budget surplus.

58. **A**—In the balance of payments statement, the capital account shows the flow of currency in physical and financial assets.

59. **C**—Import quotas protect domestic producers at the expense of the higher price paid by consumers.

60. **E**—Because an injection of dollars into the circular flow goes through the economy several times, the impact on real GDP is multiplied.

AP Macroeconomics Practice Exam 2

Free-Response Questions

Planning time—10 minutes

Writing time—50 minutes

At the conclusion of the planning time, you have 50 minutes to respond to the following three questions. Approximately half of your time should be given to the first question and the second half should be divided evenly between the remaining two questions. Be careful to clearly explain your reasoning and to provide clear labels to all graph axes and curves.

1. The U.S. economy is experiencing a severe recession and the budget is currently balanced.

   (A) One policy analyst advocates expansionary tax cuts, while another advocates expansionary government spending. Which of these policies will have the greatest impact on real domestic output? Explain how you know.

   (B) If you can choose only one of the proposed policies in part (A), explain how this policy impacts the federal budget and each of the following:
      i. Interest rates.
      ii. Investment.

   (C) Given that the economy has still not recovered from the recession, identify one tool of the Federal Reserve that might stimulate the economy.

   (D) Using correctly labeled graphs, show how the Fed policy identified in part (C) would affect each of the following:
      i. Interest rates.
      ii. Real GDP
      iii. The price level.

   (E) Explain one factor that might lessen the effectiveness of the Fed's monetary policy.

2. Assume that the European Union (EU) has experienced lower interest rates while interest rates in the United States have remained relatively high. Explain how these lower real interest rates will affect each of the following:

   (A) The purchase of EU assets by American investors.
   (B) The international value of the EU currency, the euro.
   (C) EU exports to the United States.
   (D) EU imports from the United States.

3. The competitive world price of steel is lower than the equilibrium price of steel in the United States.

   (A) In a correctly labeled graph, show the U.S. market for steel, being careful to clearly identify each of the following:
      i. The domestic price of steel in the absence of imported steel.
      ii. The world price of steel.
      iii. The amount of steel currently being imported into the domestic market.

   (B) American producers of steel are threatened by imported steel and successfully lobby Congress to impose a quota on foreign steel that reduces, but does not completely eliminate, the amount of steel imported into the U.S. market. In your graph, show the impact of the quota on each of the following:
      i. The price of steel paid by domestic consumers.
      ii. The amount of steel now being imported into the domestic market.

   (C) Suppose now that instead of a quota, Congress approves a tariff to limit, but not eliminate, the amount of steel imported into the United States. Explain the difference between the impacts of a tariff from those of a quota.

› Free-Response Grading Rubric

Note: Based on my experience, these point allocations roughly approximate the weighting on similar questions on the AP examinations. Be aware that every year the point allocations differ and partial credit is awarded differently.

Question 1 (10 points)

Part (A): 2 points

1 point: The spending policy will increase real GDP more than the tax cut policy.

1 point: The spending multiplier is greater than the tax multiplier. Tax cuts increase disposable income and some of that is saved, not spent, so the multiplier effect is smaller.

Part (B): 3 points

1 point given for acknowledging that regardless of policy, the budget will be in deficit.

i. 1 point: Borrowing to finance the fiscal policy will increase the interest rate.
ii. 1 point: Higher interest rates will decrease investment.

Part (C): 1 point

1 point is given for an expansionary monetary policy. Either lowering the discount rate, lowering the reserve ratio, or buying Treasury securities in an open market operation.

Part (D): 3 points

These are graphing points.

i. 1 point: Correct money market showing increased money supply decreasing the interest rate.

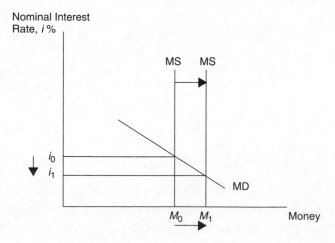

ii.   1 point: A graph showing AD increasing and increasing real GDP.

iii.   1 point: A graph showing the corresponding increase in the price level.

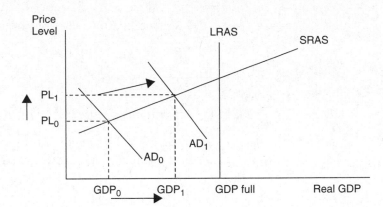

Part (E): 1 point

Identify a reason why greater money supply might not result in a large boost to real GDP.

- Money demand is very elastic.
- Investment demand is very inelastic.
- Banks hold excess reserves rather than making loans.
- Borrowers do not redeposit their loans, but hold some as cash.

Question 2 (4 points)

Part (A): 1 point: Lower interest rates make EU financial assets less attractive to American investors so fewer EU financial assets will be purchased.

Part (B): 1 point: Decreased demand for the euro depreciates the euro vs. the dollar, and appreciates the dollar against the euro.

Part (C): 1 point: A depreciating euro makes EU goods look like a bargain to American consumers, increasing demand for EU goods. The EU exports more goods to the United States.

Part (D): 1 point: An appreciating dollar makes American goods look more expensive to EU consumers, decreasing demand for U.S. goods. The EU imports fewer U.S. goods.

Question 3: (7 points)

Part (A): 4 points

These are graphing points. 1 point for a correctly labeled steel market.

 i.   1 point: The domestic price is at the intersection of domestic demand and supply.

 ii.   1 point: The world price of steel is below the domestic price.

iii.   1 point: Imported steel is the difference between domestic demand and supply at P_w.

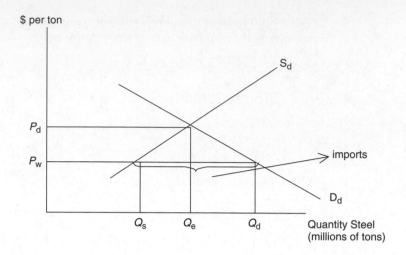

Part (B): 2 points

Also graphing points. The question notes that there are still some imports after the quota.

  i. 1 point: Showing the quota increases the price somewhere between the P_w and P_d.
 ii. 1 point: Showing the amount of imported steel is now less than before the quota.

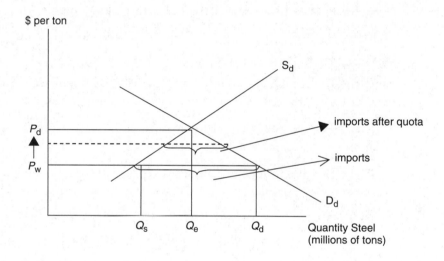

Part (C): 1 point

Explain how a tariff has the same effect as the quota but the quota does not create any revenue for the government.

Note: Recently this problem has increased in difficulty by asking you to label and discuss inefficiency and DWL created by a tariff or quota. Be sure you can do this!

Scoring and Interpretation

AP Macroeconomics Practice Exam 2

Multiple-Choice Questions:

Number of correct answers:
Number of incorrect answers:
Number of blank answers:

Did you complete this part of the test in the allotted time? Yes/No

Free-Response Questions:

1. _____/10
2. _____/4
3. _____/7

Did you complete this part of the test in the allotted time? Yes/No

Calculate Your Score:

Multiple-Choice Questions:

$$\underbrace{\hspace{3cm}}_{(\text{\# right})} - \underbrace{\hspace{3cm}}_{(.25 * \text{\# wrong})} = \underbrace{\hspace{3cm}}_{\text{MC raw score}}$$

Free-Response Questions:

$$\text{Free-Response Raw Score} = (1.5 * \text{Score \#1}) + (1.875 * \text{Score \#2})$$
$$+ (1.0714 * \text{Score \#3}) = \underline{\hspace{1.5cm}}$$

Add the raw scores from the multiple-choice and free-response sections to obtain your total raw score for the practice exam. Use the table below to determine your grade, remembering these are rough estimates using questions that are not actually from AP exams, so do not read too much into this conversion from raw score to AP score.

MACROECONOMICS #2	
RAW SCORE	APPROXIMATE AP GRADE
71–90	5
53–70	4
43–52	3
31–42	2
0–30	1

Appendixes

Bibliography
Web Sites
Glossary
Important Formulas and Conditions

BIBLIOGRAPHY

Arnold, Roger A., *How to Think Like an Economist,* Thomson South-Western, Mason, OH, 2005.

Hamermesh, Daniel S., *Economics is Everywhere,* McGraw-Hill Irwin, New York, NY, 2004.

Krugman, Paul and Robin Wells, *Economics,* 2nd ed., Worth Publishers, New York, NY, 2009.

Mankiw, N. Gregory, *Principles of Economics,* 4th ed., Thomson South-Western, Mason, OH, 2006.

McConnell, Campbell L.; Stanley L. Brue; and Sean Flynn, *Economics,* 18th ed., McGraw-Hill Irwin, New York, NY, 2008.

WEB SITES

Here is a list of Web sites that you might find useful in your preparation for the AP Economics exams.

www.collegeboard.com/student/testing/ap/about.html

www.ncee.net

www.economy.com/dismal

www.economist.com/research/Economics

www.theshortrun.com

www.bized.co.uk/learn/economics/index.htm

www.reffonomics.com

www.welkerswikinomics.com/home.html

tw.neisd.net/webpages/dmayer

absolute advantage The ability to produce more of a good than all other producers.

absolute (or money) prices The price of a good measured in units of currency.

accounting profit The difference between total revenue and total explicit cost.

aggregate demand curve The negative relationship between all spending on domestic output and the average price level of that output.

aggregate income The sum of all income earned by suppliers of resources in the economy.

aggregate spending (GDP) The sum of all spending from four sectors of the economy.

aggregate supply curve The positive relationship between the level of domestic output produced and the average price level of that output.

aggregation The process of summing the microeconomic activity of households and firms into a macroeconomic measure of economic activity.

all else equal The assumption that all other variables are held constant so that we can predict how a change in one variable affects a second. Also known as the "ceteris paribus" assumption.

allocative efficiency Production of the combination of goods and services that provides the most net benefit to society. This is achieved when the MB = MC of the next unit.

appreciating currency An increase in the price of one currency relative to another currency.

asset demand for money The amount of money demanded as an asset is inversely related to the real interest rate.

assets of a bank Anything owned by the bank or owed to the bank.

automatic stabilizers Fiscal policy mechanisms that automatically regulate, or stabilize, the macro economy as it moves through the business cycle.

autonomous consumption The amount of consumption that occurs no matter the level of disposable income.

autonomous investment The level of investment determined by investment demand and independent of GDP.

autonomous saving The amount of saving that occurs no matter the level of disposable income.

Average Fixed Cost (AFC) Total fixed cost divided by output.

Average Product (AP_L) of Labor Total product divided by the labor employed.

average tax rate The proportion of total income paid to taxes.

Average Total Cost (ATC) Total cost divided by output.

Average Variable Cost (AVC) Total variable cost divided by output.

balanced-budget multiplier A change in government spending offset by an equal change in taxes results in a multiplier effect equal to one.

balance of payments statement A summary of the payments received by the United States from foreign countries and the payments sent by the United States to foreign countries.

balance sheet or t-account A tabular way to show a bank's assets and liabilities.

base (or reference) year The year that serves as a reference point for constructing a price index and comparing real values over time.

bond A certificate of indebtedness from the issuer to the bond holder.

budget deficit Exists if government spending exceeds the tax revenue collected.

budget surplus Exists if tax revenue collected exceeds government spending.

business cycle The periodic rise and fall in economic activity around its long-term growth trend.

capital (or financial) account This account shows the flow of investment on real or financial assets between a nation and foreigners.

capitalist market system (capitalism) An economic system based upon the fundamentals of private property, freedom, self-interest, and prices.

cartel Firms that agree to maximize their joint profits rather than compete.

circular flow of economic activity (or circular of goods and services) A model that shows how households and firms circulate resources, goods, and incomes through the economy. This basic model is expanded to include the government and the foreign sector.

Classical school A macroeconomic model that explains how the economy naturally tends to come to full employment in the long run.

closed economy A model assuming no foreign sector (imports and exports).

collusive oligopoly Models where firms agree to work together to mutually improve their situation.

comparative advantage The ability to produce a good at lower opportunity cost than all other producers.

complementary goods Two goods that provide more utility when consumed together than when consumed separately.

constant returns to scale The horizontal range of long-run average total cost where LRAC is constant over a variety of plant sizes.

constrained utility maximization Given prices and income, a consumer stops consuming a good when the price paid for the next unit is equal to the marginal utility received.

consumer price index (CPI) The price index that measures the average price level of the items in the base year market basket. This is the main measure of consumer inflation.

consumer surplus The difference between a buyer's willingness to pay and the price actually paid.

consumption and saving schedules Tables that show the direct relationships between disposable income and consumption and saving.

consumption function A positive relationship between disposable income and consumption.

consumption possibility frontier The line that illustrates all possible combinations of goods that two nations can consume with specialization and trade.

contraction A period where real GDP is falling.

contractionary fiscal policy Lower government spending or higher net taxes to shift AD to the left to full employment and reduce inflationary pressures.

contractionary monetary policy Decreases in the money supply to increase real interest rates, shift AD to the left to full employment, and reduce inflationary pressures.

cost of living adjustment An annual adjustment to a salary (or pension) so that the purchasing power of that income remains constant. This adjustment is typically based upon the change in the consumer price index.

cross-price elasticity of demand A measure of how sensitive the consumption of good X is to a change in the price of good Y.

crowding out effect Typically the result of government borrowing to fund deficit spending, this is the decline in spending in one sector due to an increase in spending from another sector.

current account This account shows current import and export payments of both goods and services and investment income sent to foreign investors and investment income received by U.S. citizens who invest abroad.

dead weight loss The lost net benefit to society caused by a movement from the competitive market equilibrium.

debt financing A firm's way of raising investment funds by issuing bonds to the public.

decision to invest A firm invests in projects if the expected rate of return is at least as great as the real interest rate.

deflation A decline in the overall price level.

demand curve Shows the quantity of a good demanded at all prices.

demand for labor Shows the quantity of labor demanded at all wages. Labor demand for a firm hiring in a competitive labor market is MRP_L.

demand-pull inflation Inflation that results from stronger AD as it increases in the upward sloping range of AS.

demand schedule A table showing quantity demanded for a good at all prices.

depreciating currency A decrease in the price of one currency relative to another currency.

depression A prolonged, deep trough in the business cycle.

derived demand Demand for a resource arising from the demand for the goods produced by the resource.

determinants of demand The external factors that shift demand to the left or right.

determinants of supply The external factors that influence supply. When these variables change, the entire supply curve shifts to the left or right.

discount rate The interest rate commercial banks pay on short-term loans from the Fed.

discouraged workers Citizens who have been without work for so long that they become tired of looking for work and drop out of the labor force. Because these citizens are not counted in the ranks of the unemployed, the reported unemployment rate is understated.

disequilibrium Any price where the quantity demanded does not equal the quantity supplied.

disposable income (DI) The income a consumer has to spend or save once they have paid out net taxes.

diseconomies of scale The upward part of the long-run average total cost curve where LRAC rises as plant size rises.

dissaving Another way of saying that saving is less than zero.

domestic price The equilibrium price of a good in a nation without trade.

dominant strategy A strategy that is always the best strategy to pursue, regardless of what a rival is doing.

double counting The mistake of including the value of intermediate stages of production in GDP on top of the value of the final good.

economic costs The sum of explicit and implicit costs of production.

economic growth The increase in an economy's PPF over time.

economic profit The difference between total revenue and total economic cost.

economics The study of how society allocates scarce resources.

economies of scale The downward part of the long-run average total cost curve where LRAC falls as plant size rises.

egalitarianism The philosophy that all citizens should receive an equal share of the economic resources.

elasticity Measures the sensitivity, or responsiveness, of a choice to a change in an external factor.

elasticity along the demand curve At the midpoint of a linear demand curve, $E_d = 1$. Above the midpoint demand is elastic and below the midpoint demand is inelastic.

equation of exchange The equation says that nominal GDP ($P * Q$) is equal to the quantity of money (M) multiplied by the number of times each dollar is spent in a year (V).

equilibrium GDP The level of real GDP where real domestic production is equal to real domestic spending.

equity financing The firm's method of raising funds for investment by issuing shares of stock to the public.

excess capacity The difference between the long-run output in monopolistic competition and the output at minimum average total cost.

excess demand The difference between quantity demanded and quantity supplied. A shortage.

excess reserves The portion of a deposit that may be loaned to borrowers.

excess supply The difference between quantity supplied and quantity demanded. A surplus.

exchange rate The amount of one currency you must give up to get one unit of the second currency.

excise tax A per unit tax on a specific good or service.

expansion A period where real GDP is growing.

expansionary fiscal policy Increases in government spending or lower net taxes meant to shift AD to the right toward full employment and lower the unemployment rate.

expansionary monetary policy Increases in the money supply meant to decrease real interest rates, shift AD to the right toward full employment, and reduce the unemployment rate.

expected rate of return (r) The rate of profit the firm anticipates receiving on investment expenditures.

explicit costs Direct, purchased, out-of-pocket costs, paid to resource suppliers outside the firm. Also referred to as accounting costs.

exports Goods and services produced domestically but sold abroad.

factors of production Inputs or resources that go into the production function to produce goods and services.

fiat money Paper and coin money with no intrinsic value but used to make transactions because the government declares it to be legal tender.

final goods Goods that are ready for their final use by consumers and firms.

financial account See *capital account*.

the firm An organization that employs factors of production to produce a good or service that it hopes to profitably sell.

fiscal policy Deliberate changes in government spending and net tax collection to affect economic output, unemployment, and the price level.

fixed inputs Production inputs that cannot be changed in the short run.

foreign sector substitution effect The process of domestic consumers looking for foreign goods when the domestic price level rises, thus reducing the quantity of domestic output consumed.

four-firm concentration ratio The sum of the market share of the four largest firms in an industry.

fractional reserve banking A system in which only a fraction of the total money deposited in banks is held in reserve.

free rider An individual who receives the benefit of a good without incurring any cost for the good.

free-rider problem The lack of private funding for a public good due to the presence of free riders.

full employment Exists when the economy is experiencing no cyclical unemployment.

functions of money Money serves as a medium of exchange, a unit of account and a store of value.

game theory An approach for modeling the strategic interactions of firms in oligopoly markets.

Gini ratio A measure of income inequality. As the Gini ratio gets closer to zero, the more equally the income is distributed. As the Gini ratio gets closer to one, the more unequally the income is distributed.

Gross Domestic Product (GDP) The market value of the final goods and services produced within a nation in a given period of time.

GDP price deflator The price index that measures the average price level of goods and services that make up GDP.

human capital The amount of knowledge and skills that labor can apply to the work that they do.

implicit costs Indirect, non-purchased, or opportunity costs of resources provided by the entrepreneur.

imports Goods produced abroad but consumed domestically.

incidence of tax The division of a tax between consumers and producers.

income effect Due to a higher price, the change in quantity demanded that results from a change in the consumer's purchasing power (or real income).

income elasticity A measure of how sensitive consumption of a good is to a change in consumers' income.

inferior goods A good for which demand decreases with an increase in consumer income.

inflation An increase in the overall price level.

inflation rate The percentage change in the price level from one year to the next

inflationary gap The amount by which equilibrium real GDP exceeds full employment GDP.

interest rate effect The process of reduced domestic consumption due to a higher price level causing an increase in the real interest rate.

intermediate goods Goods that require further modification before they are ready for their final use.

investment spending Spending on physical capital, inventories, and new construction.

investment demand The negative relationship between the real interest rate and the cumulative dollars invested.

investment tax credit A reduction in taxes for firms that invest in new capital like a factory or piece of equipment.

Keynesian school A macroeconomic model that believes the economy is unstable and does not naturally move to full employment in the long run.

labor force The sum of all individuals 16 years and older who are either currently employed (E) or unemployed (U). LF = E + U.

Law of Demand All else equal, when the price of a good rises, the quantity demanded of that good falls.

Law of Diminishing Marginal Utility In a given time period, as consumption of an item increases, the marginal (additional) utility from that item falls.

Law of Diminishing Marginal Returns As successive units of a variable input are added to a fixed input, beyond some point the marginal product declines.

Law of Increasing Costs As more of a good is produced, the greater is its opportunity (or marginal) cost.

Law of Increasing Marginal Cost As a producer produces more of a good, the marginal cost rises. This is very similar to the idea of increasing opportunity costs in Chapter 5.

Law of Supply All else equal, when the price of a good rises, the quantity supplied of that good rises.

least-cost rule The combination of labor and capital that minimizes total costs for a given production rate is where $MP_L/P_L = MP_K/P_K$.

liability of a bank Anything owned by depositors or lenders to the bank.

liquidity A measure of how easily an asset can be converted to cash.

loanable funds market A hypothetical market where borrowers (investors) demand more funds at a lower real interest rate and lenders (savers) supply more funds at a higher real interest rate.

long run A period of time long enough for the firm to alter all production inputs, including the plant size.

Lorenz curve A graphical device that shows how a nation's income is distributed across the nation's households.

luxury A good for which the proportional increase in consumption exceeds the proportional increase in income.

M1 The most liquid measure of money supply, including cash, checking deposits, and traveler's checks.

M2 $M1$ plus savings deposits, small time deposits, and money market and mutual funds balances.

M3 $M2$ plus large time deposits.

macroeconomic long run A period of time long enough for input prices to have fully adjusted to market forces, all input and output markets are in equilibrium and the economy is operating at full employment (GDP_f).

macroeconomic short run A period of time during which the prices of goods and services are changing in their respective markets, but the input prices have not yet adjusted to those changes in the product markets.

marginal The next unit, or increment of, an action.

marginal analysis Making decisions based upon weighing the marginal benefits and costs of that action. The rational decision-maker chooses an action if the MB ≥ MC.

marginal benefit (MB) The additional benefit received from the consumption of the next unit of a good or service.

marginal cost (MC) The additional cost of producing one more unit of output.

marginal productivity theory The theory that a citizen's share of economic resources is proportional to the marginal revenue product of his or her labor.

Marginal Product (MP$_L$) of Labor The change in total product resulting from a change in the labor input.

Marginal Propensity to Consume (MPC) The change in consumption caused by a change in disposable income. The slope of the consumption function.

Marginal Propensity to Save (MPS) The change in saving caused by a change in disposable income. The slope of the saving function.

Marginal Resource Cost (MRC) The change in a firm's total cost from the hiring of an additional unit of an input.

Marginal Revenue Product of Labor (MRP) The change in a firm's total revenue from the hiring of an additional unit of an input.

marginal tax rate The rate paid on the last dollar earned, calculated by taking the ratio of the change in taxes divided by the change in income.

marginal utility The change in an individual's total utility from the consumption of an additional unit of a good or service.

market A group with buyers and sellers of a good or service.

market basket A collection of goods and services used to represent what is consumed in the economy.

market economy An economic system in which resources are allocated through the decentralized decisions of firms and consumers.

market equilibrium Exists at the only price where the quantity supplied equals the quantity demanded. Or, it is the only quantity where the price consumers are willing to pay is exactly the price producers are willing to accept.

market failure The inability of the free market to allocate resources efficiently.

market power The ability to set a price above the perfectly competitive level.

money demand The negative relationship between the real interest rate and the quantity of money demanded as an asset plus the quantity of money demanded for transactions.

money market The interaction of money demand and money supply determines the "price" of money, the nominal interest rate.

money multiplier Equal to one over the reserve ratio, this measures the maximum amount of new checking deposits that can be created by a single dollar of excess reserves.

money supply The fixed quantity of money in circulation at a given point in time as measured by the central bank.

monopolistic competition A market structure characterized by a few small firms producing a differentiated product with easy entry into the market.

monopoly A market structure in which one firm is the sole producer of a good with no close substitutes in a market with entry barriers.

monopsony A factor market in which there is a sole firm that has market power, i.e. a wage-setter.

multiplier effect The idea that a change in any component of aggregate demand creates a larger change in GDP.

national debt The accumulation of all annual budget deficits.

natural monopoly The case where economies of scale are so extensive that it is less costly for one firm to supply the entire range of demand than for multiple firms to share the market.

natural rate of unemployment The unemployment rate associated with full employment, somewhere between 4–5 percent in the United States.

necessity A good for which the proportional increase in consumption is less than the proportional increase in income.

negative externality The existence of spillover costs upon third parties from the production of a good.

net exports The value of a nation's total exports minus total imports.

net export effect The process of how expansionary fiscal policy decreases net exports due to rising interest rates. Another form of crowding out.

nominal GDP The value of current production at the current prices.

nominal interest rate The interest rate unadjusted for inflation. The opportunity cost of holding money in the money market.

non-collusive oligopoly Models of industries in which firms are competitive rivals seeking to gain at the expense of their rivals.

nonmarket transactions Household work or do-it-yourself jobs that are missed by GDP accounting.

non-renewable resources Natural resources that cannot replenish themselves.

normal goods A good for which demand increases with an increase in consumer income.

normal profit The opportunity cost of the entrepreneur's talents. Another way of saying the firm is earning zero economic profit.

official reserves account The Fed's adjustment of a deficit or surplus in the current and capital account by the addition or subtraction of foreign currencies so that the balance of payments is zero.

oligopoly A very diverse market structure characterized by a small number of interdependent large firms, producing either a standardized or differentiated product in a market with a barrier to entry.

open market operation (OMO) A tool of monetary policy, it involves the Fed's buying (or selling) of Treasury bonds from (or to) commercial banks and the general public.

opportunity cost The value of the sacrifice made to pursue a course of action.

peak The top of the business cycle where an expansion has ended and is about to turn down.

perfectly elastic $E_d = \infty$. In this special case, the demand curve is horizontal meaning consumers have an instantaneous and infinite response to a change in price.

perfectly inelastic $E_d = 0$. In this special case, the demand curve is vertical and there is absolutely no response to a change in price.

positive externality The existence of spillover benefits upon third parties from the production of a good.

present value The amount of money needed today, to produce, at a given interest rate, a given amount of money at some time in the future.

price ceiling A legal maximum price, above which the product cannot be sold.

price discrimination The sale of the same product to different groups of consumers at different prices.

price elasticity of demand (E_d) Measures the sensitivity of consumers' quantity demanded for good X when the price of good X changes.

price elasticity of supply (E_s) Measures the sensitivity of producers' quantity supplied for good X when the price of good X changes.

price floor A legal minimum price, below which the product cannot be sold.

price index A measure of the average level of prices in a market basket for a given year, when compared to the prices in a reference (or base) year.

prisoners' dilemma A game where the two rivals achieve a less desirable outcome because they are unable to coordinate their strategies.

private goods Goods that are both rival and excludable.

producer surplus The difference between the price received and the marginal cost of producing the good.

productive efficiency Production of maximum output for a given level of technology and resources.

production function The mechanism for combining production resources, with existing technology, into finished goods and services.

production possibilities The different quantities of goods that an economy can produce with a given amount of scarce resources.

production possibilities frontier (PPF) The graphical device used to show the production possibilities of two goods.

production possibility curve A graphical device that shows the combination of two goods that a nation can efficiently produce with available resources and technology.

productivity The quantity of output that can be produced per worker in a given amount of time.

profit maximizing resource employment The firm hires a resource up to the point where MRP = MRC.

progressive tax A tax where the proportion of income paid in taxes rises as income rises.

proportional tax A tax where the proportion of income paid in taxes is constant no matter the level of income.

protective tariff An excise tax levied on an imported good that is produced in the domestic market so that it may be protected from foreign competition.

public goods Goods that are both nonrival and nonexcludable.

quantity theory of money The theory that an increase in the money supply will not affect real output and will only result in higher prices.

quintiles When you rank household income from lowest to highest, each quintile represents twenty percent of all households.

quota A maximum amount of a good that can be imported into the domestic market.

real GDP The value of current production, but using prices from a fixed point in time.

real rate of interest The cost of borrowing to fund an investment and equal to the nominal interest rate minus the expected rate of inflation.

recession Two or more consecutive quarters of falling real GDP.

recessionary gap The amount by which full employment GDP exceeds equilibrium real GDP.

regressive tax A tax where the proportion of income paid in taxes decreases as income rises.

relative prices The price of one unit of good X measured not in currency, but in the number of units of good Y that must be sacrificed to acquire good X.

renewable resources Natural resources that can replenish themselves if they are not overharvested.

required reserves The minimum amount of deposits that must be held at the bank for withdrawals.

reserve ratio The fraction of total deposits that must be kept on reserve.

resources Also called factors of production, these are commonly grouped into the four categories of labor, physical capital, land or natural resources, and entrepreneurial ability.

revenue tariff An excise tax levied on goods that are not produced in the domestic market.

saving function A positive relationship between disposable income and saving.

scarcity The imbalance between limited productive resources and unlimited human wants.

second-hand sales Final goods and services that are resold.

shortage A situation in which, at the going market price, the quantity demanded exceeds the quantity supplied.

short run A period of time too short to change the size of the plant, but many other, more variable, resources can be adjusted to meet demand.

specialization Production of goods, or performance of tasks, based upon comparative advantage.

spending multiplier The amount by which real GDP changes due to a change in spending.

spillover benefits Additional benefits to society, not captured by the market demand curve from the production of a good.

spillover costs Additional costs to society, not captured by the market supply curve from the production of a good.

stagflation A situation seen in the macroeconomy when inflation and the unemployment rate are both increasing. Also called cost-push inflation.

sticky prices The case when price levels do not change, especially downward, with changes in AD.

stock A certificate that represents a claim to, or share of, the ownership of a firm.

subsidy A government transfer, either to consumers or producers, on the consumption or production of a good.

substitute goods Two goods are consumer substitutes if they provide essentially the same utility to the consumer.

substitution effect The change in quantity demanded resulting from a change in the price of one good relative to the price of other goods.

supply curve Shows the quantity of a good supplied at all prices.

supply schedule A table showing quantity supplied for a good at various prices.

supply shock An economy-wide phenomenon that affects the costs of firms and results in a shifting AS curve.

supply-side fiscal policy Fiscal policy centered on incentives to save and invest to prompt economic growth with very little inflation.

surplus A situation in which, at the going market price, the quantity supplied exceeds the quantity demanded.

tax bracket A range of income on which a given marginal tax rate is applied.

tax multiplier The magnitude of the effect that a change in lump sum taxes has on real GDP.

technology A nation's knowledge of how to produce goods in the best possible way.

theory of liquidity preference Keynes' theory that the interest rate adjusts to bring the money market into equilibrium.

Total Cost (TC) The sum of total fixed and total variable costs at any level of output.

Total Fixed Costs (TFC) Production costs that do not vary with the level of output.

Total Product (TP$_L$) of Labor The total quantity of output produced for a given quantity of labor employed.

total revenue The price of a good multiplied by the quantity of that good sold.

total revenue test Total revenue rises with a price increase if demand is price inelastic and falls with a price increase if demand is price elastic.

total utility The total happiness received from consumption of a number of units of a good.

Total Variable Costs (TVC) Production costs that change with the level of output.

total welfare The sum of consumer surplus and producer surplus.

trade-offs The reality of scarce resources implies that individuals, firms, and governments are constantly faced with difficult choices that involve benefits and costs.

transaction demand The amount of money held in order to make transactions.

trough The bottom of the cycle where a contraction has stopped and is about to turn up.

underground economy The unreported or illegal activity, bartering or informal exchange of cash for goods and services that are not reported in official tabulations of GDP.

unit elastic demand $E_d = 1$. The percentage change in price is equal to percentage change in quantity demanded.

utility Happiness, or benefit, or satisfaction, or enjoyment gained from consumption of goods and services.

utility maximizing rule The consumer chooses amounts of goods X and Y, with their limited income, so that the marginal utility per dollar spent is equal for both goods.

utils A hypothetical unit of measurement often used to quantify utility. A.k.a. "happy points."

variable inputs Production inputs that the firm can adjust in the short run to meet changes in demand for the firm's output.

velocity of money The average number of times that a dollar is spent in a year.

world price The global equilibrium price of a good when nations engage in trade.

IMPORTANT FORMULAS AND CONDITIONS

Chapter 5

1. Optimal Decision-Making:
   MB = MC

2. Opportunity Cost From a Production Possibility Frontier (PPF):

   Good X: the slope of the PPF

   Good Y: the inverse of the slope of the PPF

Chapter 6

1. Market Equilibrium:

   $Q_d = Q_s$

2. Shortage:

   $Q_d - Q_s$

3. Surplus:

   $Q_s - Q_d$

4. Total Welfare:

   = Consumer Surplus + Producer Surplus

Chapter 7

1. Price Elasticity of Demand:

   E_d = (%Δ in quantity demanded of good X)/(%Δ in the price of good X)

2. Percentage change:

   %Δ = 100 * (New Value − Old Value)/ Old Value

3. Total Revenue:

   = Price * Quantity Demanded

4. Income Elasticity:

   E_I = (%Δ Q_d good X)/(%Δ Income)

5. Cross-Price Elasticity:

   $E_{x,y}$ = (%Δ Q_d good X)/(%Δ Price good Y)

6. Price Elasticity of Supply:

   E_s = (%Δ in quantity supplied of good X)/ (%Δ in the price of good X)

7. Marginal Utility:

   MU = ΔTU/ΔQ

8. Utility Maximizing Rule:

   $MU_x/P_x = MU_y/P_y$ or $MU_x/MU_y = P_x/P_y$

Chapter 8

1. Accounting Profit:

   TR − explicit costs

2. Economic Profit:

   TR − explicit costs − implicit costs

3. Marginal Product of Labor:

   MP_L = Δ in TP_L/Δ in L

4. Average Product of Labor:

   AP_L = TP_L/L

5. Total Costs:

   TC = TVC + TFC

6. Marginal Costs:

   MC = ΔTVC/ΔQ

7. Average Fixed Cost:

   AFC = TFC/Q

8. Average Variable Cost:

   AVC = TVC/Q

9. Average Total Cost:

   ATC = TC/Q = AFC + AVC

10. Marginal Cost and Marginal Product of Labor:
    MC = w/MP_L

11. Average Variable Cost and Average Product of Labor:

    AVC = w/AP_L

Chapter 9

1. Profit Maximization Point:

   MB = MC or MR = MC

2. Demand for Firm's Product (Perfectly Competitive Market):

   P = MR = AR

3. Profit:

   $\Pi = TR - TC = P * q_e - TC = q_e * (P - ATC)$

4. Break-Even Point:

   P = ATC

5. Shutdown Point:

   P < AVC or TR < TVC

6. Allocative Efficiency:

   Produce output q where P_c = MR = MC

7. Excess Capacity in Monopolistic Competition:

   $Q_{atc} - Q_{mc}$

8. Perfectly Competitive Long-Run Equilibrium:

   P = MR = AR = MC = ATC

9. Monopoly Long-Run Equilibrium:

   P_m > MR = MC

Chapter 10

1. Marginal Revenue Product:

   $$= \frac{\text{Change in Total Revenue}}{\text{Change in Resource Quantity}}$$

   $= MR * MP_L$

   a. Under perfectly competitive price-taking conditions:

      $MRP_c = MR * MP_L = P * MP_L$

   b. Under conditions of market power, MR < P:

      $MRP_m = MR * MP_L < MRP_c$

2. Marginal Resource Cost:

   $$= \frac{\text{Change in Total Resource Cost}}{\text{Change in Resource Quantity}}$$

   = Wage (in a competitive resource market)

3. Least-Cost Hiring Rule:

   $MP_L/P_L = MP_K/P_K$ or equivalently,

   $MP_L/MP_K = P_L/P_K$

4. Profit Maximizing Resource Employment:

   MRP = MRC

5. Monopsony Hiring Decision:

   MFC = MRP > W

Chapter 11

1. Socially optimal output:

   MSB = MSC

2. Marginal Tax Rate:

   = (Δ taxes due)/(Δ taxable income)

3. Average Tax Rate:

   = (total taxes due)/(total taxable income)

Chapter 12

1. Nominal GDP:

   = Current year production * Current year prices

2. Real GDP:

   = 100 * (Nominal GDP)/(GDP Deflator)

3. Aggregate Spending (GDP):

   = $C + I + G + (X - M)$

4. Disposable Income (DI):

   = Gross Income − Net Taxes

5. Net Taxes:

   = taxes paid − transfers received

6. % Δ Real GDP:

   = %Δ Nominal GDP − %Δ Price Index

7. Price Index Current Year:

   = 100 * (Spending Current Year)/ (Spending Base Year)

8. Consumer Inflation Rate:

= 100 * (CPI New − CPI Old)/CPI Old

9. Real Income:

= (Nominal Income)/CPI (in hundredths)

10. Nominal Interest Rate:

= Real Interest Rate + Expected Inflation

11. Labor Force:

= Employed + Unemployed

12. Unemployment Rate:

= Unemployed/Labor Force

Chapter 13

1. Consumption Function:

C = autonomous consumption
+ MPC(DI)

2. Saving Function:

S = autonomous savings + MPS (DI)

3. Marginal Propensity to Consume (MPC):

= $\Delta C/\Delta DI$ = slope of consumption function

4. Marginal Propensity to Save (MPS):

= $\Delta S/\Delta DI$ = slope of saving function

5. MPC + MPS = 1

6. Net Exports $(X - M)$:

= Exports − Imports

7. Equilibrium in the Loanable Funds Market:

$S = I$

8. Spending Multiplier:

= $1/(1 - MPC)$ = 1/MPS

= $(\Delta$ GDP$)/(\Delta$ Spending$)$

9. Tax Multiplier (Tm):

= MPC * (Spending Multiplier)
= MPC/MPS

= $(\Delta$ GDP$)/(\Delta$ taxes$)$

10. Balanced-Budget Multiplier = 1

Chapter 14

1. Macroeconomic Short-run Equilibrium

AD = SRAS

2. Macroeconomic Long-run Equilibrium

AD = SRAS = LRAS

3. Recessionary Gap:

= Full Employment GDP − Current GDP

4. Inflationary Gap:

= Current GDP − Full Employment GDP

Chapter 15

1. Budget Deficit:

= Government Spending − Net Taxes

2. Budget Surplus:

= Net Taxes − Government Spending

Chapter 16

1. $M1$ Measure of Money:

= cash + coins + checking deposits
+ traveler's checks

2. $M2$ Measure of Money:

= $M1$ + savings deposits + small (e.g., under
$100,000 CDs) time deposits + money market
deposits + money market mutual funds

3. $M3$ Measure of Money:

= $M2$ + large (over $100,000) time deposits

4. Present Value (PV) of $1 received a year from today:

= $\$1/(1 + r)$

5. Money Demand:

= Transaction Demand + Asset Demand

6. Equilibrium in the Money Market:

Ms = Md

7. Reserve Ratio (rr)

   = Required Reserves/Total Deposits

8. Simple Money Multiplier:

   = 1/rr

Chapter 17

1. Equilibrium in the Currency ($) Market:

   Q_d for the $ = Q_s$ of the $

2. Revenue from a Tariff:

   = Per Unit Tariff * Units Imported